P9-BYN-882

THE HAWAIIAN REVOLUTION (1893–94)

THE HAWAIIAN REVOLUTION (1893–94)

William Adam Russ, Jr.

With an Introduction by
Pauline N. King

Selinsgrove: Susquehanna University Press
London and Toronto: Associated University Presses

Associated University Presses
440 Forsgate Drive
Cranbury, NJ 08512

Associated University Presses
25 Sicilian Avenue
London WC1A 2QH, England

Associated University Presses
P.O. Box 39, Clarkson Pstl. Stn.
Mississauga, Ontario,
L5J 3X9 Canada

The paper used in this publication meets the requirements of the American National Standard for Permanence of Paper for Printed Library Materials Z39.48-1984.

Library of Congress Cataloging-in-Publication Data

Russ, William Adam, 1903–
The Hawaiian Revolution (1893–94) / William Adam Russ, Jr. ; with an introduction by Pauline N. King.
p. cm.
Originally published: Selinsgrove, Pa. : Susquehanna University Press, 1959.
Includes bibliographical references (p.) and index.
ISBN 0-945636-43-1 (alk. paper)
ISBN 0-945636-53-9 (alk. paper) (paperback)
1. Hawaii—History—Revolution of 1893. I. Title.
DU627.2.R8 1992
996.9′028—dc20 91-41617
CIP

PRINTED IN THE UNITED STATES OF AMERICA

To

A. K. B. R.

CONTENTS

INTRODUCTION

Pauline N. King

The rewriting and revision in interpretation of controversial historical events are certainly common in the discipline of history. Many works written thirty or more years ago do not withstand critical analysis to remain as valuable contributions to the understanding of such events.

Points of view have changed. New material has become available. Many historical events have become a central part of contemporary political movements. The bias of the author, no doubt unrealized by him, is identified and used to eliminate a work as archaic.

Such a situation exists in relation to the writing of the history of the revolution in 1893 that abrogated monarchy and ended the sovereignty of the Kingdom of the Hawaiian Islands. The subsequent five years of a Republic of Hawaii, until annexation to the United States, is also fraught with emotional barrier reefs endangering all present interpretations of the era as well as those of the past.

Yet the two volumes by William Adam Russ, Jr., *The Hawaiian Revolution (1893–94),* published in 1959, and *The Hawaiian Republic (1894–98): And Its Struggle to Win Annexation,* published in 1961, have remained rich sources of information about this period in Hawaiian and American history. Even by modern standards the two works add significantly to the understanding of the period by the thoroughness and detail of the narrative. They deserve reprinting—the first volume in time for the one hundredth anniversary of the revolution.

In it Russ wrote in detail of the events during the period from January 1893 to about June 1894. He used as his primary sources the official documents of the United States government and those of the governments of Hawaii: Kingdom, Provisional, and Republic. Other primary sources included the collections in archives and libraries of the major figures of the period; the printed works of governments and individuals; secondary works in books, periodicals, and articles; and newspapers in key cities. He made his focus the days of the revolution, the reactions to the news in the United States, the attempts to annex the islands, the policies of the presidents and the secretaries of state, and the debates in Congress. His study ended with the failure of passage of the annexation treaty of 1893.

The narrative detail of this study is not found elsewhere even today. Therein lies the continuing usefulness of the work. His accomplishment is based on extensive scholarly research with a careful analysis and criticism of the opinions and actions of leaders of the revolution in Hawaii and Americans in Hawaii and Washington, D.C.

Can it be said that he wrote an "objective" history? Perhaps the question should be: Is there such a creation as objective history? He apparently thought there was. In American historiography the period between the two world wars was an era that believed in the possibility and necessity for the professional historian to write objective history. Russ's background and training place him among the historians who adhered to this theory.

He was a typical academic of his era. He completed his B.A. degree at Ohio Wesleyan University when he was twenty-one years old in 1924. Two years later he had received his M.A. from the University of Cincinnati. He became a history instructor at the University of Cincinnati in 1926 and an assistant professor of history at DePauw University in 1927. At the same time he worked on his doctorate degree, which he received from the University of Chicago in 1933. (None of these institutions, incidentally, was known for their innovative approaches to the study of history.) In 1933 he joined the faculty of Susquehanna University, where he remained until he retired as Professor of History and Political Science in 1967. He moved to Topton, Pennsylvania, where he died on February 26, 1981.

Other than his two books on Hawaii and an article or two, he appeared to concentrate his interests on Pennsylvania state history and the history of his community: the small, rural town of Selinsgrove. His interest in Hawaii, colleagues believe, resulted from his dissertation on the subject of the revolution. He himself stated that he had been interested in Hawaii for many years and continued his research "at intervals" until the opportunity to publish his work arose.

Perhaps because of his distance from Hawaii, it was possible for him to achieve a remarkable balance in his account. He included criticisms of Americans in Hawaii and of American policies emanating from Washington, D.C. He carefully examined controversial statements and actions in the text. He carried his analysis to footnotes, some extensive in length, for qualifications or refutations. His footnotes are a must to read as much for the references as for the meaningful information contained in them. That quality of scholarship has not been matched for that period in any similar current publication.

In his preface, Russ wrote of his approach to the work: "Now, with the material written up, I am not aware of either starting or ending with any preconceived or postconceived axes to grind. After years of thought, I am not convinced that any one reason can be given for the Revolution, or for its sequel, annexation. To the contrary, there were many causes, although all were not equally important."

He may not have had axes to grind. He did, however, have preconceived ideas and prejudices, of which he was not aware. His ideological bent was such as to approach the history of Hawaii only in terms of American interests and influence.

To him, Hawaii's story at the end of the nineteenth century was the story of America's part in the expansion of world imperialism. Candor demanded, he said, that the United States' acquisitions in the 1890s be recognized as part of that trend. And justice, he said, should be given the colonialized world. But American action was necessary, he thought, to preserve and advance its power position in relation to the imperialist nations. The ambivalence in his attitude toward the conflicts between the needs of power and justice was itself a reflection of his ideology.

The timing of the publication of his book was to coincide with the granting of statehood to the Territory of Hawaii in 1959. That fact influenced the tone of his work to exemplify the Americanization process of Hawaii that led finally to statehood. His argument was that Americans in Hawaii were the harbingers of American civilization in the Pacific. Supposedly culturally superior to the

Hawaiians, Americans were responsible for the adoption of Western culture in Hawaii. It was this group that pushed for union to the United States. To Russ, the United States government was not responsible for aggressive moves against the Kingdom. Instead, American policy followed American leadership overseas.

Russ did not write as if the United States were never mistaken and unjust in its actions. He was critical but not condemning of the actions and policies of United States leadership. If the annexation of the Hawaiian Kingdom was an extension of American imperialist expansion, it was not an official movement of the government. It was instead the final legalization of what had been decades of American dominance of Hawaii. It was the inevitable exchange of island sovereignty for American sovereignty. Russ censored the mechanism (revolution) by which the exchange was accomplished but not the end result (annexation). Thus, if the truth of the events of 1893 demanded that American actions be fully exposed, Russ did so only to clarify and condemn the deeds and misdeeds of American leadership. It is as if he were giving Americans a lesson in morality to ease the American conscience and respond to its sensibilities.

What are the defects in and limitations and omissions of Russ's work? His major failure was that he did not search for the point of view of Hawaiians about the last monarch, Queen Lili'uokalani, the Kingdom, or the revolution in sources other than official Kingdom Government documents. Yet he used the memoirs and papers of the opponents of the Queen. The primary voice he used was the published work by her, *Hawaii's Story by Hawaii's Queen* (Boston: 1898).

It was written in order to influence Congress in its consideration of the treaty for annexation before Congress in 1897. It is an important source of her interpretation of American activities in Hawaii. Other Hawaiian sources were not used. Part of Russ's problem was that Hawaiian private papers, memoirs, and translated Hawaiian language documents were not readily available.

This deficiency led him to fail to consider the rights and integrity of the Hawaiian Kingdom. Indeed, in his conclusion, "The Summing Up," he started his considerations by stating that the monarchy under Kalakaua and Lili'uokalani was "inefficient, corrupt, and undependable." He did not understand that the independent Kingdom had a right to control its own internal affairs of whatever quality. He denied that in 1898, when annexation finally was accomplished, the United States received "stolen goods" from the revolutionists who had formed a Republic of Hawaii.

Today, many if not most Hawaiian and American historians have a different approach to the era. They do contend that the islands were "stolen" from the Hawaiian people by the United States. American imperialism is identified as aggressive and destructive of colonialized cultures. In regard to the Revolution of 1893, modern historians do condemn America's role, emphasizing the aggressive actions of the American diplomat in Hawaii, John L. Stevens. They assert that the landing and use of American sailors and marines from the USS *Boston* anchored in Honolulu Harbor were the primary factors that made revolution successful. Without American active participation, these writers insist, the Hawaiian Kingdom's sovereignty would not have been broken. Nor would the Hawaiian people have lost their nationhood and their sense of identity as a people.

Oddly, Russ's evidence of the detail of events can be used by these modern interpreters to support their opposite points of view. Moreover, Russ's information is not found elsewhere outside of original documents. For example, in regard to the involvement of Stevens, Russ catalogued the diplomat's activities in favor of the annexation party and against Queen Lili'uokalani, the constituted ruler of the Kingdom. Russ also pointed out that the timing of the landing of American troops was set by Stevens even against the wishes of the annexationists. Today, that evidence is welcome reinforcement for writers who excoriate Stevens' conspiracy during the crucial days of January 1893. There is other material in Russ's work that can be used by today's partisans. Indeed, for those writers who have a critical but supportive interpretation of American policy, Russ's work is also satisfactory.

In that sense he has achieved a "relative objectivity" simply by virtue of his careful scholarship and his attempts to keep a balanced and "neutral" view. He did not even realize his limitations or his accomplishments. He stated in his preface: "If any so-called 'general reader' should ever pick up this book to peruse, let me say to him read ahead of time: The numerous footnotes are for scholars; they are not for you. Simply skip them." Yet they are vital to this work. They help all readers to understand the events and they rescue the author from his ideological narrowness.

Since the date of his publication in 1959, other historians have written about the period. The most noteworthy are the works of two historians, Ralph S. Kuykendall and Merze Tate. Kuykendall wrote *The Hawaiian Kingdom: The Kalakaua Dynasty, 1874–1893,* published in 1967, and Tate wrote *The United States and The Hawaiian Kingdom* published in 1965. Both are excellent studies, and both cover a long period of time, Kuykendall ending his text in January of 1893. Thus, neither examine the revolutionary period in its entirety as did Russ.

A more recent work by Helena G. Allen, *The Betrayal of Queen Liliuokalani: The Last Queen of Hawaii, 1838–1917,* was published in 1982 and emphasizes the drama and tragedy of the Queen's life as a whole and the arrogance and conspiracies of her opponents during the revolutionary period.

Allen has written a book from a Hawaiian point of view in the sense that much of her narrative is based on information from Hawaiian sources. These sources are primarily the reminiscenses of a dependent of the Queen. Others are statements of supporters of the Queen found in private collections to which Allen had access but which are not available to scholars. Again, her consideration of the Revolution is one short chapter in a narrative of a whole life. Historians can use Allen's book for the opinions of Hawaiians, however, but the quotes would be from a secondary source without verification from the original.

Two movements in historical writing in recent times are antagonistic to the Russ overview. One is the attack against Western-centered history; the other the use of history as a tool in political activism. In the first instance, for the history of Hawaii "Western-centered" can be translated as an American-centered or -oriented interpretation of Hawaii's past.

To critics, Americanized history of Hawaii is another form of imperialism. In this form the history of the islands is the history of the introduction and imposition of Western-American culture over a weak and disintegrating native culture. Moreover, Hawaiian leaders and people have little influence over their destiny in this story. They are but puppets made to act by the superior American advisors.

Most available published works are American-oriented, and certainly Russ's work is. So too are those of Kuykendall and Tate. They use the same and similar sources as Russ and they write narrative history. They too did not use many sources from the Hawaiian point of view other than official documents. All three describe the evolution of Hawaii as a Western-like sovereign nation primarily influenced by American culture, and the tone of the works is that this story is one of progress and positive development.

Allen's work is also Western-oriented in a sense. If her sympathies are with Hawaiians, she still looks at someone such as the Queen from the outside. Lili'uokalani's "betrayal," she wrote, was merely the inevitable outcome of one hundred years of change. It is, then, a popularized version of the fatal impact theory of Hawaiian history. Hawaiians are victims forced into alien lives without their cooperation or understanding.

Modern students are correcting what they perceive as this imbalance by promoting the Hawaiian view of Hawaiian history. This approach means the reintroduction of the Hawaiian people as major factors in their own history. It means the dependence on local sources and an overtly negative view of American policies and actions.

The use of the history of Hawaii as a tool in political activism is also changing the profile of interpretation. The modern movement proclaiming the rights of native peoples has prompted a reexamination of the Revolution of 1893. The purpose here is to prove the reluctance of Hawaiians to become a part of the United States. It is also to determine American responsibility for the success of the revolution, and the historical record will then be used to influence government policy. New publications that will consider these two concerns as scholarly books have not yet been completed.

Until new books of scholarly standard are published, Russ's work remains of value. Even then it will still be a valuable resource. Any student of the period needs the accessibility of many points of view for a thorough understanding of this important event in Hawaiian and American history.

The Hawaiian Revolution (1893–94)

I. THE AMERICANIZATION OF HAWAII

The United States annexed Hawaii in a period of world imperialism. In the mad scramble for leases, spheres of influence, enclaves, and coaling stations, in Asia and in Africa, the American republic won its share in Hawaii, Puerto Rico, and the Philippine Islands. "Candor must compel one [says Tyler Dennett] to admit that the American policy in the Hawaiian Islands was showing marked parallels to the existing and later policies of China and Japan in Korea: economic penetration under the treaties of 1875 [1876] and 1887, insistence on no disturbance of the trade, and demands for preferred commercial and political treatment."[1]

We might demand justice for China by means of the open door; and yet, as Dennett points out, by the time of McKinley's inauguration, steel rails were selling in Europe at eighteen dollars per ton, and industry was requiring markets for surpluses—not only of steel but of many other products as well. "The task for American statesmen in the last three years of the century was to obtain for Americans a real equivalent, territorial or otherwise, not merely for Hongkong but now also for Kwangchow-wan, Foochow, Tsingtao, Wei-hai-wei and Port Arthur. . . ."[2]

The story of the acquisition by the United States of the Hawaiian Islands reaches back many years before their final incorporation into the American system in 1898. American interest in the Sandwich Islands did not begin, so to speak, in a day as it did in Puerto Rico and the Philippines. United States relations with Hawaii went back at least three-quarters of a century, and became more intimate as time passed.[3] Even before the Kingdom

[1] Tyler Dennett, *Americans in Eastern Asia* (N. Y., 1922), p. 611.

[2] *Ibid.*, p. 608. Compare Honolulu *Bulletin*, Jan. 14, 1898: ". . . perhaps the Kiaochow incident has more than one point of contact with the Hawaiian question."

[3] For example, Secretary of State John Sherman told the Japanese Minister in the summer of 1897: ". . . through three quarters of a century, in which the constitution and government of Hawaii and the commerce of the islands with the world have undergone notable changes, the one essential feature of the *status quo* has been the predominant and paramount influence of the United States upon the fortunes of the group, and . . . the union of

had been recognized by the powers of the world, the United States had an influence which no other country enjoyed. In the last quarter of the nineteenth century the United States exercised what amounted to a protectorate over the islands. Hence final annexation merely legalized what before had been practical fact.[4]

The first important contact with white civilization occurred in 1778, when the islands were visited by Captain James Cook, who

that island territory to the United States, often foreshadowed and at times taking tangible shape, has been recognized as a necessary contingency, drawing nearer year by year with the passage of events" (*Literary Digest*, July 17, 1897, XV, 334).

[4] It is obvious that this book cannot offer any details regarding the history of the archipelago before 1893. That task is being well done by Ralph S. Kuykendall who has thus far published *The Hawaiian Kingdom, 1778-1854: Foundation and Transformation* (Honolulu, 1938) and *The Hawaiian Kingdom, 1854-1874: Twenty Critical Years* (Honolulu, 1953); a third volume, soon to be printed, will finish the history of the monarchy.

A short synopsis of the history of American influence was included by President McKinley in his message to the Senate accompanying the treaty of June 16, 1897. Henry E. Chambers's *Constitutional History of Hawaii* in the *Johns Hopkins University Studies*, Series 14 (Baltimore, 1896), has a number of errors. Almost every book dealing with Hawaii has at least one chapter summarizing Hawaiian history before annexation. See, for instance, "Americanization of Hawaii," which is chapter VIII of James Morton Callahan's *American Relations in the Pacific and the Far East 1784-1900*, pp. 114-134, in *Johns Hopkins University Studies*, Series 19 (Baltimore, 1901); and John W. Foster's *American Diplomacy in the Orient* (Boston and N. Y., 1903), pp. 98-133, for the early years of Hawaiian history up to the 1850's. A short account of the relations between the United States and Hawaii from 1820 to 1893 can be found in a report made by Andrew H. Allen, head of the Bureau of Rolls and Library, dated Feb. 9, 1893, printed as *Sen. Ex. Doc. 77* (52 Cong. 2 Sess.). William De Witt Alexander, *History of Later Years of the Hawaiian Monarchy and the Revolution of 1893* (Honolulu, 1896) is helpful. Some background information is to be found in Julius W. Pratt, *Expansionists of 1898: The Acquisition of Hawaii and the Spanish Islands* (Baltimore, 1936). Harold W. Bradley has written a fine book on *The American Frontier in Hawaii: The Pioneers 1789-1843* (Stanford University, 1942). Sylvester K. Stevens's *American Expansion in Hawaii, 1842-1898* (Harrisburg, Pa., 1945) is an excellent general account of the subject. Jean Ingram Brookes has written on another phase of the problem in *International Rivalry in the Pacific Islands, 1800-1875* (Berkeley, 1941); see particularly, pp. 344-365. See also Theodore Morgan, *Hawaii: A Century of Economic Change, 1778-1876* (Cambridge, Mass., 1948). For the story of Japanese immigration, see Hilary Conroy, *The Japanese Frontier in Hawaii, 1868-1898* (Berkeley, 1953).

named them after the fourth Earl of Sandwich, "the reputed noble inventor of stratified refreshments."[5] American relations, however, with Hawaii began in 1820 with the arrival of a group of Puritan missionaries and of an American whaler. Every year after that brought more foreigners to convert the heathen; and the missionaries' prestige was augmented rapidly. The second generation of these Americans often intermarried with the natives, neglecting Christian work to enter business[6] and politics.

A strong and aggressive foreign element, mainly American, purloined political power from the Kanakas,[7] and made itself wealthy by entering business, trade, and commerce. Although most of them were no longer missionaries, they were called the "Missionary Party"[8]—in derision—by the natives who saw themselves being progressively relegated to the rear. The numerically inferior, but culturally superior, Americans became not only the leading businessmen but also the chief politicians and governing officials. Royal officers after the 1850's seldom bore Hawaiian names.[9]

The charge that Christian missionaries came to save souls and stayed to become wealthy and powerful was made both before and after the Revolution of 1893. Thus H. G. Creel wrote in 1915 that Hawaii "is owned, controlled and ruled by missionaries" and that "the penny contributions of children, the proceeds of ladies' aid societies and the missionary donations of earnest men and

[5] William Elliott Griffis, "Our New Fellow-Citizens," in *Outlook,* LIX (July 23, 1898), 722.

[6] Liliuokalani, in her book, *Hawaii's Story by Hawaii's Queen* (Boston, 1898), p. 8, refers to the wealthy firm of Castle and Cooke, both of whose partners, having been sent to Honolulu by the American Board of Commissioners for Foreign Missions, resigned from their missionary work and entered mercantile activity.

[7] "Kanaka" is the native word for people. "Kanaka," "native," and "Royalist," came to be practically synonymous.

[8] The missionaries were usually called "foreigners" or "Americans." Their party was not only designated as "Missionary," but "American," "Reform," and "foreign." Later it became the Revolutionary and then the Republican party when it was in opposition to the ousted Royalists.

[9] For proof, see the list of Royal officials in *Sen. Report 227* (53 Cong. 2 Sess.), pp. 168-169. This was the report of a Senatorial Committee, under John T. Morgan, which investigated American activities in Hawaii. Hereafter designated as "Morgan."

women were made to serve the ends of Big Business in Hawaii."[10] Senator John L. Mitchell of Wisconsin said in 1898 that "Since the advent of the white man every leaf in the history of Hawaii is either red with blood or black with intrigue and jobbery."[11] Charles Nordhoff, the veteran correspondent of the *New York Herald,* who was fated to play a minor rôle in the story of the Revolution, commented, in a letter of October 10, 1893, upon "the melancholy spectacle of the degeneracy under tropical sun and circumstances[,] the quick degeneracy of the children & grand children of a noble band of missionaries, owing to the greed for wealth & abnormal profits aroused by our sugar treaty with them. They have become false to the trust the fathers left them; seeking Annexation, at the same time [they] show themselves unworthy & unfit for American citizenship."[12]

Of course there were others whose comments were kinder. A more favorable statement of the missionary influence appeared in the report of the Morgan Committee (to be discussed later): "Civilization and constitutional government in Hawaii are the foster children of the American Christian missionaries."[13] A less vitriolic reaction originated with the Singapore *Free Press* in 1897: ". . . Hawaii owes her present position in the world, her civilization, and her prosperity to the labors of the early missionaries. . . . The danger . . . is now that they make too much of their success, and endeavor to drive where they should lead. That is the complaint of the lay element in Honolulu against the present missionaries, who still have predominating influence in the affairs of the Republic."[14]

Whether this missionary influence was commendable or not, the fact remains that Hawaii became more and more American. As early as 1871 Minister Henry A. Peirce could report to Secretory Hamilton Fish that the "favorite songs and airs [of the

[10] *Hawaii An International Crime* (Girard, Kansas, 1915), pp. 19 and 27.

[11] *Congressional Record* (55 Cong. 2 Sess.), p. 6190.

[12] Nordhoff to Carl Schurz, Oct. 10, 1893, Schurz MSS., CIX, 24181 (Library of Congress). See also *Harper's Weekly,* Feb. 18, 1893, p. 163.

[13] Morgan, p. 10; cf., *House Ex. Doc. 47* (53 Cong. 2 Sess.), p. 106. The latter is the report made by Commissioner James H. Blount, who, it will appear later, was sent by President Cleveland, in the spring and summer of 1893, to investigate the causes of the recent Revolution in the islands. Hereafter cited as "Blount."

[14] Quoted by *Literary Digest,* XIV (Feb. 20, 1897), p. 499.

Kanakas] are American. Sherman's 'Marching Through Georgia' and 'John Brown's Soul Is Marching On' are daily heard in the streets and in their schoolrooms."[15] So intimate did the ties between Americans in Hawaii and those at home become that the America Minister reported in 1894 that for the past twelve years or more the Americans in Honolulu held a poll every time a Presidential election took place in the United States in order to find out which candidate would carry Honolulu. In 1892 Cleveland got seventy-four votes, Harrison sixty-six.[16] Natives referred to American naval vessels as "our war ships."[17] The Kanakas, as well as the whites, celebrated Thanksgiving.[18] The assertion of Rear Admiral George Belknap was undoubtedly true: ". . . the United States made those islands what they are—gave them all their prosperity. The town of Honolulu is as much an American town as any town in this country."[19] It would be natural to expect the Americans in Hawaii to desire annexation.[20]

As the Americans strengthened their grip upon Hawaii, a gulf developed between them and the natives, who, quite naturally, considered that the missionaries were a usurping faction. This race antipathy was partly neutralized by intermarriage between Americans and natives, but even more by the rapid passing away of native blood. Nevertheless, a mutual antagonism grew up between the foreigners who looked down upon the Kanakas because of their intellectual sluggishness, and the Kanakas, who in turn were jealous of the commanding influence held by the whites. Often, but not always, the large number of half-breeds joined the white party.[21]

[15] Morgan, p. 30.

[16] Willis to Gresham, Nov. 3, 1894, Cleveland MSS. (Library of Congress).

[17] According to Z. S. Spalding to the Morgan Committee, p. 248.

[18] Morgan, p. 552.

[19] *Ibid.,* p. 721.

[20] The natives did not think so, however. Thus former Queen Liliuokalani told a friend of Rear Admiral Beardslee's: "I cannot understand why those missionary boys, Sanford Dole, Albert Judd and Sam Damon, who were my playmates and grew up with me, should have taken my country from me." Quoted by L. A. Beardslee, "Pilikias," in *North American Review,* CLXVII (Oct., 1898), 478. Lorrin A. Thurston (*Memoirs of the Hawaiian Revolution,* edited by Andrew Farrell, Honolulu, 1936, p. 277), admits proudly that the "mission boys" led in the Revolution.

[21] Cf., Blount, pp. 106-107.

It is hardly necessary to state that this foreign clique almost always openly favored the United States and clamored for annexation at every opportunity. Later, as they became interested in sugar growing, it was to their advantage to compel the Government to secure concessions in trade for them. In brief, in the Pacific Ocean an outpost of American civilization had been created by private citizens, not by official action of the American Government. Against the frequent stand-offishness of Washington officials, these expatriated Americans worked, secretly and otherwise, for a union which would mean better government and, not the least important, commercial advantages.

* * * * *

The year 1820 also saw the first official representative of the American Government despatched to the islands. This event resulted in a treaty of navigation and friendship in 1826, the first international compact signed by Hawaii.[22] Although the convention was not ratified by the United States, Hawaii abided by it. Already the Americans had a preeminent position.

The growing influence of Americans did not, however, prevent other nations from attempting to win control of the islands which, not having as yet been internationally recognized as independent, were looked upon as fair booty for anyone. Owing to complaints made by several Englishmen of unfair treatment at the hands of natives, Lord George Paulet was sent to Hawaii to investigate in 1843. He ended by seizing the islands in the name of England and running up the British flag as a token of occupation. King Kamehameha III, finding himself helpless, appealed to President Tyler for aid. The latter, to show that he considered the islands as an independent nation, had Congress appropriate money to send a Commissioner to Hawaii. Paulet's superiors finally thought it best to repudiate the seizure and to restore the native ruler.[23] In the same year, England and France entered into an agreement, which the United States refused to sign, mutually to guarantee Hawaii's independence.[24] Denmark, England, and France signed

[22] *Sen Ex. Doc. 77* (52 Cong. 2 Sess.), pp. 4 and 31-32.

[23] Documents on this British seizure are printed in *ibid.*, pp. 41 and 103-107. See also Morgan, pp. 138-155. Ralph S. Kuykendall, *A History of Hawaii* (N. Y., 1926), pp. 157-160, tells the story.

[24] *Sen. Ex. Doc. 77, op. cit.*, p. 60. But Webster had already recognized its independence (Kuykendall, *op. cit.*, p. 157).

treaties of amity and commerce with the island Kingdom; and in 1849 a treaty of friendship between Hawaii and the United States was signed, and this time, ratified.[25]

In 1849 the French began to make demands.[26] King Kamehameha III was so closely pressed by the French that he decided to cede his patrimony to the United States, which in the past had been so friendly. A provisional deed of cession was given to the American Commissioner who sent it to Daniel Webster, Secretary of State for Fillmore. The deed was sealed and was to be opened only in case France occupied the Kingdom. An American and an Hawaiian flag were sewed together to be run up the moment French soldiers pulled down the Hawaiian emblem. Webster did not look with favor upon the sealed deed, but he did ask for explanations and assurances from France.[27] After considerable parleying, the French withdrew.

For several years after that event, agitation in favor of annexation was prevalent among the American residents of Hawaii, but no official action was taken. In 1853 a Committee of Thirteen was formed to reconstruct the Government and then to turn it over to the United States. A number of Americans memorialized the King in favor of annexation, but at the protest of France and England, the King changed his Minister of Foreign Affairs and the matter was dropped.[28]

It remained for the year 1854 to witness the most determined movement for annexation that occurred before 1893. Propaganda on the part of American businessmen in the islands had a great deal to do with creating unionist sentiment, and yet the cession policy was strongly favored by King Kamehameha III. His Government was weak, administered largely by foreigners, and at the

[25] *Sen. Ex. Doc. 77, op. cit.*, pp. 75-82, for the treaty; also pp. 61 and 64-65; and Kuykendall, *op. cit.*, p. 177.

[26] Kuykendall, *op. cit.*, pp. 180-183. The French had also created considerable trouble in 1839 and in 1842 (*ibid.*, pp. 152-155).

[27] Blount, pp. 141-164, gives the chief documents touching annexation movements in the 1850's. See also *Sen. Ex. Doc. 77* (52 Cong. 2 Sess.). Charles Callan Tansill, *Diplomatic Relations between the United States and Hawaii, 1885-1889*, in *Fordham University Studies* (Historical Series, No. 1; N. Y., 1940), pp. 1 *ff.*, gives a summary of these early years of contact between the United States and the Hawaiian Islands.

[28] Blount, p. 143.

mercy of any marauder; the natives were dying off; the ruler's control over the nation was slipping from his hands; and his own dynasty was losing the pristine vigor which it had acquired from the first Kamehameha.

Harassed by other nations and pressed by American-Hawaiians, the King was willing to abdicate provided his country united with a strong power, preferably with the United States. The movement went so far as the drafting of a treaty of cession to the United States, signed by the Foreign Minister and the American representative at the King's court. It got no further because of the rise of opposition in too many quarters. President Pierce's Secretary of State, William L. Marcy, looked with disfavor on the proceedings because the King demanded the admission of Hawaii into the Union as a full-fledged state, and because he asked compensation for himself and the royal family, amounting to several hundred thousand dollars. Furthermore, the British agent was strongly opposed to American annexation. In addition the Crown Prince, Alexander Liholiho, was prejudiced against Americans because his brother, Lot Kamehameha, had been insulted in New York where he was taken for a Negro; and, naturally, the Crown Prince was not delighted with the idea of bartering away his chance for the succession. Even Robert C. Wyllie, the Foreign Minister, was personally against the cession in spite of having signed the deed of transfer. The final blow came with the death of the King late in 1854.[29] The United States had not secured the islands, and yet its interest in them was expressed by Marcy who informed Commissioner David L. Gregg that if Hawaii's loss of independence was "unavoidable," the United States "would much

[29] *Sen. Ex. Doc. 45* (52 Cong. 2 Sess.), Richard W. Van Alstyne dug up some interesting material on this episode from the British archives which he used in his "Great Britain, the United States, and Hawaiian Independence, 1850-1854," in *The Pacific Historical Review,* IV (March, 1935), 15-25. The treaty was printed in Morgan, pp. 40-43; see also William De Witt Alexander, "The Uncompleted Treaty of Annexation of 1854," in *Papers of the Hawaiian Historical Society, No. 9,* which is filed as an enclosure of Sewall to Sherman, No. 29, Aug. 25, 1897, in Hawaii Despatches. Hereafter cited as "Despatches." The despatches from American representatives in Hawaii to the Department of State and *vice versa* are housed in the National Archives at Washington. See also Kuykendall, *op. cit.,* pp. 185-188.

prefer to acquire the sovereignty of these islands . . . than to see it transferred to any other power."[30]

The Americans who had egged on the late King were still determined to get concessions in trade from the United States, even if they could not secure annexation. Their method was reciprocity. Industry and commerce were languishing for the want of a market; and the Americans looked with longing eyes upon that of their homeland. The first attempt, in 1855, to win reciprocity failed; yet the interest of the American Government was shown in 1863 when the rank of its representative at Honolulu was raised from Commissioner to Minister Resident.[31] In 1867 a second attempt to get reciprocal trade failed,[32] largely because the United States Senate was too busy with Reconstruction matters.[33] In spite of this setback, Secretary William H. Seward wrote to the American Minister on September 12, 1867, that "a lawful and peaceful annexation of the islands to the United States with consent of the people . . . is deemed desirable by this government."[34]

With the failure of their second reciprocity effort, American businessmen in Hawaii began to look elsewhere for relief. They found it in free-trade Australia.[35] By 1873 they were sending 4,101 of their 11,595 annual tons of sugar there instead of to the United States, and the Australian market was increasing yearly. When this fact reached the ears of American officials at Washing-

[30] Marcy to Gregg, April 4, 1854, in *Sen. Ex. Doc. 77* (52 Cong. 2 Sess.), pp. 117-119.

[31] *Sen. Ex. Doc. 77, op. cit.,* p. 10. Cf., Osborne E. Hooley, "Hawaiian Negotiations for Reciprocity, 1855-57," in *The Pacific Historical Review,* VII (June, 1938), 128-147.

[32] *Sen. Ex. Doc. 77, op. cit.,* pp. 135 ff. The Senate finally refused to ratify in 1870. See also John Patterson, "The United States and Hawaiian Reciprocity, 1867-1870," in *The Pacific Historical Review,* VII (March, 1938), 14-27. Patterson attributes failure of the treaty to the fact that certain Senators believed reciprocity would delay annexation.

[33] Seward admitted this, in almost these very words, to his secret agent to Hawaii, Z. S. Spalding (Spalding, in Morgan, p. 261).

[34] Seward to McCook, in *Sen. Ex. Doc. 77, op. cit.,* p. 137; Dennett, *op. cit.,* p. 416.

[35] Morgan, p. 103. Also, Chalfant Robinson, *A History of Two Reciprocity Treaties* [.] *The Treaty with Canada* [.] *The Treaty with the Hawaiian Islands in 1876* . . . (New Haven, 1904), pp. 123-128.

ton, they saw the light at once; Australian (English) commercial supremacy in Hawaii would inevitably lead to political control. Moreover, a few American statesmen foresaw the great commercial possibilities in the Pacific; in 1871 Secretary Hamilton Fish called Honolulu a "resting spot in mid-ocean between the Pacific Coast and the vast domains of Asia which are now opening to commerce and Christian civilization."[36] In 1873, Generals John M. Schofield and B. S. Alexander reported to Secretary of War W. W. Belknap regarding Pearl Harbor from the standpoints of commerce and defensive capabilities.[37] Although the United States did not wish to annex at that time, it could neither afford to lose potential trade nor allow another nation to entrench itself in Hawaii. Thus a House Committee said there must be reciprocity in order to stave off British control.

In short, a reciprocity treaty was ratified in 1876, this time through the initiative of the United States.[38] It permitted free exportation to the United States of brown and other unrefined sugar, muscovado, sirup of sugar cane, melada, and molasses. Revenue on sugar and molasses amounting to $792,405[39] annually was given up at that time by the American Government, but the sugar trade increased so rapidly thereafter that this remitted revenue amounted to five million dollars in the late 1880's. The following figures indicate the remitted revenue on sugar and molasses:

1877	$ 792,405	1885	$ 4,799,920
1878	792,779	1886	4,276,100
1879	1,014,470	1887	4,830,067
1880	1,506,589	1888	4,764,618
1881	2,174,589	1889	4,925,588
1882	2,612,742	1890	4,535,100
1883	2,872,644	1891	5,317,238
1884	2,869,689		
		Total	$48,084,547

Under the McKinley Act—because sugar was on the free list—

[36] Dennett, *op. cit.*, p. 610.

[37] *Sen. Ex. Doc. 77* (52 Cong. 2 Sess.), pp. 165-166.

[38] Documents and text can be found in *ibid.*, 147 *ff*. Chalfant Robinson, *op. cit.*, gives the main facts about the treaty, pp. 140 *ff*.

[39] Another estimate placed the remitted revenue at $456,777 annually. See J. Laurence Laughlin and H. Parker Willis, *Reciprocity* (New York, 1903), p. 78.

the remitted revenue ceased from March 31, 1891, to August 1, 1894. The Wilson-Gorman Tariff took effect on the latter date. It restored all sugar, except Hawaiian, to the schedule, and the figures[41] on remitted revenue become interesting again:

1895	$2,499,329
1896	4,535,792
1897	5,276,175
1898	8,564,416
1899	7,767,039
1900	6,667,434
1876-1891	48,084,547
Total	$83,394,735

In spite of the loss in revenue, the United States felt that it was a good bargain, for one clause of the treaty gave to Americans ultimate control of the Kingdom's foreign policy. The clause read:

> It is agreed, on the part of His Hawaiian Majesty, that so long as this treaty shall remain in force, he will not lease or otherwise dispose of or create any lien upon any port, harbor, or other territory in his dominions, or grant any special privilege or rights of use therein, to any other power, state, or government, nor make any treaty by which any other nation shall obtain the same privileges, relative to the admission of any articles free of duty, hereby secured to the United States.

This was an early "Platt amendment" which made Hawaii virtually a sphere of influence for the United States, but the sugar planters in the islands were pleased. Z. S. Spalding, who made an estate of a million dollars for himself out of sugar, said that "before the reciprocity treaty had passed all the plantations had

[40] From Russell H. Anderson, "Some Aspects of Tariff Remissions on Sugar, 1876-1927," in *The Annals of the American Academy of Political and Social Science,* CXLI (Jan., 1929), p. 151. For other statistics, see Chalfant Robinson, *op. cit.,* p. 148. The figures as listed include the remitted revenue for the second treaty as well as the first one. Hilary A. Herbert, Chairman of the House Committee on Naval Affairs, said: "Every dollar of the . . . taxes released on Hawaiian sugar went into the pockets of the producers of that article, Mr. Claus Spreckels and others." See "Reciprocity and the Farmer," in *North American Review,* CLIV (April, 1892), 417.

[41] Russell H. Anderson, *op. cit.,* p. 153.

gone through bankruptcy. I do not think that there was a single plantation that had not gone into bankruptcy."[43] A land boom ensued as more and more acres slipped from native into sugar planters' hands. So profitable was the sugar business that by 1898 the incomes of six selected companies ran from a minimum of ten per cent to a maximum of fifty-four per cent on capital invested.[44]

The political consequences of this reciprocity agreement cannot be overestimated. When Hawaii was finally annexed in 1898, practically everybody agreed that the first real step had been reciprocity, that is to say, economic annexation. The *New York Tribune* spoke truly on March 3, 1893, when it said: "It is Reciprocity that has enabled the United States to take possession of the key of the North Pacific [Hawaii]." Yet the treaty had to be railroaded through the Senate, for many could not see the advantage in giving up so much revenue.[45]

The Blaine era in American diplomacy brought further sentiment in favor of annexation. On December 1, 1881, Secretary James G. Blaine wrote to James M. Comly, American Minister, as follows: "I have shown . . . how entirely Hawaii is a part of the productive and commercial system of the American States. . . . There is little doubt that were the Hawaiian Islands, by annexation or district [*sic*] protection, a part of the Union, their fertile resources for the growth of rice and sugar would not only be controlled by American capital, but so profitable a field of labor would attract intelligent workers thither from the United States." Blaine then asked Comly "discreetly" to turn Hawaiian thoughts

[42] The same fact is evident in the United States veto of Hawaii's action when it moved to make most-favored-nation treaties with other countries. Both Germany and Great Britain demanded their rights to no avail (Laughlin and Willis, *op. cit.*, pp. 89-90).

[43] Morgan, p. 251. Cf., Rear Admiral George Belknap, in *ibid.*, p. 721, who said: "From that moment [signing of the reciprocity pact] an era of prosperity dawned upon those islands and trade there increased several hundred per cent."

[44] Laughlin and Willis, *op. cit.*, p. 88.

[45] That Americans did not lose in the long run (because the treaty increased the commerce between Hawaii and the United States) was the burden of an unsigned review of the results of the treaty, printed in Morgan, pp. 103-113.

toward inviting American colonization by means of homestead laws for immigrants.[46]

As more and more Hawaiian sugar poured into the United States to compete with that grown in Louisiana and elsewhere, determined opposition arose to the renewal of the treaty. In spite of Cleveland's advocacy of a new treaty in his annual message of 1886, a second pact could, therefore, be pushed through the Senate in 1887 only by further concessions from Hawaii. The chief concession consisted of granting to the United States a lease upon, and exclusive control over, Pearl Harbor which was to be used as an American naval base.[47] The Pearl Harbor clause was added to the treaty in the Senate without the knowledge or approval of Secretary Thomas F. Bayard.[48]

When the amended treaty arrived in Honolulu, King Kalakaua at first refused to sign it. The Reform Cabinet then in power, representing to a considerable extent the sugar interests which had to have reciprocity in order to live, was forced to exert pressure upon the King to get his consent. Kalakaua was constrained to accept the Pearl Harbor amendment only after receiving the promise that the following proviso would be sent to the Secretary of State at Washington: "Hawaiian Sovereignty and Jurisdiction were not impaired . . . the Hawaiian Government was not bound to furnish land for any purpose and . . . the privilege to be

[46] *Sen. Ex. Doc. 77* (52 Cong. 2 Sess.), pp. 165-166.

[47] *Ibid.*, pp. 166-168. Donald Marquand Dozer has described the propaganda unleashed by Louisiana Congressmen and East Coast sugar refiners against reciprocity in "The Opposition to Hawaiian Reciprocity, 1876-1888," in *The Pacific Historical Review,* XIV (June, 1945), 157-184.

[48] For more facts see Charles Callan Tansill, *Diplomatic Relations between the United States and Hawaii, 1885-1889* in *Fordham University Studies* (Historical Series, No. 1; N. Y., 1940), pp. 19 *ff.* See also Charles Callan Tansill, *The Foreign Policy of Thomas F. Bayard 1885-1897* (N. Y., 1940), pp. 359-410 for material, similar in content, to the pamphlet. "The earliest published suggestion that Pearl Harbor be offered to the United States as an inducement for a reciprocity treaty appeared in an editorial in the *Pacific Commercial Advertiser* of February 8, 1873." Probably the first diplomatic (hence secret) hint was made by Minister James McBride to Secretary Seward in 1864. See Ralph S. Kuykendall, *The Hawaiian Kingdom 1854-1874 Twenty Critical Years* (Honolulu, 1953), pp. 200 and 250.

granted should be coterminous with the Treaty."[49] Just what validity such a unilateral interpretation of the treaty had is hard to say. But one more step had been taken toward complete control[50]—a fact which was brought out clearly in the same year when the United States refused to join England and France in a tripartite agreement to guarantee the independence of the islands.[51]

The new treaty had, however, one joker which its American proponents seem not to have taken seriously at the time. It was to last seven years, after which it could be abrogated upon a year's notice. Suppose either party denounced the pact, would the United States not lose its control over Pearl Harbor—particularly inasmuch as Kalakaua had signed the treaty with the understanding that "the privilege to be granted should be coterminous with the Treaty"? This danger might arise soon (that is, after 1891) because the treaty was dated back to 1884. The problem emerged in bold relief at the passage of the McKinley Tariff of 1890, which, by placing all sugar on the free list, and by giving a bounty of two cents a pound to domestic producers, practically nullified the reciprocity clause of the agreement of 1887.[52] Moreover, all imports from Hawaii (such as rice and tallow which heretofore had been admitted free) were subjected to the McKinley schedule.

Hawaii raised so much objection to these actions that McKinley, on December 4, 1890, offered a bill which declared that the Tariff of 1890 did not impair the reciprocity clauses of the treaty of 1887. Said he: "There are special reasons for the

[49] Minutes of the Cabinet Council, pp. 383-386, Sept. 22, 26, Oct. 20, 1887. The Minutes of the Cabinet Council can be found in the Archives of Hawaii, Honolulu, hereafter called "Archives."

[50] In spite of the conversation of Nov. 7, 1885, between British Minister Sackville-West and Hawaiian Minister H. A. P. Carter, as reported to Lord Salisbury. Carter told the Englishman that annexation was far distant, since reciprocity did not mean political control (Allan Nevins, *Grover Cleveland: A Study in Courage,* N. Y., 1932, p. 550).

[51] Dennett, *op. cit.,* p. 611.

[52] What the free sugar clauses of 1890 meant to Hawaiian sugar exports is evident from the fact that, whereas Cuba sent $21,000,000 worth of sugar to the American market in 1891, its share grew to $60,000,000 in 1892 and to $63,000,000 in 1894. After the repeal of the McKinley Tariff, Cuban exports fell in 1895 to $15,000,000 and Hawaii's increased in proportion. See Chalfant Robinson, *op. cit.,* pp. 155-156. Query: Did the loss to Cuba after 1894 help bring on the Cuban Revolution and the Spanish-American War?

maintenance of the treaty at this time." In all likelihood one of the reasons was Pearl Harbor. The bill passed on March 3, 1891.[53] Whether McKinley's "Declaratory Act" could have prevented Hawaii from denouncing the whole treaty and from demanding return of Pearl Harbor is uncertain. Would the United States have given up the lease, even if Hawaii had abrogated the treaty?[54]

The Wilson-Gorman Tariff of 1894—passed after Annexationists in Hawaii had overturned the Queen—did away with the free sugar policy by imposing a duty of forty per cent and by eliminating the bounty. This gesture returned Hawaiian planters to their strategic position under the reciprocity treaty; the country prospered; and annexationism died down considerably. Yet the sentiment for union continued; Annexationists did not wish to risk another economic crisis such as might easily occur if the United States ever placed sugar on the free list again.[55]

* * * * *

Annexation was a thing to be hoped and worked for; but if to be achieved at all, it could only be a goal in the distant future. Years before the trouble arose from the McKinley Act, it had become clear to many planters that the more immediate problem was to get economic and political control of the islands, and then perhaps annexation might follow. A more progressive race, the descendants of the missionaries who sent their children to the United States to be educated,[56] slowly and almost imperceptibly

[53] Pratt, *Expansionists of 1898, op. cit.*, pp. 43 *ff.*

[54] In 1897, while the Dingley Tariff was under debate, the reciprocity clause was retained only through considerable lobbying by Hawaiian diplomatic representatives at Washington. During this discussion President Sanford B. Dole asked Minister Francis M. Hatch about the status of Pearl Harbor. Hatch answered that some American officials said that the United States had an absolute right of control, paid for by remissions on the sugar duty. Hatch himself felt that Senator William P. Frye's idea would probably prevail if the matter ever came up. Frye believed the United States had a right to Pearl Harbor, but that to assert the right after any abrogation of the reciprocity treaty would be mean and immoral (Hatch to Dole, June 8, 1897, Dole Papers, Archives).

[55] The problem of the inconsistency between the treaty of 1887 and the McKinley Tariff is ably discussed by Laughlin and Willis, *op. cit.*, pp. 99-102; see also *Congressional Record* (51 Cong. 2 Sess.), p. 3620.

[56] For instance, Chief Justice A. F. Judd was born in the islands and studied at Harvard and Yale (Blount, p. 362); William De Witt Alexander studied at Yale and taught for a time at Beloit (Morgan, p. 262); the Rev.

wormed their way, year by year, into the King's favor until they were the power behind the throne. Controlling the business and wealth of the islands, they became the dominant minority amongst a people who only a few years before had welcomed them as visitors.[57]

Under American influence a crude Constitution was proclaimed in 1840[58] and a better one in 1852.[59] A third, that of 1864,[60] contained a bill of rights which repeated most of the inalienable privileges of Englishmen and Americans. The Ministry was appointed at the King's pleasure, although one Minister must countersign any act of the King, thus making himself responsible. The upper house, that of the Nobles, consisted of twenty men, appointed for life by the sovereign. It acted also as the court of impeachment. The lower house, the Representatives, was elective. A member must own property worth $500 or have an income of $250 annually. At first a voter was required to own $150 worth of property or have an income of $75 per annum, and be able to read and write. Later the property qualification was removed.[61] The King was given final veto over laws passed by the Legislature, and he also appointed the Supreme Court. Such a system of government gave almost unlimited opportunity for an unworthy King to misrule with impunity.

As the Americans slowly gathered economic and political power in their hands, they came face to face with many features of Hawaiian society which they could not like. One was the king-

Mr. Oliver P. Emerson, Secretary of the Hawaiian Board of Missions, was born in Hawaii of New Hampshire missionaries and studied at Williams (Morgan, p. 174); and William R. Castle, born in Honolulu of American parents, studied at Oberlin.

[57] For an appreciation of the generosity and friendliness of the natives to the early missionaries, see the deposition of former Minister Charles T. Gulick, in Blount, pp. 279 *ff*.

[58] A primitive representative chamber and an upper house, consisting of king and chieftains, were the main features. Printed in Morgan, pp. 121-127, and analyzed by Chambers, *op. cit.*, pp. 13-16. For a brief survey of Hawaiian constitutional history up to 1893, see William De Witt Alexander in Morgan, pp. 315-323.

[59] Analyzed by Chambers, *op. cit.*, pp. 17-20.

[60] Blount, pp. 338-351. Also printed in Morgan, pp. 160 *ff.*; described by Chambers, *op. cit.*, pp. 20-22.

[61] Blount, p. 105.

ship. The title of king sounded evil enough in American ears, but a decayed and pusillanimous sovereign, who was often a drunken debauchee, sounded even worse. Further, the Americans who knew that they controlled the government, felt, more and more, the insult involved in having to kowtow to a monarch who could not gain their respect; and even when they began to pull the strings which made the government function, it irked their republican sensibilities to be required to work through a bizarre monarchy whose dark-skinned king they considered their moral, intellectual, and social inferior.[62] But they put up with this tawdry royalty because it was on the scene when their fathers arrived, and because they were a small faction in the midst of a native population which outnumbered them (even as late as the 1890's) forty to one.[63] Their chance to overturn it would come only when the natives had died off sufficiently, and when the monarchy had, through its imbecility, struck itself down.

The islands had been united under Kamehameha I after fierce opposition in 1795; he ruled until 1819. The first three Kamehamehas had been strong enough; the fourth (1854-63) was weaker; and the fifth (1863-72) was not only a drunkard, but also weighed 300 pounds and was ever in danger of suffocating from obesity.[64] The dynasty became extinct in 1872, when a high chieftain, Lunalilo (1872-74), was elected to the kingship.[65]

[62] Cf., Minister Henry A. Peirce to Secretary Fish, Feb. 17, 1874: "Were it not for the serious condition of things . . . one would be amusingly reminded by the Hawaiian court and Government, their parade paraphernalia, etiquette, and diminutiveness of the nation and absence of strength, of the court and government of Offenbach's Grand Duchess of Geralstine." See *Sen. Ex. Doc. 77* (52 Cong. 2 Sess.), p. 158.

[63] The Honolulu *Hawaiian Star,* Feb. 27, 1897, explained the situation as follows: "What was the Monarchy here? Merely a tolerated system of government, because it suited several powers to have the Islands kept independent . . . who were the real rulers? By no means the Hawaiians. The Government was either conducted by Anglo-Saxons entirely, or with an occasional dummy Hawaiian set up and the work done by the Anglo Saxons [*sic*] behind him." From 1842 to 1854, there was only one native in the Cabinet, that is, John Young II, and he was a half-caste; and from 1842 to 1872 there were only two Hawaiians, half-caste or full-blood, in the Cabinet.

[64] Morgan, p. 31.

[65] Lunalilo was no better. He was under the guardianship of the banker, Charles R. Bishop, who controlled his property, and allowed the new King twenty-five dollars a month for spending money (Liliuokalani, *op. cit.,* p.

Dying without issue and without appointing a successor, he left the task of choosing a sovereign to the Legislature. Two candidates were available. The whites, mostly American, were not yet strong enough to abolish the monarchy, and had to content themselves with supporting the candidate who promised to be most amenable to American influence.[66] They worked in favor of a distant relative of the last sovereign, Prince David Kalakaua,[67] as against Emma, the Queen Dowager, who being English, was reputed to have English favor. Owing to the active interference of Americans, and to the feeling that if Emma were chosen no reciprocity treaty could be expected from the United States,[68] Kalakaua was selected. Immediately upon election, he was faced with a revolt led by the disappointed partisans of the Queen Dowager. Nevertheless the new sovereign was established on his throne by British and American troops which were landed from battleships in the harbor.[69] This interference in the internal affairs of the Kingdom not only showed the weakness of the native government, but set a precedent which would be referred to when American troops were needed in future insurrections.[70]

37). For details on the election of Lunalilo, see Sanford B. Dole, *Memoirs of the Hawaiian Revolution,* ed. by Andrew Farrell, Honolulu, 1936, pp. 1-33; and Thurston, *Memoirs, op. cit.,* pp. 1-11.

[66] Following the deposition of the monarchy, the Honolulu *Pacific Commercial Advertiser* said that after "the Kamehameha line became extinct the rulers of Hawaii have been allowed to continue the monarchical form of government as a matter of courtesy rather than right" (enclosed in Severance to Quincy, No. 200, May 9, 1893, Consular Letters, which are housed in the National Archives, Washington, D. C.).

[67] Later rumor had it that Kalakaua had been suggested by Mark Twain (New York *World,* Dec. 1, 1893). The direct line of Kamehamehas having become extinct, Kalakaua, whose ancestor had been a first cousin of Kamehameha I, was the founder of a new line. His dynasty was called the Keawe-a-Heulu line (Liliuokalani, *op. cit.,* p. 105).

[68] Blount, p. 108. For details see Kuykendall, *op. cit.,* pp. 236-238.

[69] *Sen. Ex. Doc. 77* (52 Cong. 2 Sess.), pp. 155-158; W. D. Alexander, in Blount, p. 180; testimony of Commander Theodore F. Jewell, who was on the U.S.S. *Tuscarora* during the period of Kalakaua's election, in Morgan, pp. 418 *ff.;* also Rear Admiral George Belknap, who was in Honolulu at the time, in *ibid.,* pp. 711 *ff.* Liliuokalani gives the episode some attention in *op. cit.,* pp. 177 *ff.*

[70] Liliuokalani (*op. cit.,* p. 48) vehemently denies the justice of this precedent. She maintains that in 1874 troops were landed to protect the constitutional government and that in 1893 they were to aid in overthrowing

Much to their disgust, the American adherents of Kalakaua, who had thought him to be a liberal, found that he was an ardent reactionary who began to rule as if he were a Bourbon.[71] Moreover he was a roué whose scandalous life irritated the whites.[72] The Americans stood him as long as they could; finally in what came to be known as the Revolution of July 1, 1887, they demanded a new Constitution which would make him responsible to the white element. When he saw his opponents in arms against him, Kalakaua accepted and proclaimed the Constitution which the whites had drafted.[73]

it. For amusing facts about the landing of the troops and the riot, see Dole, *Memoirs, op. cit.*, pp. 33-44, and Thurston, *Memoirs, op. cit.*, pp. 11-20.

[71] For the misrule of adventurers such as Moreno, Gibson, and Spreckels, see W. D. Alexander, the Hawaiian historian, in Blount, pp. 179-196; see also, Thurston, *Memoirs, op. cit.*, Chapters III-IX.

[72] For instance, in 1887 he was accused of accepting a bribe of $71,000 (Chambers, *op. cit.*, p. 24). A handwritten account of this affair can be found in Thurston Papers for 1887, in Archives. Isobel Field, the artist, denies the scandal about Kalakaua's excessive drinking and discredits the stories about Palace orgies. The King, loving companionship, held parties that were, she says, perfectly decent. When American and Russian officers tried to outdrink him, they always failed because he first took poi and milk before imbibing the stronger liquor. See Isobel Field, *This Life I've Loved* (N. Y., 1937), pp. 165, 173. On the other hand, the King's own Minister to the United States, H. A. P. Carter, informed Secretary Thomas F. Bayard time and again that Kalakaua was untruthful, corrupt, and weak. For instance, see Tansill, *Diplomatic Relations . . . , op. cit.*, p. 34, note 95.

[73] For Chief Justice A. F. Judd's description of how this Constitution was extorted from the King, see Blount, pp. 109-110. Some of the Revolutionists wanted a republic, but the more conservative participants "said that the King and the Hawaiians should have another opportunity" (George Belknap, who was in Hawaii at the time, in *ibid.*, pp. 711 *ff.*). It is clear from a handwritten proclamation (in Thurston Papers, Archives) drafted by Thurston in May, 1887 that he wished to depose Kalakaua and establish a republic. He seems to have found less support for this policy than he felt to be necessary but in all likelihood he used this paper of 1887 as a specimen for the drafting of the proclamation of Jan. 17, 1893. Many of the names included as putative officeholders in the republic, after the expected dethronement of Kalakaua, appear as leaders in the Committee of Safety of Jan., 1893. More will be said of this later. Isobel Field maintains that she played an important part in the uprising by acting as secret messenger between the King and Gibson, the Foreign Minister. She believes that she saved the throne for Kalakaua (Isobel Field, *op. cit.*, pp. 208-214). For inside details see Thurston Papers for 1887 and Minutes of the Cabinet Council, 1864-1891, pp. 376-381, both in Archives. The leader in this, as well as in the Revolu-

The Americans, who had been responsible for the *émeute* by which a new Constitution was made possible, of course tried to see to it that the new system would give them legally the control of the Royal Government. The Cabinet, composed of four Ministers, was removable only upon a want-of-confidence vote by a majority of the Legislature, or by being convicted of felony, or by impeachment. No act of the sovereign was effective until countersigned by at least one Minister, who then made himself responsible for the act. The Cabinet members had the right to sit in the Legislature, to debate and to vote, except in case of a resolution of lack of confidence in themselves. The Legislature was bicameral, composed of twenty-four Nobles and twenty-four Representatives, sitting together. The Royal veto might be overcome by a two-thirds vote of both houses. A Noble must be twenty-five years of age, have resided three years in the Kingdom, and must own property worth $3,000 or have an income of $600 a year. The Nobles sat as a court of impeachment. They were given six-year terms, but received no pay. To qualify as a voter for a Noble, a subject must have the same property qualifications as the man running for the office. A Representative was required to have resided three years in the country, and own property worth $500 or enjoy an annual income of $250. The Supreme Court was appointed by the King.

This "Bayonet Constitution,"[74] which set up a Government savoring of the English variety, was a clever device for securing to the whites the control of the Kingdom. The ruler (on paper at least) was tied down so completely that it was hoped good government might be possible even though he be dissipated and profligate. It was supposed to give to the whites (mostly Amer-

tion of 1893, was Lorrin Andrews Thurston (1858-1931), descended from Puritans who settled in Massachusetts in the 1630's. Both parents were missionaries in Hawaii. He attended private school, Oahu College, and Columbia University law school. Returning to Honolulu he set up a law practice with W. O. Smith, and was elected to the Legislatures of 1886 and 1892. His experiences therein made him an Annexationist. The story of Hawaiian annexation is largely a story of Thurston's activities. After 1898 he became principal owner and editorial director of the *Advertiser*. R. S. Kuykendall has a sketch of him in the *Dictionary of American Biography,* edited by Allen Johnson and Dumas Malone (N. Y., 1928-37), XVIII, 517-518.

[74] Thus designated by Liliuokalani (*op. cit.,* p. 182) who avers that the conspirators originally plotted to assassinate the King and set up a republic.

icans) almost complete domination in the upper house, because few natives had much property; and, even if the natives might have a majority in the lower house, the Nobles could block bad legislation. To control the Ministry they needed only one Representative, provided they controlled every vote in the upper chamber.[75] Moreover, the three-year residence requirement made it easy for newly-arrived Americans soon to take part in the political affairs of the Kingdom. Finally, it was hoped that a counter-revolution to secure a new Constitution by King or natives had been made practically impossible, because the sovereign could proclaim no decree or law which did not have the signature of at least one Minister. This was the Constitution, which, according to John L. Stevens (soon to be the American Minister to Hawaii), "was gained by the people, especially by the property holders and businessmen . . . much as the Magna Charta of England was gained by the barons from King John in 1215."[76]

When the trouble arose, the incumbent American Minister, George W. Merrill, asked Secretary of State Thomas F. Bayard for instructions as to what attitude he should take in such domestic crises. On July 12, 1887, Bayard answered in a letter which was later used as precedent for acts of the American Minister in 1893. After asserting that there must be peace and quiet so that American commerce to Hawaii would not be disturbed, and after referring to the intimate relations between the two countries, Bayard said: "Your own aid and counsel, as well as the assistance of the officers of our Government vessels, if found necessary, will therefore be promptly afforded to promote the reign of law

[75] Blount, p. 112, says the property qualifications for membership in the upper house gave three-fourths of the vote for Nobles to the whites, and one-fourth to the natives.

[76] Stevens to Blaine, Aug. 19, 1890, in *House Ex. Doc. 48* (53 Cong. 2 Sess.), p. 67. Both old and new Constitutions are printed in Blount, pp. 338-351; the new Constitution is analyzed by Chambers, *op. cit.*, pp. 25-27. Dole, *Memoirs, op. cit.*, pp. 44-58, describes the Revolution and the new Constitution. The best brief analysis of the Constitution of 1887 is "Cabinet Government in Hawaii 1887-1893" by Thomas M. Spaulding, in *University of Hawaii Occasional Papers No. 2* (Honolulu, 1924), pp. 1-22. Spaulding showed that the weaknesses grew out of the haste in which the Constitution was written. The King still had the power to appoint Cabinets and to veto. For these reasons the system was not true cabinet government on the English model.

and respect for orderly government in Hawaii."[77] This instruction was tantamount to saying that if the Minister thought American lives and property were being endangered by domestic violence, troops from any United States naval vessel in port might be used.

Under the old Constitution, there had been no property qualifications; therefore natives had been in a majority in both houses of the Legislature. Now they were disgruntled.[78] Moreover, under the old Constitution, the Cabinet was responsible to the crown, and the ruler had real power. Now reduced to a mere figurehead, he too was disgruntled. A new feeling of sympathy grew up between the natives and their sovereign, both of whom saw themselves thrust into an inferior position by the new system. Although, at the time, the King had to accept the new fundamental law or face armed revolution led by the whites, he used every subterfuge to evade the restrictions that had been placed upon him. The remainder of Kalakaua's reign was characterized by a running contest between the Reform party which desired to control the Government and the King who fought to regain his prerogatives.

In 1889 a revolt was planned and started in the interest of the old order by a half-caste named Robert W. Wilcox, an inveterate revolutionary.[79] It is not clear whether Wilcox wished to depose the King and place his sister Liliuokalani in power, or whether he intended to restore the King to his authority under the Constitution of 1864.

At first the Cabinet thought it was the former, because on July 22, 1889, the Cabinet Council discussed "the alleged conspiracy of R. W. Wilcox and others to create a revolution in favor of placing H.R.H. Liliuokalani on the Throne." As a preventive, the Cabinet

[77] *Foreign Relations of the United States 1887,* printed as *House Ex. Doc. 1* (50 Cong. 1 Sess.), part 1, pp. 580-581.

[78] Cf., S. M. Damon's statement in Blount, pp. 44 *ff.;* also Wilcox's testimony in *ibid.,* pp. 549-550.

[79] For the Wilcox affair see statement of Volney V. Ashford, in *ibid.,* pp. 202 *ff.;* and Merrill's report on the insurrection to Blaine, in *House Ex. Doc. 48* (53 Cong. 2 Sess.), pp. 16-20. Alexander gives more information in his testimony to the Morgan Committee, pp. 284 *ff.* Liliuokalani, *op. cit.,* pp. 198-202, has some data on Wilcox. Dole, *Memoirs, op. cit.,* chapter IV, and Thurston, *Memoirs, op. cit.,* chapter X, offer further information.

on July 29 unanimously voted that the King must turn over all Government arms to the Minister of Foreign Affairs. Kalakaua refused because he said he was commander in chief under the Constitution; he would consent only if the Supreme Court so decided.[80]

On July 31, while the strong man of the Cabinet, Lorrin A. Thurston, was making an official visit to the leper colony on Molokai, Wilcox occupied the Palace. Marshal John H. Soper was awakened at three in the morning with the news: "By Jesus[,] Marshal, Wilcox is in the Palace, with two hundred men." Soper organized a party of volunteers who drove the insurrectionists out by means of dynamite sticks.[81]

United States troops went ashore to protect American lives and property, and the commander of the U.S.S. *Adams* lent the Government 10,000 rounds of ammunition. Impressed by the instability of the existing Government, the United States maintained a naval vessel in Honolulu from that time on, ready to protect lives and property at a moment's notice.[82]

The plot failed, and for the moment constitutional government was assured. The Cabinet, however, decided that the King must be brought under control. On August 3 it presented the following statement to him: "The Government in all its Departments must be conducted by the Cabinet, who will be solely and absolutely responsible for such conduct. Your Majesty shall in future sign all documents and do all acts which under the laws or the Constitution require the signature or act of the Sovereign, when advised so to do by the Cabinet, the Cabinet being solely and absolutely responsible for any signature of any document or act so done or performed by their advice."

[80] Minutes of the Cabinet Council, pp. 401-402, in Archives.

[81] See unsigned manuscripts in Thurston Papers, Archives, entitled "Wilcox insurrection 1889" and "Biography of R. W. Wilcox."

[82] An American war vessel had usually been stationed in Honolulu, but not always. As early as May 8, 1889, Minister Merrill had asked that a warship be retained permanently in Hawaiian waters because of "the large American interests . . . the absence of cable communication, the comparatively isolated condition of the islands, and . . . an approaching political campaign." In *House Ex. Doc. 48* (53 Cong. 2 Sess.), pp. 5-6. Blaine saw to it that a vessel was sent. See also, *ibid.*, pp. 14-15 and 32-35; Morgan, pp. 526 and 721; and *Senate Report 681* (55 Cong. 2 Sess.), p. 117.

The King objected, saying he had the right to withhold his signature from commissions and papers if he disagreed with their contents. Again he declared he would refuse until the Supreme Court decided the issue. The Court unanimously supported the Cabinet's position by declaring that the Government was a constitutional monarchy. "There can be no dual Government," it said. "There can be no authority without responsibility. The King is without responsibility. The Constitution confers the responsibility of the Government upon the Cabinet: they therefore have the authority." When this decision was read to the King, with the request that he accept the principles laid down in it, he apologized for his "rather high words" and promised to abide by the Court's opinion.

The Minister of Foreign Affairs then informed Kalakaua that all military equipment and munitions would be taken from the Palace and barracks, except what was needed for the King's Guard; that the Commander of the Guard would be removed; and that a letter of thanks to the volunteers who put down the insurrection would be issued.[83] Already the Privy Council had appropriated money to pay for the expenses of quelling the revolt.[84] All of which must have been gall and wormwood to Kalakaua.

Having won this victory over the sovereign, the Cabinet proceeded to make use of it by endeavoring to secure an extension of the reciprocity treaty which was about to end in accordance with its terms. In September, 1889 the Cabinet voted to instruct Minister H. A. P. Carter to proceed with a new treaty, subject to final ratification by the King. Kalakaua was stubborn and refused to sign the commission. The Cabinet reminded him of the Supreme Court's opinion that he was to follow the decisions of his Ministers. The King replied that the Court's directive applied only to internal matters, and that "it was not his duty to sign a document presented by the Ministry in relation to a Treaty if he

[83] These proceedings can be found in Minutes of the Cabinet Council, Archives, for Aug. 3 and 5, 1889, pp. 403-404, 405 *ff*.

[84] Minutes of the Privy Council, Archives, Aug. 2, 1889, pp. 265-267; see also Oct. 26, 1889, pp. 272-276. For another disagreement between King and Cabinet over the signing of an exequatur for H. W. Severance to act as Consul General for the United States, see Minutes of the Cabinet Council, July 31, 1889, pp. 402-403. The Cabinet finally had its way and the paper was signed.

had reasons satisfactory to himself for declining to do so." The ire of the Ministers can be gauged by the words in the minutes of the Cabinet Council:

> The Minister of the Interior [Thurston] said that this was not the first instance of His Majestys [*sic*] refusal to comply with the advice of his Ministers, that the experience of the Cabinet had been one continued struggle to get him to do his duty, and that the history of such action on the part of Sovereigns in the past had had the uniform result of bringing disaster upon the Sovereign and the Country. His Majesty said I' am willing, Let it come.
>
> The Minister then said, Your Majesty, distinctly refuses to do your duty.
>
> His Majesty answered, It is not my duty. I have the Constitutional right to decline to sign the document.
>
> The Council then adjourned[.][85]

This was plain talking on the part of both the King and his aggressive Minister. From the incident it is not difficult to foresee a time when Thurston would become the leader of the Revolution to abolish the monarchy. The conflict between the desire of the sovereign for personal power and the determination of the Reform party, working through the Cabinet, to secure democratic government was slowly leading to a rupture. The attitude of the King is shown in Isobel Field's recollection of a conversation which she had with Kalakaua some two years before this event.[86] Said the King: "What they want is my country. They are hoping to annex Hawaii to the United States. It has been a steady fight ever since I came to the throne." She then asked whether he thought they would take Hawaii from him. "Not while I live," said the King.

As long as the Cabinet remained a unit it had the advantage over the sovereign; but if there was division, he could play both ends against the middle. In 1890 the Attorney General, C. W. Ashford, seems to have gone over to the Royal side. In any event, the Cabinet divided three to one (the one being Ashford) on the question of granting to V. V. Ashford a commission as Colonel of Volunteers. The Attorney General naturally desired the post

[85] Minutes of the Cabinet Council, Archives, September, 1889, pp. 408-413.
[86] *Op. cit.*, pp. 208-214.

for his brother. The King's sly satisfaction can be gathered from the minute which reads: "His Majesty said that the failure of unanimity in the recommendation of the Cabinet placed him in an embarrassing position." He desired a written opinion from each member.[87]

A short time later the same problem arose over the old question of commissioning H. A. P. Carter to enter into a new reciprocity treaty with the United States. Again the vote was three to one, Ashford in the minority. By that time the agile-minded Thurston had advanced a step further in his theory of Cabinet responsibility. He told Kalakaua that the King should follow the advice of a majority; and added that three Supreme Court Justices had told Thurston informally that they thought unanimity was unnecessary.[88] The dispute this time arose over the appointment of another man as Colonel of Volunteers. Said Ashford: "I advise Your Majesty to decline to follow the advice of the majority of the Cabinet and that of the Supreme Court." The King was undoubtedly delighted to inform his Ministers he would not sign the commission unless there was unanimity within the group.[89]

Another instance, unimportant in itself, of this conflict between Cabinet and sovereign concerned the seemingly innocuous desire of Kalakaua to visit Kona on the Island of Hawaii in April, 1890. The Cabinet advised him not to go because there were disquieting rumors of uprisings around Honolulu and he might be needed. Said Thurston: "If Your Majesty leaves it will be against the advice of the Cabinet." On the margin of the Minute Book the Council secretary wrote dryly: "*H.M.* decides to go [.]"[90] This is the last entry in the Council's Minute Book for over a year. The reason was that an election had overturned the Reform party's majority in the Legislature and the ruler secured a friendly Cabinet which sympathized with Royalist ideas of government. The Cabinet Council was an active body only when the American or Reform party was in power.

By 1890, then, the Americans who had been responsible for the new Constitution of 1887 learned that they had been defeated in

[87] Minutes of the Cabinet Council, March 21, 1890, pp. 414-415.
[88] *Ibid.*, April 10, 1890, pp. 416-417.
[89] *Ibid.*, p. 417.
[90] *Ibid.*, April 17, 1890, p. 418.

their endeavor to secure control of the executive department of the Government. In spite of the heavy property qualifications and other disabilities imposed upon the natives, the white or Reform party was able to squeeze only one Legislature out of the new Constitution. In the first one elected under the new dispensation the whites secured a majority (and therefore controlled the Cabinet) because they were still armed and were able to overawe the natives.

The Legislature of 1890, however, elected in favor of a pro-native Constitution, showed how completely the white party had wrought in vain; the intelligent laboring class of Honolulu failed to support the Reform party, which lost control even of the Nobles. As a consequence, a Cabinet composed of Royalists resulted.[91]

Thus, despite the Americans' hopes that under the Constitution of 1887 they had made inescapable provisions for hamstringing the King, they failed. In the first place, they forgot to write into the new document in so many words that the King must follow the advice of his Cabinet. This they secured as an aftermath of the Wilcox insurrection of 1889 when the King, after the Supreme Court turned against him, promised to accept the principle of Cabinet responsibility. But hardly had this victory been won before the King found a loophole: was the advice of the Cabinet to be given by a mere majority or must it be unanimous? Suppose the Cabinet divided, two to two? In the second place, the constitution-makers of 1887 were unable to prevent their enemies from getting into control of the Legislature and therefore of the Cabinet in the first free election held.

In all of these matters the King and his advisers were considered by the white party to be chiefly to blame. Because of Kalakaua's evasions of what the Reform party considered to be his obligations, more and more leaders of the whites began to conclude that the only way to secure good government was to get rid of the monarchy altogether. One of the first to come to this decision, if he did not believe it already, was Thurston who had been attempting, with futility, to reduce the King to an innocuous place in the administration. Within two years after his failure, Thurston was organizing a secret movement to unseat the

[91] Stevens to Blaine, Feb. 7, 1890, in *House Ex. Doc. 48* (53 Cong. 2 Sess.), pp. 35-36; also same to same, pp. 37 and 55.

monarchy. In addition, it is significant that the Revolutionary Committee of Safety of 1893 would proudly state, in a sworn affidavit, that the same men who carried through the Revolution of 1887 were, in 1893, the supporters of the Provisional Government.[92]

Kalakaua, intensely disliked by Americans both because of his tendency towards reactionary absolutism and because of his dissolute life, died of obesity in San Francisco on January 20, 1891. He had gone there for his health. Of him the New York *World* later said: ". . . there was no Keeley cure in Hawaii, then, and he proceeded, with truly royal disregard of the proprieties, to drink himself to death in a year."[93] He was brought back with royal honors on the American man-of-war *Charleston*. His sister, Liliuokalani, known in everyday life as Mrs. John Dominis, wife of a man of part Italian blood from Boston, succeeded him.[94]

The Americans accepted Liliuokalani with some misgivings, but hoped for the best because she was supposed to have been influenced by Christianity and by her American education. She had composed several hymns which were used in Hawaiian Protestant churches, and yet her personal morality remained a moot question until 1936 when Julius W. Pratt gave convincing proof that her evil reputation arose from deliberate reviling by Annexationists, especially by Minister John L. Stevens and the Reverend Mr. Sereno E. Bishop.[95]

It profited those republicans who later deposed the Queen to paint her in as unfriendly terms as possible. Even the New York *World* which criticized the republicans for having perpetrated a crime in dethroning her, said she lived the life of a heathen and married a "mongrel," named John Dominis; furthermore, that she was the "granddaughter of the first man ever hanged in Hawaii for wife murder. She is the daughter of a drunken Kanaka, a Honolulu bummer who was elevated to the throne without the

[92] Morgan, pp. 590-591.

[93] Dec. 1, 1893.

[94] She was called Lily of Killarney by Americans who could not pronounce her name. Liliuokalani meant "preservation of the heavens." She was born Lydia Kamakaeha Paki on September 2, 1838.

[95] Julius W. Pratt, *Expansionists of 1898, op. cit.*, pp. 160 *ff*. See also *Harper's Weekly* (Dec. 2, 1893), p. 1146.

least shadow of claim."[96] The same paper, at another time, described Dominis as "a sailor . . . who . . . possessed something of a Turkish fondness for tobacco and women." After his death, Liliuokalani tried to find out about his family history. She received a letter from "the fellow's former wife, or one of them, in this country, and she promptly suspended all further inquiry."[97] It is hardly necessary to remind the reader that these charges were mere mud-slinging which was so characteristic of the yellow journalism of the time.

Liliuokalani was not a good Queen. That is certain. And the vengefulness she showed towards those who deposed her gave more fuel to her enemies, like the American Minister John L. Stevens, who covered her with abuse and vilification. Senator George F. Hoar recorded that, when he wrote the platform of the Massachusetts Republican party in 1894, he included a plank which read: "No barbarous Queen beheading men in Hawaii." But he admitted that later he found out she was a true Christian woman, and on several occasions he publicly retracted his statement deriding her.[98]

The Queen had both good and bad points, as James Schouler showed many years ago.[99] Theophilus H. Davies, guardian of the heir apparent, Kaiulani, admitted that Liliuokalani was "ill-advised" and "unwise, if not disreputable."[100] However, inasmuch as he wanted his ward to be made Queen, his evidence is clearly

[96] Dec. 1, 1893. Liliuokalani, in her autobiography, of course spoke highly of Dominis and denied all rumors of either his or her unchastity. His father was a sea captain who left Honolulu in 1846 on a voyage and was never heard of again. The son, whose first important Hawaiian post was General on the staff of Prince Lot, died in 1891, seven months after Liliuokalani's accession (*Hawaii's Story,* pp. 13, 23, 29).

[97] Jan. 29, 1893.

[98] George Frisbie Hoar, *Autobiography of Seventy Years,* two volumes (N. Y., 1903), II, 263-265. Isobel Field (*op. cit.,* p. 218) defended the Queen's morals. See also Albert Pierce Taylor's appreciation of Liliuokalani at the time of her death, in his *Under Hawaiian Skies*: *A Narrative of the Romance, Adventure and History of the Hawaiian Islands*: *A Complete Historical Account* (Honolulu, 1922 and 1926), pp. 523-528.

[99] "A Review of the Hawaiian Controversy," in *Forum,* XVI (Feb., 1894), 677.

[100] "The Hawaiian Situation," in *North American Review,* CLVI (May, 1893), 607.

partisan. Perhaps the most reasonable attitude was taken by Representative (later Senator) Hernando Money of Mississippi when he asked: "With how many courts of Europe would we have diplomatic relations, if we were to go into the private character of their rulers?"[101] After all, it was hardly the business of either Minister Stevens[102] or of the American people.

* * * * *

As matters shaped up in Hawaii on the eve of the Revolution, there were many causes for that event in addition to political ones. Possibly as potent a reason as any is what might be called big business. The entire industry of the islands was in the hands of foreigners, of whom the influential element was American.[103]

Foreigners also owned most of the land; in fact the natives were almost landless. Out of 4,695 landholders in the Kingdom in 1891-92 the largest part was non-native.[104] It is only fair to state that the landless condition of the natives was nothing new, and that it was due as much to the domestic land system as to American greed. When the Puritan missionaries arrived, a feudal régime prevailed. Allodial title was nonexistent. In theory the King was suzerain, or feudal lord, to whom the chiefs paid a rent for their land in recognition of the fact that it had been distributed to them by Kamehameha I. Tenants and sub-tenants then held smaller portions on feudal tenure from each chief; in many cases there were several ranks of vassals and sub-vassals who

[101] Memorandum Notes in Gresham MSS., Box 6, Library of Congress.

[102] Immediately upon the Queen's accession, Minister John L. Stevens undertook to lecture her on the duty of following constitutional procedures during her reign. In his statement to Blount, Marshal C. B. Wilson said: "Picture to yourself the time and scene. An elderly editor of an obscure country journal [Stevens had been editor of the *Kennebec Journal* of Augusta, Maine], accidentally pitchforked into the position of the national representative of one of the greatest nations on earth—and a republic at that—lecturing a monarch born and educated to the purple, a woman in the hour of deepest bereavement [because of the death of her brother], in the style and with the ideas that he would have used to a Sunday school class of little children or possibly to a benighted heathen from the depths of barbarism" (p. 554).

[103] Z. S. Spalding, one of the great sugar men, estimated that in good times American investments in Hawaii would amount to fifty millions of dollars (Morgan, p. 249).

[104] Blount, p. 77.

held the usufruct of the land from the one immediately above. Finally the mass of the people lived as squatters upon the land of the tenant or chieftain, whose serfs they were, and to whom they paid a kind of feudal rent in the form of two days' work a week—one day for the landlord and one for the King. The entire scheme savored of the conditions in Western Europe during the Christian Middle Ages.

As a result of the influence of American missionaries, King Kamehameha III, in the late 1840's, was persuaded to abolish this feudal ownership by dividing all the land and by giving patents for much of it in fee simple. The Privy Council resolved, on December 18, 1847, that the King might retain his own private holdings, which thereafter should be called the crown domain. All the rest should be divided into three parts: one-third was to go to the Government which would hold it in trust for all subjects, one-third was to be granted to the chiefs, and one-third was to be given to the common people. In order to carry this policy out, the chiefs, in much the same way in which serfdom was abolished in Russia by the Czar Liberator in the early 1860's, were required to give up their feudal titles, and all land so freed was placed in a common pool.

When the division (called the Great *Mahele*) was finally put through on March 8, 1848, the results were as follows: the crown lands (private domain of the King) amounted to 915,000 acres; government lands totaled 1,495,000 acres; that granted to the nobles or chieftains accounted for 4,010,000 acres; and the common people received a mere bagatelle, that is to say, 11,132 squatters received 28,658 acres, or about two and a half acres each. In the words of Commissioner James H. Blount: "The majority received nothing. The foreigners soon traded the chiefs out of a large portion of their shares, and later purchased from the Government government lands and obtained long leases on the crown lands . . . the native never had much of the land."[105] The indigent native, unable to raise a sufficient living on a plot which

[105] Blount, p. 134. These facts have been gathered from *ibid.*, pp. 84-89, 106, 199-201, 404-408, 420-430, and 639-642. See also Sanford B. Dole, "Evolution of Hawaiian Land Tenure," in *Papers of the Hawaiian Historical Society, No. 3,* printed in Morgan, pp. 92-103; and testimony of Z. S. Spalding, in *ibid.*, pp. 233 *ff.*

totaled less than three acres, soon lost his patrimony through debt; and the rich foreigners bought large blocks from the royal domain, such as the 24,000 acres which Claus Spreckels purchased for $10,-000 in 1880. Z. S. Spalding, another great sugar planter, acquired 12,000 acres and leased 15,000 more from the chiefs.

The census figures for 1891-92[106] indicate that Europeans and Americans, owned 1,052,492 acres (65.77%), natives 257,457 acres (13.89%), half-castes 531,545 (28.67%), Chinese 12,324 (0.66%), and Japanese 200 acres (0.01%). In other words, the natives accounted for 34,436 out of a total population of 89,990, yet owned only 257,457 acres of the total (1,854,018). It must be remembered that the ordinary Kanaka was practically landless, for the 257,457 acres were owned largely by a few rich native chieftains.

From the standpoint of taxation,[107] the disparity is also marked. Americans and Europeans paid, in 1891-92, $274,516.74 (51.98%), natives $71,386.82 (13.52%), half-castes $26,868.68 (5.10%), Chinese $87,266.10 (16.54%), Japanese $67,326.07 (12.75%), and all others $729.82 (0.12%). The Chinese paid more taxes than did natives. Americans argued that because they paid over half the taxes, they should control the spending of the money. Something will be said later in regard to taxes paid by Annexationists who used the statistics to prove their right to offer Hawaii to the United States.

By 1890 the main industry in Hawaii was sugar raising; all other enterprises were subordinated to it,[108] and the chief market

[106] Blount, p. 77.

[107] *Ibid.*, pp. 76 and 605. On Oct. 25, 1897, the Honolulu *Hawaiian Star* gave the following figures from the assessment books, as of January 1, 1897: 106 American business concerns were assessed for $2,250,907; six British ones for $382,239; five German ones for $374,400; eighteen Portuguese for $21,200; one Hawaiian for $2,200; 281 Chinese for $446,950; and fifty-five Japanese for $77,700. These made a total of $3,556,596.

[108] In 1897 the exports in pounds and in dollars were:

Sugar	520,532,192 lbs.	$15,390,223.09
Rice	5,448,700 lbs.	255,055.60
Coffee	288,228 lbs.	89,813.36
Wool	204,720 lbs.	17,750.44

From William Fremont Blackman, *The Making of Hawaii* (N. Y., 1899), p. 253. Truly did the sugar grower, Spalding, say that sugar "is the only

was the United States.[109] Here also figures picture the supremacy of foreign, and especially, American interests. The unincorporated sugar industry was valued at three million dollars.[110] Of this total, the British controlled $1,195,000; Hawaiian-born Americans $500,000; Americans $415,000; Germans $515,000; and Norwegians $375,000. The natives seem to have had no holdings at all. The following table indicates the dominance of Americans in the incorporated sugar business as well in other corporations, most of which were concerned in land and sea transportation:

Nationality	*Capitalization of sugar interests in 1893*[111]	*Capitalization of non-sugar interests in 1893*[112]
Americans	$18,594,695	$2,690,994
Hawaiian-born Americans	2,960,280	948,107
British	4,303,218	1,289,520
Hawaiian-born British	196,200	233,006
Germans	1,233,935	299,523
Hawaiian-born Germans	39,165	28,839
Chinese	259,700	44,640
Portuguese	49,500	420
Kanakas	38,991	51,620
American-Hawaiian half-castes	88,900	33,473
British-Hawaiian half-castes	160,098	201,639
German-Hawaiian half-castes	2,058	4,701
Chinese- and Portuguese-Hawaiian half-castes	34,000	36,763
All other foreigners	3,550	13,565
Total capital stock	$28,274,000	$6,150,705

interest I know of in the country" (Morgan, p. 258). William De Witt Alexander said: "Sugar engrosses everything, monopolizes everything" (*ibid.*, p. 265).

[109] In 1891 Hawaii exported 274,983,295 pounds of sugar to the United States, but only 285 pounds to all other nations; 4,894,752 pounds of rice were shipped to the United States, but only 5,698 pounds to all others (*New York Times*, March 27, 1893). See also *Sen. Ex. Doc. 76* (52 Cong. 2 Sess.), pp. 67 *ff*. In 1891 Hawaiian imports were valued at $7,439,483, of which $6,495,608 were from the United States. In the same year its exports totaled $10,258,788, of which $10,196,278 were to the United States (*ibid.*, p. 68). Of the total tonnage (274,852) in the Hawaiian carrying trade, 169,472 were American (*ibid.*, p. 69).

[110] Blount, p. 615.

[111] *Ibid.*, pp. 616-617.

[112] *Ibid.*, p. 644.

The reciprocity treaties gave to sugar culture a tremendous boom, which the following figures[113] will illustrate:

1876-77	25,576,320 lbs.	1883-84	143,233,520
1877-78	40,896,680	1884-85	171,351,140
1878-79	47,452,160	1885-86	216,270,000
1879-80	63,584,640	1886-87	212,800,000
1880-81	93,608,800	1887-88	224,000,000
1881-82	114,177,280	1888-89	268,800,000
1882-83	115,819,200	1889-90	268,000,000

These statistics seem to prove that it would be profitable for all American sugar interests in the islands to agitate for annexation, and, failing that, for reciprocity. Such a conclusion, reasonable as it appears, is too easy. All important sugar men did favor reciprocity, but not all by any means wished annexation. Many were opposed to union with the United States because of what they feared would happen to their labor supply if American exclusion laws applied to Hawaii.

It is hardly necessary to say that such a complex movement as that which resulted in the overthrow of the monarchy and finally in annexation cannot be explained by any one cause—whether that cause be sugar (or business), the desire for good government (or a plot), or any other single explanation. All of these, including the race question (that is, Japanese and Chinese immigration), played their parts. However, the chief cause for the Revolution of 1893 and for final annexation was one in which sugar and immigration were entwined together. In other words, cultivation of sugar had produced a situation in which there was danger that Orientals would shortly overwhelm white civilization in the islands.

To forestall this event, the Revolutionary leaders (not including most of the planters) found it necessary to overturn the monarchy in order to be in a position to offer the islands to the United States. It is to a certain extent true that the Revolution was the result of a plot to secure good government, because it was clear to men like Thurston that good government could never be gained under a monarchy; and granted that the monarchy could be purified (which they did not grant), a purified monarchy could never give good government for the reason that it would

[113] Russell H. Anderson, in *Annals of the American Academy of Political and Social Science, op. cit.*, p. 152. See also *House Ex. Doc. 48* (53 Cong. 2 Sess.), p. 51.

be too weak to handle the hordes of contract laborers who were pouring in. Nor could men like Thurston stomach the thought of government under Japan, even though it might be good. By "good government" they meant government by whites.

Thus in its largest implications, sugar becomes of great significance in explaining the Revolution of 1893 and its sequel, annexation. Sugar was endangering white civilization by necessitating the importation of thousands of Asiatics; tobacco and cotton had performed a like service in the American South by making it profitable to bring in black slaves. In Hawaii the Mongolians were there, were needed, and could not easily be deported; but they would inevitably smother American or white dominion unless Hawaii was under the aegis of a power strong enough to keep the whites in the saddle, with or without exclusion. It is little wonder that in 1894, when a republican Constitution was being framed, Thurston advised President Sanford B. Dole to study the Mississippi Constitutional Convention of 1891 in order to learn how to keep the upper hand over a large, troublesome element in the population.[114]

[114] Thurston to Dole, March 10, 1894, Minister and Envoys, Archives. For the connection between sugar and immigration in more detail, see William A. Russ, Jr., "The Role of Sugar in Hawaiian Annexation," in *The Pacific Historical Review,* XII (Dec., 1943), 339-351.

II. MINISTER STEVENS AND THE DEVELOPMENT OF ANNEXATION SENTIMENT

For years the Hawaiian mission had been one of the least important diplomatic appointments which a deserving Democrat or Republican could secure. It was a sort of exile for four years because Honolulu, without cable communications with the outside world, was so isolated that it was a week behind the news if sent by telegraph to San Francisco and then by letter on shipboard, and ten days or two weeks behind if news went by letter the entire distance. There was little in the tiny Polynesian Kingdom to attract first-rank men. Of course the American Minister was almost as important as the sovereign, for he represented the power which exercised a virtual protectorate over the islands; in social affairs he ranked high among the small, but powerful and wealthy American colony. If he favored annexation, he was welcomed as a brother; for Americans in the Kingdom found it wise to be clannish among themselves and to lionize the Minister if he deserved it. If he was opposed to annexation, his reception was formally correct but cold. The diplomatic corps was small and anything but brilliant. England and the United States were represented by Ministers, France and Japan by Commissioners, Portugal by a *chargé d'affaires*.[1] Other nations had consuls and commercial agents, usually chosen from persons residing in the islands.

John L. Stevens, who represented the United States when the Revolution of 1893 took place, was a good choice[2] if President Harrison wanted a man on the scene who would forward American interests, including annexation.[3] Partly because he was an ex-

[1] Stevens to Foster, No. 79, Jan. 18, 1893, Despatches (National Archives).

[2] Originally appointed as Minister Resident, his status was improved in Hawaiian eyes when, in the summer of 1890, he was made Envoy Extraordinary and Minister Plenipotentiary. See *House Ex. Doc. 48* (53 Cong. 2 Sess.), p. 69.

[3] The Royalist, Charles T. Gulick, a former Cabinet Minister, told Blount (p. 300) that upon being presented to King Kalakaua, Stevens made such an offensive lecture that the King had a mind to ask for his recall. From then on "the American legation was the rallying point for the missionary annexation party," Gulick continued. During 1892 Annexationists like Hartwell, Smith, Waterhouse, Thurston, Dole, and Judd met there often to plot

clergyman and partly because he hailed from Maine which had had such close connections with Hawaii, Stevens soon ingratiated himself with the missionary, sugar-planting clique which completely dominated the economic activity of the islands. The letters he wrote back show clearly that he confided in them, and they in him, on all their aspirations, political and otherwise. If the success of a diplomat can be gauged by the degree to which he associates himself with the ruling aristocracy of a country; if his success can be gauged by his popularity with that aristocracy; and if his success can be gauged by his ability to interpret, for his home Government, the feelings and opinions[4] of that aristocracy—then Stevens was a most successful Minister. He knew what the sugar planters and the Annexationists were thinking about; he listened to and reported on all the scandalmongering and rumors about the sins of the native dynasty; he praised the virtues of the American ruling class; he wrote detailed despatches on changes in the Government; in short, he became an Annexationist of Annexationists,[5] representing Hawaii to the United States rather than *vice versa*. Indeed, Queen Liliuokalani, after her dethronement, declared that as soon as Stevens landed in the islands he began to urge annexation, and that his daughter was drowned (by a tragic accident) while he was in the interior canvassing for annexation among the natives.[6]

and plan. Gulick added that Stevens was the "cat" who pulled the chestnuts out of the fire for the Annexationists. For more in a similar vein by Gulick, see *ibid.*, pp. 351-353. In a Decoration Day address, Stevens spoke in such an undiplomatic manner favoring annexation that E. C. MacFarlane, member of the House of Nobles, asked the Government what steps had been taken to rebuke Stevens (*ibid.*, pp. 430-431 and 558).

[4] For instance, the confidential despatch to Blaine, March 20, 1890, in which he predicted the complete Orientalization of the islands unless annexation took place, in *House Ex. Doc. 48* (53 Cong. 2 Sess.), pp. 49-50; also May 20, 1890, discussing the necessity of aiding the sugar planters, in *ibid.*, pp. 53-54; also Oct. 22, 1890, urging the establishment of a naval coal depot at Honolulu, in *ibid.*, p. 71; and Sept. 5, 1891, pressing for a new reciprocity treaty and pleading for annexation before Hawaii was gobbled up by some other power, in *ibid.*, pp. 84-86.

[5] It is true that Stevens, when testifying before the Morgan Committee (p. 551) denied "promoting or accelerating" the annexation movement, but the facts prove that his assertion was faulty.

[6] *Op. cit.*, p. 244; for an account of the accident, see Young, in Morgan, p. 325.

Stevens[7] was born at Mt. Vernon, Maine, in 1820, the year in which the first American missionaries arrived in Hawaii. Ordained as a Universalist minister, he soon gave up preaching because of his health. In 1855 he became associated with James G. Blaine on the *Kennebec Journal,* published at Augusta;[8] from then on he was a personal friend and protégé of Blaine, always getting ahead when Blaine did. Blaine, who very early had become an Annexationist (having written an editorial urging acquisition of Hawaii in the first number of the *Kennebec Journal* which he edited), passed this interest on to Stevens. The latter was sent to the lower house of the Maine Legislature in 1865, remaining there until 1868 when he was elected to the State Senate.

By that time Blaine was a prominent national figure, and Stevens was sent as Minister to Uruguay and Paraguay where he served from 1869 to 1874. From 1877 to 1883 he was Minister to Norway and Sweden and from 1889 to 1893 he served as Minister to Hawaii.[9] Stevens believed, along with Blaine, that England must be circumvented in its design of acquiring Hawaii.[10] Stevens had never received any national attention until late in life, that is, during the last few months of his Hawaiian mission. As the *Boston Journal* said, he came into public notice just as Blaine died. It continued, in relation to these "Two Great Men," that Stevens "was indebted largely to the friendship of Hon. James G. Blaine for the position he holds, as well as his former

[7] Thomas M. Spaulding wrote the account of his career in the *Dictionary of American Biography,* edited by Allen Johnson and Dumas Malone (20 volumes, N. Y., 1928-37), XVII, 618-619.

[8] The *Kennebec Journal* had an important bearing on the history of Hawaiian annexation. Luther Severance of Augusta, a close friend of Blaine, and appointed by President Taylor as Commissioner to Hawaii in 1850, was part owner of the *Journal.* Blaine, at one time the paper's editor, had Stevens chosen as Minister to Hawaii. Stevens was connected with the *Journal* until his death. During his residence in Hawaii this small paper became nationally known and was widely quoted because of its intimate relationship with Stevens who, during the Revolution of 1893, was the leading figure in Hawaii. See New York *Sun,* July 8, 1898; Henry Kingsbury and Simeon L. Deyo (editors), *Illustrated History of Kennebec County Maine* (N. Y., 1892); and David Saville Muzzey, *James G. Blaine: A Political Idol of Other Days* (N. Y., 1934), p. 27.

[9] *Harper's Weekly,* Feb. 25, 1893, p. 175.

[10] Muzzey, *op. cit.,* p. 203.

appointment as minister to Sweden."[11] In short, Maine could look upon Hawaii as its own child, for the influence of that State's citizens upon the destiny of the islands is nothing less than remarkable.[12]

When Stevens arrived in Honolulu on September 20, 1889, affairs were quiet enough, although the Royalist *émeute* under Wilcox had happened the previous July 31. For about two years his despatches were devoted mostly to arguments in favor of annexation, rather than to describing events, except for those covering the trial of Wilcox and his confederates,[13] the funeral of Kalakaua, and the accession of Liliuokalani. They were filed away in the proper place in the State Department without much attention being paid to them. In short, the Hawaiian Legation produced little business, no notice, and few letters that needed to be answered by anybody except a subordinate.

Suddenly in 1892 the number of Hawaiian despatches began to grow to enormous proportions. Whereas one volume now contains all the letters that had been received for a period of years, soon two or three or even more volumes were required for one year when permanent filing took place. By 1893 the Hawaiian Legation

[11] Quoted by *Kennebec Journal,* Feb. 6, 1893.

[12] Maine people were proud of what scions of their State had accomplished in Hawaii. Besides the above-mentioned Maine men (Severance and Stevens), it was a Maine man, Harold M. Sewall who was the last American Minister to Hawaii; he received the islands for the United States when they were annexed. The Consul General under Stevens, H. W. Severance, was the son of Luther Severance, already referred to. Frank P. Hastings, *chargé* in place of Hawaiian Minister Thurston, at Washington, was a native of Calais, Maine. Moreover, the first and only President of the Hawaiian Republic was Sanford Ballard Dole, whose parents came from Maine. The Bowdoin College catalogue of 1836 carries the name of David Dole, born at Skowhegan, graduate of Bangor Theological Seminary, who went to the Sandwich Islands as a missionary. He married a Miss Ballard of Bath; became President of Oahu College; had two sons (one of them the President of Hawaii); and died in 1878. The son who became President of Hawaii married Anna P. Cate of Castine, Maine. The *Kennebec Journal* of Feb. 2, 1893, gave these facts under the title, "Maine at the front again, sure!" See letter of "An American" from Honolulu which was used as an editorial on Feb. 1, 1893; also, the issue of Feb. 16, 1893. See also Ralph S. Kuykendall, "Sanford Ballard Dole," in *Dictionary of American Biography* (20 volumes, N. Y., 1928-37), V, 358-359.

[13] Cf., *House Ex. Doc. 48* (53 Cong. 2 Sess.), pp. 29-30 and 31-32.

became as important as any with which the State Department did business—probably sending as many or more despatches than those at London or Paris. In due course of time a diplomatic pouch was used for mail to and from Honolulu. Then the Minister was given a translation of the State Department secret code so that he need not depend upon the naval code.

The Government at Washington had three official sources of information on Hawaiian affairs. First, consular reports, which gave facts on economic and commercial matters, although when political events became hectic, the Consul General (who also served as Secretary of Legation) often sent newsletters of general interest, which were of value to American officials, and which are of service in giving information to the historian. Second, the naval officers stationed at Honolulu, besides transmitting routine reports on their ships and sailors, offered political information as well; when despatches of political significance arrived at the Navy Department, almost invariably copies were forwarded to the Secretary of State and sometimes to the President. Third, and most important, there were the official, confidential, and private despatches and letters from the Minister to the Secretary of State. In the case of an ardent Annexationist like Stevens, the despatches were usually full of political gossip, accompanied by copious clippings from the Honolulu newspapers. Sometimes entire newspapers and pamphlets were sent to the Department at Washington.

Much of what Stevens wrote home concerned his rivalry with Major James H. Wodehouse, the English Minister to Hawaii. This personal mistrust of the English representative soon developed into a fear, in Stevens's mind, of British aggression. Stevens was merely reflecting the American dislike of England, a dislike that would enable the American press in the first days of February, 1893, to be certain that the British were determined to prevent annexation to the United States. There was probably as little real foundation for this press bugbear as there was for Stevens's idea that Wodehouse was trying to gain the Kingdom for England.

It is true that Cook discovered the islands, giving to England a primary claim; nevertheless after American influence became paramount, there is little indication that England cast covetous eyes at Hawaii—although it goes without saying that had the archipelago come into English control without effort and without international dispute that country could hardly have refused. After the London Government repudiated the seizure of the islands by Lord George Paulet in 1843, its policy was rather that of helping the country to continue independent. Hence there was some official objection to American attempts at annexation in the 1850's. In 1874 British marines aided United States bluejackets to seat the American candidate, Kalakaua, as against the British candidate, Emma, on the throne.

After the reciprocity treaty of 1876, which gave to the United States a virtual protectorate, England's objections to American interference ceased entirely. Even Stevens in one place said that a majority of the English in Hawaii followed the Americans in their desire for union with the United States.[14] Moreover, there were English-born members of the Revolutionary party, like Henry Waterhouse. Annexationists, both in the islands and on the mainland, were not above using England's supposed interest in Hawaii as a fulcrum to further annexation efforts by the United States.[15]

* * * * *

That trouble was brewing in Hawaiian air can be gathered from the despatches sent by American representatives as early as 1890. Letters describing the chaotic political situation became more and

[14] An important exception was Theophilus H. Davies, guardian of Kaiulani.

[15] On Feb. 25, 1893, W. R. Castle, one of the Annexation Commissioners sent by the Provisional Government to secure a treaty, suggested to President Dole that, in view of the failure to win ratification of the treaty, perhaps an overture to England for either annexation or a protectorate might awaken the American public to the value of the gift which was being offered to it (United States, Ministers and Commissioners to Washington, Archives). Whether Castle was serious about this suggestion is uncertain. Discouraged at the refusal of the United States to act, he was in all likelihood indulging in mere talk. For the last thing the Americans in control of the Provisional Government wanted was English interference in the islands.

Hastings, Secretary of Legation and *chargé* at Washington, sent an undated memo, sometime after July 10, 1893, to Dole declaring that there was talk among Washington officials about intimating to Honolulu leaders they might force the issue by appealing to some foreign power for annexation. Hastings thought Canada would not do (Dole Papers, Archives). There are many references to similar threats in Tansill, *op. cit., passim.* Compare J. Franklin Jameson's thesis in "Typical Steps of American Expansion," in *History Teacher's Magazine,* V (Feb., 1914), 39-44.

more frequent. For instance, Felix McCurley, American naval commander at Honolulu, told the Secretary of the Navy on August 22, 1890, that there were rumors of disorder because the natives desired a new Constitution. He went on to say that, in case of rioting, American Minister Stevens and English Minister Wodehouse "propose to land the men from the American and British vessels of war, to prevent it, and think this display of force will prevent further trouble." McCurley added that he had asked Stevens if that would not be an interference with Hawaiian autonomy; Stevens thought not, if the local Government authorized the intervention. McCurley concluded by saying that "as my instructions direct me to support him with the available force at my command . . . I shall in accordance with such instructions fully cooperate and sustain him in any action he may take."[16]

McCurley's words would indicate that a definite understanding existed between the State and Navy Departments, namely, when the judgment of the American Minister deemed it necessary, the Hawaiian Government (as established under the Constitution of 1887) was to be upheld by American intervention if the local Government asked for help. Such authorization would probably not be difficult for Stevens to secure as long as the dominant, property-holding, white element controlled the Cabinet.

By 1892 the American Minister smelled revolution *against* the present system, *led by the whites who had established it in 1887*. On February 8, 1892, he wrote to Blaine in his regular report:

> There are increasing indications that the annexation sentiment is growing among the businessmen as well as with the less responsible of the foreign and native popula-

[16] McCurley to Secretary of the Navy, No. 37818½, Aug. 22, 1890; filed under the same No. 37818½ are two other despatches giving political information of interest: Rear Admiral George Brown to Secretary of the Navy, Sept. 26, 1890, and E. M. Shepard to Secretary of the Navy, March 9, 1891. Both have clippings from Honolulu newspapers. Such despatches from naval commanders to the Secretary are now, for the most part, to be found in Records of the Department of the Navy in the National Archives. Record Group 24, *Records of the Bureau of Naval Personnel* (Bureau of Navigation), General Correspondence of the Division of Officers and Fleet, 1887-1895. Hereafter this source is to be cited, in short form, as Bureau of Navigation.

tion of the Islands. The present political situation is feverish, and I see no prospect of its being permanently otherwise until these Islands become a part of the American Union or a possession of Great Britain. . . . At a future time . . . I shall deem it my official duty to give a more elaborate statement of facts and reasons why a "new departure" by the United States as to Hawaii is rapidly becoming a necessity, that a "Protectorate" is impracticable, and that Annexation must be the future remedy, or else Great Britain will be furnished with circumstances and opportunity to get a hold on these Islands which will cause future serious embarrassment to the United States. At this time there seems to be no immediate prospect of its being safe to have the harbor of Honolulu left without any American vessel of war. Last week a British gunboat arrived here, and, it is said, will remain here for an indefinite period.[17]

On March 8, 1892, Stevens described to Secretary Blaine how a revolution might work: first the police station would be seized, then the palace, and finally the Government Building. He then asked for information:

> If the Government here should be surprised and overturned by an orderly and peaceful revolutionary movement, largely of native [white] Hawaiians, and a Provisional or Republican Government organized and proclaimed, would the United States Minister and Naval Commander here be justified in responding affirmatively to the call of the members of the removed Government to restore them to power or replace them in possession of the Government buildings? Or should the United States Minister and Naval Commander confine themselves exclusively to the preservation of American property, the protection of American citizens, and the prevention of anarchy? . . .
>
> I have information which I deem reliable, that there is an organized revolutionary party in the Islands. . . . This party is hostile to the Queen and to her chief confidants, especially opposed to the coming to the throne of the half-

[17] Stevens to Blaine, No. 46, Feb. 8, 1892, Despatches. "Copy to Secy. of the Navy, for his *Confidential* information." When printed in *Sen. Ex. Doc. 77* (52 Cong. 2 Sess.), p. 177, and in *House Ex. Doc. 48* (53 Cong. 2 Sess.), p. 87, there were some unimportant changes in punctuation and capitalization.

> English heir-apparent now being educated in England. . . .[18]

Blaine, ever the Annexationist, seems to have asked his friend Stevens to write what he thought about the growing Annexationist feeling among the whites; for, on March 25, 1892, a noteworthy personal letter was written to "Bro. Blaine" by Stevens. It indicates beyond cavil that the Minister had, by that time if not before, absorbed completely the viewpoint and the psychology of the American aristocracy in Hawaii. Businessmen, he said, believed that annexation would not only bring prosperity but would also protect their property much better than it was protected at present. In addition, American workmen in the islands felt that the United States would defend them from Asiatics who were "now a menace to the future American civilization of the Islands." All "thoughtful" men with families looked upon the incoming hordes of Orientals as a threatening "cloud."

Moreover, Stevens continued, sugar-growing could never again be so profitable; there was need of diversified farming which could materialize only if the United States, by annexation, took over the crown lands (amounting to 200,000 of the best acres in the Kingdom) and divided them among the common people. Furthermore, the Americans objected to the possibility of an overwhelming English influence in the Government when the half-English Crown Princess, Kaiulani,[19] came to the throne. Her father was a Scotsman, Archibald Scott Cleghorn, who served as Governor of Oahu Island. "In his younger days Cleghorn, the reputed father, was no more exclusive in his domestic relations than was the mother of the princess." Gossip had it that the real father

[18] Stevens to Blaine, No. 48, March 8, 1892, Despatches. According to a notation by Assistant Secretary A. A. Adee, this despatch was never answered. Printed in *Sen. Ex. Doc. 77* (52 Cong. 2 Sess.), p. 178, and in *House Ex. Doc. 48* (53 Cong. 2 Sess.), pp. 88-89.

[19] The Princess's full name was Victoria Kawekiu Kaiulani Lunalilo Kalaninuiahilapalapa. She was the daughter of Cleghorn and Princess Like-Like who was a sister of Kalakaua. In everyday life she was known as Miss Cleghorn. On March 9, 1891, she was declared heir apparent. Stevens's predictions of Liliuokalani's early death were poor, for she lived until November 11, 1917. On the other hand, Kaiulani died in a short time, on March 6, 1899.

of Kaiulani was an American naval officer from Maine.[20] Inasmuch as the reigning Queen was not expected to live long, Kaiulani's accession would bring a strong English influence into the Palace. Wodehouse, the English Minister, was closely associated with both the Government and the dynasty. One son had married a half-white sister of the Princess, and several other sons had important political jobs.

In the face of these reasons for annexation, Stevens concluded: "To me it is very plain after a careful study of all the facts in the case that the present state of things cannot continue—that the time is not distant when the United States must say *yes* or *no* to the question of 'Annexation'—that the moral and pecuniary welfare of these Islands will demand an affirmative answer." He submitted that the future was dark for Americans, "With England in . . . control of the Palace [and] with the young Princess heir placed on the throne. . . . If you See no objections to my doing So, I intend ere long to Send an official dispatch, giving a detail of facts Sustaining the opinions I have expressed in this letter." Finally he asked Blaine to write him what he thought. Was he for annexation or against it?[21]

In March, 1892, there was an abortive revolution led by the Ashford brothers and Robert W. Wilcox of the Liberal party.[22] The aim was to establish a republic, and then educate the people for future annexation to the United States.[23] The Royal Palace was sand-bagged and nineteen conspirators were arrested, including the Ashfords and Wilcox.[24] In a confidential despatch, Stevens said that the Queen was losing prestige because she had

[20] He should perhaps be listed as another of Maine's scions in Hawaii.

[21] Stevens to Blaine, March 25, 1892. It is passing strange that this personal letter was sewed into the volume of official despatches, between Nos. 50 and 51. The fact that Blaine left it with the official correspondence would indicate that he perceived its significance and additionally that he would want to show his favor towards annexation.

[22] Same to same, No. 52, April 2, 1892, Despatches. Partly printed in *House Ex. Doc. 48* (53 Cong. 2 Sess.), pp. 90-91.

[23] Testimony of Wilcox, in Blount, pp. 550-551.

[24] Rear Admiral George Brown to the Secretary of the Navy, May 23, 1892, filed under No. 37818½, Bureau of Navigation; statement of the Hawaiian Patriotic League, in Blount, p. 454; and Stevens to Blaine, May 21, 1892, in *House Ex. Doc. 48* (53 Cong. 2 Sess.), pp. 91-92.

made a half-caste Tahitian, named Charles B. Wilson,[25] her Marshal. He continued with a passage which, when the Hawaiian correspondence was printed, was ordered to be omitted: "It is a general and long held opinion here, that this man, Wilson, was for years her paramour, during the lifetime of her invalid American husband, who died eight or nine months Since"; perhaps they were having "illicit relations" now,[26] for Wilson[27] lived in or near the Palace. "The great lack here now is an intelligent and efficient Executive, which it is impossible to have with the existing monarchy"; scandal and corruption had inhabited the Palace for the past twenty years.[28]

Stevens's strictures upon Liliuokalani's personal morals were unfair, of course, but she found it more difficult to be "Her Majesty" than to be merely Mrs. John Dominis. It is only just to say that the new sovereign confronted many problems. The

[25] Nicknamed "King Bolabola."

[26] Commissioner Blount emphatically denied that the Queen had had improper relations with Wilson. Fred W. Wundenberg, one of the early Revolutionists, and under the Provisional Government, a clerk of the Supreme Court, defended Wilson's bravery and efficiency, as well as his personal relationship with the Queen (pp. 68 and 92 ff.). But Volney V. Ashford, a chronic Hawaiian agitator, declared the Queen's and Wilson's actions were scandalous (*ibid.*, p. 208). Liliuokalani (*op. cit.*, pp. 227-229, 274, 291-292) defended herself against the charges of improper relations by saying that Wilson had married one of the young women whom she had educated and who was lady-in-waiting at the time Wilson was serving as Marshal. Because their duties required frequent attendance upon the Queen, she gave them a cottage near her mansion; Liliuokalani admits, however, that she had numerous reasons later to doubt Wilson's loyalty and truthfulness.

[27] It is clear that Wilson had as little love for Stevens as Stevens had for Wilson. In his statement to Blount, the former Marshal related several instances of Stevens's boorishness and dictatorial methods. On one occasion, "at a state dinner at the palace, he [Stevens] signalized himself by killing mosquitoes, clapping both hands together with a loud report, letting the mosquitoes fall into his soup, from which he afterward picked them out. The onlookers and others at the table were simply paralyzed by his coarse breach of etiquette" (p. 555). In another instance, according to Wilson, Stevens came into the Queen's presence, "flinging one leg over the arm of the chair" and announced that it "was the President of the United States of America addressing the Queen of Hawaii" (p. 557). Liliuokalani (*op. cit.*, pp. 379-380) told of a visit by Stevens who "seated himself in a manner which no gentleman would assume in the presence of a lady."

[28] No. 52, *op. cit.*

nation was in debt; the civil list was overtaxing the ability of the people to pay for the Government's running expenses;[29] many American businessmen who were losing money because of the McKinley Tariff were maneuvering for annexation; natives were disgruntled and wanted more rights. In short, the Kingdom was politically, economically, and socially in a chaotic condition, with little chance of a sovereign of Liliuokalani's wilfulness and love of power saving the situation.

The Queen and her Cabinet did try to ameliorate one of the difficulties under which the islands were laboring, that is, the decline of trade resulting from the McKinley Tariff. It has already been seen that as early as 1889 the Reform Cabinet attempted to get the treaty renewed; after passage of the McKinley bill instructions were despatched in 1891 to the Hawaiian Minister at Washington asking him to secure relief.[30] All of these ventures failed. No doubt Liliuokalani and her advisers perceived the importance of winning release from the hardships imposed by the free sugar clauses of the American tariff; for, if they succeeded, Annexationist sentiment would to that extent be allayed. In any case, overtures for a new reciprocity treaty could be made with as much grace by a Royalist Cabinet as by a Reform one, because, in one sense, the longer there was reciprocity the less demand there would be for annexation.

On February 6, 1892, Foreign Minister Samuel Parker instructed J. Mott Smith to enter into negotiations with the United States Government for a reciprocity treaty.[31] Mott Smith soon answered that, much to his chagrin, both President Harrison and Secretary Blaine were not interested in the matter. Parker replied that it looked as though the United States, in spite of knowing it had broken a treaty, did not care to do justice because it felt Hawaii was so securely tied to American interests it would have to take its medicine.[32] Harrison had, however, reimposed duties

[29] For a discussion of the extravagance and overtaxation under the monarchy, see testimony of John A. McCandless, in Morgan, p. 604.

[30] See instructions of Aug. 4, 1891, signed by the Queen on Aug. 24, in Minutes of the Cabinet Council, pp. 420-421, Archives; also *House Ex. Doc. 48* (53 Cong. 2 Sess.), pp. 73, 86-87.

[31] Parker to Smith, Feb. 6, 1892, filed under United States, Minister to Washington, in Archives.

[32] Same to same, March 9, 1892, *ibid.*

on sugar coming from Colombia, Haiti, and Venezuela because these countries refused to lower duties on American goods; the Hawaiian Minister thought this action would help island planters a little.[33] Having interviewed Senator Nelson W. Aldrich, Mott Smith learned there was no hope for a reciprocity treaty in the Senate.[34] His efforts were harmed by published rumors of a coming revolution back in Honolulu. Blaine told Smith there would be no use in negotiating a treaty if the Hawaiian Government was about to be overturned.[35] Parker hastened to assure Smith that everything was quiet and that no uprising was expected.[36]

Nevertheless, rumors would not down, especially when Thurston's arrival in Washington caused much speculation about annexation. Consul A. Hoffnung cabled from London asking whether an article in the London *Times,* in reference to proposed annexation, had any foundation.[37] Somehow or other two Honolulu papers, the *Bulletin* and the *Pacific Commercial Advertiser,*[38] received the information that Mott Smith had told Washington interviewers he felt Hawaii might accept annexation if it was offered. When Foreign Minister Parker demanded a retraction, much of Smith's usefulness was weakened. A great deal of his time thereafter was expended in making denials that he had ever issued such a statement.[39]

The resignation of Blaine from, and the appointment of John W. Foster to, the State Department made Smith more hopeful of getting a sympathetic hearing on reciprocity. But Foster told him nothing could be done until after November, this being an election year.[40] The Democratic victory under Grover Cleveland elated Smith who told Parker that it meant a chance to get "fairer and freer trade"; the Republicans were "fettered by obligations—

[33] Smith to Parker, March 21, 1892, *ibid.*

[34] Same to same, May 6, 1892, *ibid.*

[35] Same to same, March 24, April 14, and April 22, 1892, *ibid.*

[36] Parker to Smith, May 10, 1892, *ibid.*

[37] Smith to Parker, May 20, 1892, *ibid.*

[38] Hereafter this paper will be referred to simply as the *Advertiser.*

[39] Parker to Smith, May 23, June 16, June 20, 1892; Smith to Parker, July 13, 1892, United States, Minister to Washington, Archives.

[40] Smith to Parker, July 15, 1892, *ibid.*

to gigantic Trusts—and manufacturing monopolies."[41] This hope of relief from the Democrats was finally realized with the passage of the Wilson-Gorman Tariff of 1894, but by that time it was too late to save the monarchy in Hawaii.

During these futile negotiations, Liliuokalani was immersed in political troubles in Honolulu. She managed to keep in the saddle without much trouble until the Legislature met on May 28, 1892; when it convened, turbulent days ensued. The first subject of dispute was whether the Queen had the power to remove Kalakaua's Cabinet. She, asserting that the death of the former sovereign released his Ministers from duty, had laid the case before the Supreme Court. The Court decided for the Queen.[42]

This Legislature, composed of three parties, had been elected in February, 1892. The line-up in the House of Nobles indicated how impotent the white party was, in spite of the restrictions laid down in 1887. The National Reform party, of nine members, wanted a new Constitution which would reduce the property qualifications of Nobles so that more natives could be elected. The Reform party—that is, the white, American, or planter-missionary element, led by Lorrin A. Thurston, H. P. Baldwin, and W. O. Smith—had fourteen. The Liberals, who represented the native group purely, wished to have the Nobles appointed by the sovereign. There were four independents. Commissioner James H. Blount later said that in this Legislature, "There was never a time when the reform party had any approach to a majority of members."[43] Thurston, hoping that a better Cabinet could be secured, formed an alliance with his sworn enemies, the Liberals, to oust the Ministry which the Queen had appointed. Furthermore, he enunciated the doctrine that she was constitutionally required to appoint a Cabinet selected by the majority.[44] The fact that dozens of petitions were coming in from natives in favor of a new Constitution; the unstable three-party situation which lent itself to deals, bribery, and jockeying for position; the Queen's desire to have a Cabinet which would serve both her and the natives; and

[41] Same to same, Nov. 18, 1892, *ibid.*

[42] Blount, p. 373; Liliuokalani, p. 218.

[43] Blount, p. 114. Another estimate gave eighteen Nationals, seventeen Reformers, fourteen Liberals, and three independents (*ibid.*, p. 672).

[44] C. B. Wilson's statement, in *ibid.*, p. 559.

the determination of the Reform party, i· spite of its minority position, to secure a Cabinet of its own—all these, and many others, let to a riotous session in which Cabinet after Cabinet was appointed, installed, and then thrown out in a welter of parliamentary ineptitude.

These Cabinet crises[45] so lengthened the session that it became the longest in the country's history; moreover, the repeated deadlocks between the executive and the legislative departments made constructive lawmaking impossible. The situation provided plenty of news for the American Minister, Consul General, and Naval Commander to write home about. The State Department, as well as the Navy Department, received fat despatches on every ship from Hawaii, and was well posted on what was doing. All of the goings-on supported Stevens in the opinions he had already expressed. The naval despatches were of a similar import.[46]

The deadlock began to take on dangerous proportions in September, 1892. One of the Queen's Cabinets, which included E. C. MacFarlane and Charles T. Gulick both of whom were distrusted by the American party, was described by the *Hawaiian Gazette* as having been appointed "in defiance of the will of the Legislature and of the people." This paper, criticizing the Queen for her bad government and worse advisers, predicted: "Unless promptly abandoned, they will dig the grave of the Hawaiian monarchy. Will the Queen listen to her true friends?" It thought that in the "Case of the Queen against the Constitution," the worst influence came from her Marshal, C. B. Wilson, who was instigating her in these usurping activities.[47] Stevens agreed that the impasse was the work of the half-caste Wilson who dominated the Queen; but

[45] Described by Chief Justice A. F. Judd and by E. C. MacFarlane in Blount, pp. 377 and 430-435.

[46] For instance on Sept. 6, 1892, George Brown, Rear Admiral, Pacific Station, wrote to the Secretary of the Navy: "This subject of annexation has been freely discussed by individuals for a long time, but until very recently there has been no combined concert of action. There now exists in Honolulu an organization comprising the most prominent annexationists which has for its object the formulation of some plan by which a change of government can be affected [*sic*] quietly, and with the consent and co-operation of the Queen and the members of her cabinet and staff" (*Sen. Ex. Doc. 77,* 52 Cong. 2 Sess., p. 179).

[47] Enclosed in Severance to Assistant Secretary of State W. F. Wharton, No. 148, Sept. 13, 1892, Consular Letters, National Archives.

he added that another culprit was one Whaley who headed a ring of smugglers and opium dealers. The better element in the Legislature voted the MacFarlane Cabinet out.[48]

The leaders of the American party who, by means of the Constitution of 1887, had hoped to entrench themselves in the upper house of the Legislature, shortly received a psychological setback. In the bye-election on October 4 to fill two vacant seats in the House of Nobles, the American or Reform party lost both of them. Consul General H. W. Severance interpreted the American defeat as resulting from opposition which "found expression through the native vote aided by the political demagogues who use the Word 'Annexation' for their Capital stock, and race prejudice has manifested itself as I am led to believe through English influence against the American people, from whom they have never received anything but Kindness."[49] Of course the native-Royalist combination was delighted. The Royalist or Government organ, the Honolulu *Bulletin,* said that the election victory was "a killing blow to the traitorous agitation for selling the independence of the kingdom. It shows that the great mass of people on the premier island [Oahu] takes no stock in the unsettling conspiracy to have the islands annexed to a foreign power."[50]

The Annexationist paper, the *Advertiser,* reminded Hawaiians that, because of the continued disturbances, Government bonds were declining on the London market; moreover, the "election yesterday resulted in a complete victory for the Ministerial-Lottery candidates. . . . The result is a setback to the cause of representative government, to clean and honest administration and to every sound and healthy interest of Hawaii." Honolulu, it declared, was being run by the "boodle" element.[51]

Stevens attributed the situation to the influence of English Minister Wodehouse, whose wife intervened in favor of the appointment of bad Cabinets. "The English Minister and wife," said he, "have resided here nearly twenty five years, and the latter

[48] Stevens to Foster, No. 65, Sept. 14, 1892, printed in *Sen. Ex. Doc. 77* (52 Cong. 2 Sess.), pp. 179-180. Marshal Wilson, a prejudiced authority, told Blount (pp. 560-561) that all these anti-Reform Cabinets had been overthrown by the use of planters' gold for bribing purposes.

[49] Severance to Wharton, No. 155, Oct. 7, 1892, Consular Letters.

[50] Enclosed in *ibid.*

[51] Enclosed in *ibid.*

has an unsavory reputation in all the best circles here." The most objectionable member of the recent Cabinet was a German-Jew who was a "cast-off politician of San Francisco, a gambler" and who was "believed to be in the pay of the opium ring, whose ramifications reach to Hong Kong, to San Francisco, and to Vancouver." A lottery ring also added to the distrust in which the Queen and her advisers were held. The "gang," in which some of the Cabinet as well as Marshal Wilson were interested, was trying to sell a franchise to a New Orleans lottery ring. Stevens ended his despatch with a most revealing sentence: "I know that this Legation has the confidence and earnest support of a majority of the Legislature and of the chief men of the Islands."[52] It is understandable that when President Cleveland allowed publication, at the request of the Senate, of all Hawaiian correspondence since 1889, this despatch was omitted.[53]

When the deadlock continued, Stevens wrote that the issue was whether the Tahitian favorite (Wilson) could nullify the Constitution. The Queen's "infatuation for him is now so excessive that he is believed to have almost absolute control of her official action"; added to this, he had English influence behind him because the English were opposed to seeing American fortunes advance. "There is a prevalent anxiety in the public mind as to the actual state of things. The Tahitian favorite, of half English blood, does not mean to yield, and were there not an American Ship of war here, he would perhaps try to use his police and a mob of 'hoodlums' to break up the Legislature, restore the old Constitution, and thus render the Palace master of the situation."[54]

The *Advertiser,* speaking for the whites, declared the deadlock was a repetition of "the features of the pre-revolutionary [that is, pre-1887] regime. . . . If political rights in Hawaii are not to be reduced to the mockery which is all they were six years ago, the friends of the people must insist first and foremost upon the formation of a Cabinet by strictly constitutional means."[55] Nevertheless the Queen continued her attempts to rule with a Cabinet

[52] Stevens to Foster, No. 70, Oct. 8, 1892, Despatches.

[53] *House Ex. Doc. 48* (53 Cong. 2 Sess.), p. 1.

[54] Stevens to Foster, No. 71, Oct. 19, 1892, Despatches; printed in *House Ex. Doc. 48* (53 Cong. 2 Sess.), pp. 96-97.

[55] Enclosed in Severance to Wharton, No. 161, Oct. 19, 1892, Consular Letters.

which could not win a vote of confidence in the Legislature. "Thus," averred Stevens, "there is here, on a small scale, the old historic issue between autocracy and parliamentary responsibility." He thought that it was actually only a minority which was holding out; and added that if the majority had its way Liliuokalani would be forced to appoint a strong American Ministry.[56]

To make matters worse, other factors entered. Theophilus H. Davies, guardian of the Crown Princess, Kaiulani, arrived from England in the midst of the constitutional struggle. Stevens was certain that he intended no good, for, being a rich Tory in England and a powerful landholder in Hawaii,[57] Davies would bulwark the pro-English tendencies of the Queen. Rumor said that he was the agent of the Canadian Pacific Railroad and had been sent to the islands to secure rights for a transpacific cable. Meanwhile there was talk that the recently rejected Cabinet had asked for Consul General Severance's recall. Said Stevens: "But influential parties have called at this Legation, who say, that if any such step has been taken by this rejected Cabinet, the American merchants and business men, as well as other leading citizens, will send a strong memorial to the Department of State against any such action of a dead Ministry. . . . So far I am supported here by all the responsible Americans and others."[58]

The Queen tried a new Cabinet with Joseph Nawahi as Minister of Foreign Affairs, W. H. Cornwell as Minister of Finance, Charles T. Gulick as Minister of the Interior, and Charles Creighton as Attorney General. When this Ministry received a vote of no confidence, the *Advertiser* commented: "The maker of these Cabinets is a practical joker of much humor, and one would be very ready to fall in with his mood if his jests were not so unconscionable."[59] Later testimony, which is not unimpeachable, attributed the fall of this Cabinet to bribery of native members of the Legislature by rich planters.[60]

Finally, after months of friction, the Queen capitulated and ap-

[56] Stevens to Foster, No. 72, Oct. 31, 1892, Despatches; printed in *Sen. Ex. Doc. 77* (52 Cong. 2 Sess.), pp. 181-182.

[57] Davies owned $707,800 of sugar stock and $53,000 of other stock.

[58] Stevens to Foster, No. 72, *op. cit.*

[59] Enclosed in Severance to Wharton, No. 164, Nov. 2, 1892, Consular Letters.

[60] Colburn to Blount, in Blount, p. 31.

pointed four Americans who represented the propertied interests of the country. They were confirmed by the Legislature on November 8, 1892. Severance reported that representative government had won a victory; Stevens said it was an American triumph over Tahitian and English influence. The Cabinet included G. N. Wilcox (Interior), M. P. Robinson[61] (Foreign Affairs), P. C. Jones[62] (Finance), and Cecil Brown (Attorney General). These men, as Stevens proudly reported, represented property worth a million dollars.[63]

During this hubbub in the islands, Stevens was preparing the official despatch which he had promised Blaine on March 25. It showed him to be a downright, one-hundred-per-cent Annexationist. Not only was he able to interpret the wishes of the Hawaiian Annexationists to the State Department, but he was also a propagandist in favor of union in his own right. His official position made it possible for him, acting as an agent of the American clique in Hawaii, to preach annexation better than could any private Hawaiian. Accordingly, in a forty-four page letter written in longhand, with appendices, he wrote an essay to Foster (who had by that time succeeded Blaine as Secretary of State) on the "financial, agricultural, social, and political conditions of these Islands." He emphasized the weakness of the Government,[64] the bankruptcy of the sugar industry which was seeing

[61] Robinson owned more than half of the Oahu Railroad and Land Company.

[62] For Jones's story of the bribing of legislators by the Queen's party and of her personal solicitation to get the new Cabinet voted out, see Morgan, pp. 201-209. "The Queen interested herself and labored earnestly among the native members to secure their votes, going down on her knees to Hoapili, noble from [the Island of] Hawaii, so, he said, to get him to vote us out" (p. 206).

[63] Stevens to Foster, No. 73, Nov. 8, 1892, Despatches; printed in *House Ex. Doc. 48* (53 Cong. 2 Sess.), p. 110. See also Severance to Wharton, No. 167, Nov. 10, 1892, Consular Letters.

[64] His statement regarding the decayed monarchy will bear quoting: ". . . the monarchy here is an absurd anachronism. It has nothing on which it logically or legitimately stands. The feudal basis on which it once stood no longer existing, the monarchy now is only an impediment to good government—an obstruction to the prosperity and progress of the islands. . . . Hawaii has reached the parting of the ways. She must now take the road which leads to Asia, or the other, which outlets her in America, gives her an American civilization and binds her to the care of American destiny."

evil days consequent upon abrogation of the reciprocity treaty by the McKinley Tariff,[65] and the general need of American aid if Hawaii was to advance. "To postpone American action many years is only to add to present unfavorable tendencies and to make future possession more difficult."

Again Stevens stressed the danger of English influence when Kaiulani succeeded to the throne. In the last section of the brochure he asked: *"What Should Be Done?"* His answer was that there were only two possibilities. One was the outright annexation which was the better of the two. The other was closer relations with Hawaii by means of a customs union, an ocean cable, perpetual cession of Pearl Harbor—in short, a definite American protectorate.[66] He considered the despatch of such significance that in a special letter to Foster he asked that it be read by President Harrison, Secretary of the Navy B. F. Tracy, and Senators John T. Morgan, John Sherman, and William P. Frye.[67]

In continuing his publicizing of the need of annexing the islands, Stevens perceived that his No. 74, sent as a confidential and official despatch, could hardly reach the American public, which,

[65] On the subject of the business status, Stevens bore in heavily on the need of reviving the sugar industry which had lost fully twelve million dollars because of the McKinley Tariff. He was certain that "Wise, bold action of the United States will rescue the property-holders from great losses." He believed that, if annexation took place, the chief reason for such action should be to protect the sugar interests, and he gave figures on how much the bounty should be. It ought to be limited to six mills per pound (twelve dollars per ton) and paid only so long as the United States maintained a bounty for its own producers. If objection were made to the fact that Hawaiian planters would receive only twelve dollars per ton, while Louisiana growers got twice that amount, the answer was that the latter raised twice as much from each acre. On Feb. 1, 1893, after the Revolution, he added in another despatch (Stevens to Foster, No. 82) that the consensus of opinion among leading planters, "obtained by me five or six months since, was, and is, that $12 per ton bounty will place all the Hawaiian plantations worth maintaining on the road of financial safety and success."

[66] Stevens to Foster, No. 74, Nov. 20, 1892, Despatches; printed in *Sen. Ex. Doc. 77* (52 Cong. 2 Sess.) pp. 184 *ff*.

[67] Same to same, unnumbered, Nov. 28, 1892, Despatches. Foster showed Stevens's letter to James H. Blount, Chairman of the House Committee on Foreign Affairs. Blount, who would soon play an important rôle in Hawaii, refused to take an attitude upon the matter, but did show copies of the letter to Congressman R. R. Hitt and James B. McCreary (Blount's testimony, in Morgan, pp. 403-404).

after all, counted most if union of the two countries was ever to be achieved. He contributed, therefore, to his paper, the *Kennebec Journal,* of which he was still titular editor, a long letter. In it he argued cogently for annexation and predicted in somewhat enigmatic terms that the issue was about to emerge as a problem for the American people. The letter appeared as an unsigned editorial on November 17, 1892, with the title, "The American Pacific Opportunity." "The time is near when we must decide [he declared] who shall hold these islands as a part of their national territory. . . . Their ultimate possession of [*sic*] the United States is of the utmost importance to American commerce in the Pacific, which promises vast development, if wisely cared for and without too much delay. Shall Americans sleep while others are awake to take from them these natural advantages? Time and tide wait neither for men nor nations."

Although the *Journal* did not admit Stevens's authorship until later, the editorial created something of a furor in the American press, and the rather obscure Augusta newspaper was quoted and clipped far and wide. A special despatch from San Francisco to the New York *Mail and Express* said: "The recent editorial of Minister Stevens, our representative in Hawaii, in the Kennebec JOURNAL, has created a sensation in this city."[68] The *San Francisco Examiner,* reflecting the long interest of the Pacific Coast in Hawaiian annexation, published a three-page article in favor of it.[69] The editorial was reprinted in full by the New York *Sun* which asserted that it was important.[70] The *New York Tribune* said: "In some form, and sooner or later, this [annexation] must come about."[71]

Inasmuch as the Revolution, engineered by Hawaiian Annexationists, occurred less than two months after the editorial appeared, it became even more important later when critics of Stevens would quote from it to show that, having predicted a decision would soon have to be made by Americans, he was hand in glove with the Revolutionists.

* * * * *

Stevens knew what he was talking about, because a close rela-

[68] *Kennebec Journal,* Dec. 1, 1892.
[69] *Ibid.,* Nov. 24, 1892.
[70] *Ibid.,* Nov. 30, 1892.
[71] *Ibid.,* Dec. 2, 1892.

tionship existed between him and Thurston. The latter, who was the leading figure in the overthrow of the Queen, is authority for the statement that Stevens allowed him to read the important despatch of November 20, 1892, which the Minister sent to Foster and which predicted trouble in Hawaii.[72] As a matter of fact, there had been, for months, a secret organization in Honolulu and Stevens knew of it; his assertion, "that there is an organized revolutionary party in the Islands," has already been quoted.[73] In his *Memoirs* Thurston told the story of the formation of this group, called the Annexation Club, early in 1892;[74] in spite of its name, declared Thurston, it was not to promote annexation, but to be ready for action in case the Queen made a move against the Constitution. Organized by Thurston, at the suggestion of Henry E. Cooper, it was secret and small: usually about a dozen men, never more than seventeen. "No records were ever kept by the Annexation Club," averred its founder.

The Club sent Thurston to Washington to make contact with the American authorities, and paid his expenses. He met Cushman K. Davis, Republican member of the Senate Foreign Relations Committee, and received a friendly hearing. He then inter-

[72] *Memoirs, op. cit.*, pp. 239-240. Most of the original letters can be found in the Thurston Papers, Archives. Thurston's words in reference to the way he and Stevens were acting in collusion were: "The U. S. Minister at Honolulu, Mr. Stevens, has written and forwarded by this mail, an exhaustive despatch to the State Department, concerning the Hawaiian situation. He allowed me to read it, and I heartily endorse every statement in it" (Thurston to Archibald Hopkins, Dec. 14, 1892, filed under "Foreign Office. Miscellaneous Local," Archives). In the same letter at another point Thurston said: "The American Minister, with the fullest knowledge of the facts, and himself an enthusiastic advocate of annexation, concurs in this opinion," namely, the opinion that there was no immediate probability of annexation. One is justified in wondering whether Thurston did not help Stevens to write the famous despatch of November 20, 1892.

[73] Stevens to Blaine, No. 48, March 8, 1892, Despatches.

[74] In the Thurston Papers, Archives, is a rough, handwritten draft of a constitution for the Annexation Club, dated August, 1892. The reasons for forming the organization, as given in the document, were that industries were in bad shape, unemployment rife, and poor government chronic. All these troubles were a consequence of the régime then in power. Therefore the signers felt that prosperity could not come except through a union with a larger power, the United States. It is hard to see how Thurston could say that the club was not formed to promote annexation.

viewed James H. Blount, Democratic Chairman of the House Foreign Affairs Committee, who said that if the question of annexation came up before the House it would be treated as a national, and not a party issue; and advised Thurston to see Secretary Blaine.[75] The latter suggestion was hardly necessary, because Thurston carried a letter of introduction from Stevens to Blaine.[76] He informed the Secretary of the unsettled conditions arising from Royalist misrule, of the expectation that Liliuokalani might start trouble at any time, and of the intention of the Annexation Club to seek union with the United States, if the Queen gave the least provocation. Blaine sent him to the Secretary of the Navy, B. F. Tracy, who took him to the White House. President Harrison thought it best not to meet Thurston personally, but through Tracy sent word that annexation would receive a sympathetic hearing. "That," reported Thurston, "was all I wanted to know."

Before leaving for Hawaii, Thurston appointed Archibald Hopkins as the Washington representative of the Annexation Club at a salary of seventy-five dollars a month. Hopkins kept in touch with Washington officials and made reports to Thurston. Soon he

[75] When he was interrogated by Senator George Gray of Delaware during the Morgan investigation as to whether he had ever heard of annexation before 1893, Blount answered in the affirmative and said Thurston had been his informant in 1892. Gray asked him what Thurston had said. Blount studied the floor and replied that he could not recall. Thurston, who tells the story in his *Memoirs, op. cit.*, pp. 478-479, relates that he does not know whether Blount really had forgotten or whether he "lied like a gentleman" in order to protect Thurston who had talked to him in strict confidence. Thurston's comment on the incident is disarmingly frank and quite significant: "His [Blount's] silence was of great moment to us of the Provisional Government; if he had divulged, at that stage, our preliminary contemplation in 1892 of overthrowing the Monarchy, the fact would have scored in favor of the royalists and the Cleveland administration."

[76] It will be recalled that Thurston arrived in Washington and was interviewing high officials at the very time the Hawaiian Minister, J. Mott Smith, was working feverishly to get a reciprocity treaty. It will also be recalled that Smith wrote to Foreign Minister Parker that Thurston's arrival had caused all kinds of speculation and had interfered with the campaign to secure reciprocity. With Thurston interviewing Blaine, it is little wonder that the Secretary told Smith on April 14, 1892, it was useless to enter into sugar negotiations. Said Blaine: "*I* expect to hear of a revolution there." See Smith to Parker, April 14, 1892, in United States, Minister to Washington, Archives.

was writing that he had learned from high authority the United States would pay the Queen $250,000 if she turned Hawaii over to the American Government. On December 14, 1892, just before the Revolution broke out, Thurston informed Hopkins that the Annexation Club considered the sum preposterously high and would not agree to it. He declared, however, that a treaty of annexation could perhaps be pushed through the Hawaiian Legislature if the United States paid the bill. Some of the members would vote for annexation gladly; the "remainder would have to be subsidized to the amount of $500 to $5,000 each, as would also some twelve to twenty of the native leaders outside of the house."

Thurston admitted that many planters feared annexation because it would end the penal labor system whereby workmen could be punished for breaking their contracts. The drain on the labor supply was so great that it was necessary to import between three and five thousand plantation workmen every year. Twenty thousand Japanese had been brought in, each laborer costing the planter seventy-five dollars. The planter got his money back by means of the penal contracts. Thurston was afraid that such a system would not be allowed by the United States, which excluded Chinese entirely; therefore, if the islands were annexed, the planters would face chaos because of labor shortage.[77] Hopkins showed Thurston's proposition to Secretary of State Foster, who, while interested, said nothing could be done because Cleveland's administration was coming into power in a few months. Before this reply from Hopkins, dated December 28, 1892, reached Thurston, the Revolution had already occurred, and the Annexation Club was the Hawaiian Government.[78]

* * * * *

During December, 1892, affairs in Hawaii, now that the American party had a respectable Cabinet in office, continued calm. It was announced that the legislative session would end on January 14, 1893. The last despatch before the Revolution, of Captain G. C. Wiltse (Commander of the *Boston,* and soon to play a leading rôle in Hawaiian affairs), said that things in Honolulu

[77] Thurston to Hopkins, Dec. 14, 1892, filed under "Foreign Office. Miscellaneous Local," Archives.

[78] The facts about the organization and activities of the Annexation Club can be found in Thurston, *Memoirs, op. cit.,* pp. 228 *ff.,* 237 *ff.,* 251.

were quiet and unchanged, although there was rumor of a vote of want of confidence in the Wilcox (American-supported) Ministry.[79] Stevens took his family for a trip through the islands on the *Boston* in the interest of his health; as the vessel left, "everything was perfectly quiet."[80] The sugar baron, Z. S. Spalding, who left Hawaii on January 4 for Paris, later deposed that there seemed to be less chance of trouble than for years, else he would hardly have left; that he had heard of no conspiracies to overthrow the monarchy; and that W. C. Wilder, in a few days to be one of the leading Revolutionists, told him that "Nothing of the kind [was] contemplated at that time."[81]

Because prorogation of the Legislature was at hand, each party was anxious to have its Cabinet in office when that event occurred, for it would control the Government during the next two years until a new Legislature met.[82] With this fact in mind, the Queen's supporters[83] made the necessary party deals, and suddenly on January 12, 1893, things began to happen.[84]

When a vote of lack of confidence (representing a coalition of the Liberal and National Reform parties) passed the Legislature, the Wilcox Ministry was forced to resign next day. The Queen was pleased, for, as she later asserted, she felt she was "simply a nonentity" under the Wilcox Cabinet.[85] One member of the Reform party subsequently charged that the Legislature was bribed with $7,000 of Samuel Parker's money.[86] In any event, Liliuokalani appointed Parker as Minister of Foreign Affairs in a new Ministry which was supposed to end all troubles (as she hoped) by representing both native and American elements. Parker and John F. Colburn (Interior) were to speak for the native interests. For the Americans she offered W. H. Cornwell

[79] Wiltse to Tracy, Jan. 4, 1893, No. 37818½, Bureau of Navigation; also *Advertiser,* Jan. 5 and 9, 1893.

[80] Young, in Morgan, p. 325.

[81] Morgan, pp. 243-245.

[82] Blount, pp. 114-115.

[83] Z. S. Spalding attributed the fall of the Wilcox Cabinet to a Noble from Kauai who, although elected as a member of the Reform party, changed his vote at the behest of Paul Neumann, one of the Queen's minions (Morgan, p. 256).

[84] The Royalist version is given by Marshal Wilson, in Blount, pp. 559 *ff.*

[85] Blount, p. 395.

[86] Henry Waterhouse's statement, in *ibid.,* p. 48.

(Finance) and A. P. Peterson (Attorney General). This coalition was opposed ardently by the Americans, but was welcomed with enthusiasm by the Kanakas who supposed it to mean the end of factional strife.[87]

The *Advertiser* on January 14 gave a thumbnail sketch of each new Minister. The Minister of Finance (Cornwell),[88] declared the *Advertiser,* "does not know enough about accounts to keep those of a poi shop." The Attorney General (Peterson) had capacity, but had forfeited his reputation in the eyes of all men. Of Parker, it said: "We have nothing to say against 'genial Sam' —it is a Hawaiian tradition that brains are not needed in the Foreign Office." Of Colburn, the Minister of the Interior, the editor thought that "perhaps the less said the better. It is sometimes charity to be silent."[89] Obviously the two Ministers who were to represent the American interests did not do so. Consul General Severance reported that the new Cabinet would not increase the respect for representative government, but added that Honolulu was quiet.[90] Likewise, the Annexationist *Advertiser* opined that the "change of Ministry will not . . . lead to any political disturbance or unrest."[91]

The criticism of the *Advertiser* was, at the start, directed against the Legislature as much as against the Queen. "The late Cabinet," it said, "was removed, as every one knows, by a combination of opium smugglers, disappointed office seekers, intriguing office holders and haole hunters, and by the powerful influence of the Court and

[87] See reaction of the *Advertiser* of Jan. 13, 1893, under the title "A New Deal," in which article the editor asked: "Is not this the year 1886 over again?"

[88] James W. Girvin, Hawaiian Consul at San Diego, California, wrote to Thurston a similar thumbnail sketch, part of which said: "I remember hearing Will Castle say once that Cornwell's head was like a wart on the end of a neck and that he had not brains enough to make a speech on any subject. . . . Sam Parker got switched off early in life or he might have made a man" (Girvin to Thurston, Jan. 30, 1893, in file entitled United States, Ministers and Commissioners to Washington, Archives; hereafter designated as "M&C").

[89] Enclosed in Severance to Wharton, No. 174, Jan. 18, 1893, Consular Letters.

[90] Severance to Wharton, No. 173, Jan. 13, 1893, *ibid.*

[91] Enclosed in *ibid.* Alexander later said there would have been no revolution if the Queen had demanded no more than the lottery and opium bills (Morgan, p. 301).

the Police Department [that is, Marshal Wilson], and the free use of bribery." It felt that the Legislature deserved as little confidence as did the new Cabinet. "The balance of power is held by a group of bribe takers, and the result is that the men of honor, intelligence and standing, of whom there are happily not a few, are condemned to vote in a minority. The capacity of the Hawaiian for self government has been put to a crucial test during the last days, and the outcome is not encouraging to the friends of the native race." The editor then referred to the Constitution in a way which made it plain that a new revolution was the only solution. The Constitution of 1887, he declared, was a failure; the Queen was just as tyrannical as Kalakaua had ever been; and Hawaiian-Americans were in the same position as in 1886, that is to say, in a state of "suppressed revolution." "The condition of the Hawaiian Government might be compared to that of a ship of war, which has been captured by pirates."[92] This was plain and significant talk from the oldest Annexationist organ in Hawaii. It was an admission that the supposed political domination acquired by the American party in 1887 had come a cropper. That Constitution had been formulated for the purpose of giving to the whites everything except the kingship. The question now was, in view of the fact that this one concession to the natives had proved to be a mistake, could the 637 American voters get real control without abolishing the monarchy?

Having secured a Cabinet she liked, Liliuokalani signed two bills which created such opposition[93] on the part of the Americans that their passage brought the first step in the movement to dethrone her. The ruler's income[94] added up to $70,000 annually: salary amounted to $20,000 and $50,000 came from the crown lands. Jealous of her dependence upon the Legislature for a portion of her income, she desired to make herself more independent financially. Furthermore, she was looking for some permanent source of revenue whereby the Government would not

[92] *Advertiser,* Jan. 14, 1893, enclosed in Severance to Wharton, No. 174, Jan. 18, 1893, Consular Letters.

[93] There was also criticism of a distillery law to aid the rum industry (Morgan, pp. 176-177).

[94] The Queen had $4,700 invested in sugar stock, $12,000 in the Hawaiian Construction Company, and $350 in the Mutual Telephone Company (Blount, pp. 619-670 *passim*).

have to resort to loans as it had in the past. One opportunity presented itself in the form of a lottery concern, which, having been driven from Louisiana, was seeking a promising city where it could locate.[95] Liliuokalani was willing to have a national lottery bill enacted into law provided she and the Government were compensated. The company promised an annual subsidy of $500,000, part of which was to be used to lay a cable from Honolulu to California.[96] A second method by which funds could be raised emerged in the form of an opium combination which wished a charter. In spite of the entreaties of her American friends who tried to persuade her to recognize the evils of such legislation, the Queen affixed the Royal "R" to both bills after they had been passed.[97] In the defense which she published in 1898, Liliuokalani attempted to justify both laws. The funds from the lottery were to be used for public works which would benefit the natives, while the opium measure was an endeavor to regulate a traffic which could not be suppressed.[98] United States Minister A. S. Willis

[95] A few months before this, President Paul Conrad of the Louisiana Lottery Company had stated that his concern would not leave Louisiana; that the rumor which asserted it was seeking a concession in Hawaii was wrong; and that it would fill out its chartered time in Louisiana (*Kennebec Journal,* Aug. 30, 1892). Thurston *Memoirs, op. cit.,* pp. 219-226, printed the lengthy defense which the lottery interests published under the title, "The Golden Era. Honolulu, H. I. Sept. 1, 1892. That $500,000 Offer."

[96] Chief Justice A. F. Judd, in Blount, p. 378; see also testimony of Samuel Parker, in *ibid.,* pp. 437-438. A copy of the lottery law, in Morgan, pp. 761-764, shows that the franchise was granted to D. H. Cross of Chicago, W. B. Davenport of St. Louis, John Phillips, J. J. Williams, and Dr. Gilbert Foote—the last three of Honolulu. The annual subsidy of $500,000 was to be used for the following purposes: $100,000 for an ocean cable, $50,000 for railroads on Oahu, $50,000 for railroads on Hawaii, $50,000 for improving Honolulu harbor, $150,000 for roads, bridges and wharves, $50,000 for the promotion of business, and $50,000 for encouragement of tourist travel.

[97] The Honolulu Chamber of Commerce petitioned the Queen against the lottery measure, before and after its passage. Both appeals were enclosed in Stevens to Foster, No. 79, Jan. 18, 1893, Despatches. John R. Musick, in *Hawaii . . . Our New Possessions* (N. Y. and London, 1898), pp. 350-351, said that the Queen was begged by American ladies not to sign the two bills. She knelt down to pray, and even wept, but as soon as they were gone, approved the legislation just the same. Alexander testified to the same fact before the Morgan Committee, p. 292.

[98] Liliuokalani, *op. cit.,* pp. 239-241. She added, in justification of signing the lottery bill, that she felt she ought to give her approval because the

later explained the Queen's acts as an attempt to dislodge the dominant whites from the financial hegemony which they had exercised over the banks for thirty years. Because the Government was always borrowing, the banks held it in subjection. The two laws were to free the Government, by "destroying the domination of the whites." Willis concluded: "This, in my judgment, was the most potent reason for the 'revolution' and also greatly strengthened the opposition to restoration [of the monarchy] as that would have left those two laws in force [.]"[99] Whatever the explanation of the Queen's actions might be, they had important consequences.

The Americans were as enraged at the method of passing the laws as they were at the laws themselves. The Queen knew (said they) that such legislation would never get through the House of Nobles; therefore, she delayed its submission until late in the planting season when many of the reliable members had returned home to attend to sugar growing.[100] The *Advertiser* made a frontal attack upon the recent procedure and, undoubtedly speaking for the American party, threatened retaliation: "THE business community is entitled to a voice in the management of affairs, and it

Cabinet had presented the measure to her; and that, inasmuch as many shopkeepers had petitioned for a lottery, the project was popular. Blount (pp. 674-684) brought back seven certified copies of such petitions which had been signed by numerous citizens and presented to the Legislature. Some of the signers became members of the second Annexation Club; that is to say, the public one which was formed after the Revolution and which will be discussed later. These included John S. McGrew, afterwards editor of the violently Annexationist *Hawaiian Star;* several officers of the Provisional Government army; F. Wilhelm, who was on the original Advisory Council; the Assistant Secretary of the Annexation Club; and many others. In regard to the opium bill, the Queen declared that the traffic needed supervision because of the machinations of Chinese smugglers, and that the law was copied from a British statute for the control of the opium trade in the colonies. Yet even the Royalist *Bulletin,* Jan. 10, 1893, called the lottery project a "foul" measure. For another condemnation of the opium law, see *The Friend,* LI (Jan., 1893), 3.

[99] Willis to Gresham, private, Sept. 20, 1894, Gresham MSS., Library of Congress.

[100] It will be remembered that the American or Reform party did not have a majority of that body, even if all members of the party were present. Six of the best members had left Honolulu for business and for other reasons (Morgan, p. 442).

has the power to make its rights respected. . . . It is unfortunate for the Sovereign that her advisers should lead her into a course which must hasten the downfall of the Hawaiian Monarchy."[101]

Minister Stevens, having returned from his junket on the *Boston* in haste, at once visited the Cabinet to protest the acts of the Government in his absence. The Ministers and the Queen later deposed that he "pounded his cane upon the floor" and asserted that the United States had been insulted.[102] In his report to Foster, Stevens said that the Queen, taking advantage of his absence on a trip to Hilo, allowed her unscrupulous advisers to force the lottery law through the Legislature by having the opium ring distribute lottery stock among the native members. She signed it gladly.[103]

The selection of the Parker Cabinet and the enactment of the lottery-opium laws set the white party seething with discontent.[104] One last straw was needed, and this was provided on the following day. At noon, Saturday, January 14, 1893, the Queen prorogued the Legislature a few hours after Stevens's return. Amidst a great deal of pomp and finery (she herself drunk, according to an important onlooker),[105] the Queen officially ended the session. American members were almost entirely absent, partly because many

[101] Jan. 14, 1893, enclosed in Severance to Wharton, No. 174, Jan. 18, 1893, Consular Letters.

[102] The Queen and Cabinet used this incident as another example of Stevens's domineering tactics.

[103] Stevens to Foster, No. 79, Jan. 18, 1893, Despatches.

[104] This is true, in spite of Thurston's statement (*Memoirs, op. cit.*, p. 227) that the lottery-opium legislation and the fall of the Wilcox Ministry did not produce any desire to overthrow the monarchy: "Nothing was further from my thoughts, at that time, than an overthrow of the Monarchy or any forceful move against the Queen." He may not have had any "forceful move" in mind, but he had been a leader in the Annexation Club since early in 1892, and had just written Hopkins that the members of the Legislature might be bribed to ratify an annexation treaty.

[105] Lucien Young, *The Boston at Hawaii* (Washington, D. C., 1898), p. 165. Young's statement is to be taken *cum grano salis*. He described the prorogation ceremony as follows: ". . . about the funniest thing I ever saw in my life—a circus. The procession was headed by two or three lackeys, and then followed the governor of Oahu, father to the heir apparent, dressed in a gaudy uniform covered with gold." Then came the Queen with a long train borne by four attendants. Again Young said she was drunk (p. 328).

of them had not been present for some time, and partly because the rest wished to show their distaste for the recent antics.

Rid of the Legislature, the Queen on the same day took a final step—the one which brought about the revolution against her. Disliking the way in which her hands were tied by the Constitution of 1887, she had been planning to proclaim a new one.[106] She had also been impressed by numerous petitions from natives who had submitted their requests to the Legislatures of 1890 and 1892.[107] To make the deed appear more popular, thirty delegates of the Hawaiian Patriotic Association,[108] who said they represented 8,000 natives, called upon their sovereign to promulgate a new Constitution which would restore the Royal prerogative, and at the same time remove the property qualifications so that natives could regain control of the Legislature. Stevens explained the affair as a deal between the Queen and the native members of that body. In return for approving the opium and lottery laws, "She was to be immediately compensated by being allowed to proclaim a new Constitution restoring to the Crown the old despotic prerogatives in direct violation of the existing Constitution."[109]

The changes in the Constitution included these items: two princes were to be added as heirs to the throne; the Legislature was to meet in April of each year; the Queen should appoint the twenty-four Nobles; the pay of Representatives was to be raised; the membership of the lower house might be increased from twenty-four to forty-eight; only subjects might vote and the qualifications for voting were lowered[110] (one witness before the Morgan Committee said that those whites not married to native women were to be disfranchised); the term of Supreme Court judges should be reduced from life to six years;[111] and several

[106] Blount, pp. 114-115; also Alexander, in Morgan, pp. 295 *ff*.

[107] Blount, p. 115.

[108] Cf., Blount's interview with officials of the Association, pp. 379-380.

[109] Stevens to Foster, No. 79, Jan. 18, 1893, Despatches.

[110] Morgan, p. 176. The qualifications included: all taxes paid, age twenty, domicile of one year, property worth $150 or rent income of $25 or other income of $75, and registration.

[111] After his return to the United States, Stevens wrote that the Queen was afraid the Supreme Court would declare the lottery act unconstitutional, and hence she wanted a new Constitution in order to rearrange and control the Court (John L. Stevens and W. B. Oleson, *Riches and Marvels of Hawaii . . .*, Phila., 1900, p. 275).

other changes, all of them of course in the interest of sovereign and natives, and to the disadvantage of the American party.[112] The best evidence points to the conclusion that the Queen prepared the document herself, basing her ideas largely upon the autocratic Constitution of 1864.[113]

Liliuokalani called the Cabinet to the Palace in order to inform the members of her intention of proclaiming[114] a new Constitution. According to the Constitution of 1887 she was required to secure the countersignature of at least one Minister before any act was valid. Although she stressed the idea that she was working in the interest of a large group of her native subjects,[115] neither of the two Ministers who presumably spoke for the Kanakas would sign the paper. All four said they were afraid of the white party. Moreover, they declared they had never read the Constitution which she intended to proclaim, and that promulgation of any new fundamental law would be crass foolhardiness at such a time. She

[112] The projected Constitution, with changes indicated, was printed in Blount, pp. 581-590. Where Blount got this copy is uncertain, for, on Jan. 31, 1893, Liliuokalani told S. M. Damon that all copies had been destroyed by her order (*ibid.*, p. 593; see also p. 115). P. C. Jones deposed that the Provisional Government had offered $500 for a copy, but could not secure one (Morgan, p. 221). Blount admitted to the Morgan Committee that he did not know where the Cabinet secured the version given him (p. 393). William De Witt Alexander (writing in 1896) said that Blount's copy was correct. He added that the Republican Government had a copy, partly written by Joseph Nawahi, one of the Queen's native adherents, and endorsed in her handwriting (*History of Later Years of the Hawaiian Monarchy and the Revolution of 1893, op. cit.*, p. 36. Hereafter this book is cited as *History*). Blount's version was read and certified, on July 16, 1893, by Parker, Peterson, and Cornwell. They stated, however, that according to their recollection, the original draft contained no voting qualifications. Chambers, who discussed the Constitution (*op. cit.*, pp. 31-33) made many mistakes, especially in designating clauses and sections.

[113] Morgan, p. 608. In her book (pp. 229-231) the Queen declared that Marshal Wilson was the first person ever to mention the need of a new Constitution; that she had never thought of such a thing before he broached the subject. Shortly thereafter, others—such as Samuel Nowlein (head of the Household Guards) and Joseph Nawahi (former Cabinet member)—also urged it.

[114] Constitutions were always proclaimed, never voted upon.

[115] She later defended her act by showing that, out of a possible 9,500 native voters in 1892, 6,500 asked for a new Constitution (Liliuokalani, *op. cit.*, pp. 230-231).

answered that they had been studying the projected Constitution for a month.[116] In spite of pleas and threats, they refused to budge, two of them stealing out of the Palace in fear of their lives when she appeared ready to read the Constitution without their consent.[117] After conferring with the diplomatic corps, the Cabinet decided finally and absolutely not to sign.[118]

The Foreign Minister, Samuel Parker, was able to prevail upon the Queen to do nothing rash for the moment; consequently, still drunk,[119] according to Young, she announced at about 4:00 p.m. to the delegates that it was out of the question to give them at that time what they desired. She dismissed her native adherents by ordering their peaceful dispersal and by exhorting them to await a more propitious time. As reported in one of the Honolulu papers, she spoke as "the voice of the Sacred Chief, of Hawaii, Liliuokalani, the tabued one," as follows:

> O, ye people who love the Chief, I hereby say to you, I am now ready to proclaim the new constitution for my Kingdom, thinking that it would be successful, but behold obstacles have arisen! Therefore I say unto you, loving people, go with good hope and do not be disturbed or troubled in your minds. Because, within the next few days now coming, I will proclaim the new constitution. . . .
>
> Therefore, I hope that the thing which you, my people, so much want will be accomplished; it is also my strong desire.[120]

[116] Cf. Liliuokalani's statement in Blount, pp. 397-398; also Parker's version, p. 441.

[117] Alexander, in Morgan, p. 296. Young said that the Queen threatened to shoot Peterson and Colburn, who fled to W. O. Smith's office (*ibid.*, pp. 330-331). See also W. R. Castle's statement in *ibid.*, p. 585. Liliuokalani (*op. cit.*, p. 385) states that Peterson, Cornwell, and Colburn hastened to tell Thurston. She says nothing about shooting them.

[118] Severance to Wharton, No. 174, Jan. 18, 1893, Consular Letters.

[119] Young, *op. cit.*, p. 165. Lieutenant Young was on shore during the entire day, part of the time in uniform, part of the time in plain clothes, in order to keep Captain Wiltse of the *Boston* informed of what was doing. No other authority charges the Queen with being intoxicated on that day. Many Royalists later swore that Liliuokalani was not drunk at the time, and that Young himself was a notorious toper. Copies of the affidavits can be found in the Spaulding Collection, volume 7, Library of the University of Michigan, Ann Arbor.

[120] Morgan, pp. 9-10.

III. THE FALL OF THE MONARCHY

The opposition of the Ministry to the Queen's projected Constitution secured for it the temporary support of the Reform or American party, and more specifically, of the Annexation Club. Thurston later reported: "On the morning of Saturday, January 14, 1893, I went to my almost abandoned law office [almost abandoned because of his activities during the past year in connection with the Annexation Club] and began sorting papers preparatory to resuming law work." Suddenly his friendly opponent,[1] Minister of the Interior John F. Colburn, excitedly rushed into Thurston's office to tell him about the Queen's intention to proclaim a reactionary Constitution. Said he: "Lorrin, we've been having a hell of a time up at the Palace, and I have come to tell you about it."[2]

After hearing Colburn's story, Thurston suggested that they go to Judge (General) A. S. Hartwell's office, where Colburn told his story again. Hartwell and Thurston cautioned him to stand firm and to see W. O. Smith, another member of the Annexation Club.[3] After lunch, about one o'clock, Smith and Thurston went to see Attorney General Peterson, who gave the same facts as had Colburn. At this meeting, besides Smith, Thurston, and Peterson, there were Cornwell, Fred W. Wundenberg, MacFarlane (already introduced in another connection), Colburn, and some others. Thurston advised the Cabinet members to declare the Queen in revolution against the Constitution, proclaim the throne vacant, and call upon the people for support. At this point Foreign Minister Parker entered, and rather reluctantly agreed to the facts as

[1] Colburn and Thurston had grown up together and were close friends. Colburn's acceptance of a Royal position made them political foes, but they remained personally sociable. Colburn's support of Liliuokalani until 1895, when she abdicated, was, as he said, a matter of duty. As soon as she resigned the throne, he informed Thurston that he was in favor of annexation, and that the same held for Samuel Parker (Thurston, *Memoirs, op. cit.*, pp. 532-533).

[2] *Ibid.*, p. 245.

[3] *Ibid.*, p. 246. In all likelihood, Colburn knew nothing of the existence of the secret Annexation Club.

given by the other Ministers. The Queen's messenger then arrived with an order for the Cabinet to return to the Palace. Colburn refused, saying he was afraid. Parker, however, maintained he was not timid, and went back. Thurston, who already had offered to draft a declaration containing his ideas, if the Cabinet assented, now advised the three remaining Ministers that they should ask Stevens for American troops to prevent violence by the Queen's adherents. The draft was made by Thurston, who offered to deliver it personally; Peterson said he would take it, and so, much against his will, Thurston entrusted the paper to Peterson. The latter failed to carry out his promise, and Thurston never again saw the document.[4]

Smith and Thurston returned to Smith's office, where a crowd of several dozen men were discussing what to do, exchanging views, and denouncing the Queen.[5] As one eyewitness later said: "The feeling was so intense that it was a spontaneous sentiment that something radical would have to be done."[6] It was then about two o'clock.[7] Colburn and Peterson asked what support they could

[4] *Ibid.*, pp. 246-248; testimony of Smith, in Blount, pp. 491-492. Alexander, *History, op. cit.*, p. 33, printed a letter written by Thurston to Stevens and Wiltse, in which the Cabinet appealed for assistance.

[5] Young, *op. cit.*, p. 172; Thurston, *Memoirs, op. cit.*, p. 248.

[6] Dr. Francis R. Day, a Honolulu physician who served in the Provisional Government's military organization (Morgan, p. 735).

[7] There is such conflicting testimony on what happened during this hectic day, and those immediately following, that definite statements as to time and as to some facts cannot be made. Royalists would say one thing; Revolutionists exactly the opposite. Commissioner Blount, who was sent by President Cleveland to find the real facts about the Queen's removal, took depositions from both sides. Other testimony and many affidavits appear in the report of the Morgan Committee which investigated the rôles played by American officials in the Revolution. In piecing together the story, use has been made of the following Royalists and Revolutionists whose testimony disagreed the least:

Fred W. Wundenberg: Attended most of the Revolutionary meetings until Wednesday, Jan. 18, when he withdrew because he did not sympathize with the forced surrender of the Queen; commanded the police station after it was evacuated by Royal forces; his interview was signed and certified. Blount, pp. 26-27, 90-97, 575-578.

William A. Cornwell: Minister of Finance in the last Royal Cabinet; spoke from the Royalist angle. Blount, pp. 27-30; 166-168.

John F. Colburn: Minister of the Interior in the last Royal Cabinet; a

expect against the Queen,[8] and Thurston answered by drafting a proclamation which upheld the Cabinet, declared Liliuokalani in attempted revolution, and pronounced the throne vacant. He was aided by Hartwell, Smith, and the two Cabinet members. About a hundred persons signed the declaration,[9] and then it disappeared. Thurston later said he thought Paul Neumann, one of the Queen's minions, stole it from the desk.[10] Meanwhile Colburn made a speech (seven or eight persons being present)[11] outlining Liliuokalani's plans for a *coup d'état* and asking for cooperation.[12]

By that time Henry E. Cooper and Thurston had agreed that it was time for the Annexation Club to take the lead and have itself elected by the crowd as a committee of safety. At the end of Colburn's plea, someone, getting his cue from either Thurston or Cooper, moved that such a committee be formed. Cooper, an American who had arrived in the islands hardly a year before,

half-caste who spoke from the Royalist angle. Blount, pp. 30-35.

S. M. Damon: A citizen of foreign extraction; Vice President of the Provisional Government, and on the Revolutionary committee which persuaded the Queen to surrender; gave the Annexationist side. Blount, pp. 39-47.

J. O. Carter: Liliuokalani's friend and adviser, present when she capitulated. Blount, pp. 56-57.

C. Bolte: A leading Revolutionist. Blount, pp. 249-265; Morgan, pp. 452-453.

P. C. Jones: Minister of Finance under the Provisional Government. Morgan, pp. 201-233.

A. F. Judd, Chief Justice of the Supreme Court; spoke from the Revolutionary angle; sworn affidavit in Morgan, pp. 438-447.

John A. McCandless: A prominent Revolutionist; gave to the Morgan Committee some of the inside story of the formation of the Committee of Safety and the details about the organization of the Provisional Government. Morgan, pp. 619 *ff*.

William De Witt Alexander: Hawaiian historian who wrote from the Annexationist viewpoint; Morgan, pp. 262-325 and Blount, pp. 179-202; also his *History,* already cited, pp. 37 *ff*.

Lorrin A. Thurston: *Memoirs, op. cit., passim.*

Sanford B. Dole: *Memoirs, op. cit., passim.*

Liliuokalani: *Hawaii's Story, op. cit., passim.*

[8] McCandless, in Morgan, p. 607.

[9] *Loc. cit.*

[10] *Memoirs, op. cit.,* pp. 248-249.

[11] McCandless, in Morgan, p. 608.

[12] *Loc. cit.*

having been made chairman of the meeting, chose thirteen men from the crowd to form the desired committee.[13] All thirteen were members of the Annexation Club, save one who soon resigned, and then the Club, acting as the Committee of Safety, controlled every member. Thurston frankly says that the Annexation Club appeared "in the guise of the committee of safety at the deposition of the Queen."[14]

By this time the position of the Cabinet was an anomalous one. It had feared the consequences of the Queen's proclaiming a new Constitution and had appealed for protection to the white party. But the latter, by forming a Committee of Safety, was moving too fast. Thurston's charge that Paul Neumann, who had cooperated thus far, stole the proclamation deposing the Queen, would indicate that Liliuokalani's friends began to doubt the motive of Thurston and his group. McCandless, a participant in the movement and a member of the Committee of Safety, explained the failure to issue the proclamation by saying that the Cabinet was not sincere in its alliance with the American party; and that it was experimenting to discover which was the safe side, finally choosing for the Queen.[15] In all probability, both Thurston's and McCandless's reasons are valid; Colburn and Peterson might have helped in drawing up the statement to depose their sovereign in the heat of the moment, but a second sober thought indicated the folly of going too far: if for no other reason than that they would lose their jobs. Then of course the Queen's announcement that she would proceed no further with the movement at that time also mollified her Ministers. Next day, Sunday, Liliuokalani patched up her differences with them and they abandoned the Revolutionists.[16]

The failure to issue the proclamation of deposition did not,

[13] Thurston, *Memoirs, op. cit.*, pp. 249-250; McCandless, in Morgan, p. 609. The story is partly told in the words of the three leaders (Smith, Cooper, and Castle), in a conversation written out and handed to Blount, pp. 489-503.

[14] Thurston, *op. cit.*, p. 240.

[15] McCandless, in Morgan, pp. 614-615.

[16] *Ibid.*, p. 614. Stevens later wrote that the Queen's "four Ministers were in the plot" to issue a new Constitution (Stevens and Oleson, *op. cit.*, p. 276). The fact that the Cabinet immediately sought the aid of the American party would seem to nullify Stevens's assertion.

needless to say, end the activity of the American party, even if it did mean loss of Ministerial cooperation. The Annexation Club, now the Committee of Safety, felt that the Queen's retreat amounted to little because she had promised her native subjects that she would promulgate her Constitution "in a few days."[17] As soon as elected, therefore, the Committee of Safety proceeded to go to work; if the Cabinet wished to come along, well and good; if not, the Committee would act alone. Smith's office was cleared of the crowd, and the thirteen men held their first meeting at about four o'clock. Thurston's proposal to make annexation their chief aim was accepted.[18] Thurston, W. C. Wilder (rich shipping magnate), and H. F. Glade (the German Consul),[19] were appointed to see the American Minister and find out what attitude he would take in case of armed opposition to the present régime.

The delegates asked Stevens which party he would support: the Queen's or that of the citizens opposed to the Queen. He answered that always in the past he had supported the legitimate Government, but that this time he thought the Cabinet and the "people" were on the right side; therefore he would not take the Queen's part. He would recognize the Cabinet as long as it was supported by a sizable number of the responsible citizens.[20] In case of trouble he would protect property and recognize "the existing government whatever it might be."[21] Henry E. Cooper, who had been sent to interview Captain G. C. Wiltse of the

[17] Some discussion arose later about the interpretation of the Hawaiian words which the Queen used in her statement. Most translators said it meant "in a few days." The original was "ma keia man la" which meant "hereafter" or "one of these days"; it could refer to a few days, or few months, or a few years (Judge H. A. Widemann, in Blount, pp. 538-539).

[18] Thurston, *op. cit.*, p. 250.

[19] Glade soon withdrew from the movement because of his official post. Later he was naturalized and then made Hawaiian Consul General and *chargé* at Berlin (Minutes of the Executive Council, May 12, 1894).

[20] This interview is described by Thurston himself in Thurston to Foster, Feb. 21, 1893, Notes from Hawaii (National Archives). See also Smith's testimony, in Blount, p. 122.

[21] In sworn testimony W. C. Wilder deposed: "Mr. Stevens replied that if we obtained possession of the Government building and the archives and established a Government, and became in fact the Government, he should of course recognize us" (Morgan, p. 448).

Boston, was just as favorably impressed by Wiltse's attitude as was Thurston's delegation at that of Stevens.[22]

That evening Thurston invited a group of prominent men to his home, including W. R. Castle, A. S. Hartwell, S. B. Dole, Fred W. Wundenberg, C. L. Carter, and W. O. Smith.[23] Several of these were not members of the Committee of Safety; it was undoubtedly Thurston's purpose to inform them of what had been done, in order to secure their cooperation. This is the first mention of the involvement of Sanford B. Dole, the future President, in the movement. Thurston very likely told the group of Stevens's friendly attitude, for Dole remarked rather significantly in his *Memoirs*: "We knew that the United States minister was in sympathy with us."[24] Plans were informally drawn up for a Provisional Government;[25] and Wundenberg was appointed to find rifles and ammunition.[26] As a result of his activity, the old military organizations of 1887, which had been officially disbanded by the King in 1890 but which had continued to hold secret meetings, were notified to be ready.[27] As soon as the meeting broke up, Stevens heard about what had been going on. Said Smith in his testimony to Blount:

> After we adjourned Mr. Thurston and I called upon the American minister again and informed him of what was being done. Among other things we talked over with him what had better be done in case of our being arrested, or extreme or violent measures being taken by the monarchy in regard to us. We did not know what steps would be taken, and there was a feeling of great unrest and

[22] Cooper's deposition, in Blount, p. 496.

[23] Thurston, *op. cit.*, p. 251.

[24] *Op. cit.*, p. 74.

[25] Smith's testimony, in Blount, p. 497.

[26] Thurston, *op. cit.*, p. 251.

[27] McCandless, in Morgan, p. 611. An interesting statement, showing the connection between the Revolutionists of 1887 and of 1893, is the unsigned affidavit of the Committee of Safety, which was used by Annexationists in the Morgan investigation to disprove Blount's statement that Wiltse and Stevens promised aid to the Revolutionists. The document went on to say that the armed force of 1887 "had retained its organization, and turned out under the command of its old officers, constituting a well drilled, disciplined and officered military force" (Thurston Papers, Archives).

> sense of danger in the community. Mr. Stevens gave assurance of his earnest purpose to afford all the protection that was in his power to protect life and property. He emphasized the fact that while he would call for the United States troops to protect life and property, he could not recognize any government until actually established.[28]

The next morning, Sunday, January 15, 1893, Thurston, having interpreted the statements of the American officials as assurance of sympathy, if not of aid, continued with the plan of resistance.[29] He first interviewed Minister Colburn; then both of them called upon Attorney General Peterson at his home at 6:30 a.m. Thurston said the Committee of Safety had decided that the Queen must go; that "they did not propose to sit over a volcano" any longer; and that Stevens had promised to land troops and support the Revolutionists if a proclamation was issued. Would Colburn and Peterson join the movement and would the Cabinet take the lead? The two Ministers asked time to think it over, but refused next day.[30] Meanwhile both Cabinet members, despite Thurston's cautioning them against informing their colleagues, Parker and Cornwell who were hostile to the American party, at once told Parker and Cornwell. All four proceeded to devise a program to crush out what they by that time considered to be a treasonable and infamous plot.[31]

At nine of the same day the Committee of Safety met at W. R. Castle's residence, where Thurston informed the members of his conversations with Colburn and Peterson. His action was approved. Thurston refused to head a new government because he felt his reputation for radicalism might weaken it.[32] A mass meeting was suggested for the next day, and Thurston was instructed

[28] P. 122.

[29] McCandless, in Morgan, p. 618.

[30] This early morning conversation is described by all three participants in Thurston to Foster, Feb. 21, 1893, *op. cit.;* Thurston, *Memoirs, op. cit.*, pp. 251-252; and Colburn, in Blount, p. 33. See also Neumann to Foster, Feb. 21, 1893, Notes from Hawaii.

[31] It is possible that the two Ministers did exactly what Thurston expected them to do; in other words, if he intended to smoke them out and force them to show their colors, he succeeded. For the counter activities of the Royal Government, see Marshal Wilson's story in Blount, pp. 561 *ff.*

[32] *Ibid.*, p. 498.

to draw up a statement to be read to the people.[33] After the conference Thurston, Castle, and Smith again asked Stevens for aid in case of their arrest; he replied that he would use all his power to protect life and property, but could not recognize the new government until it was *de facto* and in possession of the city.[34]

Stevens had callers from the other side also. That evening Parker and Peterson inquired whether he would stand by the Queen in case of an insurrection. He was supposed to have answered that he did not see how he could assist her as long as C. B. Wilson was Marshal of the Kingdom.[35]

Next day, Monday, January 16, 1893, the Committee of Safety met all morning in Thurston's office, planning for the mass meeting. McCandless later testified that by Monday all agreed that this time it had to be dethronement. There must be no more 1887's.[36] During the meeting, Marshal Wilson called Thurston out of the room, and informed him that the Committee was ordered to disband. In return he offered the olive branch by promising to see to it that the Queen did no more foolishness.[37] According to Thurston, his words were: "I will guarantee that she will not [proclaim a new Constitution], even if I have to lock her up in a room to keep her from doing it; and I'll do it, too, if necessary."[38] When Thurston refused to abandon the movement, Wilson replied that he had done his duty by warning him. After the Revolution, Wilson told Thurston that he wanted the Queen's Cabinet to declare the Committee of Safety traitors and have them arrested, but "the damned cowards" were afraid to issue the warrants.[39]

After Wilson left, A. S. Cleghorn, father of the heir apparent and Governor of Oahu, came to plead for his daughter's cause. If Liliuokalani was to be deposed, said he, Kaiulani should be made

[33] Thurston, *Memoirs, op. cit.*, p. 252.

[34] *Ibid.*, pp. 252-253 and Blount, p. 498.

[35] Neumann to Foster, Feb. 21, 1893, Notes from Hawaii. Peterson told Blount that the reason Stevens hated Wilson was that the latter had recently arrested Stevens's Chinese coachman for carrying concealed weapons. Thurston denied the allegation against Stevens (Blount, pp. 439-440 and 555; and Thurston to Foster, Feb. 21, 1893, Notes from Hawaii.

[36] Morgan, p. 611.

[37] McCandless, in Morgan, p. 612.

[38] In *ibid.*, pp. 598-599.

[39] Thurston, *Memoirs, op. cit.*, pp. 253-254.

Queen under a board of regents; things would be different from what they had been. Thurston answered that the movement had gone too far and that he and his friends wanted no monarchy at all. The Committee approved his answer to Cleghorn, who was quite heart-broken. Castle and Thurston were instructed to draft a proclamation dethroning the Queen when the proper time came.[40]

Because Marshal Wilson had warned the Committee of the danger of holding the intended mass meeting,[41] the Revolutionists sent an official request to Stevens for aid. It read:

> We, the undersigned, citizens and residents of Honolulu, respectfully represent that, in view of the recent public events in this Kingdom, culminating in the revolutionary acts of Queen Liliuokalani on Saturday last, the public safety is menaced and lives and property are in peril, and we appeal to you and the United States forces at your command for assistance.
>
> The Queen, with the aid of armed forces, and accompanied by threats of violence and bloodshed from those with whom she was acting, attempted to proclaim a new constitution; and while prevented for the time from accomplishing her object declared publicly that she would only defer her action.
>
> This conduct and action was [*sic*] upon an occasion and under circumstances which have created general alarm and terror.
>
> We are unable to protect ourselves without aid and, therefore, pray for the protection of the United States forces.[42]

The document was signed by thirteen whites (the Committee of Safety), none of whom had any native blood. According to citizenship, six were Hawaiian, five were American, one was English, and one was German. A careful perusal of the stockholders of the various corporations in Hawaii at the time reveals that several

[40] *Ibid.*, pp. 255-256.

[41] A copy of the poster calling the mass meeting was printed in Morgan, p. 753.

[42] Blount, pp. 55-56. It is instructive to note that Alexander, *op. cit.*, p. 43, says that "inadvertently the last sentence, (which as coming from the Committee of Safety was inconsistent with the facts), was allowed to remain" after certain other portions were stricken out.

of the members were rather heavily interested in sugar; and yet it is important to note that by no means did sugar interests dominate the group. Six owned no sugar stock at all. The following table[43] gives the name, nationality, citizenship, sugar stock, and other investments:

Name	*Nationality*	*Citizenship*	*Sugar Stock*	*Stock Other Than Sugar*
Henry E. Cooper	American	American	None	None
F. W. McChesney	American	American	None	$ 600
W. C. Wilder	American	Hawaiian	None	$ 41,500
C. Bolte	German	Hawaiian	$ 38,000	$ 50,100
A. Brown	Scotch	English	$ 3,000	None
W. O. Smith	Haw. born Am.	Hawaiian	$ 22,900	$ 9,500
Henry Waterhouse	English	Hawaiian	None	$ 10,400
Theo. F. Lansing	American	American	$ 3,000	None
Ed. Suhr	German	German	$ 26,100	$ 6,000
L. A. Thurston	Haw. born Am.	Hawaiian	$ 9,200	$ 85,000
John Emmeluth	American	American	None	None
W. R. Castle	Haw. born Am.	Hawaiian	$ 86,500	$ 55,900
J. A. McCandless	American	American	None	$ 5,500
			$188,700	$264,550

In the afternoon of the same day, the Committee of Safety held its mass meeting in order to test public sentiment and to create popularity for the undertaking. It was estimated by Annexationists that 1,260 were present. After long and fiery speeches by leading insurgents, Thurston read the report of the Committee of Safety and a set of resolutions by which they "do hereby condemn and denounce the action of the Queen and her supporters." The work of the Committee was endorsed. The speakers included Thurston, Alexander Young,[44] H. F. Glade, C. Bolte, John Emmeluth, and R. J. Greene. But one of the most telling addresses was delivered by H. P. Baldwin,[45] who, along with Claus Spreckels,[46] was the

[43] Blount, pp. 121-122 and 619-670 *passim; Congressional Record* (53 Cong. 2 Sess), p. 2288.

[44] Young was of British nationality and owned $648,700 of sugar stock.

[45] For Baldwin's reasons for favoring annexation, see his letter to Blount, April 25, 1893, in Blount, pp. 601-604. He owned $1,293,900 of stock in the sugar industry and $78,550 in other enterprises (*ibid.*, pp. 619-670 *passim*).

[46] Spreckels controlled, in his own name, $955,730 of sugar stock; this

greatest sugar mogul in the islands. There was little hint to the crowd of plans for dethroning the Queen; it was merely her action in trying to overthrow the Constitution that was questioned.[47] Perhaps few at the meeting actually wished to go any further, since the Queen had capitulated.[48]

The Cabinet had already made its next move by printing and scattering all over Honolulu at 11:00 a.m., January 16, a so-called "By Authority" notice,[49] which read as follows:

> Her Majesty's ministers desire to express their appreciation for the quiet and order which have prevailed in this community since the events of Saturday, and are authorized to say that the position taken by Her Majesty in regard to the promulgation of a new constitution was under stress of her native subjects.
>
> Authority is given for the assurance that any changes

gave him a half interest in the Hilo Sugar Company, the Kilauea Sugar Company, the Paauhau Plantation Company, and the Waikapu Sugar Company. Besides these sugar investments he owned $211,500 of the stock (equal to a half interest) of the William G. Irwin Company (Blount, *loc. cit.*). Spreckels was no Annexationist. He did, however, favor reciprocity. See Claus Spreckels, "The Future of the Sandwich Islands," in *North American Review,* 152 (March, 1891), 287-292. In spite of the fact that he was opposed to annexation, Spreckels called on the Hawaiian Commissioners who, after the overthrow of the Queen, went to Washington to secure annexation; when they arrived at San Francisco, he expressed his support and even tendered to them the use of his private railroad coach for their trip across the continent. Thurston, who reported the fact in his *Memoirs, op. cit.,* p. 284, added that the Commissioners of course declined with thanks.

[47] Thus P. W. Reeder, who, as a tourist in Honolulu was present at the mass meeting, declared to the Morgan Committee that the sessions of the Committee of Safety were so secret that the first real intimation he received of its intentions was in the proclamation of Jan. 17, 1893 (which will be discussed presently). His articles, which he sent home to the *Cedar Rapids Republican* and the *Cedar Rapids Times,* were widely quoted (Morgan, pp. 676-691).

[48] Thurston admitted that, although the mass meeting adopted his resolutions, the phrases "dethronement of Liliuokalani" and "abrogation of the Monarchy" were not used at the assembly. He explained, however, that everyone there understood that such action was to be taken (*Memoirs, op. cit.,* p. 267). The *Advertiser,* Jan. 17, 1893, carried a long report of the meeting, quoting freely from the speeches. Enclosed in Stevens to Foster, No. 79, Jan. 18, 1893, Despatches. The resolutions were printed in Morgan, pp. 616-617.

[49] Signed by the Queen and four Ministers. Printed in Blount, p. 116.

> desired in the fundamental law of the land will be sought only by methods provided in the constitution itself.
>
> Her Majesty's ministers request all citizens to accept the assurance of Her Majesty in the same spirit in which it is given.

It is evident, from the lengths to which the Americans had gone, that they thought this statement had come too late, or else that the Queen's promise amounted to little. Alexander, the Hawaiian historian, said later: "This retraction came too late."[50] Be that as it may, the Royalists did not curtail their activity with this public proclamation. Taking their cue from the white party, they also held a public rally almost simultaneously with their opponents.[51] Parker testified that the purpose was "To draw the crowd away from your meeting."[52] The affair was no less noisy and enthusiastic, although the audience of 500 was composed almost entirely of Kanakas. Two resolutions were adopted:

> . . . That the assurance of Her Majesty the Queen contained in this day's proclamation is accepted by the people as a satisfactory guaranty that the Government does not and will not seek any modification of the constitution by other means than those provided in the organic law. . . . That accepting this assurance, the citizens here assembled will give their cordial support to the administration, and indorse them in sustaining that policy.[53]

In view of the facts that these resolutions were passed by the natives and that it was they who wished the Queen to change the Constitution, the basic grievance of the white party had apparently been removed. Yet, the Annexationist *Advertiser,* speaking for the Committee of Safety, next day made fun of the native meeting.[54]

[50] Morgan, p. 297.

[51] For the flier calling the meeting, see *ibid.,* pp. 37-39.

[52] *Ibid.,* p. 613.

[53] Blount, p. 116; and Neumann to Foster, Feb. 21, 1893, Notes from Hawaii. Next day the Queen and her Ministers sent to Stevens "solemn assurance that the present constitution will be upheld and maintained by me and my ministers, and no changes will be made except by the methods therein provided" (Blount, pp. 116-117).

[54] The Annexationists might deride the native meeting, but at least one American official was afraid of bloodshed if the two mass meetings clashed. Consul General Severance had already sent to Captain Wiltse a precautionary warning that troops might be necessary. It read in part: "In case

It declared that the Queen, by violating her oath, had absolved her subjects from allegiance; therefore the throne was vacant.[55] This doctrine of self-abdication by violation of her oath became the official justification of the Provisional Government for the Revolution. In other words, the Queen was the first revolutionist and had deposed herself. President Dole later said: "The Queen was an insurgent. She had rebelled against her own government."[56] The *Advertiser's* assertion is significant because it indicated that the opponents of the monarchy had moved to that stage of activity where they were talking publicly of deposition.

Following the successful mass meeting, the Committee of Safety gathered at 4:00 p.m. in Smith's office for the purpose of determining the next move. After careful deliberation, Smith and Thurston were sent to the American Minister to ask delay in landing American troops whose protection they had just requested. This most peculiar gesture has puzzled both historian and statesman.[57] The reason as given was that the insurgents had no forces at hand.[58] Stevens told the Committee: "Gentlemen, the troops of the *Boston* land this afternoon at 5 o'clock, whether you are ready or not."[59]

of any outbreak or collision with the committee of safety at the mass meeting to-day and the Government forces with a view of suppressing said meeting, it might be necessary to land a force to preserve order or protect our property. In such case, should the telephone wires be cut, I can send you a signal by lowering my flag at half mast, and you will, of course be governed by instructions from Minister Stevens." This letter played a conspicuous part in the Morgan investigation, p. 538.

[55] Enclosed in Severance to Wharton, No. 174, Jan. 18, 1893, Consular Letters.

[56] Quoted by Julius A. Palmer, Jr., *Memories of Hawaii and Hawaiian Correspondence* (Boston, 1894), p. 61.

[57] Senator George Gray of Delaware later said he had searched in vain for the Committee's reasons for requesting Stevens to delay (*Congressional Record,* 53 Cong. 2 Sess., p. 2085).

[58] McCandless deposed that some of the Committee did not want the troops yet because they feared "a changed condition" (Morgan, pp. 617-618). Thurston (*Memoirs, op. cit.,* pp. 268-269) declared that their plans were still inchoate and that they needed time. Stevens's answer was Thurston's first information that the troops were to be landed. Minister W. R. Castle, questioned at Boston in the fall of 1895, said: "I feared that when the troops were landed, just at the critical time, before we had obtained possession of all the branches of the Government, the act would be open to misconstruction" (interview printed in the *Advertiser,* Oct. 2, 1895).

[59] Wundenberg's statement, in Blount, p. 26.

He gave as his excuse that he intended to protect American life and property, as well as the Queen and the Cabinet. At five o'clock, therefore, American troops, numbering 162 officers and men,[60] disembarked and marched fully armed through the streets, to the wonderment of the populace.[61] The larger portion, consisting of three companies of bluejackets, was quartered in Arion Hall,[62] just opposite the Government Building. That left the marines to guard the Consulate and the Legation,[63] and they were divided equally for that purpose. When Blount investigated the part which American troops had taken in the deposition of the Queen, the Royalists pointed out that inasmuch as the great majority of the force were a third of a mile away from both Legation and Consulate, Stevens's primary purpose for landing troops could not have been protection of American property. Young, however, who was in command of a portion of the landing party, stated that the men were so placed as to make both sides respect American property.[64] In his note to Captain Wiltse, January 16, asking for troops, Stevens gave his reasons as follows:

> In view of the existing critical circumstances in Honolulu, indicating an inadequate legal force, I request you to land marines and sailors from the ship under your command for the protection of the United States lega-

[60] Lt. Young said a battalion disembarked. It included one company of artillery, two of bluejackets, one of marines, with musicians and hospital corps. Each man carried from sixty to eighty rounds of cartridges (Young, *op. cit.*, p. 184). Lt. Fox gave similar figures to Blount, p. 131. See also Alexander, *op. cit.*, p. 52.

[61] Wundenberg's testimony, in Blount, p. 576.

[62] Blount, while investigating the matter, asked Admiral J. S. Skerrett, then commanding at Honolulu, what he thought of the disposition of troops from the viewpoint of strategy. Skerrett asserted that the forces were ill placed if their primary purpose was to defend Americans and to protect United States property (Blount, p. 72).

[63] Stevens later declared that he had the Legation guarded because he feared the work of incendiary cranks (Morgan, p. 537).

[64] *Op. cit.*, p. 190. Perhaps the difference in opinion can be attributed to the difference in what each thought American property to be. The Royalists were probably thinking of property of the United States Government (Legation and Consulate) and Young was thinking of the property of American citizens as well.

tion and the United States consulate, and to secure the safety of American life and property.[65]

The Cabinet and Cleghorn,[66] Governor of Oahu, remonstrated at once against the disembarking of the military force without the knowledge or request of the Queen. The words of Foreign Minister Parker were: "As the situation is one that does not call for interference on the part of the U. S. Government, my colleagues and myself would most respectfully request of Your Excellency the authority upon which this action was taken. I would also add that any protection that may have been considered necessary for the American Legation or for American interests in this city would have been cheerfully furnished by Her Majesty's Government."[67] But Stevens paid no attention to their objections, and the only answer they could secure was the equivocal assertion, sent the next day, that "In whatever the United States diplomatic and naval representatives have done or may do at this critical hour of Hawaiian affairs, we will be guided by the kindest views and feelings for all the parties concerned and by the warmest sentiments for the Hawaiian people and the persons of all nationalities."[68] Little wonder that Alexander said: "There is a diplomatic ambiguity in this language which was not reassuring."[69]

[65] *House Ex. Doc. 48* (53 Cong. 2 Sess.), p. 487. Wiltse's order to Lieutenant Commander W. T. Swinburne, Jan. 16, 1893 (which played an important part in the later debates on Hawaii), read: "You will take command of the battalion and land in Honolulu for the purpose of protecting our legation, consulate, and the lives and property of American citizens, and to assist in preserving order. Great prudence must be exercised by both officers and men, and no action taken that is not fully warranted by the condition of affairs and by the conduct of those who may be inimical to the treaty rights of American citizens" (*ibid.*, pp. 487-488). Young, *op. cit.*, pp. 185-186, says that the request of the Committee of Safety for protection had nothing to do with landing the troops, because Stevens had already visited the *Boston* before receiving the appeal. He declares that the decision to land was Wiltse's alone; he made the decision because he feared a clash between the two mass meetings.

[66] Cleghorn's protest is printed in Blount, p. 572.

[67] Parker to Stevens, Jan. 16, 1893, in Neumann to Foster, Feb. 21, 1893, Notes from Hawaii. Printed in Blount, p. 591.

[68] In Neumann to Foster, *ibid.* Printed in Blount, p. 592; Stevens's answer to Cleghorn is also in Blount, p. 572.

[69] *Op. cit.*, p. 53.

Perceiving that their hand had been forced, the Committee of Safety met that night at 7:30 in the dwelling of Henry Waterhouse to form a new Government.[70] Abdication of the Queen was a foregone conclusion and officers for the new Government were chosen. John H. Soper, after some hesitation because he saw no soldiers to command,[71] accepted appointment as commander of the Revolutionary army.[72] The choice for executive of the new régime was Sanford Ballard Dole,[73] an Associate Justice of the Supreme Court, who thus far had not taken any active part in the movement against his sovereign.[74] When approached by C. Bolte, he was reluctant to tie himself up with the Revolutionists for he was not certain that the time for doing away with the monarchy had arrived. He admitted that the future destiny of the islands was with the United States, and agreed with the insurgents that

[70] It was later thought to be of significance that Waterhouse's residence was next to the American Legation.

[71] Wundenberg to Blount, in Blount, pp. 26-27. Soper owned $10,600 of sugar stock and was an American citizen (Blount, p. 129).

[72] When investigation of these affairs was undertaken, several of the Committee of Safety asserted that Soper refused the command until he had gone over to see Stevens and had received assurance of American assistance (for instance, Wundenberg, in Blount, p. 576). Soper later denied this allegation by saying that he had merely walked out on the porch to get a drink of water (Blount, pp. 505-506). He did admit that he refused to accept until he was sure Stevens had promised support. The reader should keep Soper's rôle in mind; for the question whether he talked to Stevens or got a drink of water became one of the most controversial points in the Morgan investigation of 1894. Dole later described what happened in the following words: Soper ". . . said if I accepted he would act as the head of the army to be created. I guess he and I went out doors and talked it over out there under the trees." At the same meeting, continued Dole, "A messenger was sent over to Minister Stevens' house to inquire if the report was correct that he was in sympathy with us—and he was, I gathered" (Taylor, *Under Hawaiian Skies, op. cit.*, p. 461).

[73] A résumé of Dole's Maine ancestry has already been given. Born, in 1844, of American parents in the islands, he was a Hawaiian citizen by birth; as was customary, he was sent to the United States for his education. After a year at Williams College, he entered a law office and was in due course admitted to the bar. He then returned to Hawaii to practice law. He was a member of the Legislatures of 1884 and 1886. In 1887 he was appointed to the Supreme Court bench. See *Advertiser,* Jan. 6, 1898, enclosed in Sewall to Sherman, No. 99, Jan. 11, 1898, Despatches.

[74] He knew what was going on, however, for he had attended the meeting at Thurston's the previous Saturday evening.

Liliuokalani had forfeited her throne. Like Theophilus H. Davies,[75] he felt that a regency for Princess Kaiulani would be the best immediate solution. However, he reserved the right to think the matter over and promised his answer by noon of the morrow.[76]

The night meeting at Waterhouse's was also important, for, after it, S. M. Damon, the future Vice President, announced to the Queen that he had decided to leave her party. She, thinking he might be serviceable to her, asked him to try to obtain an appointment in the new Government.[77] This may account for the weight she gave to his arguments when she was persuaded to surrender to the Revolutionists next day.

The climax of the movement occurred on Tuesday, January 17, 1893, with the final overthrow of hereditary monarchy in the Hawaiian Islands without the loss of a life.[78] At a meeting in Smith's office at 10 a.m. organization of the Provisional Government was completed and more officers chosen. Furthermore, orders were given for the chartering of W. C. Wilder's vessel, the *Claudine,* to carry despatches to the United States.[79] At eleven o'clock Judge Dole came over to the Revolutionary side as titular leader, materially strengthening its hand by lending a certain degree of dignity and judicial conservatism to the cause.[80] Meanwhile

[75] Davies, "The Hawaiian Situation," in *North American Review,* CLVI (May, 1893), 608.

[76] Bolte's testimony in Blount, pp. 251-252; Alexander, *op. cit.,* p. 54; and Young, *op. cit.,* p. 192.

[77] Damon was one of Liliuokalani's closest advisers. He told her that, although he had always supported the monarchy, her recent actions forced him to change his allegiance. McCandless said that Damon also advised her to give in, for her cause was hopeless. She assured him that she would (Morgan, p. 624). This story seems to be somewhat inconsistent with the larger facts in the case. See also Liliuokalani, *op. cit.,* pp. 386-387, and Alexander, *op. cit.,* p. 54.

[78] This was not unusual. In all the revolutions and insurrections in Hawaii since 1875 only seven persons had been killed and seven wounded. See James Schouler, "A Review of the Hawaiian Controversy," in *Forum,* XVI (1893-94), 683.

[79] Smith's testimony in Blount, p. 501. Alexander, *op. cit.,* p. 55, said that at this meeting Samuel Parker, Foreign Minister, announced his willingness to accept the presidency of the new government if it was offered to him.

[80] Dole, in his *Memoirs, op. cit.,* p. 78, related that after a night of thought he decided to accept the leadership of the new Government. He resigned from the Supreme Court, sent his resignation to the Royal Cabinet, and went

Charles L. Carter saw W. T. Swinburne, who commanded the American troops, and informed him as follows: "It is the intention of the committee of safety to take possession of the Government building. You will recognize them by Mr. Dole; you know Mr. Dole; he is the tallest man in the party; if you see him in the party you will know what he is doing."[81] Swinburne replied: "If the Queen calls upon me to preserve order, I am going to do it."[82]

As the Revolutionary star waxed, the Royal one waned. At two in the afternoon, the Cabinet drove to the American Minister's residence, declaring it was the legal Government and asking for support. Alexander, who wrote what amounted to an official history of the Revolution, is authority for giving Stevens's answer thus: "Gentlemen, these men were landed for one purpose only, a pacific purpose, and we cannot take part in any contest. I cannot use this force for sustaining the Queen or anybody else."[83] Parker and Peterson, however, deposed afterwards that, when they asked for his aid if they declared the Committee of Safety to be rebels, he refused, adding that he had made up his mind that if any large number of responsible citizens organized a Provisional Government, he would recognize and uphold it.[84] Failing to obtain any satisfaction from the American Minister, the Cabinet returned to prepare for exigencies, but the Revolution was upon them before they were aware of it.

According to the *Advertiser* in an article entitled, "New Era!

at once to the headquarters of the Committee of Safety. Shortly after that he called on Stevens and gave him a copy of the announcement of the abrogation of the monarchy, the original of which he hoped to be able to provide later. It was sent that very afternoon. Stevens commented: "I think you have a great opportunity."

[81] Swinburne's testimony in Morgan, p. 470.

[82] Alexander, *op. cit.*, p. 57. The Queen did ask for aid on that day in a note which was sent to all diplomatic representatives and which amounted to an abject surrender. It said in part: "It is now my desire to give Your Excellency . . . the solemn assurance that the present Constitution will be upheld and maintained by Me and My Ministers and no changes will be made except by the methods therein provided" (Foreign Office Files, Archives).

[83] *Ibid.*, p. 56; and Stevens in Morgan, p. 548.

[84] Neumann to Foster, Feb. 21, 1893, Notes from Hawaii; printed in Blount, pp. 439-440.

The Revolution Terminated by the Establishing of a Provisional Government," the precipitation of the putsch occurred at 2:30 in the afternoon, when several members of the foreign or American party, who had been taking a supply of ammunition to the proper rendezvous, were accosted by three policemen. They refused to halt; when policeman Leleialoha moved to draw his gun, he was fired upon by Captain Good of the Revolutionists, and was wounded—the only casualty of the uprising. A running fight ensued until the ammunition wagon reached its destination.[85] At once the Committee of Safety decided it was time[86] to read the proclamation overthrowing the monarchy and establishing a Provisional Government.

For personal safety the twenty Revolutionists divided into two bodies which advanced upon the Government Building by different routes. Neither one had any arms whatever. The long proclamation was read by Henry E. Cooper at 2:40 to a few clerks and porters who loitered nearby.[87] Lieutenant Young, who was watching, estimated that there were fifty armed volunteers as the reading began, and that this number had grown to 175 by the time it was finished.[88] His figures are rather optimistic when compared to those given by some of the men who took part in the event. Another account reports that at the beginning of the proclamation only one individual was armed, but that, towards the end, a few

[85] Enclosed in Stevens to Foster, No. 79, Jan. 18, 1893, Despatches; printed in *House Ex. Doc. 48* (53 Cong. 2 Sess.), pp. 129-130. Good was later officially exonerated for his act and was allowed to enter upon his duty as captain in the new Provisional Government army. The moral effect of his shot was stressed in his favor. (Proceedings of the Executive and Advisory Councils of the Provisional Government, Archives, Honolulu, Jan. 20 and 21, 1893, pp. 31 and 36. This source is hereafter referred to as EAC.)

[86] McCandless in Morgan, p. 625, said the Committee thought this was the time because the crowd, hearing the shot, had rushed to the scene, and the streets leading to the Government Building were deserted. Dole (*Memoirs, op. cit.*, p. 79) stated that, just as he was about to proclaim the new Government, he saw several Royal policemen across the street, and he hesitated. Hearing Captain Good's shot, the police hurried to the scene of the disturbance, and the way was open for the Revolutionists.

[87] Damon's testimony, in Blount, p. 39.

[88] Young, *op. cit.*, p. 200. Wundenberg informed Blount (p. 577) there was "practically no audience whatever" at the start. Alexander, a witness, later deposed that the audience consisted of several Government clerks and one native member of the Legislature (Morgan, p. 298).

so-called Revolutionary troops, armed with shotguns, were arriving. When hard pressed by Secretary Walter Q. Gresham, Thurston who was the real spirit behind the Revolution, asserted that 274 men were present and were armed with "Springfield rifles—that is to say, they were mostly armed."[89] Dole, who ought to know, wrote later that the Government Building was deserted except for a few clerks. The Royal Cabinet was at the police station. When the Committee arrived, there was one soldier only, according to Dole; in Dole's words: "We got to the court-house [Government Building] and the only 'force' we saw was Oscar White, carrying a gun, standing on the town side of the Government house. But soon afterward some of our men commenced to arrive."[90]

The Royal commander[91] was there waiting for the Cabinet to

[89] Miscellaneous Archives, Memoranda of Conversations with the Secretary of State 1893-1898, National Archives. Conversation of August 14, 1893.

[90] As told to Taylor, *op. cit.*, pp. 462-463.

[91] This was Charles J. McCarthy, later Governor of Hawaii under President Wilson. McCarthy expected Royal soldiers to arrive, but the division within the Cabinet prevented such action. An interesting document, now in the Dole Papers, was presented to the Hawaiian Archives by Professor R. S. Kuykendall on Nov. 28, 1931. It shows that McCarthy was ready to resist. Though so hastily written that the day of the month is illegible, the words "January 1893" are clear enough. It reads:

> Mr. C. B. Wilson,
> Marshal of the Kingdom etc
> Dear sir,
> I believe that it would be advisable to send up to the Government Building after dark about 20 stand of arms, and about 300 or 400 rounds of ammunition with the idea of storing them in the office of the Attorney-General, in case of necessity.
> I have sufficient employees here to take care of the building in case of attack.
> Yours respectfully
> C. J. McCarthy

On the reverse is the following endorsement in pencil:

> Capt. Parker was detailed for this duty. was there all night. Peterson stopped its continuance this morning. Jan 17th 1903.
> C. B. Wilson

Just why Wilson wrote "1903" for "1893" is hard to say. Perhaps he endorsed the statement in 1903 from memory, forgetting that he was referring to 1893. If the endorsement is genuine, the Annexationists owed more to Peterson than they knew, because if the order had not been countermanded by Peterson, it is likely that bloodshed would have occurred. Peterson was

send a force of armed men and arrest the insurgents. The Cabinet, however, was too divided to take a stand, and the Revolutionists acquired possession of the Government Building without difficulty. The clerks gave up readily and accepted positions under the new administration. Frank P. Hastings and Prince David Kawananakoa, who were serving in the Foreign Office, began to make out commissions for officeholders under the changed conditions. Towards the end of Cooper's reading of the proclamation, Dole sent his announcement to Stevens, a copy of which he had already presented to the American Minister several hours before.[92]

The American troops leaned on a picket fence across the street, with arms stacked nearby,[93] but did not offer to give any effective aid.[94] Damon testified to Blount: "I was perfectly nonplussed by not receiving any support. I could not imagine why we were there without being supported by American troops. . . . We were not supported in any way."[95] Charles L. Carter crossed the street and asked Swinburne for a guard. Swinburne's reply was, "I remain passive." Swinburne's colleagues, Lieutenant Young and Captain Wiltse, were watching the proceedings; and Wiltse refused to recognize the Provisional Government until it controlled the police station and the military forces. Young recorded: "Several persons asked me if we were not going to stand by them. I replied, 'Gentlemen, you heard what I said.' A few looked at each other in surprise. . . ." Wiltse refused two requests for aid,[96] although he did tell Young: "I will not allow any fighting in the city."[97]

The lengthy proclamation,[98] deposing the Queen and setting up the new régime, was at once printed and scattered broadcast. It

always reviled by the Annexationists. For instance, the *Advertiser* on Jan. 11, 1893, castigated those who voted for the infamous lottery bill. It said that only natives voted for it on its second reading, except Arthur P. Peterson, whose "political career . . . began in honor and ends in shame."

[92] *Memoirs, op. cit.,* pp. 81-83.

[93] Testimony of Dr. Nicholas B. Delamater of Chicago, a tourist who witnessed the event, and Dr. Francis R. Day, who stood guard while the proclamation was read (Morgan, pp. 729 and 738).

[94] Testimony of J. C. Quinn and Edmund Norrie, in Blount, pp. 600-601.

[95] Blount, p. 40.

[96] Young, *op. cit.,* pp. 201-202.

[97] Young to Blount, July 16, 1893, in Blount, p. 673.

[98] Enclosed in Stevens to Foster, No. 79, Jan. 18, 1893, Despatches.

gave a historical review of the tyranny and inefficiency of the Royal Government under Kalakaua and Liliuokalani, whose Legislatures were "replete with corruption" and bribery.

The new policy was outlined as follows: (1) absolute abolition of the Hawaiian monarchy; (2) establishment of a Provisional Government to rule until annexation by the United States; (3) composition of the new Government: an Executive Council of four members, namely, Sanford B. Dole (Chairman and Minister of Foreign Affairs), James A. King (Interior), P. C. Jones (Finance), and W. O. Smith (Attorney General), and an Advisory Council of fourteen members;[99] (4) all officials except the

[99] The membership of the new Government, nationality, and business connections are instructive. Exactly half of the Advisory Council were not even Hawaiian citizens; not one was a native. Bolte was born in Bremen, Emmeluth in Cincinnati, McChesney in Iowa, McCandless in Pennsylvania, Morgan and Tenney in New York. A glance at the following statistics will indicate that sugar interests were represented, although the stock owned by even the largest holder was modest in comparison, for example, to that owned by Claus Spreckels and by H. P. Baldwin.

Name	*Citizenship*	*Nationality*	*Sugar Stock*	*Other Stock*
Executive Council				
S. B. Dole	Hawaiian	Haw. born Am.	$ 800	$ 2,800
J. A. King	Hawaiian	American	200	-------
P. C. Jones	Hawaiian	American	1,600	35,000
W. O. Smith	Hawaiian	Haw. born Am.	22,900	9,500
Advisory Council				
A. Brown	English	Scotch	3,000	----------
J. Emmeluth	American	American	-----	----------
C. Bolte	Hawaiian	German	38,000	50,000
J. F. Morgan	Hawaiian	Haw. born Am.	2,000	4,200
H. Waterhouse	Hawaiian	English	----------	10,400
S. M. Damon	Hawaiian	Haw. born Am.	5,000	800
W. G. Ashley	American	American	----------	3,800
E. D. Tenney	American	American	6,500	200
F. W. McChesney	American	American	----------	600
W. C. Wilder	Hawaiian	American	----------	41,500
J. A. McCandless	American	American	----------	5,500
W. R. Castle	Hawaiian	Haw. born Am.	86,500	55,950
L. A. Thurston	Hawaiian	Haw. born Am.	9,200	85,000
F. J. Wilhelm	American	Haw. born Ger.	500	----------
			$176,200	$305,350

(From Blount, pp. 129 and 619-670 *passim.*)

Queen, her Ministers, and Marshal were to remain; (5) laws not inconsistent with the new order of things were to continue.[100]

The new Government, having no support except for a few citizen soldiers armed with rifles and shotguns, perceived that the next step was to demand surrender of the Queen's Government. The Cabinet had been at the police station, for some time, holding a council of war with the Marshal. S. M. Damon, C. Bolte, and others, who were sent to the station house to demand its surrender, informed the Cabinet that the new Government had been recognized by the American Minister. The Queen's Ministers, however, were skeptical and declared that they did not believe Stevens had given countenance to any new régime; and that if they had only the insurgents to face they would not capitulate. Damon urged that inasmuch as the Provisional Government had the support of the American forces, it would be wise for the Royal Government to give up, so that useless bloodshed might be averted. Marshal

[100] Thurston, *Memoirs, op. cit.*, p. 271, gave the origin of this remarkable document. He and Castle had been instructed to draw up a proclamation at the meeting of the Committee of Safety on Monday morning. Both had been too busy to comply. In the meeting at Waterhouse's the night of the landing of the American troops, the Committee (Thurston being absent because of severe illness) ordered him to draw up the document for use next day. The following morning, his secretary at about nine o'clock brought him the Committee's request. Too ill to write, he had his secretary hurry to his office to secure a typewriter; having returned with the machine, the secretary typed the proclamation as the prostrate Thurston dictated. The first draft was not completed until eleven o'clock and there was no time to revise. It was sent at once to the Committee which adopted Thurston's unrevised version, changing only one word. A few minutes later Cooper was reading it at the Government Building.

The proclamation did not, however, come out of thin air. It will be recalled that Thurston had drafted a proclamation to depose King Kalakaua on May 17, 1887, and it is not too much to assume that he had this 1887 document at hand. Few changes had to be made except as to date and the names of persons. "Kalakaua" became "Liliuokalani"; "republic" became "provisional government"; "council of state" became "advisory council," and so on. Indeed some of the names under the projected 1887 plan of government appear again as officials in 1893. Many of the orders which the contemplated republic was to issue were similar to those first proclaimed by the Provisional Government in 1893, such as: suspension of the writ; prohibition of any vessels leaving port, except foreign vessels of war; forbidding the sale of liquor, *etc.* The 1887 document can be found in Thurston Papers, Archives.

Wilson was even more stubborn, replying that he could withstand both Americans and Revolutionists. He refused to submit without the Queen's order. The Cabinet, determined to find out whether Stevens had recognized the insurgents, despatched a note to him, a little after three o'clock. It read:

> Her Hawaiian Majesty's Government having been informed that certain persons to them unknown have issued proclamation declaring a Provisional Government to exist in opposition to Her Majesty's Government, and have pretended to depose the Queen, her cabinet and marshal, and that certain treasonable persons at present occupy the Government building in Honolulu with an armed force, and pretending that your excellency, in behalf of the United States of America, has recognized such Provisional Government, Her Majesty's cabinet asks respectfully: Has your excellency recognized said Provisional Government? and if not, Her Majesty's Government, under the above existing circumstances, respectfully requests the assistance of your Government in preserving the peace of the country.[101]

Alexander, the Hawaiian historian who observed the events of the Revolution, asserted that by 3:00 p.m. Colonel Soper had managed to collect a hundred volunteers and by 4:00 p.m. two hundred.[102] These numbers may be exaggerated, but if not, two hundred raw minute men represented the new Government's sole claim to power. It is little wonder, then, that at 4:30 when Dole asked Captain Wiltse to recognize the new state of affairs, the Captain first wanted to know whether the Provisional Government had possession of the barracks. Dole, in his request, justified recognition on the basis of what he told Young: "You see we have possession of the government building, the archives and the treasury, which is the government of Hawaii." Young replied: "I see you are here, but how about the police-station, police and barracks, and the armed forces at those places?" Dole's reply was that he would soon have those points. When Wiltse received Dole's answer, "at about 5 o'clock p.m.," he said: "Very well, gentlemen, I cannot recognize you as the de facto government until you have

[101] Blount, p. 63.
[102] Alexander, *op. cit.*, p. 62.

possession of the police station and are fully prepared to guarantee protection of life and property."[103]

Meanwhile, the note sent by Dole at the end of the reading of the proclamation had arrived at the American Legation. Asking aid and recognition, it read as follows:

> The undersigned, members of the Executive and Advisory Councils of the Provisional Government this day established in Hawaii hereby state to you that for the reasons set forth in the Proclamation this day issued, a copy of which is herewith enclosed for your consideration, the Hawaiian Monarchy has been abrogated and a Provisional Government established in accordance with the said above mentioned Proclamation. Such Provisional Government has been proclaimed; is now in possession of the Government Departmental Buildings, the Archives and the Treasury, and is in control of the City. We hereby request that you will, on behalf of the United States of America, recognize it as the existing de facto Government of the Hawaiian Islands and afford it the moral support of your Government, and, if necessary, the support of American troops to assist it in preserving the public peace.[104]

Stevens thereupon sent his aide to see whether the Revolutionists were really in possession of the Government Building. Learning that they were, he forthwith despatched to the Provisional Government a note which read:

> A Provisional Government having been duly constituted in the place of the recent Government of Queen Liliuokalani, and said Provisional Government being in full possession of the Government building, the Archives and the Treasury and in control of the Capital of the Hawaiian Islands, I hereby recognize said Provisional Government as the de facto Government of the Hawaiian Islands.[105]

Therefore, when the letter asking aid came from the Cabinet,

[103] Young, *op. cit.*, pp. 201-202. See also Young's testimony before the Morgan Committee, p. 488. Swinburne gave Blount the same facts, p. 57; also in Morgan, pp. 471 *ff*.

[104] Enclosed in Stevens to Foster, No. 79, Jan. 18, 1893, Despatches. The original of this note (in the files of the Foreign Office, Archives) contains the directions which were given to the clerk who was to make copies and send them to the diplomatic officials in Honolulu.

[105] *Ibid.*

Stevens had already repudiated the Government which it represented. He jotted down the following memorandum[106] when that note arrived:

> UNITED STATES LEGATION,
> Honolulu, January 17, 1893.
>
> About 4 to 5 p.m. of this date—am not certain of the precise time—the note on file from the four ministers of the deposed Queen, inquiring if I had recognized the Provisional Government came to my hands, while I was lying sick on the couch. Not far from 5 p.m.—I did not think to look at the watch—I addressed a short note to Hon. Samuel Parker, Hon. Wm. H. Cornwell, Hon. John F. Colburn, and Hon. A. P. Peterson—no longer regarding them ministers—informing them that I had recognized the Provisional Government.
>
> John L. Stevens,
> United States Minister.

Upon receiving Stevens's recognition the Provisional Government sent a committee, composed of Sanford B. Dole, Charles L. Carter, S. M. Damon, Rev. S. G. Beckwith, and James A. King, accompanied by the Cabinet, to the Palace for the purpose of announcing to the Queen that she was deposed, and of demanding the surrender of the station house and all her forces.[107]

J. O. Carter, friend of the Queen, expressed his sympathy, but advised against any demonstration on her part for that would precipitate a conflict with the American forces. He further persuaded that her case would have a careful hearing at Washington, and that a peaceful submission would aid her cause.[108] S. M. Damon, future Vice President, made the same promise. The Queen who, according to one estimate,[109] had fifty soldiers in her Palace, eighty in the barracks, and two hundred in the station house,

[106] Blount, p. 63. Young told the Morgan Committee that by 6:30 Wiltse knew Stevens had recognized; and that about 7:30 he (Young) was informed the police station had been peacefully acquired by "citizen troops" of the Provisional Government (p. 488).

[107] Amongst others who were present, the story of the interview was given in a sworn statement by E. C. MacFarlane, in Blount, pp. 171-172; also in a sworn statement by Paul Neumann, in *ibid.*, pp. 172-174.

[108] Carter to Blount, in Blount, pp. 56-57.

[109] Minister Colburn later deposed that the Royal forces amounted to 600 men with 30,000 rounds, eight brass Austrian cannon, and two gatlings;

could not see why she should surrender to the Provisional Government. However, when even Judge H. A. Widemann, her confidant, impressed upon her that if she resisted, she resisted the United States, she began to weaken. She was finally convinced that, because Minister Stevens had already recognized the insurgents, and it had been his policy to uphold the Government which he recognized, her only hope was an appeal to Washington. At last she was persuaded to surrender under protest (she did not abdicate), if allowed to lay her case before the President of the United States. Dole, the head of the new Government, was present and agreed to the terms of the surrender.[110] The capitulation[111] read as follows:

> I, Liliuokalani, by the Grace of God and under the Constitution of the Hawaiian Kingdom, Queen, do hereby solemnly protest against any and all acts done against myself and the Constitutional Government of the Hawaiian Kingdom by certain persons claiming to have established a Provisional Government for this Kingdom.
>
> That I yield to the superior force of the United States of America whose Minister Plenipotentiary, His Excellency John L. Stevens, has caused United States troops to be landed at Honolulu and declared that he would support the said Provisional Government.
>
> Now to avoid any collision of armed forces, and perhaps the loss of life, I do under this protest and impelled by said force yield my authority until such time as the Government of the United States shall upon the facts being

another estimate gave 272 men in the barracks, 224 in the station house, and fifty at the Palace—all of these being equipped with fourteen pieces of artillery, 386 rifles, and sixteen revolvers. Samuel Nowlein, Captain of the Household Guards, testified that he had under him 272 men (Blount, p. 174). Marshal Wilson swore he had 224 men at the police station (*ibid.,* pp. 176-177).

[110] Miscellaneous Archives . . . , *op. cit.* Conversation between Gresham and Thurston, Aug. 14, 1893. For Damon's endorsement of the terms of the surrender, see his testimony to Blount, p. 43.

[111] Printed in *Advertiser,* Jan. 18, 1893, and enclosed in Stevens to Foster, No. 79, Jan. 18, 1893, Despatches. Young says that this paper was drawn up by the Queen's lawyer, Paul Neumann, who laid her capitulation to the United States forces as "a pretext" (*op. cit.,* p. 204). Alexander, *op. cit.,* p. 67, admits it was a mistake for Dole to endorse the document; and that an unqualified abdication "even at the cost of a little bloodshed" would have been better. In any event it was a surrender and not an abdication, and occurred on Jan. 17, 1893, and not on Jan. 19, as stated by Henry James in his *Richard Olney and His Public Service* (Boston and N. Y., 1923), p. 82.

presented to it undo the action of its representative and reinstate me in the authority which I claim as Constitutional Sovereign of the Hawaiian Islands.

Done at Honolulu this 17th day of January, A. D., 1893.

Liliuokalani, R.
Samuel Parker,
Minister of Foreign Affairs.
W. H. Cornwell,
Minister of Finance.
Jno. F. Colburn,
Minister of the Interior.
A. P. Peterson,
Attorney General

The Queen then ordered Marshal Wilson to hand over the police station to the Provisional Government.[112] Thus final capitulation of the Royal Government occurred between 7:00 and 7:30 p.m., whereas recognition of the insurgents by Stevens took place between 4:00 and 5:00.[113] Control of the station house was given to the Provisional Government at once and the Royal forces marched out. They were disbanded and paid off by Colonel Soper next day. It had all been so easy that P. C. Jones's statement can be understood: "It was a surprise to us to see how quickly and quietly they yielded, and it is an evidence of the rottenness of the monarchy which fell as soon as any resistance was made."[114]

Annexationists in Hawaii were jubilant. The *Advertiser* said: "The Hawaiian monarchy perishes by its own fault. It dies for

[112] The Queen's order to Wilson, signed by her Ministers, read: "You are hereby authorized to surrender to the so-called Provisional Government this day established, headed by S. B. Dole, esq., the police station and Oahu prison and Government property in your possession or under your control" (Blount, p. 573).

[113] Stevens later set the time of recognition at five o'clock; his wife and daughter thought it was at five-thirty; and McCandless was sure it occurred between four and four-thirty (Morgan, p. 626).

[114] To the Morgan Committee, p. 203. Thurston, writing in his *Memoirs* (*op. cit.*, p. 273) years later, said: "Knowing every detail of what happened, I still do not comprehend exactly how it all came about, yet happen it did. I cannot but believe that it was the result of fate, foreordained from the beginning of things." Two pages farther on he explained it by saying that the Royal Government simply lacked the heart to fight. In the Thurston Papers, Archives, is an undated memo written and signed by Dole in praise of Thurston's part in the uprising. In it are the words: "We certainly owed much . . . to circumstances entirely out of our control."

lack of the vital virtues which alone can keep any system of government in being. . . . On the day when the connection of a half century becomes closer, and Hawaii enters into the family of States [that is, is annexed to the United States], as a territory or otherwise, her political troubles will be at an end."[115]

The new Government at once legislated to protect itself.[116] Order No. 1 of the Provisional Government of the Hawaiian Islands commanded all citizens to hand in their arms and ammunition so "that efficient and complete protection of life and property" might be secured. Order No. 2 suspended the writ of *habeas corpus* and declared martial law throughout the Island of Oahu.[117] The Queen was directed to retire to her private residence and to lower the Royal standard; but she was informed that she would be permitted to draw her salary at the end of the month.[118]

Because the *raison d'être* of the Provisional Government was to gain union with the United States,[119] it at once appointed a Commission which was to proceed to Washington and ask for annexation. The ship *Claudine* was chartered at a cost of $300 a day, and the Commission was granted $4,000 for its expenses.[120] The members were Lorrin A. Thurston, of Connecticut parentage, the real leader of the Revolution; J. Marsden, of English extraction, a Noble in the Legislature and the owner of $50,000 worth of sugar stock; William R. Castle, of New York descent, a lawyer; W. C. Wilder, President of the Inter-Island Steamship Company of Hawaii and owner of the vessel which carried the Commission to San Francisco; and Charles L. Carter, son of a recent Hawaiian Minister to the United States. Thus no second-rate men were sent

[115] Enclosed in Severance to Wharton, No. 174, Jan. 18, 1893, Consular Letters.

[116] The new Government had no money because of a peculiar circumstance. On Jan. 18 it was necessary to borrow $1,000 from Bishop and Co. to defray ordinary expenditures until "George Smithies, who has the combination and key of safe, is able to get out of bed." His illness tied up the sum of $50,000 which was much needed (EAC, Jan. 18, 1893, pp. 10 and 22, Archives).

[117] Enclosed in Stevens to Foster, No. 79, Jan. 18, 1893, Despatches.

[118] EAC, p. 11; see also pp. 24, 34.

[119] Cf., McCandless, who declared that the one object was annexation, and that otherwise not enough men could have been secured to organize a Government or form an army (Morgan, p. 632; *Advertiser,* Jan. 19, 1893).

[120] EAC, p. 11; instructions to Commissioners are on pp. 13 *ff.;* original of instructions is in Dole Papers, Archives.

on this important mission;[121] but, as Julius A. Palmer, Jr., pointed out later, they had no legal mandate from even the 637 American voters in Hawaii. They would speak merely as Revolutionists.[122]

The instructions to the Commission were to secure a treaty of annexation on the following terms: (1) territorial government, or a régime similar to that of the District of Columbia; (2) all appointments, except governor or executive commission, to be chosen from persons who had resided for five years in the islands;[123] (3) the Hawaiian debt to be assumed by the United States; (4) public and crown lands to be the property of the island government; (5) a cable to be laid within a year, or within a set time; (6) the entrance of Pearl Harbor to be opened and a coaling station established; (7) Hawaiian sugar planters to receive any bounty which might be paid to American sugar men; (8) importation of laborers into the islands not to be prohibited; (9) local laws, not inconsistent with American laws, to remain in force; (10) compensation to Liliuokalani and Kaiulani.[124]

True to their promise, the officials of the Provisional Government permitted the Queen to send her protest on the same steamer, although they refused to allow a Royalist commission to go with them. The letter[125] read in part:

> To His Excellency, Benjamin Harrison,
> President of the United States.
> MY Great and Good Friend.
> It is with deep regret that I address you on this oc-

[121] Their biographies were given in Stevens to Foster, No. 80, Jan. 19, 1893, Despatches. Copies of their commissions, signed by Dole, appear in Notes from Hawaii. See also Dole to Mott Smith, Jan. 18, 1893, Ministers and Commissioners, Archives (hereafter cited as M&C); and *Harper's Weekly*, Feb. 18, 1893, p. 163.

[122] Palmer, *Memories of Hawaii, op. cit.*, p. 134.

[123] Dole was particularly concerned over this item. On Feb. 10, 1893, he wrote to Thurston: "I need hardly caution you against any arrangement which would make it possible for the U. S. Government to saddle us with political bummers or decayed politicians in important government positions" (M&C).

[124] EAC, pp. 14-15. There is a typewritten copy of instructions in the Dole Papers, Archives, dated Jan. 18, 1893, with the last two stipulations added in Thurston's handwriting.

[125] The letter was filed in Notes from Hawaii, under date of Feb. 3, 1893. The reader will observe an inconsistency in the appeal despite its legalistic terms. If Stevens had been authorized to interfere, what hope was there that the Government would disavow him?

casion. Some of my subjects aided by Aliens have renounced their Loyalty and revolted against the Constitutional Government of my Kingdom. They have attempted to depose me and to establish a Provisional Government, in direct conflict with the organic Law of this Kingdom. Upon receiving incontestable proof that His Excellency the Minister Plenipotentiary of United States aided and abetted their unlawful movements and caused United States troops to be landed for that purpose, I submitted to force believing that he would not have acted in that manner unless by the Authority of the Government which he represents. This action on my part was prompted by three reasons: the futility of a conflict with the United States; the desire to avoid violence, bloodshed and the destruction of life and property; and the certainty which I feel that You and Your Government will right whatever wrong may have been inflicted upon us in the premises. . . .

I pray you, therefore, my good friend, that you will not allow any conclusions to be reached by you until my Envoy arrives.

I beg to assure you of the continuance of my highest consideration,

Liliuokalani, R.

She also sent an appeal to President-elect Cleveland.[126]

* * * * *

The peculiar position and the important, if behind-the-scenes, rôle played by Minister Stevens demand that some space be given to a discussion of the degree of culpability (or credit) he merits in connection with the Revolution of 1893. More must be said later when the investigations by President Cleveland and by the Morgan Committee are related.

Stevens was maligned and censured by Democrats and anti-Annexationists; praised and commended by Republicans and imperialists. To begin with, was he a culprit in the so-called "Crime of 1893,"[127] that is, in the illegal overturning of the Royal Gov-

[126] Liliuokalani, *op. cit.*, pp. 389-390; and EAC, pp. 16-17. Frank Godfrey, on the editorial staff of the Royalist *Bulletin,* was brought before the Councils on Jan. 19 and forced to retract a statement, made in his paper, to the effect that the promise to allow a Royalist commission to go along on the *Claudine* had not been kept. No such promise was ever made (EAC, pp. 20-21).

[127] The Revolution was thus designated by Amos K. Fiske in the *New York Times,* July 8, 1898.

ernment? Is McElroy justified in saying that Stevens "began consciously working by political means in the direction of the annexation of the country to which he was accredited, while the American Secretary of State failed to rebuke, if he did not actually encourage, this ambition"? Again is the same author correct when he says: "Eagerly Stevens awaited the psychological moment for a brilliant stroke which would land the islands in the lap of his own country—waited, worked, and planned"?[128]

There is little doubt, on the basis of letters from the American Minister to the Secretary of State (already quoted) that McElroy's first statement is correct: Stevens did work for annexation. The intimation in the second assertion, that Stevens plotted, is more difficult to isolate. In brief, did he have secret understandings with the Revolutionists like Thurston and Smith and did he promise aid?

When prominent Revolutionists interviewed Stevens just before the outbreak, in several secret meetings, his answers seem to have satisfied them. Likewise, Royalists and members of the Queen's Cabinet declared that he announced his intention to support a revolutionary government, properly proclaimed. From Young's statements it is clear that the insurgents fully expected the marines to defend them during the proclamation proceedings. These facts are certain. It is harder to discover the source of the insurgents' supposition; for no documents, signed by or addressed to Stevens, are extant to prove his guilt. If there was a secret agreement, it was verbal. Stevens himself denied categorically, time and again, any complicity, although he admitted, and there is written evidence to prove, that he had expected such a movement for some time. It will perhaps always be a moot question whether he was in a plot, strong as the circumstantial evidence is that he was. Com-

[128] Robert McElroy, *Grover Cleveland The Man and the Statesman An Authorized Biography,* two volumes (N. Y. and London, 1923), II, 48-49. McElroy stated further: "It is . . . interesting to discover that he [Stevens] returned just as the revolution needed the support of American marines" (II, 50). On the other hand, the Hawaiian historian, R. S. Kuykendall, does not believe there was a plot or a conspiracy. Said he: "I have never been able to believe that there was anything that could be properly called a conspiracy, though Stevens probably knew about everything that was going on" (Kuykendall to Thomas M. Spaulding, Sept. 8, 1932, in volume 5 of the Spaulding Collection, Library of the University of Michigan, Ann Arbor).

missioner Blount, President Cleveland, Secretary Gresham, and many others, firmly believed that a plot was hatched between Stevens and the Revolutionists. F. Wundenberg, one of the leading Revolutionists who took command of the station house for the Provisional Government, deposed as follows to Blount:

> During all the deliberations of the committee [of safety], and, in fact, throughout the whole proceedings connected with plans for the move up to the final issue, the basis of action was the general understanding that Minister Stevens would keep his promise to support the movement with the men from the *Boston,* and the statement is now advisedly made (with a full knowledge of the the lack of arms, ammunition, and men; also the utter absence of organization at all adequate to the undertaking) that without the previous assurance of support from the American minister, and the actual presence of the United States troops, no movement would have been attempted, and, if attempted, would have been a dismal failure, resulting in the capture or death of the participants in a very short time.
>
> Having been present at the several meetings referred to in this statement, I hereby certify that the same is correct in every essential particular.[129]

Based on such assertions, Blount's conclusions in his formal report are emphatic:

> Mr. Stevens consulted freely with the leaders of the revolutionary movement from the evening of the 14th. These disclosed to him all their plans. They feared arrest and punishment. He promised them protection. They needed the troops in short to overawe the Queen's supporters and Government. This he agreed to and did furnish. They had few arms and no trained soldiers. They did not mean to fight. It was arranged between them and the American minister that the proclamation dethroning the Queen and organizing a provisional government should be read from the Government building and he would follow it with a speedy recognition. All this was to be done with American troops provided with small-arms and artillery across a narrow street within a stone's throw. This was done.[130]

[129] Blount, p. 577.
[130] *Ibid.,* p. 128.

The historian, James Schouler, just after the Revolution, went through all the literature that was available, including Blount's report, and said that he failed to see how any conclusion different from Blount's could be reached.[131] And yet the Morgan Committee, as will be learned presently, went over the same material and exonerated Stevens.

In the absence of guilt-laying documents, probably the best solution of the question is that Stevens wanted annexation, disliked the Royal Government, and would do anything he could, without completely entangling himself, to aid the class into which he had been received and with which he was in entire sympathy.[132] No fool, he knew that letters and papers could not well be explained away, whilst verbal statements could be denied. It is perfectly conceivable that, while talking to Thurston or Smith, he could give a mere nod, a glance of the eye, or special emphasis to a sentence, which would mean more to the Revolutionists than anything set down on paper.[133] And besides, they themselves would hardly wish written words to plague them later.[134] In any case, they knew their man; they had entertained him, talked annexation with him, condemned the Royal Government just as he had done. Knowing that he favored annexation, they perceived he could not officially espouse their cause, although he would stretch his diplomatic privileges to the extreme limit. They did feel certain of securing all the aid they really needed,[135] that is, American troops

[131] James Schouler, "A Review of the Hawaiian Controversy," in *Forum,* XVI (1893-94), 686.

[132] This is a mild indictment compared to that of Taylor, in *Under Hawaiian Skies,* p. 474: "History must justly record, at this late day [1922] that United States Minister Stevens, who was always disliked and mistrusted by the Hawaiians, played the role of a meddler in Hawaiian politics as his messages to Secretary Foster indicate. He desired that the monarchy should fall, and that the Islands should be annexed to the United States."

[133] Cf., E. B. Winans, former Governor of Michigan: "While ex-Minister Stevens may not directly have helped to unseat the Queen, I am of the opinion he winked at the proceedings" (quoted by Honolulu *Hawaiian Star,* Feb. 10, 1894).

[134] Cf., McCandless in Morgan, p. 610, who said the Committee of Safety kept no notes or minutes because "We were going in to a ticklish business."

[135] This is well brought out in W. R. Castle's statement, printed in Morgan, p. 586. Castle asked Stevens that the Revolutionists might "at least have the moral assistance of the United States by a recognition of the

to keep order. If the Committee of Safety, which was practically unarmed, had not felt sure of Stevens, it could hardly have dared to declare a new Government.

After all, Stevens was bound by long-existing instructions from Washington to use American forces to keep public order and to protect American lives and property. Senator William Lindsay of Kentucky was correct when he said in 1898 that "anybody can overturn a government if somebody else is going to be there to preserve public order whilst the government is being overturned."[136] The mere assertion that no fighting would be permitted made Stevens an ally of the Revolutionists, for it prevented the Royal forces from suppressing the uprising. As Julius A. Palmer, Jr., a correspondent of the *Boston Evening Transcript* put it later: "Although taking no active part, the presence of the troops did intimidate the Queen."[137] Dole later said that A. S. Hartwell did not think the Revolutionists had sufficient forces to win; but, continued Dole, "the rest of us thought we had [sufficient forces], particularly with the friendly sympathy of the American government, in Mr. Stevens, the American Minister."[138] Little wonder that the Revolutionists saw to it that the Provisional Government paid the expenses for Camp Boston, amounting to $251.86,[139] and served the American troops with hot coffee on the night of the Revolution.[140]

The same trick of using troops to keep order during an uprising would be used later in the Panama Revolution when American naval officers in Panamanian waters, by declaring that there was

Provisional Government which was proposed to be established." McCandless declared, however, that the Revolutionists never expected any aid and had no understanding with the American Minister. The new régime called for soldiers merely to prevent looting and incendiarism; moreover, affirmed McCandless, the Revolution could have succeeded whether American forces had been present or not (Morgan, pp. 634 and 636). Thurston (*Memoirs, op. cit.*, pp. 276, 309, and 310) took pains in three separate places to deny there was any understanding with Stevens.

[136] *Congressional Record* (55 Cong. 2 Sess.), p. 6672, July 5, 1898.

[137] Julius A. Palmer, Jr., *Memories of Hawaii . . . op. cit.*, p. 133.

[138] Taylor, *Under Hawaiian Skies*, p. 459.

[139] EAC, Feb. 4, 1893, p. 94.

[140] McCandless, in Morgan, p. 630.

to be no public disorder, prevented Colombian soldiers from putting down the insurrection.[141]

Joseph Chamberlain's knowledge or ignorance of the Jameson Raid was in principle the counterpart of Stevens's attitude in 1893. Chamberlain explained his position to Lady Lugard as follows:

> You put me on my honor. Very well. The fact is I can hardly say what I knew and what I did not. I did not want to know too much. Of course I knew of the precautions, the preparations, if you like, in view of the expected trouble in Johannesburg, but I never could have imagined that Jameson would take the bit between his teeth.

"Then you did not know about the Raid?" asked Lady Lugard. "I did not," answered Chamberlain.[142]

Stevens probably knew more about the Hawaiian Revolution than Chamberlain did about the Raid, but he, too, could not afford "to know too much"—in papers and documents.

That the Revolutionists appreciated the delicacy of Stevens's position and understood that he must not know too much is evident from Stevens's testimony to the Morgan Committee. On four separate occasions he stressed the statement that the insurgents would not wish to embarrass him. (1) President Dole "was a man of too much culture to embarrass me with the knowledge that he was to take part in the revolutionary movement."[143] (2) Henry Waterhouse "was a gentleman who would not embarrass me, and he knew how cautious I was."[144] (3) The "leaders of the Provisional Government were men of brains, and they did

[141] There is a close parallel between the Revolutions in Hawaii of 1893 and in Panama of 1903. See John H. Latané, *America as a World Power, 1897-1907* (N. Y. and London, 1907) in *The American Nation: A History,* XXV, 216-217. Latané said drily of the order emanating from the American naval commander that he would allow no fighting between Colombian troops and Panamanian rebels: "It can hardly be denied that this was creating a situation very favorable to revolution." Forgetting the Hawaiian incident, Latané averred that the "hasty recognition of a new government [Panama] was . . . without precedent in the annals of American diplomacy."

[142] J. L. Garvin, *The Life of Joseph Chamberlain* (London, 3 vols., 1932-34), III, 83.

[143] P. 571.

[144] P. 573.

not embarrass me by coming there [to his home] and letting me know their plans."[145] (4) Senator George Gray of Delaware: "Did you say to him [Thurston] when the Government was established and actually in possession of the archives and buildings that you would recognize it?" Stevens: "It was not necessary. He and those acting with him knew perfectly well that the *de facto* government would have to be recognized, and Judge Dole and Mr. Thurston understand international law and usage as well as any of us. Judge Dole was too intelligent to ask me what I would do in the contingency named."[146]

One fact, and one only, lessens Stevens's guilt. This is the testimony of Lieutenant Lucien Young, close confidant of Captain Wiltse. Young maintained, both in his book[147] and to the Morgan Committee, that the landing of the American force was the work entirely of Wiltse, rather than of Stevens. Learning of the untoward development of events on shore, Wiltse called Young into conference touching the wisdom of occupying the city. They carefully examined the instructions of the Department of the Navy, which Wiltse's predecessor, Admiral George Brown, had passed on to him. After some discussion, Wiltse and Young decided that these orders covered the present situation.[148] At 10:30 a.m., as a result, Wiltse gave Young orders to get his men ready to land.[149] When Stevens arrived on board at 3:00 p.m., with the request of the Committee of Safety that troops be disembarked, he was told by Wiltse that orders had already been issued for them to go ashore at 4:00.[150] Young says Stevens was delighted with this decision.

Stevens corroborated Young's testimony by admitting that upon going aboard he found the orders already written out and copied from Bayard's instructions to Merrill of July 12, 1887. Stevens added, however, that Wiltse's orders (which told Swinburne to protect American life and property and to preserve public order) went further than his (Stevens's) request for the landing of troops.

[145] P. 574.

[146] P. 575.

[147] *Op. cit.*, pp. 182 *ff*.

[148] Morgan, p. 334.

[149] *Ibid.*, p. 333; Swinburne, executive officer of the *Boston*, asserted that Wiltse's order to get ready was issued at 10 a.m. (*ibid.*, p. 467).

[150] *Ibid.*, p. 336. The hour was, for some reason, changed to 5:00.

Stevens asked only for protection of American life and property.[151] Young went further by maintaining that there was absolute necessity for landing the troops and that neither Stevens's request nor the Committee's appeal had anything to do with the matter.[152] Young's testimony does tend to lighten Stevens's responsibility, and yet the responsibility still remains with American officials collectively. There is no reason to doubt that Wiltse and Stevens had talked over the possibility of such a crisis long before, and had agreed upon what should be done; certainly they must have mutually determined what course should be pursued as they hurried back to Honolulu. Stevens said: ". . . we had discussed it running up to Hilo and back."[153]

Nevertheless Stevens usually claimed the credit for bringing the marines and bluejackets ashore, and justified his action by citing the appeal of the Citizens' Committee. Young's story, therefore, was wiser than was Stevens's claim. If it could be proved that the American forces had been sent into the city before the plea of the Committee arrived, or that the decision to land was made apart from the Committee's request, the charge of collusion between American officials and the Revolutionists could be minimized. In other words, the Citizens' Committee asked for protection; the Committee became the Provisional Government; if the troops were furnished in answer to the Committee's appeal, they were to that extent, helping to establish the new Government, and might be charged with being in league with the Queen's enemies. On the other hand, if it could be shown that the forces were disembarked merely to keep order and defend American property and lives, and not to protect the Committee (Provisional Government), less conspiracy could be alleged. It is instructive to note that the naval officers (Wiltse, Swinburne, and Young) always declared that the decision to occupy the city was arrived at apart from the request either of Stevens or of the Committee. Nevertheless when Wiltse said he would permit no fighting in the city, he was aiding the insurgents.

* * * * *

In the matter of recognizing the Revolutionists, there is sure

[151] *Ibid.*, pp. 632-633.
[152] *Ibid.*, p. 346.
[153] *Ibid.*, p. 535; also 576.

ground for definitely stating that Stevens was guilty. On the day following the successful *coup d'état,* he sent a despatch[154] to Secretary Foster in which he said:

> As soon as practicable a Provisional Government was constituted, composed of four highly respectable men, with Judge Dole at the head. . . .
>
> The committee of public safety forthwith took possession of the Government buildings, archives, and treasury, and installed the Provisional Government at the heads of the respective departments. This being an accomplished fact, I promptly recognized the Provisional Government as the *de facto* Government of the Hawaiian Islands. The English Minister, the Portuguese chargé d'affaires, the French and the Japanese commissioners promptly did the same; these, with myself, being the only members of the diplomatic corps residing here.

Consul General Severance, in his first letter after the Revolution, made a similar statement: "Following this Proclamation the citizens took peaceable possession of the different Departments of the Govt House—and are now in possession of all the archives, treasury Dept &c [.]"[155]

The first noticeable defect in both reports is that they failed to mention the facts that the Queen had not surrendered and that her army was still intact when Stevens recognized the insurgents. Depositions[156] of both Royalists and Revolutionists to Commissioner Blount indicated that Stevens committed an international crime in recognizing a small faction which had neither the support of the majority will, nor a vestige of armed control over the country. In fact the crux of Blount's investigation centered around the question whether the Provisional Government was in control of the station house, the strongest point of defense of the regular Government, before the Provisional Government received Stevens's countenance. His premature recognition was in direct contravention of international law, for it meant intervention and fomentation of rebellion by a Minister against the Government to which he was accredited. Royalists later pointed out that the very fact

[154] Stevens to Foster, No. 79, Jan. 18, 1893, Despatches.

[155] Severance to Wharton, No. 174, Jan. 18, 1893, Consular Letters.

[156] For instance, J. O. Carter, pp. 56-57; Colburn, pp. 30 *ff.;* Peterson, p. 58; Damon, pp. 39 *ff.;* Wundenberg, pp. 26-27; and Marshal Wilson, p. 59.

Stevens recognized the insurgents so precipitately proved he was in league with them.[157] This is of course a matter of opinion, but Theodore S. Woolsey, in 1894, also looked askance at the haste in which the thing was done:

> Before the people of Oahu had a chance to pronounce upon their desire for the change, before the other Islands could even hear of it, before the new régime could demonstrate its capacity for fulfilling the obligations of the State, before it had gained possession of all the Government buildings and proved its power, its recognition was granted by the United States.[158]

Statements of both sides would indicate that, had recognition not been accorded so soon, the Royalist forces could have put up a good fight. Thus Wundenberg asserted that the insurgents acted upon the basis of Stevens's promise of support; that without the presence of the marines and bluejackets, it would have meant death to all concerned. Lieutenant Young, although stating that "If ever a situation warranted the landing of troops to protect American interests, this was such an occasion,"[159] admitted in two separate places in his book that the Royalists might have won out, had it not been for the presence of American troops and for Stevens's recognition. In one connection he averred that had the Royalists been able to use their forces, "it is extremely doubtful if the counter-revolutionists [he calls the insurgents counter-revolutionists because they were opposing the Queen's first revolution] could have taken the government building or palace that day, and it would have necessitated the proclaiming of the new government from some other place"; they had enough men, he continued, to capture the city, but only after a fight.[160] In another place he agreed that if Marshal Wilson had been able to carry

[157] But compare Alexander's statement (Morgan, p. 299) that the act of the Cabinet in abandoning the Government Building and in fleeing to the station house proved they had given up hope.

[158] In the *Yale Review,* II (Feb., 1893), 348, cited by James, *Olney, op. cit.,* p. 82, footnote 1. Woolsey (1852-1929) was professor of international law at the Yale Law School.

[159] Young, *op. cit.,* p. 182.

[160] *Ibid.,* p. 199. Thurston (*Memoirs, op. cit.,* p. 274) admitted that, if the Queen had listened to Wilson and used force, a desperate fight would have resulted.

out his plans, the Provisional Government would have suffered severe loss of life.[161]

Stevens's statements regarding his action corroborate those of critics who charged that his recognition was premature. In his book he later said that he would have landed troops, even if the Committee of Safety had not asked for them, "in conformity to the rules and instructions of the Legation."[162] But he must have known that he was wrong when he said, in the same book, that he recognized the new Government only when it was "in full possession of the Hawaiian capital and complete master of the political and military situation."[163] Yet, on at least two occasions before writing this volume, Stevens had admitted that he did not consider a little thing like the station house of any difference either way; therefore, because the Provisional Government was bound to win out, he recognized it in order to save bloodshed.[164]

It is difficult to see how Stevens ever could have made the claim that the insurgents were "complete master of the political and military situation," when he himself received the following communication[165] on January 17, 1893, from Dole, Chairman of the Executive Council. It speaks for itself:

> I acknowledge the receipt of your valued communication of this day, recognizing the Hawaiian Provisional Government, and express deep appreciation of the same.
>
> We have conferred with the ministers of the late government and have made demand upon the marshal to surrender the station house. We are not actually yet in possession of the station house, but as night is approaching and our forces may be insufficient to maintain order, we request the immediate support of the United States forces, and would request that the commander of the United States forces take command of our military forces so that they may act together for the protection of the city.

At the end of the above note, the Minister wrote for his files:

[161] *Ibid.*, pp. 204-205.

[162] Stevens and Oleson, *op. cit.*, p. 280.

[163] *Ibid.*, p. 296.

[164] Blount, pp. 60 and 126; Morgan, pp. 556-580.

[165] Blount, p. 99. This letter would seem to nullify Chambers's assertion, *op. cit.*, p. 29, that "The revolutionists . . . soon made it evident that they were amply able to maintain themselves, unaided by outside authority."

"The above request not complied with.—Stevens." His answer to Dole was: "Think Capt. Wiltse will endeavor to maintain order and protect life and property, but do not think he would take command of the men of the Provisional Government. Will have him come to the legation soon as possible and take his opinion and inform you as soon as possible."[166] Blount had considerable difficulty in procuring a copy of Stevens's reply. Receiving no answer to his first request, he applied to President Dole in person. Dole put him off, and Blount informed Secretary Gresham that "all people here . . . exaggerate and mislead in political questions." Dole finally sent a copy.[167]

Besides omitting to give to Secretary Foster all the facts regarding the situation of the Royal Government when the Revolutionists were recognized, Stevens is subject to another charge of omission. He intimated that the other diplomatic and consular representatives recognized the Provisional Government at the same time he did. The records show, however, that Stevens alone recognized the new régime on January 17. Most of the consular representatives sent notes on January 18; these include Glade, who acted both as German and Austro-Hungarian Consul; Schaefer, the Italian and Chilean Consul; Hackfeld, who was Belgian Consul and Russian acting Vice Consul; Renjes, the Spanish Vice Consul (who was also Mexican Consul); Schmidt, the Swedish Consul; Paty, the Dutch Consul; MacFarlane, the Danish acting Vice Consul; Cartwright, the Peruvian Consul; and Goo Kim Fui, the Chinese commercial agent. The Portuguese *chargé* and the French Commissioner sent notes on January 18,[168] also. But, strange to say, the Japanese Commissioner and the English Minister did not recognize the Provisional Government until January 19, the day after Stevens wrote his letter.[169] It is passing strange that he knew the Japanese Commissioner and the English Minister had recognized the Provisional Government two days

[166] Blount, p. 141.

[167] *Ibid.*, pp. 139-141.

[168] Actually the arrival of the letters of recognition from these two was not noted in the Provisional Government records until about 8:45 a.m. of Jan. 19 (EAC, p. 17).

[169] Enclosure D in Hawaiian Commissioners to Foster, Feb. 3, 1893, in Notes from Hawaii; printed in Morgan, pp. 743-750.

before their notes of recognition were dated, and the day after he wrote his despatch to Foster.[170]

* * * * *

The changes brought about in less than a week were momentous in the eyes of Hawaiians, and would mean five years of controversy and trouble for the United States. Without the loss of a life, the throne was overturned, a new Government was established, and its right to exist recognized and guaranteed by outside aid.[171] Most of this had been accomplished in a few hours. Whether the blame lay with the United States or not (Stevens was its agent), that country soon found itself in a nasty mess, largely through him, but partly also through the obtuseness of the Revolutionists in permitting the Queen to lay her surrender directly to the machinations of the American Minister and American forces. The

[170] The inconsistency is partly but not wholly explained by the difference between verbal recognition and written recognition. Roswell Randall Hoes, chaplain of the U.S.S. *Pensacola,* testified that Minister Wodehouse informed him that he had recognized the new Government informally, that is, verbally, by whispering in Sanford B. Dole's ear (Morgan, p. 751). Commander Swinburne was told by Wodehouse that he would recognize the Revolutionists as the *de facto* Government, pending advice from London. Wodehouse added, somewhat curtly: "I found it necessary to ask them, if they were the *de facto* Government, why it was necessary to bring foreign troops on the soil." To this Swinburne said nothing (*ibid.,* p. 472). McCandless asserted that the English Minister and Japanese Commissioner called at the Government Building, immediately after the proclamation, and expressed the hope that their nationals would be protected (*ibid.,* p. 626). All of these witnesses made the point that Stevens's note of recognition arrived *after* Wodehouse had recognized the new order verbally. It is questionable whether such informal recognition (as whispering in somebody's ear) amounted to much, but Stevens heard about it, and so informed Foster that the English Minister had recognized the Provisional Government at the same time he did. This was not quite true. The fact is, as shown in the Proceedings of the Executive and Advisory Councils for Jan. 18, p. 18, that at 10:30 a.m. Wodehouse called and verbally recognized the Provisional Government, adding that he would send a written recognition later in the day. He also commented upon the presence of American troops and asked how long they would stay. Instead of sending the note later in the day, he sent it next day, Jan. 19.

[171] At 11:15 a.m., Jan. 19, Captain Wiltse called to congratulate the new officials for instituting the change without bloodshed "and wished to know how many of his troops he should keep ashore to assist the Provisional Government in the protection of life and property." He was told that three companies were sufficient (EAC, pp. 19-20).

Queen was undoubtedly sincere in her belief that she had yielded to the overpowering naval strength of the United States; and she fully expected that the wonted justice and fair play of the American people would restore her to the throne. Her attitude is well put by Commissioner Blount as follows:

> The Queen finally surrendered . . . to the Provisional Government on the conviction that the American minister and the American troops were promoters and supporters of the revolution, and that she could only appeal to the Government of the United States to render justice to her.
>
> The leaders of the revolutionary movement would not have undertaken it but for Mr. Stevens's promise to protect them against any danger from the Government. But for this their mass meeting would not have been held. But for this no request to land the troops would have been made. Had the troops not been landed no measure for the organization of a new Government would have been taken.
>
> The American minister and the revolutionary leaders had determined on annexation to the United States, and had agreed on the part each was to act to the very end. . . . Her [Liliuokalani's] uniform conduct and the prevailing sentiment amongst the natives point to her belief as well as theirs that the spirit of justice on the part of the President would restore her crown.[172]

All Hawaiians, Royalist and otherwise, were wondering what the United States would say.

[172] Blount, pp. 128 and 130.

IV. THE FIRST REACTION OF THE UNITED STATES

It took the steamer *Claudine* ten days to reach San Francisco with its Hawaiian Commissioners and news about the startling events that had taken place in Honolulu on January 17, 1893. San Francisco papers printed the facts on January 28,[1] but the news did not reach the columns of Eastern journals until next day, a Sunday. Hawaiian matters at once found space in the press amidst accounts of Gladstone's Home Rule Bill, the formation of the Cleveland Cabinet, the Chicago Fair, the scarcity of money in the Treasury, the need of repealing the Sherman Silver Purchase Act, and the death of James G. Blaine.

Not all editors were so well informed about Hawaii as was he of the *Kennebec Journal,* who, on January 31, declaring that the United States needed the islands and that no other nation was going to get them, was able to assert that the news "comes as no surprise." The *New York Herald,* January 29, in its first article, copied at length the *Hawaiian Gazette* of January 18, in which the causes of the overturn were chiefly laid to English influence and the Queen's attempt to promulgate a Constitution which would have disfranchised foreigners. The *Herald* reported that Washington was thinking of sending another war vessel to Honolulu; it informed its readers "WHERE THE ISLANDS ARE"; and recalled that Henry Waterhouse (a prominent Revolutionist) had said in the United States in 1892 that "annexation is inevitable. . . . It is impossible for them [the islands] to continue as an independent nation."

The first editorial of the *New York Times,* January 29, was factual; the Queen had only herself to blame and the monarchy was bound to fall sometime. The *Tribune* of the same date thought that American views on isolation must "give way to the necessities of our increasing commerce." The *World* headline ran: "Hawaii

[1] Annexationist opinion was well represented by the *San Francisco Chronicle,* Jan. 29, 1893, which said the Commission spoke for a majority in the islands; and that the people were all ready for a revolution, hence the Queen's threat of proclaiming a new Constitution was merely the excuse that the Annexationists needed.

is free. Liliuokalani Upsets the Constitution and is Herself Overthrown." That of the *Sun* read: "Hawaii Asks to Come in. Revolution Successful, She Seeks Annexation." In its very first editorial the *Sun* proclaimed its jingoism (with particular disregard for the history of Texan annexation): "The State of Hawaii may thus be the first independent foreign country to be annexed to the American Union; and we dare say it will not be the last. And how long will it be before the nations east of the Atlantic and north of the Mediterranean become weary of the state of armed hostility and suspended warfare in which they live, and resolve to end it by joining together in the confederation of the United States of Europe?"

Next day, January 30,[2] the press began to follow the *Sun* in taking a more partisan attitude. The New York *Evening Post* forecast its position on the question of annexation when it said that the United States had enough to do at home, and that the revolution was achieved by the sugar planters. "It is a revolution on a strictly cash basis. . . . The sugar-planters want that bounty."[3] The *Tribune* hoped that the Senate and President could get the job of annexing done before Harrison left office. "There is no reason for deferring action on such a matter because of the approaching change of Administration." The *Times* denied the need for hurry because no foreign nation would beard the United States by interfering in Hawaii, and, furthermore, there was no in-

[2] On this day the papers were full of the details about Blaine's funeral.

[3] The close editorial connection between the *Post* and the *Nation* is indicated by the statement of the latter in its first comment: "The upheaval is in the American quarter altogether. It is a revolution on a strictly cash basis. When the McKinley tariff put raw sugar on the free list, it gave a bounty of two cents per pound to the producers of sugar in the United States. This was sufficient to revolutionize the Hawaiian Islands any day. The sugar-planters want that bounty. They have a delegation, or an embassy, or whatever it may be called, en route to Washington city now to place the sovereignty of the kingdom at our disposal and the sugar bounty at their disposal" (*Nation,* Feb. 2, 1893). The *New York Times,* Jan. 31, 1893, spoke in similar terms. It said that "Commercial profit or political expediency would either of them constitute a sufficient reason for annexing Hawaii," and yet it would be foolish not to study the matter first; "there is no question involved of delivering an oppressed people from bondage. The Hawaiian revolution was a business operation purely." The planters "want to make something out of us. Can we make anything out of them? . . . We should annex Hawaii, if at all, as we should buy a ham."

formed opinion on the matter either in Congress or in the country at large.[4] The *Sun* asked: "Shall we annex Hawaii? If we don't the commissioners will apply to England." The *World* brought in a different slant by heading a news article with the words: "The Warship Boston cut a Big Figure in Hawaiian Revolution," and by declaring editorially that it was "a perplexing question." If Hawaii had been offered by its Queen, well and good; but it was being offered by a foreign minority who overthrew the Queen. Moreover, continued the editor, the Commissioners were admitting that democratic suffrage in Hawaii was impossible; if it were annexed, there would have to be "a provincial aristocracy—something very different from anything else in our system." The *Herald* had its headline read: "Minister Stevens Helped Overthrow Liliuokalani"; and it printed not only her surrender but Stevens's premature recognition.

By January 31 the Annexationist papers of New York had worked themselves into a dither about England's intentions. Thus the *Tribune* thought annexation was necessary because "We cannot turn [Hawaii] adrift" and allow some other nation to take it. The *Sun* felt that if the United States refused the islands, England would not. "In Hawaii the story of Gibraltar would be repeated at our expense." It then described the American Pacific fleet, giving tonnage and guns. The *Post,* however, repeated that there was no reason to annex, because the United States already had all the advantages through its protectorate; and the editor reminded the American people with what unhappy results the Federal Government had tried to govern Louisiana and South Carolina during reconstruction.

The campaign against England on the part of the Republican and Annexationist press of the country is an interesting commentary, not only upon American journalism, but also upon the long-standing enmity of Americans toward the British. Without one iota of proof or justification, some spread-eagle papers soon were hinting at war with England. The supposed affront consisted in the fact that the English Minister, in spite of Stevens's statement,

[4] This point was admitted by even some of the Annexationist papers. Thus, on March 9, 1893, the *San Francisco Chronicle* used its entire first and second pages for information and drawings on Hawaii. Likewise, the *New York Herald* (anti-Annexationist) contained, on Feb. 12, 1893, half a page with drawings devoted to Hawaiian legends, tools, and customs.

had not recognized the Provisional Government when the first despatches left Honolulu. The *Herald,* which was anti-Annexationist, declared on January 31 that the English Minister to the United States, Julian Pauncefote, had been instructed to protest to Secretary Foster about Stevens's acts in Hawaii; and that the deposed Queen had appealed to England for aid. Next day, however, the *Herald* said that Pauncefote was not so instructed; but the *Tribune* of even date reported that he was expected to protest. The *Sun,* which led in this anti-English attack, declared on February 1 that if the United States refused to take Hawaii, it would turn to England, just as Texas had done; that in American hands, the islands would be strategically valuable, but in England's they would be a perpetual threat to the United States. It tried to prove the assertion by quoting the London *Times* which said that "the maritime power that holds Pearl Harbor and moors her fleet there, holds the key of the North Pacific." The *Herald,* January 30, reported the London *Daily News* as declaring that other nations, besides the United States, needed coaling stations; and the London *Daily Telegraph,* commenting upon "American intriguers," was quoted as saying: "We could not allow the United States to annex the islands, even if the established policy at Washington permitted the idea to be entertained."[5] The London *Chronicle* thought it would be piratical for the United States to annex.[6]

The New York *Sun* led the way in twisting the lion's tail. "The United States is able to take care of this business without interference from Great Britain," it proclaimed; and added that Americans would do better than "the honey-hearted philanthropists" of London had done in Jamaica.[7] The *San Francisco Chronicle* asserted that "if England wants us to annex Hawaii, all she has to do is to tell us that she will not permit it."[8] The same journal called attention to the fact that the countries of continental Europe were saying nothing against American acquisition of the islands; the "English, however, with that stupidity which is well called insular, and with a conceit begotten of conquest of naked and half-

[5] Clipped by *New York Herald,* Jan. 30, 1893.

[6] Quoted by *San Francisco Chronicle,* Feb. 2, 1893, which thought that England was a fine one to be pointing the finger of scorn at the United States.

[7] Feb. 1, 1893.

[8] Jan. 31, 1893.

starved savages" and "with a true John Bullish hum and haw," say that the United States may not annex.[9] The New York *World* pooh-poohed the English peril, and yet even it carried a cartoon[10] of a huge Negress labeled "Lilly" who was offering John Bull a bouquet of flowers marked Hawaii, while a little Negro was giving a round box called annexation to Uncle Sam. The caption read: "Queen Lilly—If you'se gwine take it at all, you best take it foh it's wilted." A few days later the same paper printed another cartoon[11] showing Hawaii as a child kneeling before Uncle Sam who was holding its hand, while John Bull, with all his possessions behind his burly bulk, reached for Hawaii, too. Uncle Sam was saying: "I guess I had better take care of this one." The New York *Sun* declared for either annexing or letting the islands go; the "protectorate idea is bosh." It recalled that the United States always had to fight for its rights against England. Two days later the same journal was asking, "Is There a Secret Treaty of Partition?" between England and Germany to divide up Hawaii; and it reminded Americans that their lease on Pearl Harbor would continue only so long as the treaty of reciprocity with Hawaii lasted.[12] J. Mott Smith, the Hawaiian Minister to Washington, thought England would use the navy to show its objection to annexation.[13]

The New York *Evening Post* laughed at the uproar created by the *Sun* and the *Tribune* against England; and the San Francisco *Morning Call* counseled taking rumors of England's interference "with caution."[14] When Britain failed to protest, the *Post* said that the *Tribune* was angry because the protest was not forthcoming.[15] The *Tribune* subsided, but the *Sun* belligerently continued to raise up a straw man. It quoted the *Ottawa Citizen* which maintained that some means must be used by England to prevent the absorption of Hawaii by the United States; the *Sun* answered: "Canada's interest lies in becoming part of the United States."[16] When

[9] Feb. 1, 1893.
[10] Feb. 2, 1893.
[11] Feb. 5, 1893.
[12] Feb. 2 and 4, 1893.
[13] New York *Post,* Jan. 31, 1893.
[14] Feb. 1, 1893.
[15] Feb. 2, 1893.
[16] Feb. 6, 1893.

news arrived from Honolulu that the English Minister had finally recognized the new régime, most of the anti-English hubbub ceased, although certain Anglophobes, like the *San Francisco Chronicle,* continued to howl. As late as February 17 it was saying: "Had England attempted to interfere in Hawaii any time during the past quarter of a century she would have gotten into such hot water that all the ice in Canada would have been insufficient to cool it."

This journalistic rabble-rousing[17] against England was, as the *Post* said, funny. The fact is that, in spite of some loose talk in the London and Canadian press, England never lifted a finger against American intentions in Hawaii. It would be nearer the truth to say that London favored American annexation. Thus, on diplomatic day, February 2, 1893, the Ministers from foreign countries called upon Secretary Foster who at once made notes of their conversations. The Japanese Minister said that, even though Japan was interested in Hawaii because of the large number of its nationals there, it did not oppose American annexation; Tokyo would, on the other hand, protest its acquisition by a European power. The French Minister "was fully persuaded that Great Britain would not passively permit the transfer of these Islands to the United States"; he expected the British to impose obstacles. The German Minister stated that Germany would make no objections whatever. The stenographic notes conclude: "The British Minister, in his call at the Department to-day, made no reference to the Hawaiian question."[18]

The Anglo-Russian rivalry was brought out on March 16, 1893, when Prince Cantacuzene called to talk with the Secretary of State about Hawaii and to inform him that Russia was really a friend of the United States. Russia, he said, was "pleased" that the United States had extended its authority over Hawaii, and he hoped the trend would be completed by annexation. Not so with England, he added. She might seem to be peacefully inclined, but "she was watching and hoping for an opportunity to gain

[17] Representing the same kind of anti-English public opinion which would support Cleveland and Olney, two years later, in their jingoistic attitude during the Venezuela controversy.

[18] Memorandum, Department of State, Feb. 2, 1893. "Confidential. Not to be published. By order of the Sec'y: *Feb. 11. '93*—A.A.A. [Alvey A. Adee]" in Miscellaneous Archives, *etc., op. cit.*

the Islands for herself; . . . she might, cat-like, purr at our feet, and rub against our legs, but we should remember that she had claws."[19]

Yet on the same day, Julian Pauncefote made an official call at the Department of State and "assured the Secretary of State that his Government was only interested in seeing stable authority maintained on the Islands; that it had no desire or intention to interfere in the domestic affairs of the Islands and that it knew of the close relations existing between the government of the Islands and this country." Secretary Walter Q. Gresham suggested that better relations between Great Britain and the United States would be possible if England changed Ministers to Hawaii, because Major Wodehouse had "entangling relations with the natives." Pauncefote answered that Wodehouse had very little ability, he was not of much consequence anyway, and would be relieved if the Secretary of State requested.[20]

If further proof were needed to show the utter absurdity of the newspaper campaign against the British, it might be added that the correspondent of the New York *Nation* interviewed a number of members of Parliament, and Mr. Bryce[21] as well, but none evinced any criticism of American annexation. In fact, as the *Nation* pointed out, England could not possibly occupy Hawaii without war, because of the position which the United States had gained by the treaty of 1876.[22]

By February 1 the New York press, which set the pace for the newspapers of the rest of the country because it was so frequently quoted, had framed the attitudes which would be taken regarding Hawaii, with little exception, for the next five years. The Republican journals, the *Tribune* and the *Sun,* would fight consistently for annexation and against England. The Democratic *Post, World,* and *Times,* and the independent *Herald* would be anti-imperialistic and would favor allowing Hawaii to go its own way. The *Literary Digest* summed up press reactions towards annexation as follows: "Some influential journals speak decidedly

[19] *Ibid.*

[20] *Ibid.*

[21] Bryce wrote an article in the *Forum,* XXIV (Dec., 1897), pp. 385-396, in which he stated that in 1893 he had never heard any objection in official London circles to American acquisition of Hawaii.

[22] *Nation,* LVI (Feb. 2, 1893), 75.

for annexation, but the majority are inclined to question the expediency of the step, or, at least, advise careful consideration."[23]

* * * * *

The *Claudine* brought important news not only for the press but for the Departments of State and Navy as well. Wiltse sent a report to the Secretary of the Navy giving the facts about the Revolution.[24] Consul General Severance wrote Wharton a fat despatch with documents and clippings from the Honolulu papers.[25] Stevens not only prepared a long letter with numerous enclosures, but also composed a telegram which was to be sent from San Francisco. This telegram,[26] received on January 28, ten days after it was written, gave to the Department of State its first official notice of what had been doing in Hawaii. It read:

> Events in Hawaii in the past few days have moved rapidly. An entire overthrow of the Hawaiian monarchy and the establishment of a Provisional Government in the interests of the whole people of the islands without the sacrifice of a single life. The new Government is in full possession of the Islands and was promptly recognized by all the diplomatic representatives. The four men of whom it is composed, are of high character, one of whom resigned his position as one of the Supreme Judges to assume the place. Full despatches by the mail leaving Honolulu today by special steamer.

In light of what Stevens had been writing to his superiors at Washington, the news thus received could hardly have been surprising, although it was undoubtedly considered significant. The writer of the Washington despatch to the *New York Tribune* of January 29, 1893, said: "The news of the revolution was not a surprise in Administration circles."

The despatches which Stevens mentioned in his telegram arrived

[23] VI (Feb. 4, 1893), 389-390. For other newspaper canvasses see *New York Herald,* Feb. 1 and *Times,* Feb. 2 and 5, 1893.

[24] Wiltse to the Secretary of the Navy, Jan. 18, 1893, in Ciphers Received No. 1 (Nov. 5, 1888, to Dec. 14, 1897), p. 254 in Records of the Department of the Navy in the National Archives.

[25] Severance to Wharton, No. 174, Jan. 18, 1893, Consular Letters.

[26] Filed in Despatches; printed in *Sen. Ex. Doc. 76* (52 Cong. 2 Sess.), p. 10; and in *House Ex. Doc. 48* (53 Cong. 2 Sess.), p. 119.

several days later; they are of especial interest because they gave his version of the Revolution in full. He laid precipitation to the lottery and opium bills when "unscrupulous adventurers around the Queen improved the opportunity to push through the Legislature an astonishing lottery franchise with the obvious intent to sell it out to the Louisiana lottery men." The reasons for disembarking the troops were the call of the Committee of Safety for aid and the "existing critical circumstances." The situation required the adequate protection of American life and property; and the "landing of the men of the *Boston* . . . promptly gave immediate relief to the public anxiety" over "what might be done by irresponsible persons in the night." Continuing:

> All is quiet here now. . . . Language can hardly express the enthusiasm and the profound feeling of relief at this peaceful and salutary change of government. The underlying cause of this profound feeling among the citizens is the hope that the United States Government will allow these Islands to pass to American control and become American soil.[27]

To Stevens's telegram of January 18 Secretary of State Foster replied on January 28 as follows:

> Your despatch, telegraphed from San Francisco, announcing revolution and establishment of a provisional government, was received to-day. Your course in recognizing an unopposed de facto government appears to have been discreet and in accordance with the facts. The rule of this Government has uniformly been to recognize and enter into relation with an actual government in full possession of effective power with the assent of the people. You will continue to recognize the new Government under such conditions. It is trusted, that the change, besides conducing to tranquillity and welfare of the Hawaiian Islands, will tend to draw closer the intimate ties of amity and common interests which so conspicuously and necessarily link them to the United States. You will keep in constant communication with the Commander of the United States naval force at Honolulu, with a view to acting, if need be, for the protection of the interests and property of American citizens and aiding in the

[27] Stevens to Foster, No. 79, Jan. 18, 1893, Despatches.

> preservation of good order under the changed conditions reported.[28]

When Foster gave this reply to the press, he made a public statement in which he defended the landing of the troops, with the argument that it had been done before.[29]

Along with Stevens's letter of January 18, went the Queen's protested surrender. The Provisional Government allowed her to send the message on the same vessel which had been chartered to carry the Commissioners, but it refused to permit her to send a delegation on the same steamer, pointing out that if she wished to have representatives at Washington she must secure her own vessel. After some delay she sent Paul Neumann, along with Prince David Kawananakoa and E. C. MacFarlane, on a special steamer to lay her case before the American Government. To Neumann she gave her power of attorney, commissioned him her envoy extraordinary, and ordered him to win for her whatever advantages he could. If her throne were not to be restored, he was to gain for her as high compensation as possible in return for her rights; he was also to try to prevent annexation. Stevens reported that when Neumann called upon him before sailing, "I . . . impressed on him the logic of the situation and the absolute impossibility of restoring the deposed Queen." The American Minister was certain that Neumann hoped to gain a large fee out of the indemnity which the Queen expected the United States to pay her, in case she was not restored. As if this were not enough, Stevens went to great lengths in describing Neumann's vile character.[30]

A few days later Stevens learned that Liliuokalani was sending two more delegates to aid her cause before Harrison and Cleveland. These were H. A. Widemann and C. O. Berger, whose pedigrees were given by the American Minister. Both were Germans who supported the native side because of marriage ties; and Berger was a son-in-law of Widemann. The latter was attached to the English Minister and had a bad reputation; Berger had

[28] Foster to Stevens, Hawaïi Instructions, III, 161 (National Archives); printed in *House Ex. Doc. 48* (53 Cong. 2 Sess.), p. 133. Cited hereafter as "Instructions."

[29] *New York Herald,* Feb. 5, 1893.

[30] Stevens to Foster, No. 81, Jan. 26, 1893, Despatches; printed in *House Ex. Doc. 48* (53 Cong. 2 Sess.), pp. 132-133.

voted "with the thieves" in the Legislature. The "Palace Group" was getting signatures of those natives who were against annexation "by paying so much a head"—the lottery men doing the paying. These signatures were being secured by "utterly false representations" and by "dirty work." When finished, the petition would probably be taken to Washington by two native leaders of evil repute, J. E. Bush and Joseph Nawahi,[31] who were members of the "palace gang." It was rumored that Antone Rosa, who had "a doubtful reputation," would go, too.[32] On March 7 Stevens had his say about E. C. MacFarlane who, at that time, was in Washington trying to win Cleveland's ear in favor of the Queen's cause. Stevens asserted MacFarlane belonged to an English commercial company in Honolulu, was tied up with the English-Royalist clique, and had been "a party to defrauding the Hawaiian Government of more than $100,000, in negotiating a loan with a London house."[33]

There were now two delegations, either on the way or at Washington: the Annexationist Commissioners, and the Queen's emissaries. A third was chasing across the continent to be heard. This consisted of one member, John M. Cleghorn of San Francisco, the uncle of Kaiulani. He elected himself to the duty of hurrying to Washington to press his niece's claims to the throne.[34] The *San Francisco Chronicle* thought it immensely amusing to watch Cleghorn's race with the Commissioners through the country; it was "the most novel and important long-distance race in American history"; and the stakeholder was the United States.[35]

* * * * *

Meanwhile, the Provisional Government had not been inactive.

[31] Incorrectly spelled Namahi in *House Ex. Doc. 48* (53 Cong. 2 Sess.), pp. 136-137.

[32] Stevens to Foster, No. 83, Feb. 1, 1893, Despatches. Such letters, though probably telling no untruths, would seem to indicate that Stevens was consciously trying to besmirch the Queen's case before it had even been given a hearing. The contents of No. 83 were considered significant enough for a copy to be sent to President-elect Cleveland (in Cleveland MSS., Folio marked Feb., 1893).

[33] Stevens to Gresham, No. 91, March 7, 1893, Despatches; printed in *House Ex. Doc. 48* (53 Cong. 2 Sess.), pp. 148-149.

[34] New York *Evening Post,* Feb. 2, 1893; hereafter called *Post.* John M. Cleghorn was a brother of Archibald Scott Cleghorn, former governor of Oahu.

[35] Feb. 4, 1893.

Numerous laws were passed, all of which buttressed the new régime in its rather uncertain hold on Hawaii. Act I stated that all powers formerly exercised by the sovereign were now in the hands of the head of the Provisional Government, and all powers of the Royal Cabinet were now in the hands of the Executive Council. Act II provided an oath which all officeholders would be required to take; they must swear to "support and bear true allegiance to the Provisional Government." Another law placed all legislative powers with the Executive and Advisory Councils. Still another made it treason to plot against the new Government, to organize armies, to withhold information, or to help restore the monarchy. Importation of firearms, except by the Government, was prohibited. The lottery law was repealed.[36]

Nevertheless the Provisional Government was afraid of its hold on the populace. The appeal for arms, declaration of martial law, suspension of the writ, and the laws mentioned above, did not assure it the military stability and complete control which were deemed necessary. Nowhere is the Government's weakness more evident than in its haste and anxiety for annexation. Face to face with troubles over freedom of the press and rumors of counter-revolution, all concerned agreed that the only solution was union with the United States. Hence Stevens on January 24 told Dole that the Annexation Commission ought to have been granted fuller powers.[37] Soon the Councils were discussing the modification of some of the instructions that had been given to the Commissioners; for all felt that annexation must not be held up on any account whatever. The chief bugbear was the sugar bounty question. After much debate, it was decided (eight to seven) to instruct the Commissioners to accept a lower bounty; this vote was then reconsidered. In the end it was determined to tell the Commissioners not to insist on a full sugar bounty, but "strenuously endeavor to obtain as favorable terms as possible in this matter." With this problem out of the way, it was not difficult to agree that the Commissioners should not insist on a cable if such insistence would kill the treaty. The third new instruction was to

[36] Enclosed in Severance to Wharton, No. 175, Jan. 30, 1893, Consular Letters; Dole, *Memoirs, op. cit.*, p. 91.

[37] EAC, Jan. 24, 1893, p. 52.

ask for a protectorate during the negotiations if necessary.[38] To carry these revised directions to Washington, the Government chose Charles M. Cooke, a member of the Advisory Council; if upon arriving at San Francisco he found that the Commissioners had not reached the United States (because of shipwreck,[39] for instance), he should hasten to Washington where he was to proceed with negotiations for annexation.[40] If he found that the Commission had arrived, he was to get in touch with the members at once and deliver the revised instructions. Cooke disembarked at San Francisco on February 9.[41]

Another indication of the weakness of the Provisional Government was the trouble which was caused by the press. The editor of the Royalist *Bulletin* was told that the Government desired the "closest and sharpest criticism," but that it would not tolerate "mere *innuendo and abuse.*"[42] Of course it was difficult for an opponent of the Government to keep safely between the two extremes; and the Government itself was the final authority on what was criticism and what was innuendo or abuse. A special phase of the problem was the native press, whose editors could, with more impunity, criticize than could the English-language papers. Within a week after establishment of the new régime, Dole instructed W. L. Wilcox to go over the native press and report periodically on its political disposition and temper.[43] The very next day, J. G. M. Sheldon, one of the editors of the native *Hawaii Progress Holomua,* was ordered to appear before the Councils because of an inflammatory editorial.[44] Three days later the Coun-

[38] *Ibid.,* Jan. 28 and 31, 1893, pp. 70-71 and 76 *ff.* A pencil draft of the revised instructions, written in Dole's hand, can be found in M&C.

[39] The first word the Government received of the Commissioners was a note saying that Claus Spreckels had treated them well in California; also a telegram they sent from Fort Wayne, reporting all were in good health (EAC, Feb. 10, 1893, p. 107).

[40] *Ibid.,* Feb. 1, 1893, pp. 84-85.

[41] Cooke to Castle and Thurston, Feb. 9, 1893, M&C. He arrived on the mainland the very day that Secretary Foster handed to Thurston the rough draft of the treaty of annexation as Foster thought the Senate might ratify it. Already the Commission had been forced to back down on more points than even Cooke's revised terms permitted.

[42] EAC, Jan. 19, 1893, pp. 20-21.

[43] *Ibid.,* Jan. 23, 1893, p. 45.

[44] *Ibid.,* Jan. 24, 1893, pp. 51 and 53. Hereafter the paper is called *Holomua.*

cils directed J. E. Bush, editor of the native-language *Ka Leo,* to present himself and retract a statement which he had made to the effect that a motion in the Councils to discharge all native employees of the Government had lost by only one vote. Bush was instructed to publish a retraction of this falsehood; he promised to do so, but, as his recantation was unsatisfactory, he was told to appear again.[45]

The *Bulletin,* which had earlier been in trouble for its editorials, got into difficulties once more when, on January 31, it adverted to the unfairness of a Provisional Government's presuming to force all citizens, most of whom had no say in its establishment, to pay taxes to keep it going. The editor was called before the Councils and denounced for "discussing the situation absolutely unwarranted by the facts."[46] These press troubles added to the general feeling of insecurity and instability.

The bitterness of the opposition press, particularly the native sheets, helped to cause the Provisional Government officials some concern about the attitude of the Kanakas. The military establishment was too weak, the authorities knew, to handle any large-scale uprising of Hawaiians, unless the Government had the aid of the United States forces. Rather strangely, as early as January 23 Dole asked the Councils whether a reduction of the American forces would not make a good impression. His suggestion was vetoed almost unanimously. Councillors Smith, Damon, Ashley, Cooper, and others agreed, as the minutes have it, that such a move might "necessitate a fight and bloodshed to recover our position." Councillor Brown said that the Provisional Government forces had been short-handed the previous night and that Royalist enemies had been in the Government Building, hearing and seeing everything. "Further desultory discussion and statements emphasized the need of maintaining every precaution and of perfecting the most efficient organization."[47]

The Government was worried about the activities of native leaders like Joseph Nawahi, William White, and others "of their kind"; it was decided to watch their movements "narrowly."[48]

[45] *Ibid.,* Jan. 27, 30, 31, 1893, pp. 66, 73, 76.
[46] *Ibid.,* Feb. 1, 1893, p. 81, and *Bulletin,* Jan. 31 and Feb. 1, 1893.
[47] EAC, Jan. 23, 1893, pp. 42-43.
[48] *Ibid.,* Jan. 24, 1893, p. 55.

In order to help maintain Provisional Government sentiment in the Island of Hawaii, the Councils ordered that two dozen rifles be sent to the Sheriff at Hilo. However the Commander in Chief protested that he could not spare that many rifles, because an inventory of the arms taken from the Royal Government showed a shortage of 200 stand of those recently purchased by Wilson, the late Marshal.[49] It was clear to the Councils that if these missing guns were in the hands of the natives the situation was dangerous. There was some demand for the establishment of a detective system, although the Government's chief hope for future military support rested in the National Guard law which was being debated.[50] To add to the feeling of insecurity, considerable criticism was arising among the country people who asserted that Honolulu did not take the needs of the rural areas into account; and a protest came from Molokai regarding the lawless conduct of Government officers.[51]

These evidences of weakness culminated on January 30 with a statement to the Councils by Attorney General W. O. Smith who reported rumors afloat concerning an attempt on the part of the Queen's adherents to capture the Government Building. He said that *"special precautions"* had been taken to repel such a movement, "including a communication to United States Minister Stevens to be used only in case of an actual outbreak which would ensure the prompt assistance of United States troops." Smith argued for "the *protection of the American flag."* The minutes of this important meeting go on to say: "Considerable desultory discussion followed upon the subject of such protection . . . terminating with a *motion* by Mr. Bolte that *Mr. Stevens should be asked to afford us* the *protection of the United States Government."* The motion did not pass, but next day, January 31, it was renewed and accepted unanimously, except that C. Brown was excused from voting. The following appeal for military protection was sent to Stevens by Dole and the Executive Council:

> Believing that we are unable to satisfactorily protect life and property, and to prevent civil disorder in Honolulu and throughout the Hawaiian Islands, we

[49] *Ibid.,* Jan. 24 and 26, 1893, pp. 54-55 and 64.

[50] *Ibid.,* Jan. 24, 1893, pp. 55-56. The law passed on Jan. 27.

[51] *Ibid.,* Jan. 31, 1893, p. 76 and *Advertiser,* Jan. 30, 1893.

> hereby, in obedience to the instructions of the Advisory Council, pray that you will raise the flag of the United States of America, for the protection of the Hawaiian Islands for the time being, and to that end we hereby confer upon the Government of the United States, through you, freedom of occupation of the public buildings of this government, and of the soil of this country, so far as may be necessary for the exercise of such protection, but not interfering with the administration of public affairs by this government.[52]

Upon receipt of this abject appeal, Stevens sent a note[53] to Captain Wiltse who agreed to land more marines and occupy the country in the name of the United States. That afternoon the Councils learned that Stevens would answer their request by taking over the islands at nine o'clock the following day.[54] Soper was called before the Councils and instructed on the procedure at the flag-raising.[55]

Next day, which was February 1, 1893,[56] Stevens had the following proclamation[57] read as the American colors were hoisted:

> BY AUTHORITY TO THE HAWAIIAN PEOPLE!
>
> At the request of the Provisional Government of the Hawaiian Islands, I hereby, in the name of the United States of America, assume protection of the Hawaiian Islands for the protection of life and property, and occupation of Public Buildings and Hawaiian soil, so far as may be necessary for the purpose specified, but not interfering with the administration of public affairs by the Provisional Government. This action is taken pending, and subject to negotiations at Washington.

[52] Enclosed in Stevens to Foster, No. 84, Feb. 1, 1893, Despatches; printed in *House Ex. Doc. 48* (53 Cong. 2 Sess.), p. 139.

[53] Enclosed in *ibid.*

[54] EAC, Jan. 30 and 31, 1893, pp. 73-74, 75, 78. It will be recalled that the Government was at that very time, Jan. 31, voting new instructions to the Annexation Commissioners; one of the new orders was to ask for a protectorate during the treaty negotiations.

[55] *Ibid.*, Feb. 1, 1893, p. 80.

[56] C. S. Olcott, in *The Life of William McKinley,* two volumes (Boston and N. Y., 1916), I, 376, makes the mistake of saying the flag was raised on Feb. 9.

[57] Enclosed in Stevens to Foster, No. 84, Feb. 1, 1893, Despatches; printed in *Sen. Ex. Doc. 76* (52 Cong. 2 Sess.), pp. 44-45.

Dole, who acted as Foreign Minister, at once sent to all diplomatic representatives, except Stevens, a note explaining that "this action on the part of the United States authorities in no way affects the status of the present Government and will not interfere with the purpose for which the Provisional Government was formed or the negotiations now in the hands of the Commission at Washington. The Hawaiian flag still flies from the staff in front of the Government House and will be displayed on all the Government offices on customary occasions."[58]

Stevens's assumption of a military protectorate put an entirely different light upon insular affairs. Just as his No. 79 (giving details of the Revolution) arrived at Washington, and three days after Foster received his telegram of January 18, a new state of affairs existed in Hawaii. The United States, merely because there was no cable, was slipping deeper and deeper into the mire of Hawaiian problems—so deep in fact that it would be 1898 before a solution emerged. Unwittingly, the American people were being entangled by their agent who made the islands *de facto* American soil before he even knew whether his original act of recognizing the Revolutionists had been confirmed by the Department of State.

Moreover, Stevens's assumption of an outright protectorate added one more count which his critics would have against him. He later justified his act in the following words: "Should the American representative run the risk of anarchy and bloodshed when it was certain he would be held rigidly responsible if catastrophe and calamity come?"[59] Young attributed the appeal of the Provisional Government to fear of what the Japanese and British men-of-war in the harbor, acting in collusion, might do.[60] But there is little reason to go any further, for explanation, than the situation of the new Government: Stevens was its friend, and if it fell or if it got into trouble, that would reflect upon him as well as upon the Revolutionists.

[58] Feb. 1, 1893, Foreign Office Files, Archives.

[59] Stevens and Oleson, *op. cit.* p. 298. Yet the Annexationist Alexander admitted that raising the flag was a mistake because a protectorate was not needed (Morgan, p. 306).

[60] Young, *op. cit.*, p. 214.

In any event, in the telegram[61] dated February 1, which Foster received on February 9, there was a peculiar inconsistency. The Provisional Government, declared Stevens, was gaining power and respect, and yet he felt it wise to assume a protectorate. The message read in full:

> Provisional Government of Hawaii gaining power and respect. Everything is quiet. Annexation sentiment is increasing. Dead monarchy and opposition to annexation is [*sic*] supported chiefly by lottery and opium ring. To-day at 9 a.m., in accordance with the request of Provisional Government of Hawaii I have placed Government of Hawaii under United States protection during negotiations not interfering with the execution of public affairs. Have mailed important despatches. It is advisable that Commodore Skerrett proceed at once to Honolulu, Sandwich Islands, with one or more U. S. ships as precautionary measures.

Wiltse also sent a cipher telegram to the Secretary of the Navy, announcing the assumption of a protectorate, and added: "Situation continues the same. Shall keep Battalion ashore to protect the lives and property of American citizens in neighborhood until this Government desires their withdrawal, and the Minister approves. Government of Hawaii has organized forces, and daily gaining ground."[62] Severance sent similar information to Wharton, enclosing an extra edition of the *Advertiser,* February 1, which was printed in honor of the great event of that day.[63]

In spite of the weakness of the Provisional Government, as its appeal for protection shows, Dole was instructing the Hawaiian Minister, J. Mott Smith, to impress upon Secretary Foster, not only the peaceful transfer of power from the Royal to the Provisional Government, but also the fact that in "the event of any unanticipated disturbance the Government is amply prepared with

[61] In Despatches; printed in *Sen. Ex. Doc. 76* (52 Cong. 2 Sess.), p. 26. A copy, sent to President-elect Cleveland, can be found in Cleveland MSS., in Folio marked Feb., 1893. A copy was also given to the Navy Department (Ciphers Received, No. 1, *op. cit.,* p. 255).

[62] Wiltse to the Secretary of the Navy, Feb. 1, 1893, in Ciphers Received, *op. cit.*

[63] Severance to Wharton, No. 177, Feb. 1, 1893, Consular Letters.

their own volunteer forces and enlisted troops to quell it."[64] Five days after writing this to Smith, Dole was asking Stevens to occupy the country.

The despatches which Minister Stevens mentioned in his telegram of February 1 arrived at the State Department on February 14.[65] They are interesting because they were typical of the propaganda material which Stevens would continue to send until he left office—all of it favoring annexation and justifying his acts. He exhorted the United States to annex at once and offered the terms upon which he believed incorporation of the islands ought to be based. In the first place, there should be a territorial government, like that established over Louisiana under Jefferson, with Dole as first governor; democracy could come later. He recommended that the treaty of annexation include compensation for the fallen dynasty amounting to $150,000; that is, $70,000 for Liliuokalani, $70,000 for Kaiulani, and $5,000 for each of the two princes. Above all, there ought to be provision in the treaty for a sugar bounty.

The Minister then passed on to a justification for raising the flag. "When the monarchy died by its own hand, there was no military force in the Islands but the Royal Guard of about seventy-five natives . . ." and the new Government had to have a reliable force. Businessmen stood guard. A larger army was needed, however, because the Provisional Government feared the machinations of the Chinese, Japanese, and the opium-lottery ring. Most notable was the danger from the British:

> Another important reason for our action is the possibility of the arrival here of a British war vessel, and that the English Minister here, thus aided, might try to press unduly the Provisional Government. With the Islands under our protection, we think the English Minister will not attempt to insist that his government has the right to interfere while our flag is over the government building.

Yet he admitted that annexation sentiment was growing among

[64] Dole to Smith, Jan. 26, 1893, enclosed in Smith to Foster, Feb. 15, 1893, in Notes from Hawaii.

[65] Stevens to Foster, Nos. 82 and 84, Feb. 1, 1893, Despatches; printed in *Sen. Ex. Doc. 76* (52 Cong. 2 Sess.), pp. 46-49.

the English—as well as among the Portuguese and Germans. He made his final point in a much-quoted phrase about the ripeness of the Hawaiian pear:[66]

> The Hawaiian pear is now fully ripe, and this is the golden hour for the United States to pluck it. If annexation does not take place promptly or is held in doubt and suspense for six or ten months, there certainly will be a revulsion to despair, and these people by their necessities might be forced towards becoming a British Colony, for the English here of the monarchical type would then avail themselves of their opportunity and stir up all possible opposition to annexation.

The American naval, consular, and diplomatic agents in the islands continued with their barrage in favor of annexation and in justification of their acts—even before news of the assumption of the protectorate had reached Washington. Severance sent an editorial from the *Advertiser* which declared that annexation would produce "a boom in values . . . without precedent in its [Hawaii's] history," and that permanent prosperity would result.[67] Wiltse telegraphed: "Everything is quiet at Hawaiian Islands. Hoisting the American (U. S.) flags produce good effect. . . ."[68] Stevens wrote that he believed the natives were breaking with Liliuokalani:

> The fallen Queen has conducted herself so shamefully and shown so much favoritism to foreign adventurers that all the better portions of the natives had ceased to have legal reverence for her. Her bold, unblushing association with the Tahitian half-white palace favorite [Marshal Wilson] weakened the hold of the Queen on the natives nearly as much as the official confidence she gave to the American and Australian adventurers of the lottery and opium rings.

[66] The expression about the Hawaiian pear was bandied about in the Senate debates and became the subject for several cartoons. The metaphor appealed to many even before this despatch was printed. For instance, the Philadelphia *Press* (clipped by the *New York Times* Feb. 5, 1893) said: "The apple is ripe. Let it be picked."

[67] Enclosed in Severance to Wharton, No. 179, Feb. 8, 1893, Consular Letters.

[68] Cipher, Feb. 8, 1893, in Ciphers Received, No. 1, p. 257.

Raising the flag, he continued, was having a beneficial effect upon business which was picking up in anticipation of annexation. All the native chiefs would want to become American citizens; already they were "showing an unexpected regard for our flag."[69]

Bulwarked by American troops, the Provisional Government began to feel more confident; as the *Advertiser* put it, the American flag gave a feeling of security.[70] So safe did the Annexationists consider affairs—in contrast to the near panic before February 1—that on February 8 the Councils agreed to make their meetings public. It was hoped that this gesture would not only create good will generally, but that also it would decrease the number of false editorials and articles in the opposition press. The dismissal of the musicians in the Hawaiian band because of their refusal to take the oath—which would have caused concern previously—was looked upon with nonchalance now.[71] On February 5 the writ was restored and martial law suspended. An order was issued establishing rules and regulations for a Chinese Bureau in the Foreign Office to carry out the Act of January 11, 1893, which restricted Chinese immigration. On February 15 the opium law was repealed. Meantime Dole's title of Chairman of the Executive Committee was changed to President, and the office of Vice President was created. S. M. Damon got the latter post.[72]

* * * * *

More significant than any of Stevens's propaganda notes was Secretary Foster's instruction of February 11, 1893, one of the most important documents in all the diplomatic correspondence on annexation, for it gave the policy taken by the home Government when its Minister presumed to act independently. The Secretary criticized Stevens for the brevity of his telegram announcing the protectorate, saying that the Department had had to depend for the wording of the proclamation of February 1 on newspaper articles. The phraseology "would appear to be tantamount to the assumption of a protectorate over the islands in behalf of the

[69] Stevens to Foster, No. 85, Feb. 8, 1893, Despatches; printed in *House Ex. Doc.* 48 (53 Cong. 2 Sess.), pp. 139-140. A copy was sent to Cleveland.

[70] Feb. 2, 1893.

[71] *Ibid.*, Feb. 4, 1893.

[72] Most of the orders and laws were enclosed in Severance's No. 179, *op. cit.;* others can be found in EAC, Feb. 3, 8, and 15 on pp. 92-93, 102, and 118.

United States with all the rights and obligations which the term implies . . . to this extent it goes beyond the necessities of the situation and the instructions heretofore given you. . . ." In short, said the Secretary, the use of troops in case of uprisings was to be limited to protection of American life and property, and they were not to be employed for the assumption of protectorates. He doubted that the Provisional Government, in asking military aid, intended anything more than the cooperation of the American forces. "The accordance of such measures of protection or the unsolicited taking of the needful precautions to those ends is however, not to be confounded with the establishment of a protectorate." He continued:

> So far, therefore, as your action amounts to according —at the request of the *de facto* sovereign Government of the Hawaiian Islands, the cooperation of the moral and material forces of the United States for the protection of life and property from apprehended disorders, your action is commended. But so far as it may appear to overstep that limit, by setting the authority and power of the United States above that of the Government of the Hawaiian Islands, in the capacity of Protector, or to impair in any way the independent sovereignty of the Hawaiian government by substituting the flag and power of the United States, as the symbol and manifestation of paramount authority, it is disavowed.

These must have been stinging words to Stevens, but Foster tempered them by authorizing him to keep the troops ashore for protecting lives and property, "being careful however always to make due discrimination between these functions of voluntary or accorded protection and the assumption of a protectorate. . . . No step is to be taken by you or will be sanctioned by this Government which might tend to derogate in any way from the independence of the Government of the Hawaiian Islands which the United States have recognized as sovereign and with which they treat on terms of sovereign equality."[73]

Of this document the *St. Louis Republic,* Democratic, said: "Secretary of State Foster's pretended rebuke to Minister Stevens

[73] Foster to Stevens, No. 71, Feb. 11, 1893, Instructions, III, 162-167; printed in *Sen. Ex. Doc. 76* (52 Cong. 2 Sess.), pp. 45 *ff*. See also telegram of Feb. 14, 1893, in *House Ex. Doc. 48* (53 Cong. 2 Sess.), pp. 140-141.

for exceeding his authority in establishing a Protectorate over Hawaii is equivalent to the verdict of 'Guilty, but go on doing it.'"[74]

By this time the Hawaiian Commissioners had arrived at Washington. They reached the capital on February 3. Their intentions were explained by one of their number, Charles L. Carter, even before they arrived:

> We want to join the Union. Not as a State, however, but under a territorial district form of government. A government like that of the District of Columbia, with the addition of a governor appointed by the President. . . . There is such a large number of Chinese and other cheap laborers on the islands who cannot be trusted to vote intelligently that if universal suffrage was declared the whites, who represent almost the entire business interests of the country, would be outvoted and powerless.[75]

The Commissioners immediately sent their credentials[76] to Secretary Foster with the Annexationist version of the Revolution. Feeling that the Queen's letter would cause doubt and uncertainty in regard to the legitimacy of her surrender, they perceived it was their business to allay all fears that American troops might have aided in the establishment of the Provisional Government. When the troops landed, said the Commissioners, "They neither then, nor at any time since have taken part either for or against the Queen or the Provisional Government." Regarding Stevens's recognition of the insurgents, they wrote:

> Immediately after such proclamation such Provisional Government took possession of the City of Honolulu, including the Government Buildings, the Archives and the Treasury, and within a few hours thereafter received surrender of all the military and police forces, thereby coming into full possession of the Kingdom. Immediately after such possession had been obtained notification thereof was given to the Representatives of all foreign countries represented at Honolulu, accompanied by the request that such

[74] Clipped by New York *Post,* Feb. 23, 1893.

[75] New York *World,* Jan. 29, 1893. It is apropos to say in passing that this was an unwise statement if Carter wanted annexation. Americans would likely shy away from a territory where democracy could not obtain.

[76] Printed in *Sen. Ex. Doc. 76* (52 Cong. 2 Sess.), pp. 37-38.

> representatives extend to said Provisional Government their recognition. In reply to such request the representatives of the United States of America accorded such recognition upon the same day that it was requested.[77]

They sent copies of the recognitions by other diplomats, but all were dated a day or two after Stevens's. The Commissioners requested a treaty of annexation, based upon terms which have been discussed on a previous page; and, it is significant to note, included the Queen's capitulation in the documents presented to the State Department.

In spite of receiving a sympathetic hearing from the American Government[78] and from some of the press, the Commissioners did not find their path to annexation without obstacles. The Queen's protest had caused enough unfavorable comment from such journals as the New York *Nation* to make them feel that something more was needed to counteract the impressions made by anti-Annexationist papers. As a result, on February 11, they submitted a long defense to Secretary Foster who later gave it to the press. This statement again contradicted all claims of illegality in the establishment of the Provisional Government. The arguments were based principally on the assertion that the Queen committed an unconstitutional act in initiating violence when she attempted to proclaim a reactionary Constitution. They denied that the American forces had aided the Revolutionists, and as proof offered what they called "facts": (1) At the beginning of the trouble Stevens and the *Boston* were on a trip. (2) The Queen was the first to threaten violence; that is, on January 14, "by the public parading of the Entire military force, armed with repeating rifles and carrying a full supply of cartridges." (3) The first call to arms was made by the Cabinet, not by the Revolutionists, on January 14. (4) American troops did not arrive until five o'clock

[77] Commissioners to Foster, Feb. 3, 1893, in Notes from Hawaii; original draft, revised copy, and final copy in M&C, Archives; printed in *Sen. Ex. Doc. 76, op. cit.*

[78] Thurston's enthusiasm is evident in his telegram of Feb. 2, 1893 (before the Commission arrived at Washington), to Dole, in which he said Foster was so favorable to their mission that he had given up attending the sessions of the Bering Arbitration to be available when the Commissioners reached Washington (United States, Minister to Washington). See also same to same, Feb. 9, 1893, M&C.

on Monday evening of January 16, in spite of disorder on previous days. (5) A guard was placed at the American Legation and Consulate, while the rest of the marines were stationed at a public hall. "No demonstration was made by the troops in any manner whatever. The uniform of the United States was not seen upon the streets, except upon the persons of the individual officers passing between the points at which troops were located in the execution of their business." (6) "At the time the Provisional Government took possession of the Government Buildings, no American troops or officers were present or took part in Such proceedings in any manner whatever. No public recognition was accorded the Provisional Government by the American Minister, until they were in possession of the Government Buildings, the Archives and the Treasury, supported by Several hundred armed men, after the abdication of the Queen and the Surrender to the Provisional Government of her forces." In ending the letter the Commissioners said: "It is submitted that the foregoing Statement of facts amply meets the charge by the Queen that American troops coerced her action in abdicating."[79]

Thurston's master hand at drafting documents is evident in the above statements; but he was also as adept at propaganda. He started a campaign of propagandizing the American public the moment he and the other Commissioners landed, and carried it on almost continually as long as he remained in Washington. Upon reaching San Francisco on January 27, he at once got busy supplying information to the newspapers and giving interviews to reporters. Two days later he was able to announce that most of the Pacific Coast papers favored annexation.[80] He also answered many letters from Americans who wanted to know the facts about the Revolution. In all of these, as in his dealings with the newspapers, he defended the Revolutionists. As a good propagandist,

[79] Commissioners to Foster, Feb. 11, 1893, Notes from Hawaii; printed in *Sen. Ex. Doc. 76, op. cit.*, pp. 40-42. The discerning reader will already have comprehended the fact that some of these points were tissues of falsehood; for instance, the assertion that the Queen had abdicated. A similar Annexationist version of the Revolution was printed by the *Hawaiian Gazette* in the form of a pamphlet entitled, *Two Weeks of Hawaiian History January 14-28, 1893* (Honolulu, 1893). It was sent to the United States and used as propaganda.

[80] Thurston to Dole, Jan. 29, 1893, M&C, Archives.

he was forced to cut the corners and skim around the facts that did not favor the cause. This is evident in the above-mentioned defense sent to Secretary Foster. Among the many letters to private persons, the following is typical. After telling the inquirer about the islands and the Revolution, Thurston added: "The literal truth is that the entire movement in Honolulu was spontaneous and unpremeditated."[81] Thurston must have written that with his tongue in his cheek. Busy as he was meeting Foster almost daily to discuss the terms of the treaty, he still found time to write articles for the magazines and newspapers.[82] Time and again he assured President Dole of the good relations the Commission enjoyed with the press. So well had the groundwork been laid within two weeks that Charles M. Cooke, upon arriving with special instructions as regards the treaty, wrote home admiringly: "It is a matter of congratulation to our party that the press have so generously favored annexation."[83] Most of the credit was Thurston's.

The Government of the United States had been in action for some time. As early as January 30, two days after the arrival of Stevens's first telegram, Senator William E. Chandler of New Hampshire offered a resolution asking the President to negotiate a treaty with Hawaii looking toward annexation and admission to the Union.[84] Objected to by Stephen M. White of California, it lay over, but finally was referred to the Committee on Foreign Relations on February 2.[85] In the interim, Senator Joseph N. Dolph of Oregon offered the only extended remarks which were made public[86] during this session of the Senate upon the question of annexation, and what he said was imbedded in a speech on an appropriation bill. He favored the acquisition of the islands because they were important in Pacific commerce and because they were rich; he thought that the United States must secure its share of world trade; moreover, he declared that annexation would be the natural result of a long period of closer and closer relations between the two countries. To prove these assertions he quoted

[81] Thurston to Robert McMurdy, Feb. 3, 1893, *ibid.*

[82] For instance, Feb. 9, 1893, in *ibid.*

[83] Cooke to Dole, Feb. 10, 1893, Foreign Office Files, Archives.

[84] *Sen. Mis. Doc. 36* (52 Cong. 2 Sess.); *Congressional Record* (52 Cong. 2 Sess.), p. 929.

[85] *Record,* p. 1093.

[86] Plenty was said, however, in executive sessions.

from numerous Presidents and Secretaries of State.[87] On February 6, at the request of the Senate, President Harrison had Secretary Foster send the uncompleted treaty of 1854 with all correspondence between Commissioner David L. Gregg and Secretary of State William L. Marcy.[88] Already numerous petitions were arriving in favor of annexation. The Legislature of Colorado, reminding Congress that all nations except Great Britain had recognized the Provisional Government, asked for annexation. Other petitions came from the Legislature of Oregon and from the Board of Supervisors of San Francisco.[89] At least four resolutions, all favoring annexation, were offered in the House.[90]

Meanwhile the Commissioners and Foster were working on the treaty. Duly introduced to the Secretary of State by Minister J. Mott Smith[91] for their first conference on February 4, the Commissioners offered propositions (in accordance with their instructions) which might form the basis for negotiations. The parties did not meet again until February 7. During the interval the Department was drawing up a rough draft. At the next meeting Foster objected to incorporating a clause which would bind the United States to build a cable; he felt that would come in due course anyway. Nor did he like the stipulation that the United States must improve Pearl Harbor within a set period, for a better harbor might be found. He stated that exclusion of Chinese must go into the treaty, and told the Commissioners that provision for a bounty on sugar would be a serious obstacle to be overcome in the Senate. On February 9[92] Thurston was handed a rough draft. He was told that the bounty provision[93] could not go through

[87] *Record,* Jan. 31, 1893, pp. 998-999.

[88] *Ibid.*, pp. 1174 and 1246; printed in *Sen. Ex. Doc. 45* (52 Cong. 2 Sess.).

[89] The arrival of these petitions was noted in *Record,* pp. 1170, 1563, 1605.

[90] *Ibid.*, pp. 1027, 1406, 2032, 2086.

[91] Smith to Dole, Feb. 9, 1893, M&C, Archives.

[92] It will be remembered that Charles M. Cooke arrived in San Francisco with new instructions on this day. Even if he telegraphed to the Commissioners, it is doubtful whether his new instructions had any influence on the results, except to make the Commissioners feel that if their Government was willing to retract on several demands, it would retract on more.

[93] Thurston had probably come to the conclusion that the bounty was impossible to gain and so did not make a great deal of objection to its elimination from the treaty. On March 10, 1893, he told Dole about the "utter impossibility of our ever getting a cent of bounty out of the U. S. on our sugars" (M&C, Archives).

the Senate, and that all controversial issues must be eliminated, for the Congress then in session had only a few more days in which to meet. Furthermore, Foster said that the existing labor situation in the islands might remain unchanged until Congress acted. But he did not like the fact that the deposits in the Postal Savings Bank, amounting to $800,000, had been used for public works.[94] Thurston was perturbed about the news of the protectorate, which he feared might, but hoped would not, weaken the Commission's position.[95]

On February 10 the Commissioners made a number of objections to Foster's attempt to railroad the treaty through on his own terms; they declared his proposals were not in accordance with their instructions. At a second conference on the same day, they said they would accept the treaty with the following provisoes: (1) There must be a time limit in reference to final and complete commercial union with the United States. (2) They wished to keep the Hawaiian flag as a local emblem to cater to native pride. (3) The Provisional Government should be allowed to remove officials if that became necessary during the interim period until Congress legislated on a permanent form of government. (4) Some provision should be made for the registry of Hawaiian ships. (5) Chinese exclusion should not be perpetual. (6) They wished a clause which would allow cancellation of the treaty if Congress did not eliminate duties on imports from Hawaii into the United States within a set time. Foster tentatively accepted the last and suggested that the time limit be put at one year after ratification. He also agreed to the registry clause, and promised to think the others over.

The Commissioners then had a meeting of their own to decide upon their final attitude. Thurston stressed the fact that Foster was an advocate of annexation, but that the Secretary believed it would be difficult enough to get the Senate to ratify, without loading the treaty with details. Moreover, President Harrison was demanding a vote by the electors of Hawaii on the question of

[94] Foster asked Carter to secure for him the amount of the bonded and postal indebtedness of Hawaii (Feb. 4, 1893, M&C). Carter did not get the information until after Foster had left office. See Carter to Gresham, April 23, 1893, Notes from Hawaii.

[95] Thurston to Dole, Feb. 9, 1893, M&C.

annexation, and asking for some statement to the effect that the treaty was the will of the people. All members of the Commission agreed to accept Foster's demands, rather than go back to Honolulu with nothing.[96]

On February 11 the Secretary said it would be better to strike out all references to citizenship; that it was unwise to insert any statement about the Hawaiian flag, because it might be used locally if the Hawaiians wished. He modified the article on the right of the Provisional Government to remove officials. Chinese exclusion should obtain "Until Congress shall otherwise provide"; but it was not necessarily to be perpetual. In answer to Foster's request for information about the resources of the Queen and the heir apparent, Carter reported that in 1890 crown lands amounted to 876,000 acres; Government lands (other than crown lands) totaled 875,500 acres; and there were a few acres of school lands.[97] Some changes in reference to gratuities for the Royal family were made in the final version of the treaty.[98]

On February 11 the terms were agreed upon; after being engrossed, the treaty was signed February 14, eleven days after the arrival of the Commissioners. It had a preamble and seven articles. The articles follow: (1) Cession of absolute sovereignty to the

[96] Minutes of the meeting were preserved in M&C.

[97] Carter to Foster, Feb. 11, 1893, Notes from Hawaii; printed in *Sen. Ex. Doc. 76* (52 Cong. 2 Sess.), pp. 42-43.

[98] The conversations between Foster and the Commissioners were preserved in a volume entitled the Protocol of the treaty of 1893, which is filed in the National Archives. It includes short summaries of the conversations and stenographic notes. Appended is the following memo from Adee to Foster, dated Feb. 15: "Dear Gen'l Foster: I see no objection to a set of these Stenographic Notes being left on record—They show your care, caution, and foresight and will make good history hereafter. . . ." The State Department seemed to be desirous of leaving plenty of information about the genesis of the treaty. In Notes from Hawaii are four drafts of the pact, each described by Adee as follows: The first is the "attempt of Mr. Partridge and Mr. Adee to put the shorter substitutionary form of the Hawaiian Treaty into Shape—Probable date Feb. 6—'93 AAA[.]" No. 2 is a "Revised and amended text. . . . Probable date, between Feb. 6 and Feb. 8, 1893." No. 3 is a "Copy of a draft . . . handed by the Secretary to Mr. Thurston. Date not noted thereon. . . ." No. 4 is the "Latest revised and Amended draft of Hawaiian Treaty, which served as the basis for the final agreement of the Commissioners and the Sec'y of State. Probable date Feb. 8-9, 1893. A A A [.]"

United States, with Hawaii to become an integral part of American soil. (2) Cession of all public, Government, and crown lands, public buildings, forts, naval and military equipment; but American land laws were not to apply to Hawaiian public lands; Congress was to enact a special law on that subject, provided that all revenues from the sale of lands, excepting for use of the civil and military authorities, were to be expended for local and educational purposes. (3) Until Congress legislated otherwise, all Hawaiian laws not inconsistent with the treaty were to continue, subject to the paramount authority of the United States; the President, with the consent of the Senate, should appoint a Commissioner who was to reside in the islands and have the power of veto over acts of the local Government, but subject to the President's right to approve or disapprove his vetoes; within one year after ratification, Congress must legislate upon the subjects of imports, internal revenue, commerce, and immigration. (4) Immigration of Chinese laborers was to be prohibited until or unless Congress permitted it; and Chinese excluded by law from the United States might not enter the mainland from Hawaii. (5) The public and postal debts were to be assumed by the United States up to three and a quarter million dollars; but the local Government was to continue to pay the interest as long as the present tariff law remained unchanged. (6) The United States agreed to compensate the ex-Queen and ex-heir apparent: the former to receive $20,000 upon ratification of the treaty and $20,000 each year of her life during good behavior, and the latter to be given $150,000 as a lump sum. (7) Method of ratification by both parties.[99]

In his letter submitting the treaty to President Harrison, Secretary Foster gave the Provisional Government's version of the Revolution. Regarding the influence of American troops he said:

> Their presence was wholly precautionary. . . . They were distributed that night between the legation and the consulate. . . . They thus remained, isolated and inconspicuous. . . . At the time the Provisional Government took possession of the Government buildings, no troops or officers of the United States were present or took any part whatever in the proceedings. No public recognition

[99] *Sen. Ex. Doc. 76* (52 Cong. 2 Sess.), pp. 6-9; *Record,* Feb. 17, 1893, p. 1720.

> was accorded to the Provisional Government by the United States minister until after the Queen's abdication and when they were in effective possession of the Government buildings, the archives, the treasury, the barracks, the police station, and all the potential machinery of the Government.

There was not, he concluded, the least suspicion that Minister Stevens had aided in the revolt either by "intimidating the Queen" or by "giving assurance of support" to the new Government.[100]

When the President submitted the treaty to the Senate he could do little else than follow the facts as given by the Secretary of State:

> The overthrow of the monarchy was not in any way prompted by this Government, but had its origin in what seems to have been a reactionary and revolutionary policy on the part of Queen Liliuokalani, which put in serious peril not only the large and preponderating interests of the United States in the islands, but all foreign interests, and indeed the decent administration of civil affairs and the peace of the islands.

The President saw only two courses, annexation or protectorate, and he favored the former.[101]

The treaty immediately struck snags in the Senate, where there was a conspicuous lack of public debate on the project, although considerable discussion took place in secret session. Harrison and Foster found writing the pact was easy; conditions were different when they attempted to win ratification in spite of the fact that, according to a poll of the *New York Herald,* only three out of eighty-three Senators opposed annexation.[102] It was almost universally admitted that the necessary two-thirds of the Senate existed.[103] Although reported favorably out of the Committee on Foreign Relations by Senator John T. Morgan of

[100] *Sen. Ex. Doc. 76, op. cit.,* pp. 3-4.
[101] *Ibid.,* pp. 1-2.
[102] *New York Herald,* Feb. 6, 1893.
[103] For instance, the *New York Tribune,* Feb. 25, 1893: "There is a constitutional majority in the Senate as it stands to-day in favor of . . . ratification. . . ."

Alabama, a Democrat, the treaty was never passed. There were several reasons for the failure of the Senate to ratify.

Not the least important was the arrival of the Royal delegates, headed by Paul Neumann. The Queen's protested surrender had already created much sympathy for her, as well as a great deal of doubt as to the legality of Stevens's activities during the Revolution. Furthermore, there was a feeling that, inasmuch as the treaty was signed and sent to the Senate before Neumann had arrived, the Queen's side of the story was not being heard. Neumann sent Foster a telegram from San Francisco, received February 10, in which he called himself "Envoy Extraordinary etc for her Majesty the Queen" and in which he said: "I beg to express the hope that no action will be taken by the President in relation to the affairs of the Hawaiian Islands, until my arrival."[104]

On February 21 Neumann was finally granted an audience by Foster, but not in the character of a diplomat. He started out by stating that many, who were in favor of annexation, disliked the Provisional Government, and that the Queen demanded a popular referendum on the question whether the people wished her restoration or continuance of the present Government. Foster then remarked that Neumann was not objecting so much to annexation as to the method: Neumann admitted that this was true. Asked what he thought of the personnel of the Commission, he answered that the character of each member was "unexceptional"; later in the interview, however, he declared there were not more than eighty or a hundred respectable men behind the Provisional Government. Foster wished to know if restoration of the Queen was practicable; the reply was: "Yes, providing it could be done under an American Protectorate." Would his power of attorney permit him to recognize annexation, if some provision was made for the Queen's maintenance? Neumann answered affirmatively, and added that Liliuokalani and Kaiulani were the last of their line. He admitted that if annexation came, the Royal party would have to subside and accept the situation, although it preferred a Kingdom under American protection. But "we do not want annexation that would leave the present Government there." Foster pressed Neumann to the unwilling admission that his greatest objection was to the Provisional Government, and that he felt

[104] Notes from Hawaii.

bound to defend the Queen's case.[105] He asked to have a paper, which he had drawn up for her defense, given to the Senate. Foster agreed to take the statement, but said that it was the President's prerogative to decide whether documents would be sent to the Senate.[106]

This paper was an expansion of the facts as outlined in the Queen's protested surrender. Everything was blamed upon the American forces. The people had given in because they understood that the Revolutionists were upheld by the American authorities; and yet 3,411 qualified electors later signed a petition against the Provisional Government. Continuing:

> The events which caused this belief are the following: —1st.—The landing of the forces of the U.S.S. "Boston" against the remonstrance of the Constitutional Government. 2nd.—The assurance of the U. S. Minister Plenipotentiary that in case of a conflict he would espouse the cause of the usurpers. . . . The usurpation of authority would not have lasted an hour without such armed support and encouragement by the United States Minister. . . . [The protectorate which Stevens proclaimed on February 1] demonstrates that the so-called Provisional Government has no strength of its own, either to preserve the peace or enforce obedience to its edicts. It has neither the moral nor the physical support of the masses of the Hawaiian people, who protest, with their Queen against a continuance of its usurpation, and pray for a restoration of their Constitutional Government and sovereignty.[107]

This was a rather able defense of the Queen. Neumann's mission, however, was handicapped by the fact that he could partake of no diplomatic character and by the evil repute which Stevens's letters had given him. He was forced to resort to what amounted to private lobbying in order to defeat annexation. He saw Senator William P. Frye of Maine, who, in a two-hour interview, was not

[105] Cf., what Thurston said Neumann told him: "I am just as much of an annexationist as you are, but I am going to do the best I can for my client" (Thurston to Dole, March 10, 1893, M&C).

[106] "Stenographic Notes of an Interview between the Secretary of State and Mr. Paul Neumann, at the Department of State, on Tuesday, Feb. 21, 1893," Notes from Hawaii.

[107] Neumann to Foster, Feb. 21, 1893, Notes from Hawaii.

impressed by him because of the fact that his chief appeal consisted in arguing that the United States should pay the Queen for her rights; Frye later asserted that Neumann never mentioned or intimated that either American Minister Stevens or Captain Wiltse was guilty of any wrong. Senator Joseph R. Hawley of Connecticut, who also talked with Neumann, later stated that Neumann had represented his purpose to be that of getting pecuniary compensation for Liliuokalani.[108]

The Queen had other defenders[109] besides Neumann. A letter from John F. Colburn, former Minister of the Interior, to a relative in St. Louis gave the Royalist view of the Revolution. It was widely published and sent to President Harrison.[110] Her best proponents were anti-imperialists in the United States who felt that annexation was unwise and that acquisition of the islands, through the machinations of Minister Stevens, would be unthinkable. Thus Congressman Joseph H. Outhwaite of Ohio, Chairman of the House Committee on Military Affairs, called Stevens's interference an outrage, "an act of war,"[111] and a filibustering scheme of the sugar men.[112]

The suspicion that the sugar planters and/or the sugar trust was behind annexation was a prevalent obstacle to securing popular opinion in favor of the treaty. The New York *Post* called the overthrow of the Queen "a revolution of sugar and for sugar";[113] and the *New York Herald,* in accordance with its penchant for novelty, asked in six different places on its editorial page of February 7, 1893: *"Is Spreckels & Co. the little nigger in the*

[108] Speeches of Frye and Hawley on Dec. 13, 1893, in *Record,* pp. 193-194.

[109] Even in England. See "The Revolution in Hawaii" by His Excellency A. Hoffnung, Hawaiian *chargé* at London, in *The Imperial and Asiatic Quarterly Review and Oriental and Colonial Record,* XV and XVI (Jan. and April, 1893), 406-417. It was later printed as a pamphlet, a copy of which was sent to Cleveland through his secretary, Thurber, April 15, 1893 (Cleveland MSS., folio marked "Printed Material"). Hoffnung maintained that the Revolution was the work of the sugar interests.

[110] *New York Tribune,* Feb. 9, 1893.

[111] So also the New York *Post,* March 13, 1893: Annexation would be "an act of war."

[112] *New York Herald,* Jan. 30, 1893.

[113] Feb. 22, 1893.

fence of the sugar islands?"[114] The same paper said at another time that "there is more sugar than statesmanship and more jingoism than patriotism in the hasty movement."[115] One of Senator William E. Chandler's correspondents from Albany wrote him: "I wonder what you mean by trying to sieze [*sic*] Hawaii. . . . I feel annexation to U S is not for the benefit of the native Hawaiians nor Foreign interests and only for the interests of Skinner thieves & Sneaks."[116] The *St. Louis Republic* declared that the Revolution was "For the benefit of Claus Spreckels to help him make a dollar."[117]

More objection arose from Stevens's part in what the *St. Paul Pioneer-Press* called an "artificial revolution."[118] On its front page, the *San Francisco Chronicle* of February 9 carried the headline: "Upheld by Guns, Hawaii's New Government Sustained. The Natives Terrorized by the Boston." But the New York *Sun* cried: "Sustain Minister Stevens."[119] Of course the *New York Tribune* declared that "Minister Stevens has acted with tact and good judgment . . . precisely the right thing."[120]

Nowhere did Stevens receive more praise than in the *Kennebec Journal*. On February 1 it said that the question of annexation was of especial interest to the people of Augusta, because Stevens was a citizen of that city and titular editor of the *Journal*. "Mr. Stevens' views upon the Hawaiian situation will appear from an editorial published in our issue of November 17th, 1892. As very general interest will attach to it at this time we reproduce it today in full." On February 2 it asserted: "We have no question but what the course of Minister Stevens, will be found upon close examination, to which it will, undoubtedly be subjected by the government, to have been eminently wise and proper." When the

[114] Cf., the Albany *Times-Union*, quoted by the New York *Sun*, Feb. 7, 1893: The sugar interest "is the nigger in the fence, the cat in the meal tub, the milk in the cocoanut."

[115] Feb. 24, 1893.

[116] J. S. King to Chandler, Feb. 1, 1893, in W. E. Chandler MSS., LXXXVIII, 6676 (Library of Congress).

[117] Clipped by *New York Herald*, Feb. 15, 1893. As a matter of fact, Spreckels opposed the Revolution.

[118] Clipped by *ibid.*, Feb. 15, 1893.

[119] Quoted by *Literary Digest*, VI (Feb. 18, 1893), 444.

[120] Feb. 10, 1893.

Journal heard of the raising of the flag, it reported that the act had "met with universal satisfaction and commendation," although Stevens had been forced to proceed without instructions.[121] The *Portland Daily Press,* however, said that Stevens seemed to think he was king of Hawaii. The *Bangor Commercial* answered: "Let this Maine diplomat alone and he will have Hawaii annexed before the President, or Congress, succeed in making a move"; and the *Kennebec Journal* applauded valiantly.[122] Indeed Stevens would need all the defense he could secure.

The best way of defending him and the treaty was to counterattack by maligning the Queen. A despatch from Hawaii stated that Liliuokalani was a heathen because she made sacrifices to Pele, goddess of volcanoes.[123] A vicious onslaught came from Sereno E. Bishop, editor of *The Friend,* the oldest paper in the Pacific. Bishop tried to set E. L. Godkin of the New York *Nation* right on Hawaiian affairs. He praised the recent struggle of "the noble American colony" against misgovernment; and added that "the mass of the natives have been bedevilled by palace *kahunaism* and debauched by palace impurity during the past thirty years." King Kalakaua, he went on, had started a "heathen revival" by organizing a secret sorcery society and by making himself a god.[124] Bishop also wrote a letter to the *New York Tribune* defending the whites and the Revolutionists, but it was less didactic than usual because that paper was already Annexationist.[125]

In fact the Annexationists had a legion of powerful defenders. General S. C. Armstrong, who had been born in Hawaii and who was head of the Hampton (Virginia) Institute, also tried to convert the *Post.* Pleading for annexation, he declared that the deposed Queen was a member of "the only heathen dynasty in the history of the world which has survived the transition from barbarism to a decent grade of civilization"; furthermore, "the conquest by American missionaries of the Hawaiian Islands for a degree of Christian civilization" gave to the United States its best claim to the country.[126] In view of such assertions, the *New York*

[121] Feb. 11, 1893.
[122] Feb. 14, 1893.
[123] *New York Herald,* Feb. 16, 1893.
[124] New York *Post,* Feb. 8, 1893.
[125] *New York Tribune,* Feb. 16, 1893.
[126] New York *Post,* Feb. 3, 1893.

Tribune thought that "A mind not too large for a mustard seed shell would naturally oppose any provision for the support of the late Queen and her niece, the heir-apparent."[127] The San Francisco *Morning Call,* declaring that it was unnecessary to worry about Liliuokalani's future, added: "Uncle Sam will provide for her household expenses and dressmakers' bills handsomely, and if she chooses she may join a grievance club with other queens who have been deposed."[128]

Granted, however, for the purpose of argument, that there had been no injustice done either to the Queen or to the natives, opponents of the treaty still maintained that the United States should not annex because the islands were undesirable. "We cannot [said the New York *World*] think of making Hawaii an integral part of our Union with a share in its Government."[129] The *Post* did not want any more Nevadas, Wyomings, and Idahos, which were not fit for admission, and whose Senators had lowered the character of the Senate's personnel.[130] The *St. Louis Post-Dispatch* declared against adding "another rotten borough to the Union and strengthen[ing] the forces of plutocracy, which are already too strong."[131] The *St. Paul Dispatch* thought that any sane person, with "Kansas and Oklahoma still on his hands" would "hesitate about assuming any more responsibilities."[132] The *Chicago Herald* suggested that at best Hawaii might be made into a county of California, because, "Forming a pigmy State in the Union, it would be ridiculous."[133] The New York *Post* reminded Americans that there was no place in their system for colonies.[134]

The solution of the question, as proposed by many opponents of the treaty, was to assume an outright protectorate; for, even they admitted that Hawaii must not be set adrift to float into the hands of some foreign power. Col. George W. Merrill of Los Angeles, Cleveland's Minister to Hawaii from 1885 to 1889,

[127] *New York Tribune,* Feb. 13, 1893.
[128] Feb. 12, 1893.
[129] Feb. 5, 1893.
[130] Feb. 3, 1893.
[131] Clipped by *New York Herald,* Feb. 28, 1893.
[132] Clipped by *ibid.,* Feb. 15, 1893.
[133] Clipped by *New York Times,* Feb. 2, 1893.
[134] Feb. 6, 1893.

thought this would be the best way out.[135] The New York *World* was perhaps the most articulate journalistic advocate of a protectorate; it submitted, almost daily, that the alien population and the extreme distance militated against any closer union.[136] Annexationists, however, pointed out weaknesses in the idea of a protectorate. A certain Woodhull, a frequent correspondent of Senator Chandler, observed that if Harrison, as reported, was in favor of a protectorate, it proved that he was still under the influence of Blaine. "A protectorate will give us the Maximum of responsibility, with a Minimum of power & influence."[137] The *San Francisco Chronicle* also maintained a protectorate was unthinkable; such a solution would be bad for Hawaii, because it would be neither independent nor annexed.[138]

From the standpoint of strategy, the Administration was poorly placed to secure ratification. There was simply so little time that any attempt to hasten would give the impression that the job must be done before the full story of the Revolution got abroad. There was no opportunity to evade the charge that annexation savored of the "San Domingo job of twenty odd years ago."[139] The New York *World* thought the whole thing was "an administration plot," and that Harrison and his officials had been "in it from the beginning."[140] The *Post* counselled a second sober thought, not annexation by a rush or "hoop-la."[141] The *New York Times,* which admitted it had not seen its way clear to take a real stand on the question because of lack of information, said there was too much haste.[142] What, it asked, of the Queen's side? Foster's letter presenting the treaty to Harrison, in which it was stated that there was no collusion between Stevens and the Revolutionists, proved too much.[143] The *World* called it a "set-up job" and "Snap-shot diplomacy."[144] "The haste," it said later, "which

[135] New York *Post,* Feb. 11, 1893.
[136] Feb. 2, 1893; also Feb. 3.
[137] M. Woodhull to Chandler, in W. E. Chandler MSS., LXXXVIII, 6684.
[138] Feb. 6, 1893.
[139] *New York Herald,* Feb. 28, 1893.
[140] Feb. 16, 1893.
[141] Feb. 6, 1893.
[142] Feb. 10, 1893.
[143] Feb. 17, 1893.
[144] Feb. 17, 1893.

has attended the negotiation . . . is indefensible. . . .[145] Nobody need fear that the islands will float away or be sold out to any other nation."[146] E. L. Godkin suggested that Harrison was trying to push the treaty through in order to give "a sort of sunset glory to a dying Administration" which was leaving numerous perplexing problems.[147]

On the other hand, during the early weeks of February considerable support for the treaty made itself evident. For instance, the Senate of Pennsylvania instructed the state's Senators at Washington to vote for annexation.[148] John Conness demanded of Senator Chandler that he vote for annexation and that a territorial form of government be established.[149] Senator John T. Morgan of Alabama proposed a government consisting of a governor and an advisory council.[150] Commissioner Castle furnished the press with figures on the products, population, and resources of the islands.[151] The *Kansas City Times* wept about throwing away "The Wonderful resources which are laid at our feet"; and the Troy (N. Y.) *Northern Budget* moaned that "Only a chuckleheaded chump would refuse annexation."[152] The *New York Tribune,* calling attention to "Hawaii's value as a tropical, sugar and fruit producing country, as a naval outpost, as the fortress of the Pacific and the point from which the Isthmus and the South Seas must be guarded," maintained that objectors should in all consistency say that the United States had no right either to Florida or the land west of the Mississippi River.[153] The *Sun* argued that "Annexation is American Policy" because the United States had grown by successive annexations;[154] that union would make a cable possible;[155] and that "Honolulu is nearer Washing-

[145] Feb. 18, 1893.
[146] Feb. 22, 1893.
[147] New York *Post,* Feb. 16, 1893.
[148] *New York Herald,* Feb. 1, 1893.
[149] Conness to Chandler, Feb. 5, 1893, Chandler MSS., LXXXVIII, 6697.
[150] *New York Tribune,* Feb. 9, 1893.
[151] *Ibid.*
[152] Both quoted by *New York Herald,* Feb. 15, 1893.
[153] Feb. 11, 1893.
[154] Feb. 5, 1893.
[155] Feb. 9, 1893.

ton to-day than New Orleans was in 1810, or . . . San Francisco was in 1850."[156]

Nevertheless the treaty would not move. So far as the Senate was concerned it had been born dead.

The *New York Tribune,* as early as February 11, suspected that the Democratic Senators were trying to scuttle the pact. On the other hand, Secretary Foster, before negotiating with the Commissioners, consulted the Democratic leaders, Senators Morgan and A. P. Gorman, to find out what attitude the Democrats would take. Neither Senator looked for any trouble.[157] At the beginning, the *Tribune* declared it was gratifying to see the great unanimity with which both parties favored annexation. "There is need of judicious promptness," it said, but the "popular verdict is clear, unequivocal and practically unanimous. Hawaii is welcome."[158] At the same time, the *Sun* was so certain of annexation that it started writing of "The Greater United States";[159] and there was talk of acquiring Canada as well.[160] The *Boston Evening Transcript* thought the treaty would be ratified at once.[161]

By February 22, however, doubts began to emerge.[162] The *San Francisco Chronicle* blamed the delay upon the great number of appropriation bills.[163] The *New York Tribune* declared the dilatoriness of the Senate arose not from a desire to study the treaty; rather it was a "conspiracy," growing out of the "un-American spirit" of the Democratic party which wanted to defeat the project. "It does not represent the Democratic party."[164] The *Sun* said: "It seems incredible that any Senator, who has at heart the welfare and progress of the United States, can fail to record his vote in favor of confirming the Hawaiian Treaty."[165] "To reject it [agreed the *Tribune*] would not be merely a mistake.

[156] Feb. 13, 1893.

[157] John W. Foster, *Diplomatic Memoirs,* two volumes (Boston and N. Y., 1909), II, 168.

[158] Feb. 1 and 5, 1893.

[159] Feb. 4, 1893.

[160] *New York Herald,* Feb. 2, 1893; New York *Sun,* Feb. 12, 1893.

[161] Clipped by *Kennebec Journal,* Feb. 20, 1893.

[162] For instance, *San Francisco Chronicle,* Feb. 22, 1893.

[163] *Ibid.,* Feb. 23, 1893.

[164] Feb. 21, 1893.

[165] Feb. 18, 1893.

It would be a public crime, a wrong to the future of the American Nation, the consequences of which are not measurable."[166] On February 24, the *Tribune,* perceiving that the treaty was dead, blamed the death upon "that small and queer clique of Britainized Democrats." By February 25 it was announced by the *New York Herald* that there would be "No annexation this sess[ion]. President Harrison [is] annoyed." Two days later, the same journal printed the news that "President Harrison [is] Said to have Admitted that the Jingoists will be defeated." On the same day Charles R. Bishop, the Hawaiian capitalist, wrote to Thurston what was only too clear: "The outlook for Hawaii looks cloudy."[167]

That by February 25 the Commissioners had given up hope is evident from two facts. First, they began to lobby members of the incoming Administration, like Walter Q. Gresham, John G. Carlisle, and Thomas F. Bayard. Carter later reported that, when he questioned the presumptive Cleveland officials, he found an intangible something holding up ratification.[168] Second, the Commission was breaking up. Already Marsden and Wilder had left for home, and Castle was intending to leave soon. Castle believed that, in the long pull to win annexation after March 4, a new Minister should be appointed to replace Mott Smith, and he suggested Thurston.[169]

* * * * *

It is a fair question to ask how the treaty was defeated if a majority of the Senate, as was claimed, favored ratification. The answer is that the incoming President, Grover Cleveland, indicated to the Senate Democrats he wanted them to go slowly. This was probably the intangible something that Carter felt as he lobbied. Rumor had it, early in February, that Cleveland favored annexation, not only of Hawaii, but of Canada also.[170] Foster asserted later that the real trouble came from John G. Carlisle, Cleveland's Secretary of the Treasury designate, who hurried posthaste to Washington for the purpose of influencing Senate Democrats

[166] Feb. 17, 1893.

[167] M&C.

[168] Carter to Dole, confidential, March 22, 1893, *ibid.*

[169] Castle to Dole, Feb. 25, 1893, *ibid.*

[170] San Francisco *Morning Call,* Feb. 3, 1893. Thurston (*Memoirs, op. cit.,* pp. 560-561) reported to his Government on March 10 that high officials had assured him that both Cleveland and Gresham favored annexation.

against the treaty; and that annexation was finally blocked when Carlisle brought a message from Cleveland with orders to kill the pact.[171] Who persuaded Cleveland to give the message to Carlisle? Cleveland said, before inauguration: "I have not expressed an opinion on the question of annexation, and if I had an opinion I do not consider that it would be proper for me to express it at the present time."[172] Whether he had an opinion or not, he was reading the important messages that had been coming from Stevens ever since the Revolution. Perhaps Carl Schurz had some influence in turning Cleveland's mind away from annexation;[173] in any event, he was an intimate correspondent with the President on the Hawaiian topic after March 4.

The chief influence seems to have come from Judge Gresham, who had been chosen for the post of Secretary of State, and in whose Department the Hawaiian matter would lie. It is known that he conferred with Cleveland about Hawaii at Lakewood, New Jersey, on February 22. Gresham desired a special commission to ascertain the facts.[174] Cleveland, who undoubtedly had been impressed with the injustice done to the Queen, agreed.[175] Foster attributed the decision to "Gresham's hostility to Harrison," who, according to Foster, had won the Republican nomination from Gresham; therefore Gresham would do anything to embarrass his rival.[176]

Whatever the source of Cleveland's decision, the treaty was not ratified, and he alone must take the responsibility. The New York *Sun,* though angry at the partisanship of the Democrats, believed

[171] *Memoirs, op. cit.,* II, 168.

[172] Matilda Gresham, *Life of Walter Quintin Gresham, 1832-1895,* two volumes (Chicago, 1919), II, 741.

[173] For instance, Schurz wrote Cleveland on Feb. 27 advising against annexation because any advantages gained would be at the expense of time-honored American tradition (Schurz MSS., CVII, 23633, Library of Congress).

[174] Gresham, *Gresham, op. cit.,* II, 744. News that a commission was to be appointed appeared in the *New York Herald,* Feb. 27, 1893.

[175] President and Mrs. Cleveland had entertained Princess Liliuokalani and Queen Kapiolani in 1887 while they were en route to attend Victoria's grand jubilee (Liliuokalani, *op. cit.,* p. 121). Moreover, Neumann and his two companions had interviewed Cleveland's secretary before inauguration day (Alexander, *op. cit.,* p. 77).

[176] *Memoirs, op. cit.,* II, 168; cf., Thurston, *Memoirs, op. cit.,* pp. 559-560.

that Cleveland would soon push the treaty through to get the credit. "Grover Cleveland's luck . . . is the opportunity of annexing the Hawaiian islands."[177]

The new President was being bequeathed a plethora of troublesome problems, and Hawaii was not the least of them. The question was: What would he do about it?

* * * * *

Back in Honolulu the Provisional Government had been awaiting anxiously the outcome of its overture for annexation. The earliest word from the mainland in reference to public opinion came on February 10, 1893, in the form of American newspapers. On the same ship the first reporters arrived to hear about the Revolution. The Councils decided to pay especial attention to these reporters in order to give them the right impressions.[178]

About the same time, another type of propaganda was determined upon, namely, that an educational campaign should be started for the purpose of "fully instructing the [native] Hawaiians" on the desirability of supporting the Provisional Government. The printing committee was to attend to the matter, and expenses were to be borne by private subscription.[179] In addition, in order to decrease the importance of the Queen in the eyes of her native subjects, her guard was disbanded.[180]

The one problem that would not stay settled was that of the press. The continued "disrespectful, contemptuous and insulting comments"[181] of the native sheet *Holomua* made it clear that more than an educational campaign was needed to persuade the leading Kanakas to support the new régime. The *Advertiser* marvelled that the Government was willing to suffer so much venom from unfriendly editors.[182] On February 15 the Councils ordered the arrest of J. G. M. Sheldon and G. C. Kenyon, the *Holomua* edi-

[177] Feb. 28, 1893.

[178] EAC, Feb. 10, 1893, p. 107.

[179] *Ibid.,* Feb. 13, 1893, p. 115. In spite of this determination to appeal to the natives for their favor, the editor of the *Advertiser* continued to write about the heathen propensities and barbarous condition of the Kanakas (see, for instance, Feb. 16 and March 17, 1893).

[180] EAC, Feb. 20, 1893, p. 127.

[181] The words of Attorney General W. O. Smith in a resolution which the Councils adopted (*ibid.,* Feb. 15 and 16, 1893, pp. 116 and 122).

[182] Feb. 18, 1893.

tors, who were then held in custody. Both of them secured writs of *habeas corpus* (the writ had been restored on February 5) and the trial had to be postponed until the courts took action on the matter.[183]

This defeat of the Government seems to have emboldened the Royalist *Bulletin,* for it began to beard the Councils once more. In spite of the fact that the lottery law had been repealed shortly after the Provisional Government took hold, the *Bulletin,* in a spirit of bravado, printed the old act in a column headed by the Royal arms, and defended its impudence by saying that the Royal Government had given to the *Bulletin* the contract for public printing.[184] The deed was tantamount to a refusal to recognize the legality of the Provisional Government. The paper also severely criticized what it called the hauling up of editors (as in the case of the *Holomua*) before the Councils when those editors were merely exercising their right of freedom of the press.[185]

This was by no means the last trouble which the Government had with the newspapers; indeed altercations with the press were a never-ceasing reason why members of the Annexationist group hoped for union with the United States. Only then, they believed, would the dangerous problem end.

* * * * *

The delay in dealing with the treaty worried Secretary Foster, who finally was obliged to telegraph Stevens that the "treaty of annexation is still pending in the Senate. Confirming previous instructions, you are directed, in cooperation with the naval authorities, to support the Provisional Government in the maintenance of security to life and property and good order, until action shall be taken upon the treaty."[186]

[183] The case was decided against the editors and for the Government by Justice W. F. Frear of the lower court. It was then appealed to the Supreme Court which supported Frear, and remanded the prisoners to the Marshal to be tried by the Councils. The trial ended in a vote of guilty by a large majority. But sentence was suspended and the prisoners were allowed to go free, subject to call (*Advertiser,* Feb. 16, 18, 25, April 1, 4, 1893; EAC, April 3, 1893, pp. 177-178).

[184] *Bulletin,* Feb. 20, 1893.

[185] *Ibid.,* Feb. 22, 1893.

[186] Foster to Stevens, telegram, Feb. 22, 1893, in *House Ex. Doc. 48* (53 Cong. 2 Sess.), p. 142.

Foster need not have instructed Stevens to support the Provisional Government. Stevens was doing just that. On February 27, he wrote that there was good order and that most of the natives would "readily acquiesce" in, and the whites would applaud, annexation. He added the following: "My understanding of the spirit and terms of our temporary protectorate is in entire accord with the spirit and terms of the Secretary of State's despatch to me, of February 14th."[187]

In another communication dated the same day, Stevens went into a long discourse to prove that all his fears of British pressure were justified. On February 13 the British cruiser *Garnet,* of 2,120 tons and with 240 men and officers, arrived in Honolulu harbor. Soon the ship's sailors, allowed on shore by permission of the Provisional Government, "showed marked sympathy for the fallen Queen's cause and indulged in insulting remarks towards the United States marines and sailors of the 'Boston' on duty ashore by the request of the Provisional Government and with my approval." There was a near riot, which was stopped by the officers of the *Boston* who "prevented the English sailors getting a severe beating, with unhappy incidents." The Provisional Government then ordered that "only those of one nationality Should be on Shore the Same day."[188] Stevens attributed the whole trouble to Wodehouse and the British clique in the city. "Were it not that our flag is over the Government House, there is little doubt that this British unfriendliness[189] would have done much more mischief in stirring up the 'hoodlum' element, of which the lottery and opium gang of the fallen Queen's supporters have more or less control."[190]

All these facts played into Stevens's hands; for, in his mind, they proved the necessity of having American forces on land. Quite welcome to him, therefore, was a resolution passed on February 27 by the Executive and Advisory Councils. They resolved that "the thanks of this Government are due and are hereby

[187] Stevens to Foster, No. 86, Feb. 27, 1893, Despatches; printed in *House Ex. Doc. 48* (53 Cong. 2 Sess.), p. 143.

[188] Discussed in EAC, Feb. 17 and 21, 1893, pp. 124-125 and 130.

[189] The New York *Nation,* LVI (April 27, 1893), 304, characterized Stevens's barrage against England as a scarecrow and "a thing of rags and sticks."

[190] Stevens to Foster, No. 87, Despatches; a copy went to Cleveland. See also Severance to Wharton, No. 182, Feb. 27, 1893, Consular Letters.

tendered to Gilbert C. Wiltse, captain of the U. S. Navy, now commanding the United States steamship of war *Boston,* for his gallant, well-timed, and judicious conduct in protecting life and property in the city of Honolulu, upon the occasion of his landing his forces at the request of the United States envoy. . . ."[191]

This complimentary reference was passed because Wiltse had been transferred to another station. His successor, Rear Admiral J. S. Skerrett, reported that upon his arrival at the new post he was amazed to find the American flag over the Government Building in Honolulu. "From all information gleaned I am impressed with the idea that the Provisional Government are quite able to administer the affairs of the present government, upheld as they are by the presence of our men ashore,"[192] said Skerrett.

On March 1 Stevens became so exercised over the arrival of two Japanese warships and another British man-of-war that he telegraphed: "It is advisable to send here at once the most powerful American ship available."[193] This telegram, received at the Department by Foster's successor, Gresham, was undoubtedly a nice welcome to him in his new position. On the same day Stevens sent a despatch which reported that the qualified protectorate was working famously. "It not only tends to increase American and Annexation sentiment, but it also operates to prevent foreign complications." He was certain that Major Wodehouse wished a pretext to land British troops because he was trying to form "a tripartite management" of the islands by winning over the Japanese Commissioner to his side.

The former Japanese Commissioner had been friendly to Stevens, the new one less so. The latter had telegraphed to Tokyo for war vessels, securing two; the *Kongo* arrived on January 28 and the *Naniwa* on February 23. Neither the Japanese commanders nor the British one had called upon the head of the Provisional Government. The French Commissioner and the Portuguese *chargé* were devoted to the Provisional Government, however. Stevens added: "I still hope to separate the Japanese

[191] *House Ex. Doc. 48* (53 Cong. 2 Sess.), p. 497.

[192] Skerrett to Secretary of the Navy, Feb. 27, 1893 (received March 14), filed in Bureau of Navigation under No. 26821.

[193] Stevens to Foster, telegram, March 1, 1893, Despatches; copy to Cleveland. See also, p. 259, in Ciphers Received, No. 1, *op. cit.*

Commissioner from the English Minister"; but he was doubtful of success, for he heard that the Japanese representative was connected with the middlemen who supplied contract labor to the planters, and would lose profits in case of annexation.[194]

On the next vessel which carried mail, Stevens gave the history of his assumption of the protectorate so that, as he said, the new Secretary of State would know what justified his action. Rather cleverly, he based it upon the instructions which a previous Democratic Secretary, Thomas F. Bayard, had sent to Minister George W. Merrill on July 12, 1887.[195] Stevens went on to say that the English Minister "was bitterly dissatisfied that I had acted independently of him, landing the men of the 'Boston' when they were imperatively needed, while there was then no British vessel here," although one soon arrived. "It was then too late for the English Minister to make effective any demand to land troops, or to insist on dual action."

When the two Japanese warships arrived, Stevens's foresight precluded any joint measure by the Japanese and the British. He continued: "It was found that the prompt American action had given So much moral Support to the new Hawaiian Government that neither that Government nor the United States officials here would consent to any temporary dual or tripartite arrangement. . . . I have learned positively and beyond all doubt, that had not the monarchy here fallen and this Government had remained in its former condition of weakness, it was the intention of the newly arrived Japanese Commissioner to have demanded the Same political rights in Hawaii, including the voting franchise, for Japanese as under the Constitution of 1887, have been exercised by resident foreigners of Christian nations."[196]

By March 24 the Japanese menace, in Stevens's eyes, had become so real that there would be danger of the Japanization of Hawaii if American troops were recalled. He felt that the sudden Japanese interest was being pushed by "one of the political cliques in the Japanese Capital," else there would be no reason for two

[194] Stevens to Foster, No. 88, March 1, 1893, Despatches; copy to Cleveland.

[195] Discussed previously.

[196] Stevens to Gresham, No. 92, March 15, 1893, Despatches; copy to Cleveland; printed in *House Ex. Doc. 48* (53 Cong. 2 Sess.), pp. 149-150.

Japanese war vessels. He was rather certain that the Japanese Commissioner intended to land men and make Japanese control in the islands equal to that of the United States. But his action in declaring the protectorate, twenty-three days before the *Naniwa* arrived, "completely closed the door." Now the only hope of "the Japanese jingo to carry out his suffrage scheme" was to help restore the Queen who was willing to promise anything provided she secured the throne. Stevens told the Japanese Commissioner that the landing of Japanese troops would be the same as invading the United States. Furthermore, not only the Queen, but the Queen's officials as well, were attempting a liaison with the Japanese; Paul Neumann, now in Washington, was "in the paid employ of the Tokyo contract labor importing ring, who, for years, have been bleeding the Hawaiian planters and the Japanese laborers out of large sums of money." Moreover, this Japanese opposition to annexation was being aided by English interests. "Highly-placed Englishmen . . . prefer Japanese influence . . . rather than American." He warned the Secretary that the American flag must not be removed or the troops withdrawn until "this Japanese menace" was ended. The Provisional Government agreed with that sentiment.[197]

In all likelihood there was little real danger behind the talk about the Japanese menace. Much of the campaign sounds like propaganda on the part of Stevens to justify, to the new Administration, his assumption of a protectorate and the presence of United States forces on Hawaiian soil. James H. Blount, at least, thought there was none; for, as will appear shortly, he ordered the American flag hauled down as soon as he arrived. Attorney General Smith, on the other hand, predicted that if the United States refused to annex, Japan would interfere at once;[198] and the Honolulu Annexationist press was full of hearsay about a Japanese invasion. On March 21 the *Advertiser* said: "Rumors of war were as thick about town yesterday as creditors around the Government building on a pay-day." The reason was that a Japanese murderer had sought refuge aboard the *Naniwa,* which was supposed to have brought a cargo of small arms sufficient to equip

[197] Same to same, No. 93, March 24, 1893, *ibid.;* printed in *House Ex. Doc. 48, op. cit.,* pp. 150-152; copy to Cleveland.

[198] Smith to Thurston, March 29, 1893, M&C.

two or three thousand men. According to stories going the rounds, the *Naniwa* had intended to raise the Japanese flag, but found the Stars and Stripes flying. Another tale ran to the effect that a Japanese prince was to marry Kaiulani in order to carry the islands over to Nipponese control. The editor concluded that if the American claim to the archipelago were withdrawn, "it is exceedingly doubtful whether Japan would withhold her hand any longer from the 'Hawaiian pear.' "[199] This paper admitted that what it was saying arose largely out of hearsay; Stevens's information sounds strangely similar.

In the same mail the American Minister enclosed a copy of a conversation which the captain of the Japanese warship *Kongo* had had at Hilo, on the Island of Hawaii. If the conversation was genuine, it seems that the captain admitted he had been sent from Japan to find out whether the Japanese in Hawaii took sides with the natives or with the whites. When he found they did not cooperate with the natives, he was displeased. Probably what chagrined Stevens more than anything else was the Japanese officer's reference to the U.S.S. *Alliance* as "a wooden tub."[200]

In the light of what was supposed to be a looming yellow peril, in the form of military action by Japan, it is interesting to read that Admiral Skerrett withdrew part of the battalion from shore duty because it was not needed. He reported to the Secretary of the Navy that "there are a number of persons in this country who are greatly opposed to the Provisional Government, [;] whether or not the opposition will ever amount to anything, is probably better known to the Minister Plenipotentiary, &c, than to myself."[201] Perhaps the Admiral was being sarcastic.

What Japan really wanted, at least at this juncture, was the franchise for its own nationals in Hawaii. Saburo Fujii, "His Imperial Majesty's Diplomatic Agent and Consul-General," made this request of President Dole on March 23, arguing that the Japanese were as good as other nationalities; and that, under the most-favored-nation clause of the treaty between Japan and

[199] Enclosed in Stevens to Foster, No. 93, *op. cit.*

[200] Enclosed in *ibid.*

[201] Skerrett to Secretary of the Navy, March 29, 1893, No. 28018, Bureau of Navigation. Stevens told Dole that the reason for the desire to reduce the number of troops ashore was to improve discipline (EAC, March 18, 1893, p. 155).

Hawaii, the Provisional Government could not deny political rights to Japanese subjects.[202] On April 3 the *Advertiser,* under the title, "The Japan Scare," told of an interview with Fujii in reference to Japan's attitude on annexation. The interviewer learned little except that Japan would not oppose union with the United States, provided the rights of Japanese in Hawaii were looked after. Next day the same paper announced there would be no fight between the *Boston* and the *Naniwa.*[203] Yet on April 6 the San Francisco *Morning Call* was talking about the possibility of an Anglo-Japanese combination against the United States in the islands.

In Dole's answer to Fujii, April 10, he said that if annexation occurred the United States would be the successor of Hawaii, thus intimating that if anything was to be accomplished, Japan must negotiate with the United States directly.[204] Fujii at once repeated his demand, basing his argument on the treaty of 1871 which established friendship and trading privileges between the two countries.[205] In Tokyo, Hawaiian Minister R. W. Irwin interviewed the Japanese Foreign Minister who asked that, when a permanent government was set up in Hawaii, the Japanese be given the franchise.[206] Later the Liberal party in Japan was reported to be asking for political rights for Hawaiian Japanese.[207] On July 10 a large public meeting was held in Tokyo, presided over by the president of the House of Representatives, and all speakers urged voting privileges for their people in the Hawaiian Islands. Irwin wrote that the Japanese newspapers were full of the topic and that it would come before Parliament in its next session.[208] The *Literary Digest* found that the Imperial Government had been called upon by the Japanese press to protect the rights of the Emperor's subjects in Hawaii. *Jiyu Shimpo* (Radical)

[202] Fujii to Dole, March 23, 1893, enclosed in Hatch to Day, May 22, 1897, Notes from Hawaii.

[203] Clippings enclosed in Severance to Wharton, No. 190, April 5, 1893, Consular Letters. See also *Advertiser,* April 4 and 6, 1893.

[204] Dole to Fujii, April 10, 1893, enclosed in Blount to Gresham, No. 7, July 31, 1893, Despatches.

[205] Fujii to Dole, April 18, 1893, enclosed in *ibid.*

[206] Irwin to Dole, April 27, 1893, enclosed in *ibid.*

[207] Same to same, June 26, 1893, enclosed in *ibid.*

[208] Same to same, July 13, 1893, enclosed in *ibid.*

of Tokyo, the *Japan Gazette* (Independent) of Yokohama, and *Choyo Shimbun* (Conservative) of Tokyo, all demanded active steps in defense of the rights of the 20,000 Japanese in Hawaii.[209]

Dole's answer to all these disturbing reports was that the Japanese were deprived of the vote because they were contract laborers.[210] The Hawaiian Government was getting worried at Japan's attitude and turned to American Minister James H. Blount.[211] The Minister asked whether a letter from him, disapproving of Japan's demands, would help in the negotiations. Dole answered that "He thought it would."[212]

In accordance with his promise, Blount, who was just ready to leave for home, prepared a strongly worded statement of what he considered to be the American attitude. The question of the vote for Hawaiian-Japanese, he declared, "cannot be regarded with indifference by the Government of the United States," which had declared repeatedly that "it would not acquiesce in the interference in the domestic affairs of the Hawaiian Islands by any Foreign Power." Were American rights, he asked rhetorically, "to become endangered by the gift of political power to the inferior classes of Japanese subjects, who could so little value their manhood as to enter into a labor system [contract labor] repudiated by liberty loving people everywhere?" Additionally, Minister Irwin had asserted that, with Japan, the question at issue was not a practical one, but merely a sentimental one; moreover, Irwin himself was interested in contract labor. Blount ended up his pronouncement by advising Hawaii to postpone all activity regarding Japanese suffrage until the United States made its position clear.[213] Here the matter rested temporarily.

[209] *Literary Digest,* VII (Aug. 5, 1893), 392.

[210] Dole to Irwin, July 8, 1893, enclosed in Blount to Gresham, No. 7, *op. cit.*

[211] As will appear later, Blount was sent to investigate the facts about the Revolution and was made Minister to Hawaii when Stevens left in May.

[212] Enclosed in Blount to Gresham, No. 7, *op. cit.*

[213] Blount to Dole, July 28, 1893, enclosed in *ibid.* For praise of Blount's stand, see *Advertiser,* Aug. 22, 23, 24, 1893.

V. COMMISSIONER BLOUNT'S INVESTIGATION

Before Judge Gresham had time to get securely ensconced in the Department of State, and before the Cleveland policy toward the Revolution could be put into motion,[1] Washington was besieged by another commission which invaded it with something to say about Hawaii. It will be remembered that in the first days of February, Kaiulani's uncle had raced across the continent to protect her interests against the Provisional Government's Commissioners. He accomplished nothing. Soon the Princess's guardian, Theophilus H. Davies, under whose care she was studying in England, thought she should be present at the American capital to press her claims. Armed with introductions to some of the country's prominent men,[2] the seventeen-year-old heir to the throne and her guardian arrived at New York on March 1. From that city she issued a schoolgirlish manifesto to the American people. "Unbidden I stand upon your shores," she asserted, in order to seek to prevent the Provisional Government Commissioners from taking "my little vineyard." She, "a poor, weak girl," had come over "the wintry seas" to appeal to seventy millions of people who, she was sure, "will hear my cry, and will refuse to let their flag cover dishonor to mine."[3]

Kaiulani's presence in the country was frowned upon by Liliuo-

[1] An inside glimpse of how the Hawaiian program was being discussed among the policy-laying officials of the State Department can be gained from a *"Personal"* communication written by A. A. Adee to Gresham, dated March 10, which is part of Miscellaneous Archives, Memoranda of Conversations with the Secretary of State 1893-1898, *op. cit.* It reads, in part, as follows: ". . . white labor cannot be used in Hawaii, owing to the climate —Asiatic labor is indispensable to replace the rapidly diminishing native element—Unless Asiatic laborers be in time replaced by Africans from our own states. I do not see how a large proportion of the population of Hawaii can ever become eligible to citizenship or share in the elective franchise . . . the Islands will never maintain a voting population sufficient to confer a rightful claim to state-hood—[.]"

[2] For instance, note of Thomas H. Sherman, American Consul at Liverpool, introducing Davies to Senator W. E. Chandler. Dated Feb. 20, 1893, in Chandler MSS., LXXXVIII, 6755.

[3] Her appeal is printed in Alexander, *op. cit.,* pp. 77-78.

kalani's delegation, not only because Davies wished to place his ward on the throne at the expense of the Queen, but also because the Princess's sentimentalism might put the Royalist cause under a cloud. Some Annexationists looked upon her arrival as an English move. Woodhull, Senator Chandler's frequent correspondent in Washington, wrote him: "The presence in this country of the Young Princess, just arrived at New York, & her talk about her flag, her people, & her throne, is simply an English Move to maintain the Status Quo in the Islands."[4] The San Francisco *Morning Call* thought that "With an income of $20,000 a year [as provided in the treaty] Miss Cleghorn would be much happier than Queen Kaiulani could hope to be."[5]

On March 9 Davies asked Gresham for an interview, on behalf of his ward, "with the desire that her personality might be known to the statesmen in whose hands her fate so largely rests."[6] Gresham would see him at the Arlington Hotel, but not at the State Department.[7] Davies and Kaiulani visited Cleveland on March 13;[8] how much influence they had on the President's policy is uncertain, for the outlines of it had been settled before inauguration. Davies, calling himself "Personal Guardian of H. R. H. the Princess Kaiulani of Hawaii," did what he could by publishing several articles in her interest. In one such essay, he maintained that in the Revolution, Liliuokalani should have been removed in favor of a regency for Kaiulani because "Unquestionably the

[4] Woodhull to Chandler, March 2, 1893, Chandler MSS., LXXXVIII, 6790.

[5] March 22, 1893. The editor was mistaken about the compensation as provided by the treaty. She was to receive a lump sum of $150,000. In a similar vein, the New York *World's* editor, on Dec. 2, 1893, amused himself by asking whether Kaiulani was any better than Liliuokalani. Kaiulani, he thought, was not really Royal, but belonged to a "parvenu crowd that only lately came to the throne"; and anyway she was English. "Why should we select this girl instead of another? There are lots of nice girls at Vassar, Wellesley and Barnard, any one of whom would make a better queen for our purposes. . . . An American girl might be selected whose father would 'pony up' handsomely out of the millions he had made in pork, oil or wheat for the privilege of being father to a queen. There are plenty of girls whose papas would undertake to provide not only a royal revenue but an additional sum sufficient to maintain the Hawaiian army on a war footing of forty men and to provide a new navy of one hundred canoes."

[6] Davies to Gresham, March 9, 1893, Notes from Hawaii.

[7] Gresham to Davies, March 10, 1893, Notes to Hawaii.

[8] Alexander, *op. cit.*, p. 78.

Queen had attempted to violate the Constitution which she had sworn to uphold, and the attempt justified the people's resistance."[9] Such doctrine hardly sat well upon Neumann and his colleagues. Davies and his ward returned to England on March 21.

Meanwhile the country was learning what the new President intended to do about Hawaii. His silence up to the time he took office made some imperialists think he was ignorant. Thus Woodhull told Chandler: "Mr[.] Cleveland, notwithstanding his four years in the Presidency, is densely ignorant of Foreign affairs."[10] The President's viewpoint was perhaps best summed up in a letter he wrote to one of his closest advisers, Carl Schurz, who was firing powerful anti-Annexationist explosives through the editorial columns of *Harper's Weekly*. "I read your article in the 'Weekly' with great Satisfaction and was . . . pleased. . . ." He did not believe that annexation, *per se,* was bad, "but I am Sure we ought to Stop and Look and think. That's exactly what we are doing now."[11]

When it became clear that Cleveland would delay matters in order to get more information, the *New York Herald* praised his policy. It declared: "If we should annex Hawaii now it wouldn't be long before some cranks would want to annex the South Sea Islands or get a slice of the coast of Africa."[12] A few days later the paper said: "Our diplomatic annals do not show a more extraordinary or unwarranted course on the part of an American Minister in a foreign country than that pursued by our representative at Honolulu in this annexation business."[13] All anti-Annexationists were delighted when Cleveland withdrew the treaty from the Senate on March 9.

[9] Theophilus Harris Davies, "The Hawaiian Revolution," in *Nineteenth Century,* XXXIII (May, 1893), 833.

[10] Woodhull to Chandler, March 2, 1893, in Chandler MSS., LXXXVIII, 6790.

[11] Cleveland to Schurz, March 19, 1893, in Schurz MSS., CVII, 23712 (Library of Congress). The article in question was probably that which appeared in *Harper's Weekly* on March 18, 1893, p. 246. The following week Schurz lambasted the Provisional régime as a "government of intruders, by intruders, and for intruders," and declared the Revolution was "an outrage of the first order" (Feb. 25, 1893, p. 170).

[12] March 2, 1893.

[13] March 6, 1893.

Although Cleveland said nothing about Hawaii in his inaugural address, it was fairly well understood that some kind of investigation to glean the facts about the Queen's overthrow would be instituted. Even before it was publicly known that one commissioner, rather than several, would be sent, applications for places in such a delegation were coming in; for it would be a pleasant junket. J. P. Forbes, an Ohio State Senator, wrote from Columbus to say that the best way out was a commission. He would act as a member, without pay, if Cleveland asked him, but he was not doing the asking himself.[14] Another applicant for official favor of some sort was James H. Blount of Macon, Georgia, who wrote Gresham that he wanted to be a delegate to "an international monetary conference if occasion should offer in the future." In fact, said he, "Some honorable recognition from him [Cleveland] in an appointment of a temporary nature evincing his present confidence would be gratifying to my family & myself."[15]

Inasmuch as Blount was known to be close-mouthed, he got the job,[16] even though he seems to have preferred service on a monetary delegation. Blount was almost universally admitted to be fitted for the task, even by opponents of Cleveland, because of his long public service. Born in Macon, Georgia, in 1837, his first public office of importance was as a delegate to the Georgia Constitutional Convention under President Johnson's policy of restoration. Elected to Congress in 1872, he was reelected successively until 1893, when he declined to serve any more. In his last term he had been Chairman of the House Committee on Foreign Affairs.

In the words of Richard Olney, who later explained why Blount had been chosen for the delicate task, it was his experience on that

[14] Forbes to Cleveland, March 9, 1893, Cleveland MSS.

[15] Blount to Gresham, March 6, 1893, *ibid.*

[16] Alexander thought Blount got the appointment through Secretary Hoke Smith (*op. cit.*, p. 78). This seems to be correct, for Blount testified to the Morgan Committee (p. 385) that the first intimation he received of the possibility of his being chosen was a telegram from Hoke Smith, March 10, 1893, asking him to come to Washington prepared for a Pacific trip. At first he thought of refusing; when his son reminded him that the journey might help Mrs. Blount's health, he accepted. For a sketch of his life, see "James Henderson Blount" by John H. T. McPherson in *Dictionary of American Biography*, edited by Allen Johnson and Dumas Malone, 20 volumes (N. Y., 1928-37), II, 388-389.

committee which made him available. Continuing, in Olney's words, Blount

> . . . was believed to be much better informed than people in general concerning international matters and the relations of the United States with foreign powers. Moreover, I found on inquiry that he had the reputation of being an able, clear-headed man, of resolute purpose and of absolute integrity. . . . The President wanted information—wanted to know exactly what the facts were about this remarkable revolution, and why it was brought about, and the wishes of the people as respects annexation. . . . He was sent alone because there was only one man's work to do—namely, to get at and report the facts. Two men, even if honest, would have been in each other's way and would have been less efficient and expeditious than one.[17]

The New York *Post* applauded Blount's selection because he was a man with "an independent judgment."[18] The *San Francisco Chronicle* thought there could have been "no better selection" because Blount was a man of "sterling quality."[19] Even the New York *Sun* admitted that perhaps it was just as well to send him and get the facts.[20]

The instructions, dated March 11, which were handed to Blount by Secretary Gresham gave, as Cleveland's reason for despatching a Special Commissioner, the belief that the Hawaiian situation

[17] Olney to Mrs. G. R. Minot (his daughter), Dec. 3, 1893, in James, *op. cit.*, pp. 218-219. Presumably Blount was thought to be at least lukewarm towards annexation. Yet in interviews with Secretary Gresham, on June 14 and 16, 1893, Lorrin A. Thurston declared that he had talked with Blount in February of 1892 regarding annexation. Blount seemed to favor it, advising Thurston to see Blaine and other Republicans who likewise were Annexationists (Miscellaneous Archives . . . *op. cit.*). Blount's side of the interview between himself and Thurston was given in his testimony to the Morgan Committee (p. 386). He asserted that he merely advised Thurston to see the Secretary of State. Of course Blount could have changed his mind in the interim because of the way in which annexation was then being offered.

[18] March 21, 1893.

[19] March 16, 1893.

[20] March 21, 1893.

"demands the fullest consideration of the President" who must of necessity have "trustworthy information." Gresham continued:

> You will investigate and fully report to the President all the facts you can learn respecting the condition of affairs in the Hawaiian Islands, the causes of the revolution by which the Queen's Government was overthrown, the sentiment of the people toward existing authority, and in general, all that can fully enlighten the President touching the subjects of your mission.
>
> To enable you to fulfill this charge, your authority in all matters touching the relations of this Government to the existing or other government of the islands, and the protection of our citizens therein, is paramount, and in you alone, acting in cooperation with the commander of the naval forces, is vested full discretion and power to determine when such forces should be landed or withdrawn.

No encroachment whatever upon the sovereignty of the Provisional Government would be suffered; if it should at any time be necessary to land troops for protection of American life and property, permission must first be secured from the local authorities. To guard against the Commissioner's taking things into his own hands, as Minister Stevens had done, Judge Gresham was careful to stress that Blount's powers were limited to protecting Americans and included nothing else.[21]

These instructions, which made Blount more than an investigator, are of especial significance because they gave the policy which Cleveland intended to follow. There must be no interference with sovereign Governments without prior permission from the President. Notably prominent did the word "paramount" become in the rancid debates in Congress,[22] where it was bandied and hawked

[21] Blount, pp. 101-102.

[22] And in the press. The New York *Post,* April 24, 1893, remarked that some papers were indulging in "learned wrestling" over the meaning of the word "paramount." The New York *Sun,* April 22, 1893, condemned the idea that a personal agent of the President could be paramount over the Senatorially confirmed diplomatic representative. If used to extreme, the President might supersede all regular Ministers by employing special agents. The *New York Tribune,* April 22, 1893, said that it was simply not constitutional; yet others were able to find precedents. Thus the Philadelphia *Press,* as cited by the New York *Sun,* April 26, 1893, recalled that Orville Babcock's agency to negotiate a treaty of annexation with San Domingo during Grant's time was sufficient precedent for Blount's Commissionership.

about without restraint. Such a situation wherein there were two representatives at Honolulu was anomalous, and the powers of each required definition. In instructions of March 11 to Stevens, Secretary Gresham said that the President was sending Blount in order to "obtain the fullest possible information" and that Stevens was to aid the Commissioner in every way he could. The following words were most important:

> In all matters pertaining to the existing or other Government of the Islands the authority of Mr. Blount is paramount. As regards the conduct of the usual business of the legation, you are requested to continue until further notice in the performance of your official functions, so far as they may not be inconsistent with the special powers confided to Mr. Blount.[23]

In order to give to the Special Commissioner complete powers in his task, the Secretary of the Navy, on the same day, informed Rear Admiral Skerrett, Commander of the Pacific Station, of Blount's coming and of his paramount powers. "You will consult freely with Mr. Blount, and will obey any instructions you may receive from him regarding the courses to be pursued at said islands by the force under your command. You will afford Mr. Blount all such facilities as he may desire for the use of your cipher code in communicating by telegraph."[24]

Blount was thus given authority over the regular diplomatic representative and over the naval forces as well. Much criticism later was launched against Cleveland for placing naval officers under a civil official, especially a civil official who had not been confirmed by the Senate, and who was, therefore, merely the personal representative of the President.

Blount's letter of credence to President Cleveland's "GREAT AND GOOD FRIEND," Sanford B. Dole, President of the Executive and Advisory Councils of the Provisional Government, read in part:

> I have made choice of James H. Blount . . . as my special commissioner to visit the Hawaiian Islands and make report to me concerning the present status of

[23] Blount, pp. 3-4.
[24] Morgan, p. 401.

> affairs in that country . . . in all matters affecting relations with the Government of the Hawaiian Islands his authority is paramount. My knowledge of his high character and ability gives me entire confidence that he will use every endeavor to advance the interest and prosperity of both Governments and so render himself acceptable to your excellency.
>
> I therefore request your excellency to receive him favorably and to give full credence to what he shall say on the part of the United States and to the assurance which I have charged him to convey to you of the best wishes of this Government for the prosperity of the Hawaiian Islands.
>
> May God have your excellency in His wise keeping.[25]

This letter would later receive much criticism because in it Cleveland was speaking in sweet terms to a Government which he would soon be accused of trying to overturn.

* * * * *

The withdrawal of the treaty and the appointment of Blount placed the Annexation Commission in an awkward position. Inasmuch as the Senate would not take action until December at the very earliest,[26] the entire membership felt the desirability of saving money by having the Commission recalled and a Minister appointed.[27] During the investigation, the routine tasks of the Legation as well as the propaganda activity could be performed best by Thurston whose peculiar flair for missionary work would stand him in good stead. All concerned perceived the wisdom of getting rid of the Royalist Minister, Mott Smith, who was hanging on but doing nothing. Thurston called Smith "a second-hand old fiddle, who has had his day."[28] Smith's tenure was probably coming to an end anyway, but when he went to New York City and welcomed Davies and Kaiulani—he told Dole it was done as a matter of courtesy—the Provisional Government was through with him.[29]

Commissioner C. L. Carter informed Dole that he was homesick and wanted to return to his private affairs in Honolulu which needed attention, but that he felt obligated to stay on as long as

[25] Blount, p. 3.
[26] Thurston to Dole, confidential, March 16, 1893, M&C.
[27] Castle to Thurston, March 30, 1893, *ibid.*
[28] Thurston to Dole, March 10, 1893, *ibid.*
[29] Smith to Dole, March 10, 1893, *ibid.*

Smith remained because Smith was negligent, and was not liked around Washington.[30] On March 28 Dole informed Smith that the Government intended to commission a new Minister, but requested him to remain until his successor's arrival.[31] Commissioner Marsden was back in Honolulu by March 28 and reported; likewise on April 7 Wilder and Castle gave a survey to the Councils of the situation in the United States.[32] By that time Thurston and Carter were the only ones left at Washington to carry on the work.

As part of his duties, Thurston tried in many ways to learn from the new Administration what its attitude towards Hawaii was. He found Gresham to be a sphinx. At one interview the Secretary said he was too busy with job seekers to do anything; at another he asserted that the Administration merely desired time and information. Thurston stressed the danger of too long a delay. Capital was leaving the islands because of the uncertainty; business was bad; and there was peril from possible intrigues and foreign influence. Even though the Secretary would say nothing, Thurston believed he favored annexation.[33] In four separate interviews Gresham was cordial but noncommittal.[34] Thurston found that Cleveland wanted a plebiscite, the same farcical idea which, said the Hawaiian Minister, influenced Harrison.[35]

Both Thurston and Carter were carrying on missionary work where it would do the most good. Thurston lobbied among Cleveland's secretaries; Thurston, Castle (before leaving for Honolulu), and Carter saw Don M. Dickinson;[36] and Carter met important people in a social way to tell them Hawaii's story. He found that the Portuguese Minister at Washington favored an American protectorate over the islands. Ambassador Jules Pâtenôtre of France was unfriendly. The Japanese Minister—perhaps using the Oriental tactic of being friendly to a visitor—said he would be glad to see the United States in Hawaii. Hoke Smith, Secretary of the Interior, was opposed to annexation until

[30] Carter to Dole, March 29, 1893, *ibid.*

[31] Dole to Smith, March 28, 1893, *ibid.*

[32] EAC, March 28 and April 7, 1893, pp. 162, 179, 184.

[33] Thurston to Dole, March 10, 1893, M&C.

[34] Same to same, confidential, March 16, 1893, *ibid.*

[35] Same to same, March 10, *op. cit.*

[36] Philo Parsons to Don M. Dickinson, March 12, 1893, introducing the three Commissioners, *ibid.* Dickinson, Postmaster General in 1888-89, was a close friend of Cleveland's.

he thought of the fact that it might help the South to get rid of some of its Negroes.[37] Both Carter and Thurston visited New York City; Carter saw Captain G. C. Wiltse and some friends of Cleveland;[38] Thurston conferred with several persons "who will probably be useful to us," and looked up "a pull on [David B.] Hill and [Edward] Murphy [Jr.], the New York Senators."[39] Sometimes Thurston's enthusiasm got the better of his judgment, as when an official of the American Sugar Refining Company demanded a retraction of a critical comment which Thurston had made in a speech about the trust.[40] "It is not wise to attack the Sugar Trust," advised Charles R. Bishop.[41]

After Blount left, the Hawaiian question quieted down at Washington. Thurston went to the Chicago Fair with his cyclorama of the Volcano of Kilauea. Here he spoke many times and interviewed the anti-Annexationist editors of the *Chicago Herald* and *Chicago Evening Post;* the editor of the former was opposed to annexation but was saying nothing because the paper's owners and readers were in favor.[42] Thurston's purpose was to reach intelligent persons who could bring pressure upon their Senators.[43] Carter was carrying the gospel to New England (as he put it) where he made a speech, and saw Edward Atkinson who had some sort of special scheme—which Carter did not explain in his despatch—to solve the Hawaiian problem. Carter planned to go South and carry the campaign there.[44]

It was almost inevitable that Thurston be appointed Minister to succeed Mott Smith,[45] although Carter told Dole frankly that he, rather than Thurston, deserved the post because of his strenuous work for annexation. Moreover, he was ambitious to hold the position that his father, H. A. P. Carter, had once filled. When Carter learned he was not to be chosen Minister he said he wanted

[37] Carter to Dole, confidential, March 21, 1893, *ibid.*
[38] Same to same, confidential, March 29, 1893, *ibid.*
[39] Thurston to Dole, March 10, *op. cit.*
[40] J. E. Parsons to Thurston, March 8, 1893, *ibid.*
[41] Bishop to Carter, March 8, 1893, *ibid.*
[42] Thurston to Dole, personal, April 7, 1893, *ibid.*
[43] *Memoirs, op. cit.*, p. 286.
[44] Carter to Dole, April 7, 1893, M&C.
[45] On April 6 Dole wrote Thurston a letter pleading with him to take the post for the good of the cause (*ibid.*).

to return to Honolulu, and yet felt duty-bound to stay because he was needed and was making headway with Gresham.[46]

Mott Smith, now living at Philadelphia, made periodic reports[47] on the general situation until April 27 when he notified Dole of his retirement. He said he left without regret because he had no influence with Gresham and because the Commissioners had undermined him.[48] On May 26 the Minister officially informed Gresham that, although not recalled, he was retiring.[49] It was not until June that Thurston was formally presented to Cleveland as the Hawaiian envoy. Thurston informed the Secretary of State that he was the successor of the Commission and not of Smith.[50]

* * * * *

The failure of the treaty and the appointment of an investigator placed an entirely different aspect upon affairs in Honolulu. Now that annexation was postponed, the Royalists saw an opportunity to organize in opposition to union with the United States; by the same token, the Annexationists perceived that, with annexation thrust off into the uncertain future, organization was necessary on their part to consolidate the Government's position. Could the régime, hastily composed as a Provisional Government (provisional until joined with the United States in the immediate future, as it was hoped on January 17, 1893) hold together and govern the islands? After reading letters from the Commissioners on the failure of the treaty, the Councils agreed "on the wisdom of *reduction of expenses* and of preparing ourselves for independent administration of government against possible failure of annexation."[51]

The feeling, that it might be a long time before annexation was accomplished and that therefore a more permanent kind of organization was needed, slowly grew upon the members of the Provisional Government; and it grew for many reasons. First, two Royalist or native organizations were formed to fight annexa-

[46] Carter to Dole, confidential, April 17, 1893, *ibid.*

[47] For instance, Smith to Dole, April 20, 1893, *ibid.*

[48] Same to same, April 27, 1893, *ibid.*

[49] Smith to Gresham, May 26, 1893, Notes from Hawaii.

[50] The recall of the Commission and Thurston's letter of credence can be found in Dole to Gresham, May 4, 1893, *ibid.* The speeches of Thurston and Cleveland, when the former presented his credentials, are filed in *ibid.* for June 9, 1893. See also Thurston to Gresham, June 19, 1893, M&E.

[51] EAC, March 22, 1893, pp. 161-162.

tion and the present Government. They were the Hawaiian Civil Rights League inspired by C. W. Ashford—the *Advertiser* said he was raising the Royalist "black flag"—and the Hawaiian Patriotic League headed by men like J. A. Cummins and Joseph Nawahi.[52] These gestures were answered by the formation of an Annexation Club to support the Provisional Government.[53]

The extremist wing of the Annexationist party concluded that if the natives and the Royalists were going to form parties and clubs to fight annexation, it was ridiculous to help them with a subsidy; in other words, why continue to pay a salary to the Queen, who was using the money to underwrite the Royalist press (like the *Holomua* and the *Bulletin*) and other activities? Councillor McCandless moved in the Councils to stop paying this salary because it was commonly reported that Liliuokalani was opposing the Government by "other than Constitutional methods." There was general agreement that it had been a mistake to call the payment a salary, because Liliuokalani was no longer in office; nevertheless the Councils decided to continue to give her $1,250 a month for expenses because, after all, she had to live. The Government also determined to pay $5,000 per year for the support of Kaiulani.[54] This decision was bitterly resented by the more radical Annexationists, who would not let the issue rest.[55]

Furthermore, if the Royalists intended to become belligerent, why allow them to hold jobs in the Government? This, and other questions, caused quite a split in the Provisional Government forces. The moderate Annexationists, like those controlling the *Advertiser,* were against partisan removals, declaring that if a jobholder did his work he should be permitted to remain.[56] In other words, the age-old problem of patronage—the unfriendly *Bulletin* called it boodle[57]—began to emerge within the radical wing of the Annexa-

[52] *Advertiser,* March 2, 6, 7, 14, 17, 21, *etc.,* 1893.

[53] *Ibid.,* March 16, 22, 27, *etc.,* 1893. Clippings, giving the reasons for this organization and the speeches made when it was formed, were enclosed in Severance to Wharton, No. 185, March 27, 1893, Consular Letters.

[54] EAC, March 18 and 20, 1893, pp. 156, 157-159, 160.

[55] For instance, in Honolulu *Hawaiian Star,* March 30, April 1, *etc.,* 1893.

[56] *Advertiser,* March 1, 1893. On March 9 it admitted that some Royalists should go.

[57] March 7 and 9, 1893. It pointed out that Henry E. Cooper, a newcomer to the islands, and W. F. Frear, who had not won his spurs at the bar

tionist element. These radicals not only felt it was foolhardy to allow Royalist civil servants to remain as potential danger spots within the Government, but they also wanted jobs. It was to be expected that the *Bulletin* would inveigh against the fat printing contracts and high-salaried posts going to members of the Annexationist party,[58] but for the *Advertiser* to take such a stand was unbearable.

In the eyes of extreme Annexationists, the *Advertiser* was becoming conservative, and at best it was too critical. Radicals were dismayed when it called the Councils "an oligarchy of eighteen persons" who had no right to legislate on any topic except annexation, because that was the reason for their establishment. It admitted that the transfer of the Insane Asylum to the Board of Health was a good measure, but submitted that the Provisional Government had no power to pass such a law.[59]

The upshot was the formation of an organ to speak for the more radical Annexationists. The first public notice of the new venture appeared in the *Advertiser* on March 23 which welcomed the news. The new journal, called the *Hawaiian Star,* was to be an evening paper dedicated to fight for annexation. The first issue appeared on March 28, with the following names at the masthead: Dr. J. S. McGrew, editor in chief and president; Walter G. Smith (former staff correspondent of the *San Francisco Chronicle*), managing editor; A. S. Hartwell, vice president; E. A. Jones, treasurer; John Emmeluth, auditor; and Wm. P. Tilden, business manager. McGrew resigned as editor in chief on June 3 following, and Walter G. Smith took his place. The paper soon made itself the spokesman of the most rampant Annexationists—those who wished no compromise with the United States, the Royalists, or anyone else. In fact, at the start, its belligerency had to be calmed down by the Government. Said Attorney General W. O. Smith to Thurston: "The *Star* advocated statehood at once—and we had to stop it."[60]

as yet, had received judgeships. The *Bulletin* maintained the protectorate had been made necessary by divisions within the Annexationist ranks over patronage. On April 17 it said that nine of the original Advisory Council had won good jobs for themselves. See also May 26.

[58] March 31, 1893.

[59] "Too Much Legislation," in issue of March 14, 1893.

[60] Smith to Thurston, April 8, 1893, M&C. Hereafter this journal will be referred to simply as the *Star*.

Whereas the *Advertiser's* editorial pages were staid and dignified, those of the *Star* were rambunctious and pungent. It was not above name-calling, as when in its fourth issue, March 31, it maintained that the natives were being led by the "tricksters, the boodlers and the thieves," and that the "three crows of royalty" were Cummins, Nawahi, and Bush. The editors were clever at thinking up new and unusual arguments for annexation and against independence. For instance, in its first issue the paper launched out against the charge that the natives would lose the franchise and their social position after union with the United States;[61] it reiterated the point that the Queen was not of the royal Kamehameha line, and therefore could not claim the allegiance of the Kanakas;[62] and maintained that the editors of the Royalist *Bulletin* were "British subjects."[63] It is not too much to say that the colorfulness and aggressiveness of the *Star* gave a vital lift to the spirits of the members of the Provisional Government, dampened as they were by the failure of the treaty and by the worries of carrying on the administration until Blount had finished his investigation. Started just before the arrival of the Commissioner, the paper did valiant service in printing material which, it was hoped, would convert him to the Annexationist position. The editor of *Holomua,* unfriendly to both Annexationist organs, some time later characterized the *Advertiser* as the spokesman for the missionary-planter element, while "that ephemeral twinkler, the Star" which daily served "a mess of . . . pultaceous pabulum," represented the laboring masses and the rights of the people.[64]

* * * * *

As has been seen, one of the first official intimations of what President Cleveland intended was his withdrawal of the annexation treaty from the Senate on March 9.[65] The *New York Times* praised the act because "there was no public opinion, and no means

[61] March 28, 1893.
[62] April 4, 1893.
[63] April 6, 1893.
[64] *Holomua,* Jan. 9 and March 22, 1894.
[65] *New York Herald,* March 10, 1893. The Senate was in special session to confirm Cleveland's appointments. During this short session, petitions in favor of annexation were received from the Massachusetts General Court and from the Washington Legislature (*Record,* 53 Cong. Special Session of the Senate, pp. 15 and 20).

of forming any," and because the seriousness of the question required that it be studied.[66] The New York *Post* said: "It was to have been expected that a more satisfactory solution of the Hawaiian troubles would be arrived at under a Democratic President than under a Republican Administration."[67]

The Annexationist editors took the opposite view. The *San Francisco Chronicle* advised against too much disappointment on the part of proponents of the treaty; it was natural that anything planned by Republicans would be turned down by Democrats.[68] The *New York Tribune* pointed out that "In withdrawing this treaty Mr. Cleveland assumes a grave responsibility."[69] His act, in the eyes of the San Francisco *Morning Call,* was "A STEP BACKWARD." "Cleveland's weak point in public estimation [it continued] is his tendency to what may be termed an un-American policy"; in other words, he was working for England.[70] Congressman Nelson Dingley of Maine, with the same idea in mind, declared that annexation must be achieved to keep the islands from England.[71] The *San Francisco Chronicle* found it hard to fathom what was in the President's mind; it wondered if he intended to start all over again by signing a new treaty in order to get the glory.[72] The Hawaiian Commissioners were so upset that, on March 10, they made an official call upon Secretary Gresham. Thurston, their spokesman, wanted to know if withdrawal of the treaty meant no annexation or whether it meant a desire to secure information. Gresham answered that it was done merely to give time for further consideration. Thurston replied that delay might cause trouble in Hawaii.[73] Perhaps Thurston had in mind Dole's warn-

[66] March 10, 1893.
[67] March 17, 1893.
[68] March 17, 1893.
[69] March 10, 1893.
[70] March 10 and 20, 1893.
[71] *New York Times,* March 14, 1893.
[72] March 11, 1893.
[73] Miscellaneous Archives, *op. cit.* Thurston was afraid that Cleveland's seeming unfriendliness towards annexation might unnerve the Provisional Government and cause it to compromise. He wrote Dole a number of "pep" letters during 1893. On April 7, he said: "We have got to wipe the Monarchy clear out of sight this time or it means that all our work has been in vain and that we must again resume the weary drag of fighting royal rottenness and cussedness with a rotten electorate and a worse legislature" (*Memoirs, op. cit.,* p. 294).

ing that if annexation failed a republic would have to be formed, based upon "a government by force."[74]

The recall of the treaty and the appointment of Blount not only caused a wave of newspaper controversy, but helped to get the Hawaiian problem into the periodical press. Schurz was upholding the anti-Annexationist side in *Harper's* and sent most of his editorials to the President. Schurz argued that the United States needed no coaling stations because it was too strong to be attacked and would be weakened by having them.[75] Cleveland admitted that he was impressed by Schurz's reasoning. The historian, James Ford Rhodes, told Schurz: "I still think that the authorship of those articles should be indicated by an initial . . . for cogent reasons that I can adduce the next time that I see you."[76] When Edward L. Pierce, Charles Sumner's secretary and biographer, inquired, Schurz replied: "Yes, the articles . . . are from me. It is a subject which I have deeply at heart. There are other annexation schemes in the air which will have to be met in like manner."[77]

Cleveland was getting support from many quarters. George Ticknor Curtis asked in the *North American Review,* "Is It Constitutional?" and answered that no foreign country could be incorporated into the United States constitutionally, unless the country was contiguous or unless there was a controlling necessity. Neither of these provisoes applied to Hawaii.[78] E. L. Godkin of the *Post* fought the President's fight by lashing, almost daily, at the sugar trust. "It will probably never be known how much the sugar interests in Hawaii relied on a protest from the British for the prompt success of their scheme of annexation,"[79] he said. The *Post* made much of Thurston's admission that the sugar trust had a half interest in any bounty which might be paid to the planters after annexation.[80] Likewise the *Herald* stood manfully against an-

[74] New York *Post,* March 15, 1893.

[75] Schurz to Cleveland, March 11, 1893, Schurz MSS., CVII, 23678; same in Cleveland MSS.

[76] Rhodes to Schurz, March 25, 1893, Schurz MSS., CVII, 23738-23739.

[77] Schurz to Pierce, March 27, 1893, *ibid.,* 23742.

[78] CLVI (March, 1893), 282-287.

[79] New York *Post,* March 29, 1893.

[80] *Ibid.,* March 31, 1893. Godkin's charge that sugar was at the basis of annexation had both defenders and critics. Z. S. Spalding deposed to the Morgan Committee (p. 258) as follows: "We [the backers of the Provisional

nexation. Already its special correspondent, who later would get into trouble with the Hawaiian Government over his disclosures, was sending revelatory despatches from Honolulu.[81]

The Annexationists had their innings too. Captain A. T. Mahan brought his prestige to the fore in an article which was widely commented upon by all imperialists. He argued that England's strength lay in her island fortresses, such as Malta; that Hawaii's isolated, central position made it of equal strategic value; and that already the islands were "powerfully influencing the commercial and military control of the Pacific."[82] Thurston also made use of the periodical press to advance annexation. In an article in the *North American Review* he gave a history of American interests in Hawaii since John Q. Adams recognized its independence in 1826, and showed the advantages which reciprocity had brought to the United States. He figured that Americans had profited $28,292,668 from reciprocity with Hawaii.[83] Almost daily the New York *Sun* editorialized in favor of union between the two countries. Why, it asked, be ashamed of Annexationist desires? "What great nation has ever been anything else than annexationist?"[84] The type of argument that could be used is exemplified by the *New York Press* which said: "If the United States government is good enough for the people of this country, It [*sic*] is good enough for Hawaii. . . . Does Mr. Cleveland think it is becoming in an American President to insult the flag and institutions of America

Government] are doing it [keeping the Government going] for the present, but whether we can do it with sugar a half a cent a pound lower than now is quite another question." Thurston did his best to overcome the sugar objections of the New York *Nation,* New York *Post,* New York *World, Chicago Herald,* and *Chicago Post* by interviewing their editors. He said he convinced E. L. Godkin of the *Post* and *Nation* that sugar had nothing to do with the Revolution. Godkin promised to write no more sugar editorials (*Memoirs; op. cit.*, p. 286).

[81] *New York Herald,* March 21, 1893, for instance.

[82] A. T. Mahan, "Hawaii and Our Future Sea-Power," in *Forum,* XV (March, 1893), 1-12. Mahan used this article as chapter II (pp. 31-59) in his *The Interest of America in Sea Power, Present and Future* (Boston, 1898). The New York *Sun,* March 1, 1893, thought so well of the essay that it commented at length under the title, "We Must Have Hawaii." The Morgan Committee printed the article in its report, pp. 113-121.

[83] Lorrin A. Thurston, "The Sandwich Islands," in *North American Review,* CLVI (March, 1893), 265-282.

[84] March 12, 1893.

by thrusting Hawaii back under her native tyrants or handing her over to England?"[85] "I do not believe the Cleveland administration will dare to destroy the Hawaiian annexation project,"[86] said Senator Chandler.

* * * * *

While Cleveland was choosing a fact-finding Commissioner and while that Commissioner was on his way, Stevens was still writing to the State Department the kind of bugbear despatches to which, by this time, the Department must have become accustomed. On March 7 Stevens sent in his resignation which he said he had intended to offer, even if Harrison had been reelected. "I am aware that the present Hawaiian Government and most of the Americans and friends of the United States in the Islands have a strong desire that I should continue to hold my official position here at present, owing to my thorough acquaintance with Hawaiian affairs." But, if annexation was just around the corner, no Minister would be needed; if not, he felt that Cleveland would want a new representative. Stevens suggested Consul General Severance; above all, he warned the President not to appoint a Californian, because a Minister from that state "might not be entirely unbiassed on some questions and interests."[87] A copy of the letter was sent to the President.

In another despatch in the same mailing, Stevens reported that all was quiet: ". . . the Provisional Government is getting along exceedingly well, all circumstances considered." "Of course [he continued], all are awaiting with deep anxiety the result of the action of the Senate on the Annexation Treaty." The British Minister was trying to embarrass the Provisional Government by requesting it to seek to have the American forces returned to their ship, and by suggesting that, if the United States ratified the treaty, it should be put to a popular vote in Hawaii, "though none knows better than he that such a procedure here under existing conditions would be a farce." The Hawaiian Government answered Wodehouse by pointing out Britain's course in its numerous

[85] Quoted by *Kennebec Journal,* March 15, 1893.
[86] Chandler to Woodhull, March 13, 1893, Chandler MSS., LXXXVIII, 6815.
[87] Stevens to Gresham, No. 89, March 7, 1893, Despatches; printed in *House Ex. Doc. 48* (53 Cong. 2 Sess.), p. 147.

acquisitions of territory in the Pacific. "Annexation alone," concluded Stevens, "will put an end to these ultra British intrigues and give Hawaii responsible government and great prosperity."[88]

Meanwhile, Commissioner Blount was on his way. At San Francisco he stayed only five hours before embarking on the U.S.R.S. *Richard Rush.* His refusal to talk in that city, ignoring the great importers who wanted to testify in favor of annexation, led them to declare that he "was sent out as an attorney to make a prearranged case."[89] The *Morning Call* of that city wondered "Whether or not he had a suspicion that he was going on a fool's errand. . . ." The editor hoped that he would not drift into English influence, because "as commissioner [he] was eminently agreeable to the English residents of the islands."[90] The *New York Times,* however, was more friendly, saying that every boat from Hawaii was bringing conflicting statements about the Hawaiian situation and that the report of a levelheaded man was needed.[91]

The real purpose of the investigation was unknown in Honolulu; nor could the Provisional Government's representatives at Washington tell much. Was it to be merely an inquest to gain facts, or was restoration of the Queen intended? Thurston inferred that Blount would merely investigate to find out whether Cleveland's suspicion of a plot to unseat Liliuokalani was justified or not. He told Dole that Blount was fair-minded and unpartisan; that, as a Southerner, he would appreciate the problem of an ignorant electorate; that he favored reciprocity; and that he should be brought into contact with the best people in Honolulu. The Royalists (continued Thurston) would try to fill Blount up "with manufactured evidence"; therefore, the Provisional Government supporters ought to get some of the better natives to inform the investigator that they favored annexation. Thurston himself was working on Antone Rosa, and the Annexationists in Honolulu should do the same with John and W. H. Cummins. Even if their expenses had to be paid, such good natives as Kauhane, Iosepa, Ena, and Kaulia should be brought before Blount in order to

[88] Same to same, No. 90, *ibid.* Marked "Important" and a copy sent to Cleveland. Printed in *ibid.,* pp. 147-148.

[89] Julius A. Palmer, Jr., *Memories of Hawaii, op. cit.,* pp. 13 and 27.

[90] March 31, 1893; also March 28 and April 4.

[91] March 30, 1893.

prove to him that the Revolution was not a white man's movement as the Queen had charged.[92] Castle gave to Dole the same advice, that is, to entertain Blount and his wife, get him filled with good food, and then tell him the truth over a good cigar. "People in Washington," said Castle, "are very much accustomed to social communion."[93] Aside from suggestions as to entertainment, the Washington representatives could give little advice, even after Blount had arrived. Carter *assumed* that Blount's report, once made, would be favorable to annexation,[94] but no one was sure. Before resigning, Mott Smith related that Gresham had informed him it was not the business of the United States to restore anybody or to force any reforms; moreover Smith felt that, if Blount restored the Queen, he would be disavowed.[95]

Both Royalists and Annexationists (ignorant of the fact that Blount alone was being sent) were getting ready to receive a commission. The *Star* told editorially how the women's branch of the Hawaiian Patriotic League had been organized to present the native side to the investigators. The women, said the editor with considerable sarcasm, would give a "hookupu." "It is the firm belief of the promoters of this feminine scheme that if the seductive influences of a hookupu are added to their own blandishments, the Commission will grant any boon they may ask, and it is intimated that in this manner the Hawaiian women hope to reseat Liliuokalani on the throne."[96] Severance reported that the Provisional Government was equally pleased to hear that Cleveland intended to investigate, and added: "The continuance of a native Govt under a Protectorate would be most disastrous, nothing but absolute annexation will secure the prosperity of this Country and I am confident that the results of an impartial investigation by the Commission will sustain this view of the subject."[97]

When Blount arrived on March 29, Honolulu was all dressed up for a gala day, with the Stars and Stripes everywhere.[98] Re-

[92] Thurston to Dole, March 16, 1893, confidential, M&C.

[93] Castle to Dole, March 16, 1893, *ibid.*

[94] Carter to Dole, March 22 and 29, 1893, confidential, *ibid.*

[95] Smith to Dole, April 6 and 20, 1893, *ibid.*

[96] Severance to Wharton, No. 185, March 27, 1893, Consular Letters.

[97] *Ibid.*

[98] The ceremonies were described by the *Advertiser,* enclosed in Severance to Wharton, No. 190, April 5, 1893, Consular Letters; also Blount, pp. 4 *ff.*

covering from their surprise at meeting one man, instead of several, the various parties competed for his attention. The native women tried to stage a hookupu in Hawaiian dress, but Blount made short shrift of all welcoming delegations. The newly-formed Annexation Club[99] represented that phase of Hawaiian opinion, while Royalist organizations also pressed upon him their favors. Minister Stevens and the Americans had a carriage ready to take him to a private house, but Blount went to a hotel, refusing to place himself under obligation to either party. Stevens and the Annexationists later made much of the fact that Blount stayed at a hotel, maintaining that it was owned by a Royalist.[100]

Blount found the American colors flying over the Government Building and American marines patrolling for the Provisional Government. He at once interviewed Admiral J. S. Skerrett and ordered him to withdraw both flag and troops. Upon being informed of this contemplated action, the Councils met to discuss the matter on March 31. That evening President Dole conferred with the military officials of the Provisional Government in reference to the new problems that would face the army after American troops had withdrawn. The "*sentiment of the military* was," as he informed the Councils on April 1, "that the Provisional Government should *raise the American flag* as the flag of the Provisional Government of the Hawaiian Islands after it had been lowered by the United States officers as the symbol of their protection." The Councils did not think well of the suggestion,[101] although all members were conscious of the almost desperate problem that was being tossed back to them by the United States. The *Advertiser* proposed the swearing in of the 2,000 members of the Annexation Club as soldiers.[102]

[99] In accordance with Thurston's and Castle's suggestions for entertainment, W. O. Smith wrote as follows: "The Annexation Club have arranged to have a furnished house, with servants &. to offer to the U. S. Commissioners. Mrs. Wilder's house is ready—or Dr. McGrew's. The town is to be decorated and everything done that can be thought of which is proper" (Smith to Thurston, March 29, 1893, M&C). The Smiths gave a dinner of 125 plates for the Blounts, and Mrs. Blount was later entertained at tea in the Smith home (same to same, April 8, 1893, *ibid.*).

[100] Stevens and Oleson, *op. cit.*, p. 314; *Blount,* p. 102; Alexander, p. 82.

[101] EAC, March 31 and April 1, 1893, pp. 171-172, 173-174, 174-175.

[102] April 3, 1893.

On April 1 American occupation ended, in accordance with Blount's order to Admiral Skerrett of March 31: "You are directed to haul down the United States ensign from the Government Building, and to embark the troops now on shore to the ships to which they belong. This will be executed at 11 o'clock on the 1st day of April."[103] The lowering of the American flag and the hoisting of the Hawaiian made little impression upon the populace. There was complete apathy. The description of the event by Captain Hooper, of the revenue cutter *Rush* which had just brought Blount to Hawaii, is interesting:

> There were no demonstrations of any kind as the American flag came down, and not a single cheer greeted the Hawaiian flag as it was raised aloft. The native men stood around in groups or singly, smoking, and chatting and nodding familiarly to passing friends or leaning idly against the trees and fences, while the women and children, which formed a large proportion of the assemblage, were talking and laughing good-naturedly. As the hour for hauling down the American flag approached, many people, men, women, and children, could be seen approaching the Government square in a most leisurely manner, and showing more interest in the gala day appearance of the crowd than in the restoration of their national flag. The air of good natured indifference and idle curiosity with which the native men regarded the proceedings, and the presence of the women and children in their white or bright colored dresses, was more suggestive of a country "fair" or horse race than the sequel to a "revolution."[104]

Skerrett reported to the Secretary of the Navy: "There was not the remotest evidence shown, by the crowd of natives and others about the Government building, of any feeling." A few troops were left at the Legation "to quiet the apprehensions of Minister Stevens."[105] In his telegram to Gresham, telling of the action, Blount said: "No manifestation of excitement has appeared yet."[106]

[103] Blount, p. 6.
[104] *Ibid.*, pp. 8-9.
[105] April 6, 1893, No. 28634, Bureau of Navigation; see also Skerrett to Blount, April 1, 1893, in Blount, pp. 594-595. For the meaning of the rubric "Bureau of Navigation," see footnote 16, chapter II.
[106] April 6, 1893; there is a copy in Cleveland MSS.

The Royalist *Bulletin* asserted the act proved that the United States trusted the law-abiding characteristics of the natives.[107] The *Advertiser* was at least outwardly complacent.[108] The *Star,* on the other hand, objected; its editor, accompanied by Stevens, called upon Blount to urge continuance of American occupation. The Queen and the Japanese Commissioner, said they, had agreed that, when the Americans left, the Japanese should land armed men from the *Naniwa.* Blount refused to be persuaded that there was any such danger. In due time the Japanese Commissioner sent the vessel home.[109]

Stevens of course did not like the undoing of his own work; but, with Blount made "paramount" over him, there was little to do except to prove that the protectorate, while it lasted, was a good thing. He told Gresham that during the American occupation the Government had had time to train 400 effective soldiers and to organize a police force.[110] "Had the United States Minister and the Naval Commander not acted as they did, they would have deserved prompt removal from their places and the just censure of the friends of humanity and of civilization." He concluded by stating that there was good order everywhere because the islands now had the best government in their history.[111] He later offered further defense of his acts in his book.[112]

When news of the American evacuation of Hawaii reached the United States, reaction was largely in accordance with the party allegiance of the person or paper commenting. The *Literary Digest's* summary of press opinion was: "A number of Republican journals denounce the action, though others commend it. The Independent and Democratic press, with hardly an exception, ap-

[107] April 1, 1893.

[108] April 1, 1893.

[109] Blount, p. 103. Dole had a "very satisfactory and re-assuring" interview with Blount (EAC, April 3, 1893, p. 178).

[110] On the other hand, Nicoll Ludlow, Commander of the *Mohican,* who was in Honolulu from Feb. 10 to May 1, 1893, told the Morgan Committee (p. 788): "I do not think at any time up to the time I left there they [the Provisional Government] had [an army] to exceed a hundred men. And there was nobody who could drill them in shape. They had to send to Cleveland, Ohio, to get uniforms."

[111] Stevens to Gresham, No. 94, April 4, 1893, Despatches; printed in *House Ex. Doc. 48* (53 Cong. 2 Sess.), p. 153.

[112] Stevens and Oleson, *op. cit.,* p. 298.

prove it."[113] Senator Henry C. Lodge on April 15 offered a resolution to ask the Secretary of State why the flag had been hauled down.[114] Stevens's loyal defender, the *Kennebec Journal,* called Blount's trip a "little junketing excursion."[115] The New York *Commercial Advertiser* said that "the Buffalo liliputian [Cleveland]," by ordering Blount to remove the flag, "turned back the hands on the dial of civilization."[116] The San Francisco *Morning Call,* under the title, "THE FLAG HAULED DOWN," castigated the act as "humiliating," but just what would be expected of the "proverbial dog in the manger."[117] The *New York Tribune,* calling the event a "national humiliation," said there was no need of getting more information through Blount because the five Commissioners had told the truth.[118] The New York *Sun* asserted: "When the power of this republic is exerted to crush out republican self-government in another land, and to put back a humbug queen upon a humbug throne, it will be time for popular indignation to make itself heard."[119] Yet this paper admitted that Blount's act was probably necessary, for the reason that Stevens's work had been unauthorized and later disavowed by Foster.[120] Former President Harrison thought that "the pulling down of the flag in Honolulu has created a very intense feeling throughout the country. . . . What a pity that the Senate is not in session that we might draw out from the State Department Mr[.] Blount's report. They are evidently afraid to give it out."[121]

The most amusing onslaught against Blount's action came from the *Kennebec Journal* which turned the affair into a new Confederate rebellion. "The Southern yell goes gleefully up again at the spectacle of the lowering of the American flag in Hawaii. . . . How Ex-Confederate Blount must have smiled when he witnessed

[113] *Literary Digest,* VI (April 22, 1893), 695-696.
[114] *Record* (53 Cong. Special Session of the Senate), pp. 164 and 165.
[115] April 12, 1893.
[116] Quoted by Nevins, *Cleveland, op. cit.,* p. 553.
[117] April 15, 1893.
[118] April 16, 1893.
[119] Quoted by New York *Post,* April 17, 1893.
[120] April 15 and 17, 1893.
[121] Harrison to Foster, May 1, 1893, in John W. Foster MSS., Library of Congress. The letter was written after adjournment of the special session of the Senate which had met in March to confirm Cleveland's appointments.

the lowering of the stars and stripes at Honolulu! It was a satisfaction he never enjoyed at the hands of the brave men who bore that flag amid the smoke and carnage of Southern battlefields."[122] Next day it was talking about "Southern Treason," in which connection John A. Dix's famous order was quoted: "If any man attempts to haul down the American flag shoot him on the spot!" Readers were reminded of Cleveland's former attempt to hand back the flags to "unrepentant rebels." The editor quoted, with gusto, the *Utica* (New York) *Herald* which said Cleveland was "Aping Buchanan";[123] and the *Kansas City Star* which opined that "If Mr. Cleveland orders the flag hauled down a few more times the South will be solid for a third term."[124] On May 16, Blount was a "cowardly traitor."

In spite of all this outcry, Cleveland and Blount had loyal supporters. John P. Irish, United States Naval Officer at San Francisco, wrote to say that if California were polled, it would oppose annexation and favor Hawaiian independence—even though the San Francisco papers were deriding Blount. Suggesting that Hawaii be like Switzerland, a country of "absolute neutrality," he continued: "These are the views of our people. They never did approve the seizure of Hawaii by a mob, assisted by the Boston's blue jackets. And when that mob appointed a committee to peddle the country in the markets of the world, the proportions of the crime threatened to make the division of Poland a mere international kindness on the part of the butchers who carved that kingdom."[125] The New York *Post* approved, of course, and thought that "This event, we have no doubt, will fill our newspaper Jingoes with mingled grief and rage."[126] The *Chicago Herald* said that Blount had "purged the American flag of the stain put on it by Minister Stevens."[127]

Back in Honolulu the renunciation of the protectorate left Minister Stevens in an unpleasant position. Nor did he take kindly to accepting orders from Commissioner Blount, as when Blount

[122] April 17, 1893.
[123] April 20, 1893.
[124] April 27, 1893. See also clipping from *Baltimore American,* April 28.
[125] Irish to Cleveland, April 15, 1893, Cleveland MSS.
[126] April 14, 1893.
[127] Quoted by New York *Sun,* April 19, 1893.

directed Stevens—inasmuch as the whole matter was under investigation—to cease propagandizing for annexation.[128] Admiral Skerrett, reporting that everything was quiet and that there was "no apparent indication of either uneasiness, or apprehension, on the part of the Government Officials," added drily: "The detail of Marines now at the United States Legation, gives apparent comfort and contentment to the United States Minister."[129]

As Stevens prepared to leave for Maine on May 24,[130] there was one stratum of opinion which he could count upon, namely, that of Annexationist Hawaii which gave him a royal send-off. The *Star* said: "MINISTER STEVENS will carry with him, on his return to the United States, the respect and esteem of all men on the Hawaiian Islands, white and native, whose good will is worth having."[131] Upon the eve of his departure, a delegation of three hundred prominent men, led by a band, walked by fours down the street to Stevens's home to pay him their respects and to bid him farewell. All shook hands; he made a talk; and his voice broke at the end. The *Advertiser,* in which the details of the reception were printed, added editorially that he had "faithfully served his country in Hawaii during the transition period." He had been a good friend, a wise and just counselor.[132]

Upon sailing, Stevens must have known that he was returning to the United States under a cloud. Indeed it was well that he was at long last going to defend himself in the arena of public opinion, for a storm of criticism had been arising against him. The *New York Times* was demanding the recall of the "mischief-maker."[133] Editors, like E. L. Godkin, had been harping on the charge that the treaty of 1876 gave him no right to interfere in Hawaii as he had done.[134] As a matter of record, so much carping

[128] Blount, pp. 15-16. The San Francisco *Morning Call* thought: "Very likely Stevens made the mistake of his life in submitting to Blount" (April 22, 1893).

[129] Skerrett to Secretary of Navy, April 25, 1893, No. 29329, Bureau of Navigation.

[130] Stevens to Gresham, No. 96, April 4, Despatches.

[131] Enclosed in Severance to Josiah Quincy, No. 195, April 25, 1893, Consular Letters.

[132] Enclosed in same to same, No. 201, May 22, 1893, *ibid.*

[133] April 18, 1893.

[134] New York *Post,* April 27, 1893.

had developed against Stevens that the *New York Tribune* undertook to make a special defense of his acts. The "fact [it said] that he has interpreted his duty to be the advancement of his country's influence is seized upon by a certain section of the Democratic party . . . as a ground for abusing him."[135]

In any event, what the unfriendly New York *World* called "Stevens's Own Defense" was published ahead of his arrival in the country on May 31. In this lengthy essay Stevens reviewed the sins of the semi-barbarous monarchy, the voting out of good Ministries, the refusal of the Queen to arbitrate, the mass meetings, the landing of the troops, and the strength of the Provisional Government. If the American forces had not been sent ashore, said he, their officers would have been shamefully neglecting their duty. He emphasized the fact that Christian civilization was in danger; that no race issue was involved; and that annexation would be merely copying Great Britain in its colonial policy.[136] The New York *Post* (which had already scored Stevens's criticism of the Queen's corrupt Legislature, by reminding Americans that they had legislatures of a similar type in California, Pennsylvania, and New York)[137] called his defense "scurrilous and scandalous." It "tallies [asserted the *Post*] wonderfully well with the Fra Diavolo school of politics, of which Mr. Stevens is so apt a pupil."[138]

Others, however, were kinder. The Des Moines *Iowa State Register* said: "Welcome Home the Patriot. . . . He is worthy of it."[139] The *Kennebec Journal* defended his loyalty, saying that there was much Democratic lying about his part in the Revolution.[140] Upon landing at San Francisco, he justified his course before the Chamber of Commerce,[141] in a speech whose words and ideas he later used in his book. The San Francisco *Bulletin* thought the address "a revelation" which was given "in a strictly non-partisan spirit."[142] When he got back to Augusta, his paper welcomed him profusely: "His action has been that of a farseeing

[135] April 27, 1893.
[136] Printed in New York *World,* May 24, 1893.
[137] April 27, 1893.
[138] May 24, 1893.
[139] Clipped by *Kennebec Journal,* May 18, 1893.
[140] *Kennebec Journal,* June 2, 1893.
[141] *Ibid.,* June 1, 1893.
[142] Clipped by *ibid.,* June 22, 1893.

statesman clearly perceiving the great importance of United States control of the destinies of islands that are truly said to be 'the key to the Pacific.' "[143] The public-spirited citizens of the Maine capital planned a reception in his honor. Said the *Kennebec Journal*: "One of the most notable events in the history of Augusta will occur at the Opera house this evening."[144] In what was said to be the largest gathering ever assembled in the Augusta opera house, Stevens made a long speech defending his policy in Hawaii, and refuting the charge of collusion with the Revolutionists. "The monarchy," he declared, "died by its own revolutionary hand—a suicide of blindness, incompetence and corruption."[145]

* * * * *

In Hawaii, Blount was busily investigating—and having his troubles. His method of getting the facts was to hold interviews, to receive letters and affidavits, and to listen to memorials read from interested societies.[146] The Royalists usually sent signed versions of the Revolution, always blaming it upon the American Minister. As early as March 31, two days after his arrival, the deposed Cabinet offered him its account of the overthrow of the monarchy. The Queen submitted a long statement defending her course and asking justice.[147] Both Revolutionists and Royalists were questioned in lengthy interviews, signing their names to written copies of their statements as taken down by Blount's secretary, Ellis Mills. The Commissioner was so meticulous in refraining from giving his views that the *San Francisco Chronicle* called him "That oyster-like diplomat James H. Blount."[148]

The Commissioner found that practically all the whites, including the Portuguese, were for annexation,[149] but that the overwhelming majority of the native element was for restoration of the Queen. Statistics were secured to prove that the Provisional

[143] June 19, 1893.

[144] *Ibid.*, June 28 and 29, 1893.

[145] *Ibid.*, June 30, 1893; *Star,* July 14 and *Advertiser,* July 15.

[146] He later admitted he was handicapped by lack of authority to force witnesses to testify.

[147] Blount, pp. 290 *ff*. For texts of various memorials from native organizations, see Alexander, *op. cit.*, p. 84.

[148] April 18, 1893. The *Star,* April 4, 1893, referred to him as "the American Minister Reticent."

[149] Blount, p. 133.

Government was a device by, for, and of the American minority who saw to it that the good things went to them rather than to the Kanakas.[150] On May 2, delegates from the Hawaiian Patriotic League representing natives all over the islands brought in a memorial against union with the United States.[151] A number of leading Annexationists admitted in interviews that, if the question of annexation were put to a referendum, it would be heavily defeated.[152] Although the Annexation Club sent Blount a petition in favor of annexation,[153] no Annexationist would have been willing to submit the question to a popular vote.[154]

Blount found that the Annexationists wanted neither statehood in the Union nor universal suffrage, for both of these would give to the Kanakas and Orientals the control of the Government. A

[150] For instance, the monthly payroll for the civil service of the Provisional Government (exclusive of the Cabinet, police, and day laborers) amounted to $51,148.37 for 877 persons. Natives who were employed by the Government and who accounted for 459 of the 877 (that is, 52.34%) received $18,631. On the other hand, 205 of the 877 were Americans (the 205 included 77 school teachers) and these Americans, only 23.38% of the total, received just a little less than the 459 native employees—$18,367.49. The English accounted for 110 jobholders out of the 877 (including 37 teachers) and received $9,148.74 of the total payroll (Blount, p. 609).

[151] *Advertiser,* enclosed in Severance to Josiah Quincy, No. 196, May 4, 1893, Consular Letters; Blount, pp. 25-26, 38, and 445-466.

[152] Blount, pp. 67 and 133. This was also admitted by some Annexationists in the United States, such as the *San Francisco Chronicle,* on March 30, 1893. The argument was usually based on the idea that, even though it be granted the natives were opposed to union, they were too ignorant to be taken into consideration. On March 9 the *Chronicle* said of the Kanakas: "If they can get enough to eat and drink and a place to sleep they are perfectly content, and changes of sovereignty or dynasty are wholly immaterial to them"; and on March 16 it referred to the "poi-eating Kanakas, who are as incapable of forming and expressing an intelligent political opinion as so many Piute Indians in the Sierra Neva [*sic*] mountains, or the Chinese from the Chinese quarter of this city."

[153] *Star,* April 1, enclosed in Severance to Wharton, No. 190, April 4, 1893, Consular Letters; printed in Blount, pp. 593-594.

[154] Charles Nordhoff, correspondent of the *New York Herald,* said that the 40,000 natives were solidly against annexation, and that the 1,928 Americans were in favor (quoted by New York *Post,* April 17, 1893). Even better authority was Attorney General W. O. Smith who wrote confidentially to Thurston: "The mass of the kanakas dont want annexation, and there has been a good deal of feeling about it. But as time passes they are becoming more reconciled to the idea" (March 29, 1893, M&C).

territorial form of government, similar to that of the District of Columbia, seemed to be the aim of the whites.[155] The Queen's last Foreign Minister, Samuel Parker, testified that he wished restoration, but only under an American protectorate; and that the Queen, unsupported by American authority, could not keep order.[156]

In spite of what Blount was finding out, Stevens continued to write, up to the very moment of his departure, that annexation sentiment was growing among the natives. So also Severance on April 25: "The native Hawaiians are joining the ranks of the annexationists, and the Foreign community are emphatic for closer relations with the United States as the only assurance of a good government and future prosperity."[157]

Busy as the Commissioner was in taking depositions and in receiving testimony, he had his share of problems to face. The first was the so-called Bowen-Sewall episode.[158] The trouble grew out of the fact that Neumann and his colleagues, satisfied with what they had been able to do in helping to defeat the annexation treaty, returned to Honolulu on the same vessel as Harold M. Sewall (later American Minister to Hawaii under McKinley), Dr. William S. Bowen of the New York *World* and Charles Nordhoff of the *New York Herald.* In San Francisco it had been rumored that Bowen and Sewall were representing themselves as friends of President Cleveland, and both refused to deny that they were co-Commissioners with Mr. Blount in investigating Hawaiian affairs. On the voyage, they became friendly with Neumann, persuading him to attempt to convince the Queen that she should abdicate in return for a pension. Nordhoff seems not to have been involved in the conversations, but when Bowen and Sewall landed, they added a third intriguer, Charles L. Macarthur, editor of the

[155] Cf., testimony of Albert B. Loebenstein, in Blount, p. 410. Annexationists were very frank in their admissions that they did not want a democratic system of suffrage. Z. S. Spalding doubted whether either republican or democratic government would work in Hawaii, and therefore desired that the islands be added to California and ruled from Sacramento on the basis of restricted suffrage. He admitted the Provisional Government was "autocratic" (Morgan, pp. 256 and 259).

[156] Blount, pp. 443-444.

[157] Severance to Quincy, No. 195, April 25, 1893, Consular Letters.

[158] The incident was described in Blount, pp. 13-15; Morgan, p. 393; and Alexander, pp. 84-86.

Troy (N. Y.) *Northern Budget,* who was in Hawaii for his health.[159] On April 7 they consulted with President Dole, who neither assented to nor refused the scheme, saying that he would not avoid any plan which would settle matters. He seemed to be willing to pay the Queen $20,000 a year,[160] and even visited Neumann, somewhat surreptitiously, in order to talk the plan over.[161] Blount, upon being approached by Bowen and Sewall, refused to have anything to do with the arrangement, asserting that he had not been sent by Cleveland to meddle in Hawaiian affairs. He did, however, think it best to visit the Queen for the purpose of discovering whether she had gone into any negotiations. He also felt that, in compiling his report, her personal views should not be omitted.[162]

Readily receiving the permission of President Dole, Blount called upon Liliuokalani on April 24. Hinting displeasure at the maneuverings of Bowen and Sewall, he told her that they had no right to speak for the United States Government at all. She asserted that she had gone into no negotiations with anyone, but was waiting for the Commissioner to reseat her upon the throne. He assured the Queen that he was in Hawaii neither to aid her nor to overthrow the Provisional Government; that his sole purpose was to gather information. At this point she became uncommunicative, and was willing to say only that Neumann had been sent to Washington to prevent passage of the treaty and that her present attitude would be to take no step until the United States acted.[163]

This visit created a storm of protest from the Annexationist press against Blount and Liliuokalani. There had been a feeling for some time that Blount was taking testimony from more Royalists and native organizations than from Annexationists,[164] and this incident brought the suspicion to light. Whisperings arose

[159] Testimony of Macarthur in Morgan, pp. 691-692.

[160] According to Bowen, who described his machinations in *ibid.,* pp. 666-674.

[161] Macarthur, in *ibid.,* p. 704; EAC, April 27, 1893.

[162] Blount, p. 22.

[163] *Ibid.,* pp. 22 ff.

[164] Young, *op. cit.,* p. 246. On pp. 250 *ff.* he gave examples of what he called *ex parte* evidence taken by Blount. On p. 258 there is a charge that Blount was too friendly with the English Minister. See also Blount, p. 64.

that the Queen should have been deported in the first place, and that it ought to be done now. On May 8 the *Star* prophesied that she would always be a source of trouble to the Government. Under title of "WHAT OF THE QUEEN?" it wrote a cryptic sentence which Blount deeply resented: "Certainly, her right to treat with a foreign envoy has not been denied, as witness her unhindered interviews with Commissioner Blount."[165] In a letter to Dole, the Commissioner objected strenuously to such editorial misstatement.[166] Dole hurriedly promised that the newspaper would make the *amende honorable* and apologized on his own responsibility.[167] From that time on the Annexationist press tried to gain Blount's favor.[168]

Already there had emerged a great deal of editorial propaganda, on the part of the Annexationist newspapers, to impress upon Blount the hopelessness of the Royalist cause. Almost every day some piece or other appeared; the editors knew he would read everything printed. The *Advertiser* declared that the Provisional Government was each month giving the Queen $1,250 of the taxpayers' money, in spite of the fact that she had income from her large estates. It then adverted to the injustice of permitting her to receive a gratuity with which she subsidized an anti-Annexationist paper, nominally edited by Joseph Heleluhe, one of her creatures, but actually controlled by her.[169] The *Star* took up the same complaint by saying that the Queen's agents lived on her pay. "They represent the desire of the most worthless class of the island politicians—the tricksters, the boodlers and the thieves," not one of whom had an iota of patriotism.[170]

Later the *Advertiser* turned to another front by declaring, undoubtedly for Blount's benefit: "The revolution of 1893 was ac-

[165] Blount, pp. 64-65. On May 10 the *Star* wanted to exile her.

[166] *Ibid.*, pp. 65 and 69.

[167] *Ibid.*, p. 66.

[168] *Ibid.*

[169] Enclosed in Severance to Wharton, No. 190, April 5, 1893, Consular Letters. Liliuokalani (*op. cit.*, p. 260) denied categorically that she ever received one cent either from the Provisional Government, or its successor, the Republic; furthermore, she maintained that the income from the crown lands was stolen from her. However that may be, the records show that by May 22 she was receiving nothing from the Treasury (EAC).

[170] Severance to Wharton, No. 190, *op. cit.*

complished by the people," who were against a republic or any other kind of government, except the kind they would have if annexed to the United States.[171] On April 25 the *Star* predicted that if the United States did not take Hawaii, it would become another Bermuda, that is, an alien post to be used by enemies against American territory; on the other hand, if the United States did annex, it would be as valuable as were Malta and Cyprus to England.[172]

The *Advertiser* believed the Provisional Government should inform the natives that, under American control, they would lose neither their votes nor their lands—in spite of what Royalist liars were telling them.[173] The *Star,* on May 1, thought that one could hardly reason with the Kanakas, led as they were by "demagogues" and "inspired by Kahunas"; and yet, what could "the organized weakness known as the royal government" do for Hawaii? If the Queen were restored, there would be outbreaks, riots, a decline in trade, insecurity, and general unstable government. The only reason for the Queen's desire to return was to get "free rent and big pay for doing nothing but making a pretence of dignity and royal worth."[174] The monarchical party, in short, was "fatally smitten with vacillation and weakness" because the leaders were divided.[175] It felt sure Blount would soon learn that "the royalist cause is a fake, gotten up by shrewd politicians to trade upon; and that it has had no existence in fact since the day the ex-Queen violated the constitution and BY HER OWN ACT terminated the monarchy."[176]

Of course this press campaign for the benefit of Blount did not neglect business arguments. The *Star* thought that annexation would bring good times for Hawaii because moneyed interests would rush to the islands—"men and their kind who have been following the pioneer from the Alleghenies to the Pacific States, building great cities as they went and turning vacant principalities of land into orchards and gardens." It predicted that a year after annexation the harbor would be filled with ships, Honolulu would

[171] Severance to Quincy, No. 195, April 25, 1893, Consular Letters.
[172] Enclosed in *ibid.*
[173] Severance to Quincy, No. 196, May 4, 1893, Consular Letters.
[174] *Ibid.*
[175] *Ibid.,* enclosed in same to same, No. 200, May 9, 1893, Consular Letters.
[176] *Ibid.*

be twice its present size, and railroads would cross the island of Oahu. On the other hand, only stagnation would come under a monarchy.[177] As if to support this prophecy, the special correspondent to the *New York Tribune* had already announced that "A Boom Strikes Hawaii. Values Rise at the Prospect of Annexation" and added that "speculators in Hawaiian realty and franchises have begun to cast about for bargains."[178] On June 21 Severance called attention to the fact that since Honolulu harbor had been dredged huge ocean liners could berth there; that the ships of the Pacific Mail Company, the Occidental and Oriental Company, and the Canadian Pacific Company all stopped, coming and going; and that Pacific Mail's S.S. *China,* drawing twenty-four feet, had just docked. In view of these facts, the Provisional Government, said he, indulged "the hope that the investigation of proposed Annexation will result favorably."[179]

Moreover, the *Star* went to considerable expense and trouble to prove that inasmuch as Annexationists paid most of the taxes they should have the privilege of disposing of Hawaii as they saw fit. It was found that on the island of Oahu (where Honolulu was located) assessed property (real and personal) amounted to $15,-647,334. Of this figure, Annexationists owned $12,422,389; property owned by both Annexationists and Royalists in partnership totaled $1,544,291; that held by those who designated no political preference came to $855,698; and Royalists accounted for only $824,956.[180]

On Hawaii, the largest island of the archipelago, real and personal property was assessed at $7,759,508—of which Annexationists paid taxes on $4,827,330; those divided in sentiment, $1,952,446; no politics designated, $183,374; and Royalists $796,-358. On this island, of the sixty-four persons owning over $10,000 worth of property, thirty-nine were Annexationist, thirteen were divided in sentiment, eight were Royalist, and four gave no politics.[181]

[177] Enclosed in same to same, No. 195, April 25, 1893, Consular Letters.
[178] *New York Tribune,* March 9, 1893.
[179] Severance to Quincy, No. 204, June 21, 1893, Consular Letters.
[180] *Star,* May 13, 1893, enclosed in same to same, No. 201, May 22, 1893, *ibid.*
[181] *Ibid.*

On Kauai, thirty-eight owned over $10,000; only three were Royalist. The total assessed property amounted to $4,053,674, of which Annexationists owned $3,446,728; divided in sentiment $465,476; doubtful $13,988; and Royalists $127,482.[182]

Final figures on taxpaying all over the islands showed that, of those owning $10,000 worth of property or more, three-fourths were Annexationists who accounted for $23,498,407; divided in sentiment $5,127,670; doubtful $1,151,675; Royalists, $2,289,293; and republican $270,872.[183] Such statistics were, of course, powerful ammunition for the Annexationists and they were used to the fullest extent.

The *Star,* believing that the best defense was a strong offense, tried to prove that the financial condition of the Provisional Government was excellent by contrasting it with the weakness and graft under the monarchy in 1892.[184] The Royalist *Bulletin* ridiculed the figures which purported to uncover many dirty financial deals before the Revolution of 1893; but the *Star's* exposé did much good for the Annexationist cause, particularly because Blount was on the scene.[185] The *Star* condemned the Provisional Government for not making use of these facts which it had been unearthing: "Why not bring out all the proof which has been massed up that the Monarchy of Kalakaua and Liliuokalani was little better than a 'Thieves' Paradise?"[186] Likewise the *Advertiser* commented almost daily on the excellent financial status of the Government, in spite of its having to pay the debts accumulated by Royal extravagance.[187]

The *Star* also thought it was wise to clear up, for the Commissioner's benefit, the assertion by Royalists and by Bishop Alfred Willis of the Anglican Church in the city that the Revolution had been engineered by descendants of missionaries—which descendants should be ashamed of themselves. It said, on April 8, 1893, that among the leaders of the Provisional Government, only three —Dole, W. O. Smith, and Damon—were of missionary descent; and that King, Porter, Bolte, Brown, McChesney, Morgan, Suhr,

[182] *Ibid.*

[183] *Ibid.*, enclosed in same to same, No. 204, *op. cit.*

[184] May 30, 1893.

[185] May 31, June 2 and 3, 1893.

[186] June 16, 1893.

[187] June 1, 7, 8, Aug. 12, 15, 17, 1893.

McCandless, Emmeluth, Tenney, Waterhouse, Young, Hatch, and Allen were not.[188] The *Advertiser* added its testimony by maintaining that, of the 2,000 names on the rolls of the Annexation Club, only thirty-four or about one and a half per cent were of missionary origin.[189]

* * * * *

Meanwhile Blount had inquired of Gresham whether Bowen and Sewall enjoyed diplomatic status. The Secretary, in a letter of instructions which the Commissioner received on May 17, repudiated both of them as intruders, and supported Blount's position by appointing him Minister in Stevens's stead. On the preceding day, in order to quiet the claims of both parties in the city, he had published his instructions as Commissioner. One sentence in the statement which Blount made to the press upon that occasion had a soothing effect: "While I shall abstain from interference between conflicting forces of whatever nationality for supremacy, I will protect American citizens not participating in such conflict."[190] On May 19 he printed his appointment as Minister, and presented the credentials to President Dole on May 23.

Feeling between him and the Provisional Government continued to improve, because Annexationists perceived that his purpose was

[188] The *Star* returned to the subject frequently. For instance, on Oct. 25, 1893, it gave the following figures touching the number of missionary descendants who were then in office: Out of eighteen members of the Executive and Advisory Councils, only three were of missionary origin; of seven connected with the Supreme Court, including attachés, only one was "tainted"; in the lower courts there was none; two of sixteen in the Department of the Interior; one of five in the Customs Bureau; none in the Bureau of Agriculture; two of eight in the Department of Finance; two of seven in the Department of the Attorney General; one of seven in the Board of Immigration; two of fourteen in the Board of Health; none in the Board of Education; and one in the Board of Crown Land Commissioners. These figures did not, of course, include Minister Thurston who was descended from missionaries, and who was the master mind of both the Revolution and the Government.

[189] April 10, 1893. Again on April 5, 1893, the *Advertiser* declared that, of the 101 Cabinet members since 1842, only eight were missionaries or sons of missionaries; namely, Dr. G. P. Judd, Dr. Richard Armstrong, A. F. Judd, W. N. Armstrong, Dr. Wm. Richards, E. O. Hall, L. A. Thurston and W. R. Castle.

[190] Blount, p. 68. Reasons for publishing were given in his testimony to the Morgan Committee, p. 392.

to investigate, not to overturn. His withdrawal of the two marines, who had been stationed at the Legation during Stevens's tenure, added to the feeling of good will.[191] The *Star,* which, a few days earlier, had been lashing into him, said that he was doing a good job, was getting the facts fairly, and was preparing "a judicial document." The *Advertiser* thought that as Minister he would be "capable, wise and just." And the Royalist *Bulletin* declared that his appointment as successor to Stevens was one of the friendliest acts the United States ever did for Hawaii.[192] Sewall at once wrote Minister Blount that he had never had any political powers; that he had already published a denial; and that the supposed interview at San Francisco in which he claimed diplomatic authority had never taken place. He enclosed statements from the President, the Minister of Finance, and the Attorney General of the Provisional Government to prove he had never claimed either "quasi-official" or "official" authority.[193]

The appointment of Blount as Minister helped to clear up his ambiguous position in Honolulu, but it was personally distasteful to him. When he sought "Some honorable recognition" from Cleveland, he requested that it be "of a temporary nature."[194] He meant just that. Upon receiving his commission as American representative at Honolulu on May 17, he dutifully took the oath—administered by Consul General Severance—but sent his resignation in the same despatch to the Secretary of State which contained a copy of his oath. He told the Secretary that he regretted the appointment, but supposed that it was "desirable to the President and yourself that Mr[.] Stevens' connection with the Legation should be promptly severed."[195] The *New York Tribune* thought

[191] Skerrett to Secretary of the Navy, May 23, 1893, No. 31268, Bureau of Navigation.

[192] All three editorials were enclosed in Severance to Quincy, No. 201, May 22, 1893, Consular Letters.

[193] Sewall to Blount, May 23, 1893, with enclosures, sewed into the volume which contains Blount's despatches as Minister. Sewall, who had been appointed during Cleveland's first term to several consular posts, now deserted the President's policy and joined that of the Annexationist Republicans (*Kennebec Journal,* June 2, 1893). Sewall's defection from the Democracy won him the appointment as Minister to Hawaii under McKinley.

[194] Blount to Gresham, March 6, 1893, Cleveland MSS.

[195] Blount to Gresham, No. 1, May 24, 1893, Despatches; printed in *House Ex. Doc. 48* (53 Cong. 2 Sess.), p. 155.

that "Mr. Blount's mission was a mistake" and that he ought to be brought home.[196] By that time even the Democratic New York *World* had come to the conclusion that he was not "an ideal person for the delicate work in hand there, and it is unlikely that his tenure of the office will be a long one." Moreover, he was "a man of narrow and dense mind" who did not know when to talk and when to be silent.[197] Blount kept reminding the State Department that, as he desired to be relieved, his successor should be chosen at once.[198] The *Philadelphia Inquirer* declared that if he wanted to come home, he should be permitted to do so, for, "About the only thing which he is holding down where he is is the American flag. And he ought to be hoisting that up."[199]

The twin problems of freedom of the press and Royalist factionalism continued to be chronic headaches for the Provisional Government. For instance, on April 14, while discussing the seditious editorials of the *Holomua,* the Councils expanded the debate by canvassing the entire situation. As a consequence of numerous rumors about Royalist uprisings, the Commander in Chief was instructed to organize, at his own discretion, companies of rifle and minute men for the preservation of public order.[200] There was also a demand for a housecleaning of Royalist officeholders, as a matter of self-protection; and again the *Advertiser* took a high stand, namely, that the Provisional Government was not interested in spoils, but in the great aim of union with the United States.[201] On April 27 the Councils met, this time in special session, to discuss the prevalent rumors about conspiracies. On May 1 Emmeluth introduced a resolution which provided that all agitation for the restoration of the Queen, establishment of a republic,[202] or against annexation would come within the meaning of the Sedition Act of January 30, 1893, and was punishable by

[196] May 8, 1893.

[197] May 11 and 13, 1893.

[198] Blount to Gresham, No. 4, June 1, 1893, Despatches; and telegram, May 31, 1893, in Ciphers Received, No. 1, p. 266, *op. cit.*

[199] Clipped by *Kennebec Journal,* June 15, 1893.

[200] EAC.

[201] April 12 and 21, 1893.

[202] For instance, the Royalist agitator, R. W. Wilcox, wanted an independent republic (*Advertiser,* April 17, 25, 26, 1893).

law. It was referred to the Executive Council.[203] On May 4 a law was enacted regulating the printing of newspapers.[204]

On May 4 Admiral Skerrett reported that there was every "indication that the Provisional Government is gaining and increasing their [its] friends,"[205] and yet submerged rumblings kept the Government on the alert. The Annexationists blamed the agitation on the Royalists, whose spirits had risen now that Blount was investigating the Queen's case. Two native papers had dared to become so outspoken that the editors were arrested for libel. One of them was G. C. Kenyon, already referred to as editor of the *Holomua,* who was placed in custody for speaking of Stevens as "an ambitious, seeking-for-world-fame, 'bucolic,' allegedly-senile-and-idiotic diplomat trying to [carry] out an absolutely anti-American-in-sentiment and-origin policy of Imperial Jingoism."[206] J. E. Bush, another native leader of some prominence, published in *Ka Leo* a libelous article against Stevens, copied from an Ohio newspaper.[207] He was arrested for lying about Government bonds selling below par.[208] As a partial solution of its troubles with the press, the Government made the printing committee the official medium between the Councils and the newspapers. It was hoped that this reform would prevent the sort of garbled news items that had been trickling out unofficially.[209] Admiral Skerrett, who had been so complacent on May 4, wrote on May 23 that he had found it wise not to send the *Boston* and the *Adams* on target practice, "because of the continued agitation among people of certain classes, in, and about Honolulu."[210]

This agitation was extremely embarrassing, but worse trouble was coming. At the very time the Provisional Government was trying to impress Commissioner Blount with its financial stability,

[203] EAC, May 1, 1893; also *Star,* May 1, in Blount, p. 37.

[204] *Laws of the Provisional Government . . . Acts 1 to 42,* enclosed in Severance to Quincy, No. 221, Sept. 5, 1893, Consular Letters.

[205] Skerrett to Secretary of Navy, May 4, 1893, No. 30046, Bureau of Navigation.

[206] *Star,* May 13, 1893.

[207] Clippings from *ibid.,* enclosed in Severance to Quincy, No. 201, May 22, 1893, Consular Letters.

[208] *Star,* May 13, 1893.

[209] EAC, May 25, 1893.

[210] Skerrett to Secretary of Navy, May 23, 1893, No. 31268, Bureau of Navigation.

Claus Spreckels, the sugar magnate, endeavored to throw it into bankruptcy by foreclosing on a loan. Spreckels's attitude toward the Revolution had received varying descriptions in the United States. Some papers charged him with being the wirepuller behind the overthrow of the Queen in order to gain a sugar bounty. But the truth was that he was opposed to the Revolution, and especially to annexation,[211] because he felt that if Hawaii were joined to the United States, the importation of cheap contract labor, which he used on his plantations, would be ended.

According to Alexander, the Provisional Government historian, Spreckels saw an opportunity of restoring the Queen by means of a financial maneuver. He probably knew that many people were refusing to pay taxes because they felt that, inasmuch as the Provisional Government had not been popularly elected, it was therefore illegal.[212] In any event the Treasury was so low before the Revolution that the Wilcox Cabinet had had to borrow $95,000 to pay withdrawals from the Postal Savings Bank. The money, secured from Spreckels in December, 1892, was due on June 1, 1893. In addition to this obligation, the sum of $30,000 was owed on an English loan, payable in London on July 1. Spreckels had some kind of clandestine influence with the Queen upon which he hoped to capitalize if she were restored.[213] Feeling that, with the Provisional Government Treasury empty, he could force the Annexationists out of power, Spreckels advised Liliuokalani to select a Cabinet.

As early as April 11 the finance committee of the Advisory Council had reported on the necessity of reducing appropriations to all departments in order to have a surplus of $30,000 ready to meet the interest on the London-held bonds. The report was

[211] In 1891 Spreckels outlined his attitude on Hawaiian-American relations. He believed that the Hawaiian Islands were of tremendous economic value to the United States, because both trade and shipping had been built up between the two countries. He favored the improvement of Pearl Harbor and desired closer commercial connections. But he was opposed to annexation. Said he: "No one could be more opposed to their annexation to the United States than I am." See his "The Future of the Sandwich Islands," in *North American Review,* 152 (March, 1891), 287-292.

[212] *Advertiser,* April 14, 1893.

[213] Alexander, *op. cit.,* p. 85, is authority for the statement that, during the Bowen-Sewall episode, Spreckels had seen the Queen and encouraged her to hope for his support.

adopted.[214] At a special session on May 29, S. M. Damon, the newly appointed Minister of Finance, asked the Councils how he should raise Spreckels's $95,000.[215] On May 31, Mr. Damon, in the words of Alexander, "went out on the street and raised the $95,000 for the government in half an hour. Not only was Mr. Spreckels paid in full to his intense disgust, but the $30,000 of interest on the London debt was remitted by the mail of June 6th."[216] Everyone was relieved when, a few weeks later, "Bombastes Furioso," as Spreckels was called, left for the mainland.[217] When former Minister Stevens heard about these intrigues, he penned Dole a worried letter from Augusta.[218]

In the last days of May, 1893, just as Spreckels was expecting to throw the Government into financial straits, three sticks of "giant powder," which were found near the barracks, produced fears of a native insurrection.[219] Colonel Soper had already informed Marshal E. G. Hitchcock of a petition which was going around town and being signed largely by British subjects. The petition was for the purpose of asking the British warship *Hyacinth* to stay in the harbor in order to protect the signers; and rumor said that if a hundred persons so requested the ship would remain. Those who affixed their names to the paper included C. B. Wilson, T. B. Walker, E. C. Norrie, and G. C. Kenyon.[220]

When President Dole informed the Councils that he knew about the sale of explosives to private persons, the Attorney Gen-

[214] EAC.

[215] *Ibid.*

[216] Alexander, pp. 88-89 and *Advertiser,* May 30, June 1, 7, 8, 1893. See also Skerrett to Secretary of Navy, May 31, 1893, in *House Ex. Doc. 48* (53 Cong. 2 Sess.), pp. 502-503.

[217] *Star,* June 19 and July 19, 1893.

[218] Said Stevens, in part: "What at this distance from you I now most fear is the disorganizing & damaging influence of Claus Sprecklеs [*sic*] in the Islands. The exposure of his cause & his motives in the United States helps the cause of Annexation & the Pro. Government. Can you hold your ground securely against him in the Islands? I hope you can & will, & I so pray. The fear of his insolent & corrupting domination ought to, & probably does, operate as a strong stimulous [*sic*] to unity." Stevens to Dole, July 16, 1893, President's Files, Archives.

[219] Blount to Gresham, No. 5, June 1, 1893, Despatches; *Star,* June 5, 1893.

[220] Soper to Hitchcock, May 30, 1893, "Official Dole Files 1877-1893," in Archives.

eral introduced a bill to make it unlawful to possess explosives.[221] The military weakness of the Government was so clear that on June 10 it was decided to form a Citizen Guard.[222] To allay rumors that were circulating among the natives touching Liliuokalani's safety, the Councils invited her last Foreign Minister, Samuel Parker, to present himself. He was told that all tales to the effect that the Queen would be harmed or deported were false, and that if she thought she was in personal danger the Government would offer all the protection needed.[223]

At the very time these stirring events were going on, the Provisional Government was in the midst of an unfortunate controversy with the veteran newspaperman, Charles Nordhoff of the *New York Herald,* who had arrived on the same vessel with Bowen and Sewall. Minister Blount, harried with the details of getting his investigation over, was an unwilling participant in the dispute.[224] Castle, who had returned to Honolulu, wrote to Thurston, several days after Nordhoff's arrival, that the reporter was known to be unfriendly towards annexation, but that it might be possible to reach him by showing his daughter a good time, just as the church ladies were doing for Mrs. Blount.[225] If these methods were tried, Nordhoff's daughter seemed to have as little influence over her father as Mrs. Blount must have had over her husband; for Nordhoff began to send some spicy, anti-Annexationist correspondence back to the *Herald.*

On April 25 the *Herald* had published one of his letters in which he gave a list of the members of the Provisional Government who he said had signed a petition for the lottery bill. When the Royalist *Bulletin* republished the article in Honolulu, the Provisional Government rose up in a mighty rage. There was also no little objection to Nordhoff's statement that Minister Stevens, abetted by Dole, had been trying to alarm the Queen into abdicating and into

[221] EAC, June 1 and 2, 1893. The bill became law on June 15.

[222] *Ibid.* The law did not finally pass until August 18.

[223] *Ibid.,* June 9, 1893.

[224] Documents were printed in *House Ex. Doc. 48* (53 Cong. 2 Sess.), pp. 157 *ff.;* Skerrett described the affair in his despatch of May 23, 1893, No. 31268, to the Secretary of Navy, Bureau of Navigation.

[225] Castle to Thurston, April 8, 1893, M&C.

ceding Hawaii to the United States.[226] Stevens, about to embark for Maine, called upon Blount, "exceedingly bitter" against Nordhoff's "treasonable conduct" in "conspiring with the Royalists" to overthrow the Provisional Government.[227] Almost daily the Annexationist papers published editorials during May and June castigating Nordhoff for his articles, which the *Advertiser* called "his dirty work."[228] The *Star,* in accordance with its pugnacious defense of annexation, tried its hand at poetry:

> Abou Charles Nordhoff (may his tribe catch fleas)
> Awoke one night upon the island seas . . .

This imitation of Hunt's lines ended with the choice couplet:

> . . . men who play the "liar" best:
> And lo! Charles Nordhoff's name led all the rest.[229]

At a special session of the Executive and Advisory Councils on May 22, a show of hands proved that not one had signed the lottery petition; therefore a resolution was passed ordering Nordhoff's appearance next day[230] to explain what was considered to be more than a mere breach of etiquette. Nordhoff assured Minister Blount that the republication of his letter in the *Bulletin* was without his knowledge or consent.[231] When Nordhoff did not show up, Attorney General Smith was instructed to proceed against him. Smith informed Nordhoff that the statement made in the *Bulletin* was "known to be false and is regarded as malicious and libellous. Unless you retract the same at once and give the retraction equal publicity with the libel, proceedings will be instituted against you."[232]

[226] Attorney General W. O. Smith to Nordhoff, May 22, 1893, enclosure 2, in Blount to Gresham, No. 2, May 24, 1892 (clerical error for 1893), Despatches; printed in *House Ex. Doc. 48* (53 Cong. 2 Sess.), pp. 156 *ff*.

[227] Blount to Gresham, No. 2, *ibid.*

[228] May 19, 1893. See also May 5, 22, 24, *etc.*

[229] May 6, 1893. See also May 5, 20, June 3, *etc.*

[230] EAC, May 22, 1893; enclosure 3 in Blount to Gresham, No. 2, *op. cit.* F. J. Wilhelm was on the original Advisory Council and he had signed the lottery petition. Perhaps he was not present at the show of hands.

[231] Nordhoff to Blount, May 23, 1893, sewed into the volume of Blount's despatches as Minister.

[232] EAC, May 23, 1893; Smith to Nordhoff, May 22, 1893, enclosure 2, in Blount's No. 2, *op. cit.*

Nordhoff sought refuge at the American Legation because he said he was threatened with tar and feathers. The editor of the *Star* saw Admiral Skerrett, told him about the threats, and asked him to do what he could to protect Nordhoff. Skerrett wrote to Blount that the situation was "somewhat graver" and that he hoped "you will not underrate the excitement."[233] Blount suggested that if the Provisional Government did not like Nordhoff, it should ask him to leave, but the Minister protested to Dole against the libel charge and the threats of doing the journalist bodily harm. Dole did not answer. Blount reported to Gresham that the incident had "produced intense resentment."[234]

In protesting again to President Dole, Blount said that the United States would not stand for any such treatment to one of its citizens and used as precedent the Cutting case, in which the Mexican Government at one time had imprisoned an American citizen for something he had published in the United States. American authorities demanded Cutting's release, and enforced the demand.[235] Blount said he doubted that Nordhoff would apologize and that he would not advise Nordhoff to do so. "The New York Herald is a paper not published in the Hawaiian Islands and the proposition that the government thereof can take jurisdiction of the author of the article aforesaid . . . is wholly inadmissible." The warrant to appear before the Councils was "a violation of the rights of Mr. Nordhoff as an American citizen." Blount continued in terms which showed that he was coming to some definite conclusions in reference to the subject of his inquiry:

> When I remember how, on the 16th of January last, at the request of your leading citizens, American troops were landed and brought quiet to the homes of the people of this city, it is passing strange to me to find an eminent citizen of the United States subjected to such outrage at the hands of the Provisional Government. . . .
>
> While I desire to promote the Kindliest feelings between your Government and mine I shall not forget that

[233] Enclosed in Blount to Gresham, No. 3, May 29, 1893, Despatches.

[234] Blount to Gresham, No. 2, *op. cit.*

[235] Severance to Quincy, No. 201, May 22, 1893, Consular Letters. The decision of the lower Mexican court in the Cutting case is given in Manley O. Hudson, *Cases and Other Materials on International Law* (St. Paul, 1929), pp. 585-590.

> one of the proudest reflections of the American people is their disposition and ability to protect an American citizen throughout the civilized world.[236]

This was a spread-eagle stump-speech of no mean proportion, and it seems to have brought the Provisional Government to bay. On May 23 Dole wrote that he was sorry for the threats made against Nordhoff, who would be protected to the full extent of the Government's power.[237] Dole informed Blount that the Hawaiian Government would not prosecute "for what was suggested as contempt against the Advisory Council."[238] The *Star* thought that Nordhoff's "guilt is patent," but he had been able to evade the consequences by an appeal to a law higher than the Hawaiian. It made fun of Nordhoff's running to Blount for protection, because the threats of tar and feathers were merely idle talk. The *Star* felt pretty sure that Nordhoff was trying to make a sensation for the *New York Herald*.[239]

The Councils, busy with other matters, did not take up the subject again until June 15 when the Attorney General suggested it might be wise to drop the case.[240] Councillor Emmeluth did not want Nordhoff to get off without some official criticism, and so on June 19 offered a resolution whose last shaft was that "the persistent *detractions* of this *government* and its *purposes* by *Mr. Chas. Nordhoff* have earned him the *contempt of these Councils*." The resolution was not seconded, and there the matter rested, except for unceasing press criticism. When the reporter left the islands, the *Advertiser* said goodbye and good riddance.[241] The *Star* vented its spleen upon him at every opportunity.[242] The *Bulletin* of course reprinted[243] his *Herald* articles with praise long after he had returned to the United States.

* * * * *

All these events, most of which were crowded into the last days

[236] Blount to Dole, May 22, 1893, enclosed in Blount to Gresham, No. 2, *op. cit.*

[237] Dole to Blount, enclosed in *ibid.*

[238] Enclosed in Blount to Gresham, No. 3, *op. cit.*

[239] Enclosed in *ibid.*

[240] EAC, June 15, 1893.

[241] June 21, 1893. Also June 27.

[242] For instance, July 3, and Aug. 11, 1893.

[243] For instance, July 12, 1893.

of May, 1893,[244] riled the Provisional Government, not only against its enemies in Hawaii, but against the American Government as well. For, if the annexation treaty had not been killed by the new Administration, union with the United States would have made such difficulties, through which the Provisional Government had been passing, impossible. Furthermore, if the protectorate had not been ended, conditions would have been better. The Provisional Government determined, therefore, to carry its grievances to Washington.

In two interviews, June 14 and 16, 1893, Minister Thurston attempted to present to Secretary Gresham the dismay of the Provisional Government at the dilatory tactics of American officials in reference to annexation, and to ask what they intended to do in the future. The Minister did not get very far. Gresham cleverly turned the conversation into a series of questions which soon had Thurston on the defensive. Instead of directing the guns upon Gresham, he found himself facing a barrage from his intended victim.

Gresham at once took command of the situation by forcing Thurston to admit that the Provisional Government represented only a minority, established as it was against the wishes of the majority. Thurston's answer was that he did not believe in ignorant people exercising the suffrage. Gresham then inquired whether Thurston had not made speeches in the House of Nobles on September 14 and October 17, 1892, avowing his loyalty to the Queen and predicting that the United States would never annex Hawaii.[245] His answer was that in July, 1892, he and several others held "a consultation" on Hawaiian affairs and decided that the monarchy must go. This decision, made six months (according to his reckoning) before he made the speeches protesting his fealty to Liliuokalani, was not "publicly proclaimed." The stenographer reported that Thurston was "Evidently embarrassed."

[244] Hence Skerrett's decision not to send the two American warships on target practice.

[245] Gresham probably learned about Thurston's previous protestations of support to the Queen from the Royal emissary, E. C. MacFarlane. The latter, on Sept. 13, 1893, seemingly to justify what he had formerly charged orally, sent to the Secretary certain passages from Thurston's speeches of Sept. 14 and Oct. 17, 1892 (MacFarlane to Gresham, Sept. 13, 1893, Notes from Hawaii).

Gresham then showed Thurston a letter written by Dole, in which the President had said that the Provisional Government would apply to some other foreign power, if the United States did not annex. Thurston tried to explain it away, but his effort was rather lame. In fact, he was so roughly handled that he said: "I am not satisfied with this interview, and should like to have another conversation upon the same subject."

Two days later he returned and inquired why the United States was asking whether a majority of Hawaiians favored annexation, when the Provisional Government was not questioning the United States as to whether a majority of Americans favored it. He added: "I do not think the people of the Islands are fit for self-government; nothing but a strong government, a one man power, would meet the conditions."[246]

Thurston was conscious of the fact that he had failed in his intentions; indeed, far from giving a polite denunciation to the United States for its attitude, he had been driven from pillar to post himself. He determined, therefore, upon using a method by which he could have his say without being shunted off course by annoying queries from Gresham. In a note dated June 19, he informed the Secretary that the "object for which the mission [the five Commissioners] was appointed is still the firm policy of the Hawaiian Government, the furtherance of which it has been decided to entrust to my care." He went on to say that his Government directed him to inform Gresham of the effect of the present uncertainty and to be advised of the course to be pursued. Referring to the recent crises in Honolulu, he stated that the delay of the United States in deciding upon annexation was causing "a feverish state of mind"; business was bad, capital was timid, the Government credit was endangered, enemies of the Provisional Government were encouraged, a large armed force had to be kept prepared for any exigency, and American investments in the islands were being menaced. "It is important for the Hawaiian Government to know the intention of the United States Government concerning annexation at as early a date as possible, as, if annexation is not to take place, the methods of treating local conditions

[246] Miscellaneous Archives, Memoranda of Conversations with the Secretary of State, 1893-1898, conversations of June 14 and 16, 1893.

in Hawaii must be radically different from those to be pursued if annexation is to take place." He pressed for a decision.[247]

* * * * *

During this time Blount had been sending despatches back to Gresham, giving broad hints of his growing conviction that there had been something rotten in Hawaii in the preceding January.[248] He usually enclosed copies of the most striking testimony; as a result, the Cleveland Administration had a good idea what his final report would be. Some of his letters got into the press; and of course correspondents like Nordhoff were forwarding revealing disclosures home. In April the American public began to receive proof, aside from partisan charges, that Stevens had recognized the Provisional Government before the Queen surrendered.[249]

Some of the results of these revelations were used by Judge Thomas M. Cooley in an article in the *Forum* which was widely reprinted and commented upon. He excoriated the Provisional Government for taking power without seeking popular consent. A provisional government, said the Judge, was a temporary method of securing order; and yet the Hawaiian Provisional Government was spending its time pressing for annexation instead of keeping order. Moreover, it had no delegated powers to offer the islands to the United States. If the United States made a colony out of Hawaii, such an act would be a violation of the American Constitution. It was a bad precedent to annex territory different in race, culture, and language. Texas was no precedent; and unless the minority whites could be considered as spokesmen for all the people, annexation was morally wrong.[250] These views received more extended circulation when the *Literary Digest* printed a con-

[247] Thurston to Gresham, June 19, 1893, Notes from Hawaii. No answer was ever given to the note. The last sentence would make it appear that the Provisional Government was thinking of proclaiming a republic if annexation failed.

[248] For instance, April 26 (pp. 13-24); May 4 (pp. 35-37); and May 6 (pp. 59-62). All paging as in his Report.

[249] See New York *Nation,* April 27, May 11, and May 18.

[250] Thomas M. Cooley, "Grave Obstacles to Hawaiian Annexation," in *Forum,* XV (June, 1893), 389-407.

densation of the article.[251] Honolulu papers gave the essay considerable publicity.

* * * * *

Blount received a momentary flash of popularity in the eyes of Americans for his handling of the celebration on July 4, 1893. It had long been customary for Americans in the islands fittingly to honor Independence Day. Blount printed a request for all who were interested in such an observance to meet him at his hotel to make plans.[252] The result was that "the National Holiday July Fourth was most enthusiastically observed by American residents." Minister Blount was President of the Day; the address was made by Lieutenant Lucien Young, U.S.N.; and Commander Nelson, U.S.N., read the Declaration of Independence.[253] Meanwhile, taking advantage of the occasion, the Annexation Club started the distribution among the natives of printed copies of the American Constitution, whose title, translated into Hawaiian, was KUMUKANAWAI O AMERICA HUIPUIA.[254]

Despite all this fanfare, Admiral Skerrett reported that "the stability and solidity of the Provisional Government is not considered to be all that has impressed me formerly." There had been three arrests for conspiracy; the Attorney General, unable to

[251] *Literary Digest,* VII (June 10, 1893), 142-143. The impression made upon his readers by Judge Cooley's arguments was brought out five years later, when, amidst the debates over final annexation, Senator William P. Frye of Maine secured leave to print, as a Government document, an answer to Cooley's article by the late John Dean Caton, former Chief Justice of Illinois. The reply had been written by Caton for Secretary Gresham's information, but was never printed at the time. It was found among Caton's papers and was snapped up by Frye, a rabid imperialist, for propaganda purposes. See *Sen. Doc. 214* (55 Cong. 2 Sess.), pp. 1-15. For other indications of public and private opinion see Folio marked "Printed Material," in Cleveland MSS. Crammond Kennedy, on June 16, 1893, sent to the President a pamphlet entitled, *Some Phases of the Hawaiian Question* which was a reprint of three articles he had written to the *Washington Post* and the New York *Post.* See also Detwiler to Cleveland, April 28, 1893, Cleveland MSS.

[252] *Advertiser,* enclosed in Severance to Quincy, June 21, 1893. No. 204, Consular Letters.

[253] Same to same, No. 207, *ibid.; Advertiser,* July 5, 1893.

[254] Two copies enclosed in same to same, No. 209, July 12, 1893, *ibid.*

prove the charges, kept the suspects in jail without bail.[255] The writ was suspended in two districts on the Island of Hawaii.[256] "It would appear," said the Admiral, "that the iron heel of Military Law is really what serves to keep the Provisional Government in authority." Rumors of uprisings were rife, discontent was prevalent, and the natives were easily led. Skerrett's conclusion is most revealing: the Provisional Government was "not elected by the vote of the people and it is believed, were it submitted to a popular vote, the present Government would be ousted."[257] The Admiral's statement hardly needed proof, but when Paul Neumann wrote[258] an open letter to Dole asking for a plebiscite, the *Star* declared: "The talk of a plebiscite by an aboriginal race which is lapsing into paganism and is led by unscrupulous politicians, is obvious clap-trap."[259]

In the face of all kinds of obstacles, the Provisional Government was doing its best to strengthen itself. In order to broaden the base of support and to answer charges that the Government was an American oligarchy, a Portuguese, J. P. Mendonca, and a native, John Ena, were chosen by the Councils to be members of the Advisory Council.[260] This move did not satisfy the opposition, which pointed out that neither Mendonca nor Ena had been popularly elected; but, as pliable tools for the Annexationists, they had been selected by the very body in which they were to sit. As if to prove that the critical times were over, it was decided on June 19 that the Councils should meet weekly, instead of daily or twice daily, as had been the custom ever since the organization of the régime.[261] The decision eased the burden for many members whose businesses had suffered. Another reform was the vesting in the Advisory Council of all the powers, including pardon, which pertained to the old Royal Privy Council.[262]

[255] These were T. B. Walker, Archibald Sinclair, and E. C. Crick. They were later acquitted (*Advertiser,* June 24 and Aug. 29, 1893).

[256] June 30, 1893, in President's Files, 1893, Archives.

[257] Skerrett to Secretary of Navy, No. 33568, June 28, 1893, Bureau of Navigation; printed in *House Ex. Doc. 48* (53 Cong. 2 Sess.), p. 504.

[258] *Bulletin,* July 11, 1893.

[259] *Star,* July 12, 1893.

[260] EAC, May 29 and June 29, 1893.

[261] *Ibid.,* June 19, 1893.

[262] *Ibid.,* July 8, 1893.

Minister Blount was drawing his investigation to a close. Toward the end of his stay, he took a short trip into the interior to secure information on the attitude of the natives. By July Gresham began to demand that the report be completed. Finished on July 17, it was forwarded by naval mail to the Secretary on July 25.[263]

While preparing to leave for home, Blount got into another argument—this time over a fraudulent story which made him a contributor to a fund for the purchase of a cane for Claus Spreckels who had recently tried to bankrupt the Government and who had just left for the mainland. Blount demanded that President Dole investigate at once.[264] The Minister admitted that the incident was silly, and that he would not have made it a subject for diplomatic correspondence, except "that the Republican press of the United States may attempt to discredit me on a false state of facts."[265] Dole directed that the chairman of the committee which handed the cane to Spreckels disavow the placing of Blount's name on the list. It was found that the cane had been inscribed with the words: "Ave, Claus, Morituri te Salutans. In Memoriam. From Your Fellow Citizens, Doomed to Die At the hands of the Murder Society of the Annexation Club." Under this inscription was a long roster of names, including those of Liliuokalani and Blount.[266] Chairman Charles Creighton, a former Royal Cabinet member, apologized, but the incident dragged on long after Blount left the islands.[267] The last diplomatic communication relating to it was dated November 19, 1893.[268]

Having already resigned as Minister at the time he took the oath, Blount gave to Secretary Gresham, on July 31, formal notice of his intention to leave. He said the condition of his private affairs necessitated an immediate departure. "I assume," he averred, "that neither you nor the President under existing circum-

[263] Blount to Gresham, telegram, July 25, 1893, Despatches.

[264] Same to same, No. 6, July 26, 1893, *ibid.*

[265] Same to same, No. 7, July 31, 1893, *ibid.*

[266] Dole to Creighton, July 24, 1893, enclosed in *ibid.*

[267] Creighton to Dole, July 26, 1893; Dole to Creighton, July 26, 1893, in Foreign Office Files, Archives; EAC, July 27, 1893; *Advertiser,* July 20, 21, 27, 1893.

[268] Willis to Gresham, No. 6, Nov. 19, 1893, Despatches; printed in *House Ex. Doc. 70* (53 Cong. 2 Sess.), p. 4.

stances could urge my further continuance here. . . . I have discharged my duty the best I could considering I was surrounded by persons interested in misleading me, and in my inability to compel answers from witnesses." His analysis of conditions on the islands, as he was leaving, is interesting:

> The condition of parties in the islands is one of quiescence. The action of the United States is awaited by all as a matter of necessity. This condition, it can be assumed, will remain until the proposition to annex is accepted or rejected. In the latter contingency no sudden movement is likely to occur. The present Government can only rest on the use of military force, possessed of most of the arms in the islands, with a small white population to draw from to strengthen it. Ultimately it will fall without fail. It may preserve its existence for a year or two, but not longer.[269]

As time neared for Blount's departure, all parties tried to be nice to him. Royalists, represented by the *Bulletin,* were sure he would report in favor of restoration, and the editor thought it was a studied insult for the band to play "Marching Through Georgia" as Blount embarked.[270] Annexationists, represented by the *Advertiser,* were satisfied he would make a decision favorable to them, and so he was given unstinted praise.[271] Particularly was this the case when, after Blount had called upon the Executive Council to say "goodbye," H. P. Baldwin told the members that Blount had informed him that "the United States is bound to look out for American interests here in one way or another; that he did not know the form it would take; that Cleveland had not expressed his sentiments on the subject to him."[272]

After writing Dole a letter regarding suffrage demands made by the Japanese (already discussed), Blount sailed for the United States on August 8, leaving the Legation Building in charge of Consul General Severance.[273] Skerrett was to act as diplomatic

[269] Blount, p. 164.

[270] *Bulletin,* Aug. 8 and 10, 1893.

[271] *Advertiser,* Aug. 8 and 30, 1893.

[272] Minutes of the Executive Council, Aug. 8, 1893, Archives. On the margin are the words: "Exit Blount."

[273] Severance to Blount (clerical error for Severance to Quincy), No. 216, Aug. 8, 1893, Consular Letters.

representative.[274] He arrived at San Francisco on August 15, from which place he telegraphed Gresham that he was willing to come to Washington, if required; otherwise he would proceed directly to Macon.[275]

Lest there be misunderstandings as to Skerrett's authority, Secretary Hilary Herbert at once despatched to him a cipher message which said: "I desire to impress upon you in the absence of U. S. Minister Blount that your sole duty is confined to that of an officer of the Navy. Although it is to be performed in the spirit of the instructions of Minister Blount which doubtless have been seen by you. Protect American citizens and American property but do not give aid physical or moral to either party contending for the government at Honolulu."[276]

Things were outwardly quiet, and yet Skerrett and Severance found that they had to be watchful. The Government even got into trouble with its own newspaper supporters when Arthur Johnstone, one of the editors of the *Advertiser,* was jailed for criticizing the frequent imprisonment of newspapermen without grand jury indictment. The *Star* came valiantly to its competitor's defense.[277] The *Bulletin,* which for months had been bewailing the loss of freedom of the press, no doubt enjoyed the spectacle. On August 24, Severance reported that there was considerable talk about a Royalist *émeute,* but both Annexationist papers ridiculed the rumor. "It goes without saying [said the *Star*] that, between the iron millstone of the United States and Provisional Governments the party of anarchy would be ground to powder." In spite of rumors that arms were being landed by Royalists, the *Star* minimized the reports because it believed that no one would dare break the neutrality laws of the United States; the "ex-Queen's

[274] Skerrett to Secretary of the Navy, No. 36440, Aug. 14, 1893, Bureau of Navigation.

[275] Blount to Gresham, telegram, Aug. 15, 1893, Despatches. Blount must have soon gone on to Washington because in several weeks he had an office next door to Gresham's ("Private Memo. for President Dole," written by Frank P. Hastings, Sept. 5, 1893, in M&E).

[276] Herbert to Skerrett, Aug. 16, 1893, in Ciphers Sent No. 1, p. 170; printed in *House Ex. Doc. 48* (53 Cong. 2 Sess.), p. 456.

[277] Aug. 14, 1893.

cause is now so dead that the arm of resurrection can never fathom its January grave."[278]

Notwithstanding this brave talk, the American Consulate was raided a few days later, and real fears of a Royalist uprising began to take shape. Severance found that nothing of value had been stolen from the Consulate, because all important papers were kept in the iron safe at the Legation. He felt sure that Royalists had committed the act. The Government provided a guard, but Severance apprehended no trouble. The *Advertiser* wrote up a sensational account of the burglary, which was sent as an Associated Press release to the United States.[279] The *Star,* commenting upon the raid, said that the Royalists might as well fold up, because there had been twenty-four separate rumors of movements to restore the Queen, not one of which materialized.[280] The Government took the talk seriously, however. For instance, on August 31 the Councils were informed of a rumored Royalist plot to get the natives drunk on September 2 and thus to start a rumpus.[281] The *Advertiser,* discussing the statement of many Royalists that the innate sense of justice of the United States would lead to a restoration, declared that the dynasty had never done right by Hawaii; that both Kalakaua and Liliuokalani had been weaklings; and that to re-establish the latter would be "an act of gross political injustice to the American colony and the bulk of the tax-payers of Hawaii."[282]

The incessant rumblings of Royalist factionalism caused a revival of the demand that "The Monarchists Must Go. The only Government which permits its enemies to hold office under it is the Provisional regime of Hawaii."[283] The *Star,* pointing to the fact that Dr. G. Trousseau, Royalist, was drawing $4,000 a year as port physician, declared that Annexationists had waited seven long months for the Government to place its friends on an equal footing with its enemies in reference to jobs. Nevertheless, added the *Star's* editor, the *Advertiser* continued to counsel delay in

[278] Enclosed in Severance to Quincy, No. 217, Aug. 24, 1893, Consular Letters.

[279] Enclosed in same to same, No. 218, Aug. 28, 1893, *ibid.*

[280] Enclosed in same to same, No. 223, Sept. 12, 1893, *ibid.*

[281] EAC, Aug. 31, 1893.

[282] Enclosed in Severance to Quincy, No. 223, *op. cit.*

[283] *Star,* Aug. 29, 1893.

housecleaning.[284] The *Star* denied that the Annexation Club, when it asked for patronage, was trying to copy Tammany Hall.[285]

Pressed by a resolution of the Annexation Club against monarchist partisans within the gates, the Councils were forced to do something. George Ross, the Auditor General, submitted that as a British subject he could hardly be expected to favor annexation because that would deprive him of his livelihood; an American protectorate would probably mean that he could continue his job.[286] This admission only increased the *Star's* cry to "Turn the rascals out!"[287] How, asked the editor, could the Provisional Government, in case it had to fight for its existence, maintain itself with anti-Annexationists within its own civil service? The chief result of this clamor was the dismissal of Trousseau;[288] and, in addition, official notice was taken of the rumors that Fred W. Wundenberg, clerk of the Supreme Court, was indulging in disloyal talk.[289] The statement by Ross gave point to the never-ceasing claims made by both Annexationist papers that the chief enemies of the Government were English subjects. They instanced Bishop Alfred Willis of the Anglican Church who put out an unfriendly *Honolulu Diocesan Magazine;* Theophilus H. Davies; and the editors of two of the Royalist newspapers.[290] The *Star* thought, however, that the Royalist *Bulletin* was not so dangerous because, having only a hundred and fifty readers, it was fast going under.[291]

Admiral Skerrett, in accordance with Herbert's warning of August 16, tried to carry out his instructions to the letter. At any rate, he was supposed to have told the British Minister to Hawaii that the American forces at Honolulu would not protect subjects of Britain in case of trouble. Wodehouse at once protested through diplomatic channels; and the British Foreign Office ordered Julian Pauncefote to see Washington officials about the matter. Herbert informed Acting Secretary of State, A. A. Adee, that Skerrett had not been so instructed; to the contrary he had been ordered to

[284] Aug. 28, 29, 30, 1893.
[285] Aug. 31, 1893.
[286] Minutes of the Executive Council, Sept. 2, 1893.
[287] Sept. 1, 1893.
[288] *Advertiser,* Sept. 5 and 6, 1893.
[289] Minutes of the Executive Council, Sept. 9, 1893, Archives.
[290] *Star,* Aug. 17 and Sept. 16, 1893; *Advertiser,* Sept. 16 and 18, 1893.
[291] *Star,* July 9 and *Advertiser,* Sept. 9 and 11, 1893.

"afford to British subjects and property such protection as has always been afforded by vessels of American fleets."[292] Herbert at once sent Skerrett an order to that effect.[293] Moreover, in order to end Skerrett's loose talking, Herbert wrote:

> I think I have observed from your correspondence an unconscious leaning on your part towards the new government in the Hawaiian Islands, and I write simply for the purpose of reminding you that the position the Government wishes you to occupy is that of absolute neutrality. By reviewing your instructions and the instructions given by the State Department to Minister Blount you will see that this Government does not intend to be the partisan either of the Queen or of the present government, and you are not to favor the one or the other by act, word or deed.[294]

* * * * *

Even before Blount left, the Provisional Government decided to ready itself to enter treaty negotiations, on the chance that the report favored annexation. As a result, another person to help Thurston was appointed. At first Charles R. Bishop, the capitalist and philanthropist, was approached but he refused to serve either officially or unofficially. He gave as his reasons that he felt annexation at that time was hopeless, that the sugar planters were opposed, and that if annexation was rejected finally he favored a regency for Kaiulani under a United States protectorate.[295] Professor William De Witt Alexander, who was historian, teacher, and former Privy Councillor, was then selected as co-Commissioner with Thurston. His secret instructions authorized him to be ready to negotiate the moment the time was ripe.[296] He did not take a new treaty along with him to Washington, as the *Bulletin*

[292] Herbert to Adee, Sept. 27, 1893, in Confidential Official Correspondence, No. 1, pp. 1 *ff.*, *op. cit.*

[293] Herbert to Skerrett, Sept. 27, 1893, in Ciphers Sent, No. 1, p. 174, *op. cit.*

[294] Same to same, Oct. 3, 1893, in Confidential Official Correspondence, *op. cit.*, pp. 31-32. On Nov. 16, Skerrett reported that he had communicated all the above information to Wodehouse (No. 37818½, Bureau of Navigation).

[295] Bishop to Dole, July 17, 1893, President's Files, Archives. Bishop was then in San Francisco.

[296] EAC, July 17, 1893; *Advertiser,* July 18, 1893. His commission, dated July 19, 1893, can be found in M&E.

opined that he did, nor was he ever officially presented to Gresham.[297] Frank P. Hastings, the Secretary of Legation, was at first dubious about the wisdom of choosing another Commissioner;[298] but, when no opportunity arose to negotiate, Hastings used Alexander for propaganda purposes and later admitted that the Professor's services were invaluable.[299] Alexander's main work turned out to be the aiding of Thurston and Hastings in their task of converting editors and Americans in general from opposition to belief in annexation.

During intervals when he was not needed to supervise his cyclorama at the Chicago Fair, Thurston busied himself at missionary work. He interviewed Charles A. Dana of the New York *Sun* and visited former Minister Stevens who was doing important editorial work for the cause in his Augusta paper. As a counterpart to Thurston's activity in giving facts and figures to newspapers in the United States, the Hawaiian Minister advised Dole that the Honolulu Annexationists should impress upon the natives the fact that monarchy was dead. When, said Thurston, "this idea penetrates the skulls of the great unwashed electorate," the Kanakas would become Annexationist.[300] Hastings was doing his part by looking up the stories of previous United States acquisitions. He reported that he found no arguments which could be used by the Provisional Government, because its cause was so much better than those of Louisiana, Texas, and Alaska, when they were annexed.[301] Soon another propagandist was added to the staff in the person of William B. Oleson who shortly would publish, in collaboration with John L. Stevens, a history of Hawaii written from the Annexationist angle. Oleson did good work among the Eastern editors.[302]

[297] *Bulletin,* Aug. 25, 1893; Alexander to Dole, Aug. 21, 1893, M&E.
[298] Hastings had been sent to Washington in June, 1893.
[299] Hastings to Dole, private, Feb. 25, 1894, M&E.
[300] Thurston to Dole, confidential, Aug. 11, 1893, *ibid.*
[301] Hastings to Dole, Aug. 21, 1893, *ibid.*
[302] Alexander to Francis M. Hatch, acting Minister of Foreign Affairs, Sept. 22, 1893, *ibid.*

VI. QUIXOTICISM IN FOREIGN AFFAIRS

The problem of reading and digesting Blount's voluminous report[1] was a huge one for a methodical President and a busy Secretary of State; it was made less onerous, however, because, as has been pointed out, Blount had been transmitting copies of much of the testimony along with the conclusions which he was reaching. Gresham received the complete manuscript early in August. That by August 14 he had mastered much of it is clear from a third clash of words he had with Thurston on that date. Although the Hawaiian Minister had already been badly worsted by the Secretary of State on June 14 and 16, he seems to have been determined to find out what Gresham was learning from the report. At any rate on August 14 he decided to try again. This time he was better posted.

Thurston began by stating: "The surrender [of the Queen] was complete before Minister Stevens recognized us as the de facto Government[.]" It was not true, he maintained, that Stevens had previously agreed to recognize the insurgents if they held any building whatever. In fact, said Thurston, they could have established a provisional government even if American troops had not been present. Gresham's answer was: ". . . the naval forces were landed on Monday afternoon, and the proclamation was not read . . . until the next day. If you were able to establish a Provisional Government, unaided, by the military force of the United States on Tuesday, how was it that you were so feeble the afternoon of the day before that you had to ask the protection of the naval forces?" Thurston answered that they did not desire the American forces to aid them in the overthrow of the Royal Government. Moreover, he denied definitely that he was present at the meeting when Soper refused the command of the Revolutionary army until

[1] The report, including verbatim testimony, made about half a dozen huge volumes which are now housed in the National Archives. These volumes are separate from Blount's despatches as Minister. When the report was printed at the request of Congress, it totalled 684 pages. A comparison of the written original and the printed version shows very few errors—confined to omission of commas and looseness in copying capitals. As has been indicated the published version is *House Ex. Doc. 47* (53 Cong. 2 Sess.).

Thurston was supposed to have received Stevens's promise of support. When asked if Damon and others told the Queen to surrender because she would get justice from the United States, he replied: "I can not say that that was my understanding of the situation," because he was not present. He did deny, however, that the Queen had surrendered to the forces of the United States. When Gresham reminded him that Dole endorsed the surrender, he said Dole did not know what he was doing. His answer to the question whether Stevens recognized the new Government before the Royal forces had capitulated was: "I think not." He was certain that the insurgents could have succeeded without American aid; and Stevens "had no official information" of what was going on.[2]

This argument would indicate that Gresham had made up his mind as to the guilt of Stevens whether he had been able to read through all of Blount's report by that time or not. By September 14 he had thoroughly mastered the document; for, in a *"Confidential"* letter he wrote on that day, Gresham told Schurz he expected to read the latter's forthcoming article in *Harper's,* and continued:

> I can say to you in confidence that if anything can be established by proof, Mr. Blount's reports show that the action of the American Minister and the presence of the United States troops in Honolulu overawed the Queen, —put her in fear,—and induced her to abdicate and surrender to the so-called Provisional Government, with the understanding however, that her case would be fairly considered by the President of the United States. Should not this great wrong be undone? "Yes," I say decidedly. Aside from the President and Cabinet, this is more than I have said or written to any one, and you will understand the importance of not allowing this letter to fall into other hands.[3]

In addition to proving the friendly relations between Schurz and the Cleveland Administration in its early days, this letter shows clearly that the Secretary of State was an idealist (as was Schurz,

[2] Miscellaneous Archives, Memoranda of Conversations with the Secretary of State 1893-1898, *op. cit.*

[3] Gresham to Schurz, Sept. 14, 1893, Schurz MSS., CIX, 24135.

also) whose idealism might lead him into impractical paths. Even Schurz saw this, for, on September 24, after promising that Gresham's confidence in him would not be misused, he added that the Secretary's attitude was "unquestionably the correct one. It will, however, be a very delicate task completely to undo [?] the mischief that has been done. You are no doubt aware of the demagogic outcry [or oratory?] bound to spoil every act of justice and good policy in this matter, but I am glad to Know that nothing of the Kind will frighten you."[4]

In brief, if Gresham was to have his way, some effort would be made to undo Stevens's act and restore the Queen. The policy, enlightened and altruistic as it was, might well lead to difficulties, if not to a diplomatic impasse. Who, in the final analysis, originated it? Mrs. Gresham said that Cleveland "first yielded" to Gresham in his opinion that restoration was the only just procedure.[5] President Cleveland, whatever was done or whoever concocted it, was responsible; but it is hardly true that he originated the scheme. He admitted that he was weak on foreign affairs; and yet (as Henry James pointed out) he would naturally take a sympathetic view toward the natives and their Queen because of his "tem-

[4] Schurz to Gresham, Sept. 24, 1893, Gresham MSS., Box 6, Library of Congress; and Schurz MSS., CIX, 24144. Meanwhile Schurz continued to lash Stevens and the Annexationists in *Harper's Weekly,* no doubt having a considerable advantage over other editors, owing to his inside connections with Gresham and Cleveland. On Oct. 6 Gresham wrote him about his latest article: "I think it will do a great deal of good. . . . It is the best article of the kind that I have seen, and I sincerely hope to see something more from your pen upon the same subject." James Ford Rhodes thought Schurz's essay on Manifest Destiny would "have a large influence and do a great deal of good" (Schurz MSS., CIX, 24173). Charles Nordhoff also wrote Schurz his congratulations (Oct. 10, 1893, *ibid.,* 24181). On Nov. 11, 1893, Robert W. Wilcox, "Member of the last Hawaiian Legislature," wrote "Schultz" to "express my thanks as well as that of the Hawaiians toward your patriotic letter against the 'Annexation of these Islands to the United States' in the 'Harper's Magazine' of October" (CX, 24245, *ibid.*).

[5] Gresham, *Gresham, op. cit.,* II, 759. Sereno E. Bishop, in Alexander, *op. cit.,* p. 92, suggested that E. C. MacFarlane had some influence over Gresham. MacFarlane, who had been sent on a secret mission to Washington by Liliuokalani, had "long and confidential interviews" after September 10, with Blount and Gresham; these conversations enabled him to carry back to the Queen exclusive information regarding Administration policy, information which the Provisional Government was not fortunate enough to possess.

peramental generosity toward the under dog and his previous experience in protecting Indian tribes from spoliation."[6] Looking at the question from the moral angle, Cleveland laid "a straight course by the Eighth Commandment"; but when his attention was called to the dangerous outcome of Gresham's intentions, the President appreciated the seriousness of trying to overturn the Provisional Government which had already been recognized by the United States.[7]

James thought, after reading Gresham's letters, that the Secretary was willing to use force to restore Liliuokalani.[8] Gresham, a lawyer and judge, took the legalistic view of the Hawaiian case; but his wife and biographer declared that his attitude arose from his innate chivalry: "A woman in trouble, my husband would certainly side with her against the power, greed, and lust of man."[9] James believed it was "probably right to attribute the initiative"[10] to Gresham; Mrs. Gresham, however, averred it was impossible to say whether Cleveland or her husband originated the policy of restoration. She was willing to admit that both deserved credit. "Mr. Gresham's course in the case of Hawaii is in my opinion the most creditable act to himself and to his country of the long list of distinguished public services rendered by him during his incumbency of the Department of State."[11] James suggested that the policy may have been set the previous February, when (at the Lakewood, New Jersey, meeting) Cleveland, Gresham, D. S. Lamont, and Carlisle decided to pigeonhole Foster's treaty.[12]

* * * * *

Of course, neither the Provisional Government nor its representatives at Washington knew what was jelling in reference to Hawaii. For over three months, that is, from August 8 when Blount left, to November 16 when the news reached Honolulu, a daily guessing game went on as to what Blount had said and what Gresham planned to do. The secret was so well kept that no

[6] Henry James, *Richard Olney and His Public Service* (Boston and N. Y., 1923), p. 83.
[7] *Ibid.*, pp. 88-89.
[8] *Ibid.*, p. 84.
[9] Gresham, *Gresham*, II, 741, cited by *ibid.*, p. 83.
[10] James, *Olney*, p. 88.
[11] Gresham, *Gresham*, II, 776.
[12] James, *Olney*, p. 83. This conference has been discussed earlier.

leaks occurred at Washington; even the *New York Herald,* which was supposed to have some private lead into the State Department, was wrong when it printed a story to the effect that there would be merely the proclamation of a protectorate.[13]

During August the general tack taken by the Annexationist papers in Honolulu was like that of the *Star* on August 26: "The Democratic party cannot afford to leave these jeweled islands to be picked up either by a future Republican President and Congress and added to their escutcheon of success, or by one of the rival powers on the other side of the Atlantic." In other words, Cleveland would decide in favor of annexation because it was the commonsense thing to do.

Throughout September, despatch after despatch came to Dole from Thurston, Hastings, and Alexander containing plenty of rumor and gossip; but they always began and ended with words like these: ". . . we still remain in patient waiting by the political pool for the President to trouble the waters." Hastings, who wrote this sentence, predicted that Gresham would decide upon a protectorate, and then the Provisional Government must reorganize on a more permanent basis with the vote for property holders only.[14] He believed that a protectorate would be acceptable because the present Government was the one to be protected.[15] Thurston thought likewise.[16] Alexander, whose secret credentials to help write an annexation treaty were never used, prophesied that Cleveland would demand a plebiscite and then proclaim a protectorate over the government chosen by the people.[17] Alexander did not like the idea of a plebiscite because, as he said, "The time has passed when the Kanakas had the chief stake in the future of the Islands." He added that "Gresham still remains *mum";* not even the Vice President or the Chairman of the Senate Committee on Foreign Relations knew what was coming.[18]

Hastings predicted that if the President did not soon show his hand the Senate would draw the information out of him by resolu-

[13] Hastings to Dole, Oct. 7, 1893, M&E.
[14] Same to same, Sept. 4, 1893, confidential, *ibid.*
[15] Hastings to Thurston, Sept. 8, 1893, *ibid.*
[16] Thurston to Dole, telegram, Sept. 20, 1893, Official Dole Files, Archives.
[17] Alexander to Dole, Sept. 13, 1893, private and unofficial, M&E.
[18] Alexander to Hatch, Sept. 22, 1893, *ibid.*

tion.[19] In letter after letter, Hastings (who bore the brunt of the Legation activities because Thurston was at the Chicago Fair) informed Dole that there was no news and that he could not penetrate the veil.[20] Nevertheless Hastings perceived the rise of senatorial criticism. For instance, Senator William E. Chandler of New Hampshire denounced Cleveland for making an unconstitutional appointment when he sent Blount as Commissioner without senatorial confirmation. How wide Hastings was of the mark is shown by his statement to Thurston that he had good information to the effect that it was "an absolute impossibility" for restoration to be attempted.[21] And Alexander, after saying he expected Blount's report to be a partisan attack upon Stevens but that Stevens was able to take care of himself, added: "In spite of some sinister omens, I do not believe that any attempt will be made to dictate to the Provisional Government about our internal affairs. Nothing but Annexation would justify such interference."[22]

The Hawaiian representatives in the United States could find no information about Cleveland's plans, but they did continue with the task of influencing public opinion. The significant work being done just then was in the hands of Oleson who was achieving wonders with the American Board of Commissioners of Foreign Missions and with *Harper's Weekly* over which Carl Schurz held some kind of, as Oleson put it, "occult" influence. As a result of Oleson's persuasion, the ABCFM had sent a letter to Gresham demanding annexation. In reference to his missionary activity in New England, Oleson reported: "They are scared to death about Nevada Senators! Probably think Hawaiian Senators would favor lava money and fillibuster [*sic*] New York and Massachusetts into a passion."[23] Alexander had "done no lobbying" lately.[24]

Thurston's absence from the Legation caused some criticism at home. W. O. Smith in particular suggested that he should leave

[19] Hastings to Dole, Sept. 14, 1893, and "Private Memo. for President Dole," Sept. 5, written by Hastings, in *ibid.*

[20] Same to same, Sept. 22, 30, Oct. 2, 21, 22, 1893, *ibid.*

[21] Hastings to Thurston, Oct. 5, 1893, *ibid.*

[22] Alexander to Thurston, Oct. 20, 1893, *ibid.*

[23] Oleson to Thurston, Oct. 17, 1893, *ibid.*

[24] Alexander to Thurston, Oct. 21, 1893, and Alexander to Dole, Oct. 21, 1893, enclosing copy of ABCFM to Gresham, *ibid.*

the Chicago Fair and attend to his business at Washington.[25] This comment produced a hot answer from Thurston who reminded officials at Honolulu that, when he accepted the mission, he informed them he intended to help make expenses at the Fair if nothing was doing at Washington.[26] Unfortunately for him, the great news about Cleveland's plans regarding Hawaii broke while he was still at Chicago, and he was somewhat handicapped for several days before reaching Washington.

* * * * *

Gresham brought the Hawaiian problem, as viewed from the vantage point of Blount's report, before the Cabinet early in October. Attorney General Richard Olney, who did not attend the Lakewood conference because he had not yet been invited into the Cabinet,[27] and who, up to October, played little or no part in deciding the course to be pursued in regard to Hawaii, thought someone should attempt to point out to the visionaries, like Gresham, the insuperable dangers of a policy of restoration. Partly because as the law officer of the Cabinet his views would naturally be expected, and partly because, as he wrote, an "expression of opinion from each member of the Cabinet seemed to be invited last Friday," he submitted to Gresham on October 9 a paper which had considerable effect upon Cleveland's Hawaiian policy, and which, by the way, laid down a course of procedure which was later, of necessity, followed.

"The Hawaii business," Olney began, "strikes me as not only important, but as one that may require great delicacy in the handling. There is no question, it seems to me, that a great wrong was done"; it should be rectified if possible. But the "Stevens government," he reminded Secretary of State Gresham, was established by American forces and was recognized by the United States. How get rid of it, he asked, without subjecting its members to death or banishment? After all, it was an American undertaking, for the Revolutionists would never have arisen had they not been sure of United States backing. Olney suggested four basic points in carrying out any policy of restoration. First, "All

[25] Smith's circular of Sept. 18, 1893, and Hatch to Thurston, Oct. 10, 1893, *ibid.*

[26] Thurston to Dole, Oct. 21, 1893, *ibid.*

[27] James, *Olney, op. cit.*, p. 83.

the resources of diplomacy should be exhausted to restore the *status quo* in Hawaii by peaceful methods and without force." Second, if force was necessary, that was a matter for Congress to decide. Third, the United States must require of the Queen that, if reinstated, she give full pardon and amnesty to the officials of the Provisional Government. Fourth, he did not expect that any force would be needed.[28]

Olney later explained his reasoning behind this important opinion as follows: It "assumes rather than argues that the United States put the Queen off the throne by force and fraud and is directed to the practical question what the United States ought to do on that assumption."[29] In another place, after referring to Blount's report as "ammunition," Olney continued:

> A greater outrage upon a weak nation by a strong one could hardly be imagined. If, however, the question is whether, having been wrongfully dethroned by the United States, she can properly be reënthroned by the same power, the matter is a much more complex one. I wrote that letter to Judge Gresham (a copy of which I sent you and which must be strictly *entre nous*) because I thought that, while wholly right as to the wrong done by the United States in the deposition of the Queen, he did not fully realize the practical difficulties that might attend the attempt to restore her. . . . I don't mind saying to you that the letter was timely and I think kept the Administration from making a serious mistake.

He went on to say that, although the Queen ought to be reinstated (looking at the matter from a moral standpoint), restoration might now be "impracticable" and the injustice done her "irreparable." If so, the United States would have to do the next best thing, that is, compensate her "just as many other wrongs to private persons, which cannot possibly be specifically redressed, are partially compensated for by pecuniary indemnities."[30]

On October 18 Gresham submitted to the President his official

[28] Olney to Gresham, Oct. 9, 1893, copy in Cleveland MSS.; original in Gresham MSS., marked "Very Important." It is printed in James, *Olney, op. cit.*, pp. 212-217.

[29] Olney to his daughter, Mrs. G. R. Minot, Nov. 24, 1893, in James, *Olney, op. cit.*, p. 217.

[30] Olney to his daughter, Dec. 3, 1893, in James, *Olney, op. cit.*, pp. 217-221.

recommendations, declaring that restoration was the only just action; but he did not say how it should be done. When published, this letter created such a newspaper furor that there were calls for the impeachment of Cleveland.[31]

A Cabinet meeting was held on the same day. Once again Olney, Carlisle, and "perhaps others" maintained that the use of force would create disastrous consequences; Olney repeated the ideas he had expressed in his opinion of October 9. After the meeting, in the words of James, Gresham "dashed to the end of his diplomatic tether"[32] by hastily composing instructions for a new Minister whose duty it would be to restore the Queen. Olney, however, had accomplished important results; nowhere is there any evidence that Cleveland intended to use the army and navy without the consent of Congress to overturn the Provisional Government. If the Queen were not to be reestablished by good offices and persuasion, the President would go no farther; had Cleveland made war on Hawaii in the interest of Liliuokalani he might well have been impeached and removed from office. Olney at least prevented the possibility of Cleveland's allowing himself to be persuaded by Gresham to go beyond his constitutional powers. Perhaps Gresham was willing to use force.

Nevertheless, even under Olney's restrictions, Cleveland's policy of trying to restore Liliuokalani was impractical, and, as James calls it, silly; for how was he to force a discredited native Government back upon the more intelligent whites?[33] Another writer dubbed it "a Quixotic scheme of reparation."[34] Nevins thought that the "course planned by Gresham was absurdly impractical"; and Dennett declared: "The Cleveland investigation only served to make more certain that the Hawaiians were incapable of maintaining unaided an enlightened, just and stable government."[35] In an official call, the Russian Minister, Prince Cantacuzene, asked Gresham: ". . . is it not a little singular that your Government, a Republic, should establish a Monarchy?" The Prince added that he was not looking at the matter from the

[31] To be discussed later.
[32] James, *Olney, op. cit.,* p. 90.
[33] *Ibid.,* p. 88.
[34] Mary H. Krout, *Hawaii and a Revolution* (N. Y., 1898), p. 21.
[35] Nevins, *Cleveland, op. cit.,* p. 557; Dennett, *op. cit.,* p. 612.

standpoint of American morals, but from that of American interests. Gresham answered that the "United States can[not][36] afford to treat an independent but feeble nation like Hawaii in plain disregard of the principles of justice and right." Cantacuzene replied that the moral code for nations differed from that for individuals; and that "Nations have been built up by stealing territory."[37]

* * * * *

Already the Administration had been trying to solve the problem of finding a Minister who, in the first place, would agree with Gresham's policy and, in the second place, who could be trusted with the delicate task of carrying it out. Blount had resigned as soon as he received his appointment and was out of the question. Late in August Olney had written to Cleveland, who was then at Buzzard's Bay, Massachusetts, that the best man he knew of for the vacancy was former Congressman George W. Dargan of South Carolina. He offered to inquire further, if Cleveland wished.[38] But Olney's candidate gained no consideration, probably because the policy of restoration had not as yet been fully worked out.

One of Secretary of the Treasury Carlisle's friends, by the name of Albert Sidney Willis of Louisville, Kentucky, received the appointment. Willis (1843-1897) was born in Shelby County and studied at the Louisville Law School, graduating in 1866. In 1870 he was chosen county attorney, serving until 1875, when he was elected to Congress. He served in the Forty-fifth through the Forty-ninth Congresses.

At the same time, a new Consul General was appointed in the person of Ellis Mills, who had been Blount's secretary during his investigation. Born in England, Mills had been living at Staunton, Virginia.[39] Maine's supremacy at Honolulu was over for four years.

In his final instructions to the new Minister, dated October 18, 1893, Gresham said that President Cleveland, after a careful examination of Commissioner Blount's report, was "satisfied that

[36] The word "not" was omitted in the stenographic report because of a clerical error. If Gresham actually had said "can," his entire program would have been meaningless.

[37] Interview of Nov. 11, 1893, Miscellaneous Archives, *op. cit.*

[38] Olney to Cleveland, Aug. 23, 1893, Cleveland MSS.

[39] Mills to ———, No. 1, Oct. 19, 1893, Consular Letters.

the movement against the Queen, if not instigated, was encouraged and supported by the representative of this Government at Honolulu." The President believed profoundly that Stevens had committed an international crime and that that crime reflected upon the honor of the United States. He felt it to be his bounden duty to right the wrong that had been perpetrated. Continuing, the Secretary ordered:

> On your arrival at Honolulu you will take advantage of an early opportunity to inform the Queen of this determination, making known to her the President's sincere regret that the reprehensible conduct of the American Minister and the unauthorized presence on land of a military force of the United States obliged her to surrender her sovereignty, for the time being, and rely on the justice of this Government to undo the flagrant wrong.
>
> You will, however, at the same time inform the Queen that, when reinstated, the President expects that she will pursue a magnanimous course by granting full amnesty to all who participated in the movement against her, including persons who are, or have been, officially or otherwise, connected with the Provisional Government, depriving them of no right or privilege which they enjoyed before the so-called revolution. All obligations created by the Provisional Government in due course of administration should be assumed.
>
> Having secured the Queen's agreement to pursue this wise and humane policy, which it is believed you will speedily obtain, you will then advise the executive of the Provisional Government and his ministers of the President's determination of the question which their action and that of the Queen devolved upon him, and that they are expected to promptly relinquish to her her constitutional authority.[40]

As a diplomatic document, it would be hard to equal these instructions; not only because Stevens's acts were called "reprehensible," but also because of the delicate task and heavy responsibility that were being given to Willis. It is notable, also, that Gresham placed Cleveland's right to interfere in the internal affairs of Hawaii on the basis of his being an arbiter; that is to say, when the Queen surrendered, she, as well as the Revolutionists, turned

[40] Gresham to Willis, No. 4, Oct. 18, 1893, in Instructions, III, 186-187 (which is printed); also printed in Blount, pp. XXI-XXII.

to the President as an umpire to settle the differences between the two parties. Inasmuch as Dole and the other insurgents endorsed her capitulation, Gresham believed that both factions had appealed to the President. After examination of the facts, he had decided in favor of Liliuokalani, and Willis was to carry out the decision of the mediator to whom both had appealed.

* * * * *

The Washington representatives of the Provisional Government tried, as soon as possible, to enlighten their superiors about Willis and what his appointment meant. Hastings, who thought that Willis's mission indicated that "the jig is up as far as annexation is concerned," promised Thurston that he would meet Willis and Mills as soon as he could, and then inform Thurston and the home officials what his impressions were.[41] Upon interviewing Willis, Hastings found him to be a fine man who would stick to his own ideas but who would listen to reason. He was no loud-mouthed politician. The appointment, thought Hastings, proved that the United States did not want annexation, but it did show that the Provisional Government was being recognized as *the* Government of Hawaii, and that was all to the good.[42]

The upshot was, as Thurston and his aides viewed the status of affairs, that the determination to send a Minister precluded not only immediate annexation, but it also seemed to preclude restoration. Because it might well be years before union would occur, all diplomatic officials from Hawaii stationed at Washington began to urge Dole and his confrères to form a more permanent kind of government. Both Hastings and Alexander believed that at least the word "Provisional" should be dropped.[43] Thurston said that not only he, but W. N. Armstrong and Z. S. Spalding as well, thought a regular constitution should be proclaimed. This action would not connote any surrender of annexation aspirations; in fact it could help the cause in so far as the United States might be more willing to make a treaty with a régime that had been

[41] Hastings to Thurston, Sept. 8, 1893, M&E.

[42] "Private Memo. for President Dole," written by Hastings, Sept. 9, 1893, in *ibid.* Alexander informed acting Foreign Minister Francis M. Hatch: "I don't believe Minister Willis is instructed to meddle with your internal affairs or question your title to govern" (Alexander to Hatch, Sept. 22, 1893, *ibid.*).

[43] Hastings to Dole, Oct. 13, 1893, and Alexander to Hatch, Sept. 22, *ibid.*

established constitutionally. In accordance with his knack at drafting documents, Thurston added that he was working on a proclamation and on a constitution, whose chief characteristic was that the Presidency, like that of the United States, was separate from the Cabinet.[44] Alexander went into more detail touching what he thought should appear in the constitution. Registration to vote ought to be based upon ownership of taxpaying property rather than upon income, so as to eliminate a large number of Royalists; the Advisory Council should remain; and the lower house, if it had to exist at all, should have no real legislative authority.[45] It is obvious that Alexander did not want a democracy.

Back in Honolulu, the Annexationists, who were handicapped by the lack of definite information as to what their fate was to be, were faced by a rising Royalist feeling of jubilation at the reports of a plebiscite. Theophilus H. Davies said there must be a popular vote;[46] so did the *Bulletin* and other Royalist sources.[47] Attorney General Smith reported that the deposed Royal Foreign Minister, Samuel Parker, said to the Annexationists: "Damn you fellows, we've got you now. It will be settled by votes. We will vote you all out, and put the queen back."[48] The Provisional Government leaders and their newspapers denied repeatedly that either a plebiscite or a restoration was in the offing;[49] and added that, even if Cleveland did try either policy, the present Government would fight against it. The Annexationist spirit was shown in a half-joking remark by Finance Minister S. M. Damon: "I do not propose to bow the Knee and admit, that there is [any] Queen in Hawaii but my wife"; and he declared that the last bow to royalty he ever expected to make was on January 17 last when he told Liliuokalani he was joining the Revolutionary movement.[50]

So certain was the Government of its stability that on October 5 the Councils decided to reduce the military force from 176 officers and men to 126, on the theory that, as affairs were so quiet, there

[44] Thurston to Dole, Oct. 21, 1893, *ibid.*
[45] Alexander to Thurston, Oct. 31, 1893, *ibid.*
[46] *Star,* Sept. 20, 1893.
[47] *Advertiser,* Sept. 26, 30, Oct. 3, 1893; *Bulletin,* Nov. 1, 1893.
[48] W. O. Smith's circular, Sept. 20, 1893, M&E.
[49] *Star,* Oct. 2, *etc.*, and *Advertiser,* Oct. 23, 30, Nov. 1, 4, *etc.*, 1893.
[50] Damon to Thurston, Sept. 30, 1893, M&E.

were more in service than were needed.[51] The *Star,* whose editor probably had heard of Thurston's and Alexander's suggestions for a permanent constitution, thought that a republic, called the "Commonwealth of Hawaii" might well be proclaimed.[52] When the Queen refused to allow her property to be assessed for taxing, the Executive Council, without much ado, decided to arrive at a fair valuation and tax her just the same.[53] Beginning with October 28 and continuing through November 2, the *Star* printed in bold type at its masthead the following sentence from the *New York Herald*: "The restoration of the Queen to the throne Mr. Blount never contemplated by anything he said in his report, and the administration would not favor such a course, even if he did." If, asked the *Star,* Cleveland proposed either a restoration or a plebiscite, how could he accomplish either without a war?[54] It would not be many days before the *Star* found out how wrong it and the *Herald* had been.

* * * * *

The new Minister arrived in Honolulu on November 4, 1893, in the midst of profound peace, with the Provisional Government in full control,[55] although there were rumors that it would declare a republic, with a constitution already prepared.[56] Upon being presented to President Dole, Willis mentioned nothing about his secret instructions to see the Queen and restore her if possible; instead, he said he came to "tender to your people the right hand of good will, which I trust may be as lasting as I know it to be sincere."[57] The Annexationists were delighted at these words, because the sentiments seemed to presage complete and final recognition of the Provisional Government.[58] The *Star* carried on its editorial

[51] EAC, Oct. 5, 1893, and *Advertiser,* Oct. 7, 1893.

[52] Oct. 7, 1893.

[53] Minutes of the Executive Council, Oct. 19, 1893.

[54] Oct. 18 and 31, 1893.

[55] Skerrett to Secretary of the Navy, Nov. 2, 1893, No. 40889, Bureau of Navigation.

[56] Willis sent a cipher to Gresham, on Nov. 6, which read: "Two hundred and sixty rifles and ammunition arrived by steamer Saturday. Rumor that Provisional Government will declare for a Republic, with constitution already prepared (Ciphers Received, No. 1, p. 308; printed in *House Ex. Doc. 48,* 53 Cong. 2 Sess, p. 166).

[57] Enclosure 3, in Willis to Gresham, No. 1, Nov. 6, 1893, Despatches.

[58] *Star,* Nov. 6 and 8; *Advertiser,* Nov. 6, 7, 8, 9, 11, 1893.

page for some time Cleveland's words to Dole, in bold relief: "He [Willis] will consistently endeavor to advance the interest and prosperity of both Governments and so render himself acceptable to Your Excellency." This was called "Good Cheer from Cleveland."[59]

On November 13 Willis had his first interview with the Queen. He stated the President's regret that she had been overthrown by the intervention of the United States, and his hope that he might be able to rectify the wrong. The interview with her can best be told in Willis's own words:

> I then said to her, "The President expects and believes that when reinstated, you will show forgiveness and magnanimity, that you will wish to be the Queen of all the people, both native and foreign-born, that you will make haste to secure their love and loyalty and to establish peace, friendship, and good government." To this, she made no reply. After waiting a moment, I continued: "The President not only tenders you his sympathy but wishes to help you. Before fully making known to you, his purposes, I desire to know, whether you are willing to answer certain questions which it is my duty to ask." She answered, "I am willing." I then asked her, "Should you be restored to the throne, would you grant full amnesty as to life and property to all persons who have been instrumental in overthrowing your government." She hesitated a moment and then slowly and calmly answered: "There are certain laws of my government by which I shall abide. My decision would be, as the law directs, that such persons should be beheaded and their property confiscated to the Government." I then said, repeating very distinctly her words, "It is your feeling that these people should be beheaded and their property confiscated?" She replied, "It is." I then said to her, "Do you fully understand the meaning of every word which I have said to you and of every word which you have said to me, and if so do you still have the same opinion?" Her answer was, "I have understood and mean all I have said, but I might leave the decision of this to my Ministers." To this I replied, "Suppose it was necessary to make a decision before you appointed any Ministers, & that you were asked to issue a royal proclamation of

[59] For instance, Nov. 7, 1893.

> general amnesty, would you do it?" She answered, "I have no legal right to do that and I would not do it. . . .[60] They must be sent out of the country or punished and their property confiscated." I then said, "I have no further communication to make to you now, and will have none until I hear from my Government, which will probably be three or four weeks."[61]

The Queen's attitude was such an unlooked-for rebuff to the Administration policy that Willis's only recourse was to communicate with Washington. This he did in a telegram, dated November 16, 1893, of one enigmatic sentence: "Views of first party so extreme as to require further instructions."[62]

Already Willis was evidencing some skepticism regarding the results of his mission, for he informed Gresham, in a regular despatch, that if the Queen were reinstated "there will be a concerted movement . . . for the overthrow of that constitution [of 1887] which would mean the overthrow of constitutional and limited government and the absolute dominion of the Queen." Moreover, he questioned the political ability and personal honesty of most of her advisers, such as J. E. Bush, R. W. Wilcox, Joseph Nawahi, and John Richardson.[63]

Annexationists, upon learning about Willis's visit with Liliuo-

[60] According to the penal code under the Constitution of 1887, the Queen had the right to require the lives of the officials of the Provisional Government: "Whoever shall commit the crime of treason shall suffer the punishment of death and all his property shall be confiscated to the Government." In *Hawaii's Story, op. cit.*, p. 246, Liliuokalani said she refused to grant amnesty because she could do nothing without the consent of her Cabinet. The New York *Nation,* Jan. 25, 1894, thought she was within her rights in wishing to behead traitors, for all governments had laws to punish treasonable persons.

[61] Enclosed in Willis to Gresham, No. 3, Nov. 16, 1893, Despatches; copy in Cleveland MSS.; printed in *House Ex. Doc. 70* (53 Cong. 2 Sess.), pp. 1-3. Liliuokalani, in her book, *op. cit.*, pp. 247-248, charged Willis with unfairness, if not bad faith, in having Mills secreted behind a Japanese screen to take stenographic notes of this conversation. On his next visit Willis read her the notes. She was dumbfounded because she had thought the interview was to be strictly private. In her book, written some years after the event, she denied she ever said she wished to behead her enemies, for that form of punishment was unknown in the islands.

[62] *House Ex. Doc. 48* (53 Cong. 2 Sess.), p. 168.

[63] *House Ex. Doc. 70* (53 Cong. 2 Sess.), pp. 1-3.

kalani, began to become anxious. As late as November 15 the *Star* denied that Cleveland would try anything drastic, but thought it was best to be on guard. The growing anxiety was reflected in the Executive Council where Marshal E. G. Hitchcock said he thought "there was reason to beleive [*sic*] that an attack by overwhelming numbers within the next few nights, to take possession of the Executive Building" might occur. It was voted to increase Company E.[64]

Suddenly the long period of uncertainty was ended on November 16 with the publication in the Honolulu press (the *Advertiser* got out an extra issue) of a telegram from Auckland, New Zealand,[65] to the effect that Cleveland and Gresham were going to restore the Queen. Still there was doubt that the American Government could be planning such a move. The *Star* on that date questioned the authenticity of the Auckland telegram, and next day the *Advertiser* thought it was impossible to believe: "A democratic government [exclaimed the editor] restoring a dethroned monarch bearing such a history! The whole world would cry out —shame!"

The first real uproar occurred on November 16 when the *Star* published an interview with Willis, who later used the article as an example of what he called Annexationist lying. He denied the accuracy of the words as printed, and yet the *Star's* reporter said Willis had taken fifteen minutes to look over the reporter's version of the interview. As published the statement read, in part:

> You are authorized to say from me that no change in the present situation will take place for several weeks. I brought with me certain instructions. . . . Since my arrival here contingencies have arisen which neither the United States Government nor myself were aware of when I left Washington. . . . I forwarded my dispatches

[64] Minutes of the Executive Council, Nov. 15, 1893.

[65] Sereno E. Bishop said in Alexander, *op. cit.*, p. 95, that the first intimation which Hawaiians received of Cleveland's plans was a London telegram. It reached Auckland, New Zealand, on Nov. 2 and Honolulu by ship on Nov. 16. The telegram said that the President "was drafting a message to Congress in favor of restoring monarchy in Hawaii." Dole, *Memoirs, op. cit.*, p. 104, averred that the first he heard of Gresham's intentions was in a despatch from Australia quoting an article in the *Chicago Evening Post* of Nov. 7, which declared the Queen was to be reinstated.

> to Washington by to-day's steamer, and until I receive an answer to them no change will take place in the present situation "nor will be allowed" . . . .
>
> The whole Hawaiian question is now in abeyance and nothing the newspapers can say or do will alter the situation one iota.[66]

In consideration of the fact that the Provisional Government was absolutely uninformed as to Blount's conclusions, Cleveland's plans, or Willis's instructions, these words, whether they were exactly what the Minister declared or not, would hardly quiet fears or answer doubts. At once Dole interviewed Willis who said that the newspaper had misrepresented what he had said, making it stronger than he had intended; furthermore, "That he would act only through the proper channels; . . . that his attitude towards this Government was unchanged." Sereno E. Bishop was told by Willis that when the time came to act, he would deal with only two parties, namely, the head of the present Government and the head of the former one.[67] Several days later Willis informed Damon that Liliuokalani had asked for American troops to protect her, and that he had told her to apply to the Provisional Government. She named certain policemen she desired around her residence, and the Executive Council allowed them to be detailed for that purpose.[68]

The arrival and publication on November 24 of Secretary Gresham's report (dated October 18, as already discussed) to President Cleveland on Blount's investigation added fuel to the flame. It aroused sufficient commotion in the United States,[69] but

[66] Willis declared, in a letter to the Honolulu *Bulletin* of Nov. 17, that he had not scrutinized the notes of the interview and that some of it was "misleading." The *Advertiser* criticized the *Star* for falsifying and for deliberately stirring up factional trouble (Nov. 18, 20, 21, 1893), but the *Star* stuck to its guns and maintained the correctness of its version (Nov. 18, 20). On Nov. 17 the *Star* published Willis's remarks to a delegation from the American League in the following words: ". . . the policy of the United States is already formulated regarding these islands, and . . . nothing which can be said or done either here or there can avail anything now. I do not come here as did Mr. Blount. I come here as an executive officer. I come to act. When the proper time arrives I shall act."

[67] Minutes of the Executive Council, Nov. 17 and 18, 1893.

[68] *Ibid.,* Nov. 21, 1893.

[69] To be discussed later.

in Hawaii it raised a veritable furor.[70] The document was merely a transcript of Commissioner Blount's conclusions, namely, that the Queen had been illegally dethroned by the aid of American naval forces and that Stevens had been prominent in the overthrowal. That was undesirable enough. What aroused the Provisional Government was, as Annexationists interpreted it, the intention of the Secretary to use military means to restore Liliuokalani. They believed they saw the significance of Willis's secret interview with the former head of the Royal Government, as well as the meaning of his statements to the press. The *Star* condemned Blount's findings as one-sided because he had to make a case against his predecessor. The "Georgia pettifogger," it continued, might sympathize with that "polluted woman" as much as he pleased, but she would never sit on the throne again. His report was "as full of lies as a book is full of print."[71]

Getting out an extra edition, those in charge of the *Advertiser* printed an editorial (repeated the next day) stating that "as surely as there is an Eternal Justice overruling the affairs of men, so surely will the gross outrage proposed to be done to Hawaii fail of its purpose!" Later the same paper said it was sure that "the American people will never consent to the enslavement of Hawaii under a monarchical bondage more repugnant to republican ideas than the worst form of African slavery. It is hard to conceive how an enlightened and Christian ruler can allow his political prejudices to overcome the cherished principles which lie at the foundation of American civilization."[72] On the other hand, the *Bulletin* was jubilant and said the report was impartial.[73]

Along with Gresham's résumé of Blount's report, came Thurston's letter describing his interview of November 14 with Gresham (to be discussed shortly). So disturbed was the Executive Council that it instructed Dole and W. O. Smith to see Willis and find out exactly what the United States had in mind. The Minister answered that he could not enlighten them until so ordered by

[70] Willis to Gresham, Dec. 5, 1893, in *House Ex. Doc. 70* (53 Cong. 2 Sess.). Former Commissioner Charles L. Carter wrote a twenty-five point refutation which he printed (enclosed in Irwin to Secretary of Navy, Dec. 9, 1893, No. 42967, Bureau of Navigation).

[71] Nov. 24; also Nov. 27, 28, Dec. 5, 1893.

[72] Nov. 24, 25, 27, 28, 29, 1893.

[73] Nov. 24 and Dec. 7, 1893.

Gresham. He added that since arriving he had become "cognizant of things which were not known to the U. S. Government nor to himself before he came here and which necessitated further instructions, that the whole matter was 'hung up.' "[74] All the committee got was sympathy.[75] At three in the afternoon the Councils met in special session, and, so important did the present emergency appear to be, dispensed with the reading of the minutes of the last session.[76] Next day it was decided to issue sixty rifles and 5,000 rounds of ammunition to the Citizen Guards.[77]

Aside from such governmental precautions, the immediate reaction was a mass meeting and preparation for war. At the mass meeting of "over 1200," the Revolutionary leaders denounced Cleveland and Gresham, and committed themselves to an active policy of preventing restoration of the monarchy. Francis M. Hatch, later Minister of Foreign Affairs, declared that Cleveland had no legal right to interfere with a sovereign government. "Grover Cleveland," he shouted, "has no more right, legally or morally, to undo the act of Benjamin Harrison than he had to undo the act of Abraham Lincoln." Blount came in for denunciation also. Castle, one of the Commissioners sent to Washington the previous February, jibed at the "paramount Commissioner" whose "first act . . . was to take down the American flag . . . to see us tumble." Others who made similar rousing addresses were Z. S. Spalding, Chief Justice Judd, P. C. Jones, W. C. Wilder, and W. G. Smith—all of whom have already appeared in one rôle or another in these pages. Later one hundred and fifty-one Americans signed a protest against the use of force to restore the Queen.[78]

This evident determination of Annexationists to resist was duplicated in the Executive Council which, in two meetings, dis-

[74] The obstacle that had "hung up" Willis's action was the Queen's refusal to promise clemency. Some weeks later Damon reported a conversation with former Foreign Minister Samuel Parker, who stated he and the Royalists "felt bitterly" about the Queen's folly in declining to grant amnesty. Parker added that he told her she had thrown away her only chance to be restored (Minutes of the Executive Council, Jan. 1, 1894).

[75] *Ibid.,* Nov. 24, 1893.

[76] EAC, Nov. 24, 1893.

[77] Minutes of the Executive Council, Nov. 25, 1893.

[78] *Star,* Nov. 27, 1893. Newspaper clippings are printed in *House Ex. Doc. 70* (53 Cong. 2 Sess.), pp. 7-16. The protest of the Americans will be discussed later.

cussed the general situation. There was some support for tearing down the old barracks and using the stone to build a wall around the Government Building. Considerable talk resulted on the question of how the Government should fortify itself in order to resist "foreign" troops. It was voted to use sandbags to protect the lower verandah of the Government Building and to have other bags ready to place around the entrances on the lower floor.[79] Meanwhile Dole had a discussion with the military officers of the Government, the "plan being to resist till forced to yield without firing upon the U. S. troops"—as the Minutes of the Executive Council stated his report of the conversation.[80] The degree of resistance and the lengths to which the Government should go in defending itself produced much division. Some members wondered whether Liliuokalani should not be declared a prisoner of state and then arrested. The cautious Damon suggested that before any drastic acts such as that be committed, a note be despatched to Minister Willis requesting that "any contemplated act on his part hostile be communicated to us before he acts."[81]

Thus it was clear that the Executive Council was not a unit on how far to go in resistance. The Citizen Guards, however, appeared to be ready to go to the limit in fighting the American forces, because the sergeants of that service sent a list of propositions to the Executive Council which they wanted carried out: there should be no yielding, even if firing on American troops was necessary; the Government Building should be fortified and the barracks torn down; supplies and provisions should be stored against a possible siege; Willis should be informed about the Government's intention to fight; and the Queen should be seized and held prisoner.[82]

On November 30 John Ena, the native member of the Advisory Council, "in view of the agitated state of affairs," asked the Executive Council to enlighten the members of the Advisory Council on the attitude of the Government. Damon, the Minister of Finance, in the answer which he said was made for his colleagues of the Executive Council, indicated that he wished nothing radical

[79] Minutes of the Executive Council, Nov. 27, 1893.
[80] *Ibid.*, Nov. 28, 1893.
[81] *Ibid.*, Nov. 29, 1893.
[82] *Ibid.*, Nov. 30, 1893.

or unpolitic; it was clear that he and the more radical members of the Government were not seeing eye to eye. He was very friendly to the United States, saying that acquisition of non-contiguous territory was a new departure and that the United States would naturally act slowly. He read from a letter he had written to an unnamed gentleman in San Francisco: "There is a great deal of humbug in this world, and Mr. B. [Blount] satisfied it to the full by working up the idea that Mr. Stevens was an hour too soon in recognizing the Provisional Government." The radicals could not quibble with this sentence, but they did not like the next ones. Blount, continued Damon, had done a good job in getting all kinds of statistics; and he even defended Willis against the charge of perfidy. "We are," concluded Damon, "safe in the hands of the American Republic today."

That Damon's policy of appeasement did not represent the feelings of all members of the Executive Council is clear from Attorney General W. O. Smith's affirmation "that the *Executive Council* was *determined to resist any attacks upon the government from whatever source.*"[83] In short, the army and the radical members of the Government, like Smith, were willing to shed blood if necessary; the more conservative elements, like Damon and Dole, were willing to trust the United States, and, if resistance was necessary, intended to "yield without firing upon the U. S. troops."[84]

Thus, just at the time when the Government should have had a united attitude, its able Finance Minister, representing many others, was taking a stand of non-resistance and trustfulness. Part of this trouble arose out of the old radical-conservative fight over patronage. The present crisis gave point to the radicals' demand, long and frequently made, that Royalists should be cleaned out. As early as November 13 the *Star* had begun a new campaign to get rid of Royalists in office, saying that its policy was now supported by the entire Hawaiian diplomatic corps at Washington, by the Citizens' Reserve, and by the American League. After publication of Blount's findings, few could gainsay that the *Star* and the radicals had a case, because Blount's charges had rested largely

[83] EAC, Nov. 30, 1893.
[84] Minutes of the Executive Council, Nov. 27, 1893.

upon testimony given by certain officeholders whom the Annexationists trusted.

Blount secured the most damaging information from Fred W. Wundenberg; and when this fact became known in Honolulu there was a great outcry of denunciation against the "traitor." The *Star* called him a "perjured and lottery-besmirched" Royalist spy who was holding office under the Provisional Government.[85] Wundenberg aided in the overthrow of the Queen during the first days of the Revolution, and then had withdrawn from the movement; the *Star* later declared he was disgruntled because he had not been made Marshal.[86] Probably in order to win his favor, the Councils had elected him Collector General of Customs, and the *Advertiser* applauded the selection.[87] He declined the honor. Later he was made clerk of the Supreme Court. As will be recalled, in an earlier investigation of loyalty within the Government, his attitudes had been questioned. When his testimony to Blount became known, he was dismissed from the clerkship forthwith.[88]

In order to discover the feelings of some of the native employees, the Executive Council examined Ed. Stiles, an underclerk in the Foreign Office. He said he was not in sympathy with the Royalists and was opposed to restoration of the Queen. "As to Annexation," he continued, "I dont [*sic*] Know. Under Annexation we colored people will have no vote. I would rather be as we are now. I fear that annexation would prejudice natives and halfwhites. I am in favour of the continuance of this Government." He had joined no organization on either side.[89] This proved to be the stand taken by many jobholders: they were neutral.

The Provisional Government, believing it was on trial for its life, needed active supporters who would fight. The matter came to a head on December 2 when Finance Minister Damon tendered his resignation because the *Star* demanded dismissal of one of his clerks. He said he did not hold with the idea of spoils "even for party purposes." This démarche was earnestly discussed and action on the resignation was held over.[90] On December 7, as the crisis

[85] Nov. 28, 1893.
[86] *Ibid.*
[87] April 12, 1893; EAC, April 11, 1893.
[88] *Advertiser,* Dec. 9, 1893.
[89] Minutes of the Executive Council, Nov. 28, 1893.
[90] *Ibid.,* Dec. 2, 1893.

with Willis continued, the Attorney General offered a resolution to investigate the loyalty of all Government employees; he admitted the Finance Minister was opposed to the measure. Councillor Emmeluth added an amendment which stated in effect that the standard of judgment should include *"active support* of this Government and its purposes *in the past."* The resolution was accepted, eleven to one.[91]

Because of Damon's threatened resignation, the investigation started in his Department. Three of his employees were examined. G. E. Smithies said he was neutral and would fight for neither party. Carl Widemann declared that, having taken an oath as an official, he was doing his duty and "that was enough"; he would not fight for the Government. Palmer Wood wanted restoration, but not by force; he would fight for neither side. All three were asked to resign.[92] As the investigation went on, the *Bulletin* called it an "Inquisition."[93] The Annexation Club passed resolutions of approval, offered suggestions for the filling of the vacated posts, and thought the Road Board of Honolulu should be next on the list.[94] On December 11 it was decided to postpone the examination for a while because the Executive Council was too busy with other matters. The inquest was allowed to die, although there was much protest against shelving it.[95]

* * * * *

The uproar in Honolulu, which had started out as a defensive move against possible restoration, had thus gone far afield into the question of jobholding. Both Gresham and Willis later declared that the agitation was absolutely unnecessary. In fact, they accused Dole and Thurston of deliberately attempting to raise a furor in their own interest and to embarrass the American Government.[96]

[91] EAC, Dec. 7, 1893; *Star,* Dec. 8, 1893.

[92] Minutes of the Executive Council, Dec. 9, 1893.

[93] Dec. 11, 1893.

[94] Minutes of the Executive Council, Dec. 11, 1893.

[95] EAC, Dec. 28, 1893, and Jan. 11, 1894; Geo. C. Potter to T. B. Murray, Dec. 27, 1893, President's Files.

[96] Gresham to Willis, No. 13, Feb. 8, 1894, Instructions, III, 197 *ff*. Willis believed that the Provisional Government was deliberately acting a part; that is, in order to cover up its own weakness, it was acting as if it expected American troops to invade Honolulu. See Willis to Gresham, Jan. 16, 1894, in *House Ex. Doc. 112* (53 Cong. 2 Sess.), pp. 2-4.

Their justification for charging the Provisional Government with bad faith arose out of an official call which Minister Thurston made upon Secretary Gresham on November 14, 1893.

The background of this much-disputed interview was as follows: Thurston, still at the Chicago Fair, read a despatch in the *Chicago Evening Post* for November 7, 1893, to the effect that Willis had been ordered to restore Liliuokalani. He at once telegraphed Hastings to find out from Gresham the truth about the matter. On November 9 Hastings waited upon the Secretary, who told him that, inasmuch as the newspaper story was unauthorized, there was no reason for apprehension and no ground for rumors; and that when the Government decided upon its policy, Thurston and Hastings would be the first to know about it. This was what might be called masterly diplomatic dissimulation, if not outright lying, on the part of Gresham because the Government had already decided what it intended to do. Hastings at once composed a letter to Dole telling him not to worry.[97]

On November 10, within twenty-four hours of Gresham's assurances to Hastings, the Secretary's letter to Cleveland recommending restoration was published; no official notice was sent to the Hawaiian Legation. Thurston, still busy at the Fair closing up his cyclorama, found he had stayed away from Washington too long. But he was able to leave Chicago on November 12, arriving at the capital the next day. At ten in the morning of November 14 he called upon Gresham, who said he was busy but would be glad to see the Minister at three that afternoon. Before Thurston left, however, he got into a long argument with the Secretary. Not satisfied, he called again at three.[98]

Thurston asked Gresham whether the Secretary's letter, which had just appeared in the press, was genuine; and if so, whether the United States really proposed to restore the Queen. Gresham answered that the United States meant no harm to Hawaii. In a letter to Willis, dated February 24, 1894, Gresham underlined the answer he made to Thurston on November 14, in order to prove to Willis that Thurston knew that no military force was to be used against the Provisional Government: ". . . *no action had or would be taken by our Minister, Mr. Willis, which would imperil*

[97] Hastings to Dole, Nov. 10, 1893.
[98] Thurston to Dole, Nov. 14, 1893.

the lives or property of the officers or supporters of the Provisional Government and *that if they suffered in any way it would be in consequence of their own acts or attitude.*" Gresham thought this was definite enough assurance that Willis would not make any war upon Hawaii to reinstate the Queen; whether Thurston deliberately misconstrued it, or whether he did not think it was concise enough, is impossible to say.[99] The stenographer who took down the conversation between him and Gresham noted that Thurston, dissatisfied with the vagueness of Gresham's answer, tried to procure an amplification of the statement, but Gresham would say no more.

The conversation continued with Thurston stating that he did not understand what jurisdiction the United States could claim over the internal affairs of a nation whose Government had been recognized by the United States and by all the powers of the earth. Gresham answered that the United States had recognized the Revolutionists provisionally, that is *de facto,* until justice had been done to the Queen who had surrendered her authority to the United States. Thurston denied stoutly the existence of any agreement to the effect that, if the United States refused to annex, the Provisional Government would dissolve. Gresham reminded him of the promise made by Damon and confirmed by Dole on January 17, 1893, when the Queen surrendered. Thurston answered that he knew of no such agreement until he read about it in Gresham's letter to Cleveland of October 18. (Thurston either lied at this point or else his memory was faulty, for he and Gresham had argued over this matter in their interview of the previous August 14.) The Hawaiian Minister went on to say that he did not believe the intervention of American forces in the Revolution gave

[99] Rev. Sereno E. Bishop (in Alexander, *op. cit.,* p. 101), who could not be charged with friendliness toward Gresham, admitted that the Secretary "left the impression upon Mr. Thurston's mind that such force was *not* [italics by Bishop] to be used." Perhaps Thurston did not feel that Gresham's answer was any answer at all. Indeed there is no question it was vague. Dole, in his "Letter of Specifications" of Jan. 11, 1894, after telling Willis that he had learned of the President's intentions for the first time on Nov. 29 from a despatch written by Thurston, added that the latter had reported Gresham's "refusal to state whether it was the intention of your [the American] Government to carry out its policy by force" (enclosed in Willis to Gresham, No. 31, Jan. 19, 1894, Despatches).

to the United States any right to interfere now, although he was constrained to state: "I admit that the Provisional Government is not republican." The conference ended with the assertion by Thurston that ". . . however our Government was established, it is a government *de jure* as well as *de facto,* and the United States have no constitutional authority to destroy it or interfere with it. I shall prepare a protest and hand it to you."[100]

Thurston's version of these discussions with Gresham, as given in his report to Dole and in his *Memoirs,* differs somewhat from that taken down by Gresham's stenographer. According to the Hawaiian Minister's story, the Secretary of State would say little about his intentions. In addition, Gresham averred that the United States purposed to hurt no one in Hawaii; that if bloodshed occurred it would be brought on by Thurston's friends in Honolulu and not by American forces; and that there was a vast difference between restoring the Queen and maintaining her once restored. Their argument over the right of the United States to interfere, according to Thurston, was based on the word "until"; that is, Thurston asserted the Provisional Government was provisional "until" annexation took place, whenever in the future that might be. On the other hand, Gresham thought it meant "until" the immediate claims of the Queen were found to be just or unjust; and that, Blount having found them to be just, the Provisional Government should retire, *per* its agreement in the Queen's capitulation. Thurston denied this interpretation vehemently.[101]

According to Thurston the point which impressed him most was Gresham's differentiation between restoring Liliuokalani and maintaining her on the throne once she was restored. This is an important consideration, because it would seem to indicate that Gresham was willing to replace the Queen by a display of force (in spite of Olney's cautioning him against such procedure), and then withdraw. The colloquoy follows:

> Thurston: If you attempt to restore the Queen by force, there will be no fighting with your troops. There will be no thought on the part of the Provisional Government of firing on the American flag or shooting at troops wearing

[100] Miscellaneous Archives, *op. cit.*

[101] *Op. cit.*, pp. 324-333, and Thurston to Dole, Nov. 14, 1893, M&E.

your uniform; but the Queen will be restored in no other way, and unless you are prepared to maintain a force on shore and hold her in position, she will be overthrown as soon as your troops leave.

Gresham: Ah, that's a very different thing. Restoring her to position and maintaining her in position are two different things. It is not likely that your people would fire on American troops any more than the Queen would have when she was overthrown.

Was Gresham trying to inform Thurston that any American move to help Liliuokalani would be merely a feint, and that Thurston should take the hint and so instruct his Government to withdraw temporarily, and then reinstate itself as soon as American honor had been satisfied by the undoing of Stevens's act? In spite of just declaring the Provisional Government troops would not fight those of the United States, Thurston asserted: "I tell you that when you attempt to enforce the policy which has been indicated you will find that you have a desperate community to deal with." On the other hand, Gresham had already said: "We have not done anything that you know of yet, have we?"

In any event, the next day, November 15, Thurston telegraphed his Government as follows: "Gresham said restoring Queen to possession and maintaining her in possession very different. General belief Willis not ordered to use force until further instructions and that even if force to restore Queen such force will not thereafter support her." He ended the message by advising Dole to withdraw his troops, let the Queen be reinstated, and then dispossess her when American marines withdrew to their ships.[102]

It is difficult to believe that Gresham could have been serious when he hinted to Thurston that the Queen might be reestablished by force, but not so maintained. And yet it is just as difficult to explain away his clear intimation to Thurston, who passed it on to his Government. The Secretary's distinction between restoration and maintenance was known to officials in Honolulu after the arrival of Thurston's telegram of November 15, and the knowledge had its effect upon the policies of some members of the Government at least. It is quite likely that this idea was the reason for

[102] *Memoirs, op. cit.*, pp. 333-335.

Damon's statement—"We are safe in the hands of the American Republic today"—and for Dole's plan "to resist till forced to yield without firing upon the U. S. troops."

Inasmuch as Willis had no orders to restore the Queen by either military or other coercive means, the best solution of the puzzle is that Gresham, who was both visionary and legalistic, was drawn into a theoretical differentiation between restoration and maintenance by his desire to outargue Thurston; and that, after a second sober thought, he did not believe what he had said. Of course we do not know that this is true; all we do know is that Olney and Cleveland were against the use of force, and that Cleveland had turned the Hawaiian problem over to Congress before he knew whether the Provisional Government would agree to get out or not. More will be said on this subject shortly.

Thurston, who was fearful that Dole might weaken, kept a stream of letters and telegrams going from Washington to Honolulu in order to firm up the Provisional Government's nerve. On November 19 he pleaded with the President not to give in to Liliuokalani: "I hope to God that under no circumstances have you consented to give up your organization, and that if you have been forced out that you will by force go back again as soon as possible." He exhorted the Government to get rid of the Queen by deporting her to some South Sea Island, "a la the Samoan method."[103] A second despatch on the same day advised the formation of a permanent republic, even though it "will not be a full exponent of the republican principle."[104] A third letter of the same date said again that Gresham would not support the Queen by force after she was replaced in power, and that the Secretary was supposed to have declared he did not care if she was thrown out once the United States had done its duty.[105]

On the same day, Alexander, who was still in the United States, wrote to Dole informing him of the press outcry against Gresham; he added: "I hope and pray that you will hold the fort till Congress meets. I't will be almost impossible then to restore the Queen in the face of public opinion."[106] Hastings, after pointing out that

[103] *Memoirs, op. cit.*, pp. 335-340; also M&E.
[104] *Memoirs, op. cit.*, p. 339.
[105] *Ibid.*, pp. 339-340.
[106] *Ibid.*, pp. 340-343.

Hawaii was finding many friends in the army, navy, and Democratic party, thought it looked as though "in reply to the request from us for the bread of union we were to be given a stone—and that stone, the monarchy."[107] Mills's predecessor, H. W. Severance, who was on his way home, wrote Dole from San Francisco describing the howl in the American press.[108] On November 20 Thurston had another interview with Gresham who, although affable and pleasant, would give no definite information on the use of armed force.[109]

Unable to reply to Blount's report officially, because it was a domestic matter in the United States, Thurston did write a long letter defending himself from the investigator's charges and released it to the press associations on November 21. He pointed out what, according to him, were the incorrect statements made by Blount; refuted the charge that American troops had assisted the Revolutionists; denied the Revolution was a secret conspiracy; described the widespread support for the movement; accused the Royalists of cowardice and disunity; and denounced the statement that the Committee of Safety had been made up of aliens.[110]

On December 5 Thurston submitted to Gresham the official protest which he had promised, reiterating in it what he had already said in the recent interview with the Secretary.[111] With this parting shot, he left at once for Honolulu in order to aid his Government, arriving in the midst of the fight with Willis.

* * * * *

On November 29 the Provisional Government took official notice of Willis's visit to the Queen. This gesture was in the form

[107] Hastings to Dole, private, Nov. 19, 1893, M&E.

[108] Severance to Dole, Nov. 20 and 24, 1893, President's Files, Archives.

[109] *Memoirs,* pp. 343-348; also M&E.

[110] *Ibid.,* pp. 348-360; Morgan, pp. 596-602. The *Advertiser,* Dec. 4, 1893, upon printing Thurston's defense, praised it highly. The editor admitted it was not customary for a Minister to criticize the Government to which he was accredited, but the act was justified in this instance because of the secrecy practiced by Blount and Gresham.

[111] *Memoirs,* pp. 465-472; *House Ex. Doc. 48* (53 Cong. 2 Sess.), pp. 171-176. A signed copy was enclosed in Hastings to Dole, Dec. 9, 1893, M&E. On Dec. 28, 1893, the *Advertiser* printed the protest, excusing what was admitted to be an undiplomatic act with the assertion that the United States had kept the paper secret. On the same day the *Bulletin* dissected the arguments contained in Thurston's protest.

of a note from Dole asking the Minister whether Gresham's letter of October 18 was authentic. Willis refused to discuss the matter.[112] Upon receiving this answer the Government began to prepare in earnest for contingencies. Colonel Soper was advised to confer with his officers in order to arrive at a complete understanding with them as to the plan of action in case of hostile attack.[113] Dole cancelled the permission, granted on August 7, for American marines to drill on shore at any time; thereafter a separate request would have to be made each time the American Naval Commander wished to exercise his men.[114] The Government buildings were fortified with sandbags, while pistols and guns were distributed to all supporters of the Government who would accept them. The Portuguese representative protested to Willis that promiscuous issuance of arms to the simple Portuguese farmers might cause riots and brawls; he appealed to the Minister to give out some statement which would allay the feelings of the people.[115] Willis asked the Queen if she was afraid to remain at her home, and if so, she had at her disposal the hospitality of the Legation and the American warship. She replied she was being annoyed, but that it would be better policy for her to stay at her home. Her residence, nevertheless, was connected with the Legation by telephone.[116]

Rear Admiral John Irwin, who had succeeded Skerrett, sent a cipher to Washington saying: "Confidential. Provisional Government [say] they have one thousand men under arms. Palace prepared for defence. Party feeling intense, but no outbreak anticipated at present."[117] In a regular despatch of the same date, he

[112] Enclosed in Willis to Gresham, No. 8, Despatches; printed in *House Ex. Doc. 70* (53 Cong. 2 Sess.), p. 17.

[113] Minutes of the Executive Council, Dec. 5, 1893.

[114] Dole to Willis, Nov. 29, 1893, enclosed in Rear Admiral John Irwin to Secretary of the Navy, Jan. 19, 1894, No. 44895; printed in *House Ex. Doc. 70* (53 Cong. 2 Sess.), p. 16. Irwin informed Willis on Nov. 29 that he had "already given orders that our troops were not to be landed for drill or any other purpose unless ordered by myself, as in my opinion the landing of troops for drill would have a tendency to increase the disquiet already existing" (*House Ex. Doc. 140,* 53 Cong. 2 Sess., p. 5).

[115] *House Ex. Doc. 70* (53 Cong. 2 Sess.), p. 7.

[116] *Ibid.*

[117] Irwin to Secretary of the Navy, Dec. 4, 1893, in Ciphers Received, No. 1, *op. cit.,* p. 323; printed in *House Ex. Doc. 48, op. cit.,* p. 509.

added that the Provisional Government was in full control and that its officials were asserting "they will defend themselves at all hazards against an attack, no matter from what sourse [*sic*] it may emanate. . . . The reserve [amounting to five hundred men] is also armed, the men acting as minute men and ready for instantaneous call to arms. The feeling of both parties is intensely bitter, but I do not anticipate any collision." He could not find out what forces the Royalists had.[118]

Willis finally received from Gresham the following telegram on December 4: "The brevity and uncertainty of your telegrams are embarrassing. You will insist upon amnesty and recognition of obligation of the provisional government as essential conditions of restoration. All interests will be promoted by prompt action."[119] Because this message was too brief to be satisfactory, Willis decided to await more extended instructions which he felt sure would follow by mail. He answered Gresham in a telegram of the same date reading in part: "Active defensive preparations for several days; otherwise situation the same. The feeling intense, but hope to preserve status until further instructed." He also mentioned that Dole had inquired about the authenticity of the Secretary's letter of October 18.[120]

Anxiety was at least temporarily reduced when Willis let it be known that he had received no definite orders in the telegram of December 4, and that he was awaiting final directions on the cutter *Corwin*. This information merely postponed the decision as to whether there was to be war, decreasing the excitement instead of ending it completely. During the interim the Government trained its troops and continued to fortify public buildings.

Meanwhile the Queen's party, believing that restoration was at hand, began to make plans. Samuel Parker suggested to Damon the formation of a compromise cabinet, although it is doubtful whether this was more than merely a personal suggestion.[121] On December 5 a "Proposed course of procedure upon restoration of

[118] *House Ex. Doc. 140* (53 Cong. 2 Sess.), p. 5.

[119] Gresham to Willis, telegram, Nov. 24, 1893, quoted in Instructions, III, 188; printed in *House Ex. Doc. 48, op. cit.*, p. 171.

[120] Willis to Gresham, Dec. 4, 1893 (received at Washington, Dec. 13), Despatches; also in Ciphers Received, No. 1, *op. cit.*, p. 326; printed in *House Ex. Doc. 40, op. cit.*, p. 176.

[121] Minutes of the Executive Council, Dec. 9, 1893.

the Queen" was submitted to the American Minister. According to this scheme, the former Cabinet was to meet with other loyalists who would invite the American marines to come ashore. The United States Naval Commander would then indicate to the Provisional Government the time and the place for yielding up the archives and the Government buildings. Following a Royal proclamation of the return of the monarchy to power, a commander in chief would be appointed, *habeas corpus* suspended, and martial law instituted. All loyal citizens would be required to register and to give up their arms, vessels would be sent to the other islands to announce the change in government, and then proceedings would be instituted to try the Revolutionists for treason. A list of the leading Royalists who would be called upon for aid, as special advisers, was included.

Part of Willis's comment to Gresham indicates that he was doubting, more and more, the wisdom of restoring the old régime: "An analysis of the list of Special advisers, whether native or foreign, is not encouraging to the friends of good government or of American interests. The Americans who have for over half a century held a commanding place in the Councils of State, are ignored, and other nationalities, English especially, are placed in charge."[122] Later on he added: "It is doubtful whether any of those whose names are on these lists were informed of the fact."[123]

On December 7 Admiral Irwin received the protest which had been signed by some hundred and fifty Americans at the recent mass meeting; in it they appealed to Willis, Cleveland, Gresham, Herbert, and Irwin against what they termed the projected acts of war intended by the United States. The document said in part: ". . . any such acts of war or hostility if taken, attempted or announced in the time of profound peace now existing between the United States and the Hawaiian Islands, or without any full formal and timely announcement thereof will and would cause all concerned in authorizing the same to be held responsible for all

[122] Willis to Gresham, with enclosures 1 and 2, No. 10, Dec. 9, 1893, Despatches; printed in *House Ex. Doc. 70* (53 Cong. 2 Sess.), pp. 18-20.

[123] Same to same, No. 32, Feb. 2, 1894, Despatches. Willis's conjecture proved to be true. The list, as handed to him by C. B. Wilson, included Judges R. F. Bickerton and W. A. Whiting, both officeholders under the Provisional Government. When they heard about it, they told the Executive Council that their names had been added without their knowledge or approval (Minutes of the Executive Council, Jan. 30, 1894).

the consequences that may ensue therefrom, not only before Almighty God and in the forum of conscience but by all sanctioned rules and observances of civilized nations in their dealings with each other."[124]

Whether this appeal had any influence upon Willis or not, it is clear that he was beginning to doubt the practicability of his mission to restore the Queen. The problem he had to solve was a hard one; as the New York *Sun* on November 15, 1893, had said: "If ever a diplomatist had a ticklish task, the Hon. ALBERT S. WILLIS is the man." However, it was not the difficulty that made him waver. Perhaps he was unduly downcast over his failure to persuade the Queen to accept Cleveland's terms; perhaps he began to comprehend the hopelessness of good government under a monarchy. At any rate, on December 9[125] he sent a most revealing *"private* confidential" letter to Gresham, enclosed in one to his friend, Secretary of the Treasury Carlisle, asking the latter to read it. "If you think best *destroy* it." He went on to say: "I am under not *two* but three or four fires here but thus far believe I have not been Scorched. . . . I trust this private letter will not be misconstrued. I am here promptly to Carry out the will of the President and you Know me well Enough to believe that no newspaper Clamor—that no power, here or Else*where, will Cause* Me to hesitate one moment in its Execution." Carlisle did not destroy the letter, nor did Gresham. It began with a discussion of the Queen's obstinacy: "I need not Say how Surprised And disappointed I was at the outcome. I gave her (as you will note) Several opportunities to modify or withdraw her demands, with what poor Success you are advised. . . . The disclosure of her views meant great danger to her—most probably death. I did not feel at

[124] Signed Dec. 1; copy sent to Willis; enclosed in Irwin to Secretary of Navy, Dec. 9, 1893, No. 42967, Bureau of Navigation; printed in *House Ex. Doc. 140* (53 Cong. 2 Sess.), pp. 6-7.

[125] On that very day Charles Nordhoff was writing to Gresham as follows: "Will you be hurt with me if I venture to tell you my belief that Willis has turned out a complete failure? I of course read between the lines & I see that he has been Completely Captured by the 'genial' Provisional [Government officials] & is a new tool in their hands. My only hope now is that Willis will not bring abt. a state of affairs . . . [that will] *force* annexation" (Nordhoff to Gresham, Dec. 9, 1893, Cleveland MSS. Gresham probably sent the letter to Cleveland for his perusal, and he failed to return it.

liberty to use the Naval Cipher Code lest the information would Escape (by accident,). . . ." He then described how he had called a halt in the negotiations while awaiting further instructions; but neither the Queen nor the Provisional Government had been told the reasons for the delay. Continuing:

> As now instructed I did not feel authorized to Submit an ultimatum to her. Had She responded to the questions put to her in the way you Expected I Should have felt at liberty on the Same day to ask her to Call together her most discreet & Conservative friends to Consider the terms of a proclamation, the Composition of her Cabinet &c &c—Of Course I would have been Simply a "looker on." Upon receiving her proclamation of Amnesty &c & her Suggestions as to Cabinet (in which I had hoped She would have thought it advisable at least for the present to have Mr Damon and Mr Dole [)] (both of whom are Native Hawaiians enjoying the Confidence of All Sides), I Should the next day have made Known the will of the President to the Prov. Gov. and asked its immediate acceptance. I feel perfectly Confident that this program Could *then* have been Carried out.

He believed the project could still be executed, although newspaper editorials were making it more difficult to accomplish. "My opinion is that all this is a big game of bluff & despite the 1000 men whom they *claim* & the fortifications &c &c the End will Come when the definite will of the President is Made Known." Willis said he intended to send a note to every American citizen, asking him to register and to renounce his allegiance to the Provisional Government. "In this way I believe I Can at the proper time reach one half of their forces." The Portuguese *chargé* promised to do the same with his people.

After giving his plans, the Minister passed to some interesting speculation. "While giving you the above as my opinion I do not ignore Several Sources of peril," such as the great number of military adventurers who were looking for trouble, the Portuguese and other ignorant foreigners who might refuse to give up their arms, and the possibility of the natives and the Japanese creating disorder. He then went on:

> Assuming the restoration of the Queen with the temporary acquiescence of the Prov. Gov. & its Supporters, what next? If left to itself, under existing Condi-

> tions, it would fall to pieces like a card house. Would it be just to restore her & have Another Revolution at once —which Seems probable? If restored would She not be Entitled to our protection until She was Securely Seated? How long would this require?

He proceeded with other questions: Should he demand the re-establishment of the Constitution of 1887? What should be done about the opium and lottery bills which had been repealed by the Provisional Government? Should Dole go back to the Supreme Court? Should the Queen be allowed some pecuniary allowance during her enforced suspension? What if claims should be instituted against the United States for damages by its forces in promoting the overthrow of the Royal Government? What if the Queen, under American protection, tried to proclaim a new Constitution, which she desired? "This question is uppermost in Hawaiian hearts."

Willis, like Stevens, had become infected with the fear of machinations by the English, who, said he, were trying "to increase their foothold & are not unwilling to See the Native Hawaiians And Americans Estranged." He then delved into the old story of the relationships between Wodehouse, the Queen, and the Crown Princess; and he recalled that English influence had been increased by the establishment of Honolulu as a regular port of call for the Canadian Pacific steamers.

He ended with a historical essay:

> . . . from 1840 up to the Queens [*sic*] dethronement the American power behind the throne was greater than the throne, filling her [Hawaii's] judgeships, missions, Cabinets & legislatures & dominating the policy of the Country. Whether this paramount influence Can be revived is questionable. Another fact Should be Stated. The *City of Honolulu* is the Government & 9/10 of the Social financial & Commercial influences in Honolulu are Strongly American[.] An examination of the Constitution of 1887 will disclose how this Colony so small numerically has ruled the islands. The Hawaiian politicians have made this power arising out of limited Suffrage the ground for Strong Appeals to racial prejudice & the Queens [*sic*] action was in response to the feelings thus Aroused.

Native politicians would never rest until every Kanaka was allowed to vote, regardless of property.[126]

The *Corwin* arrived on December 14 with orders written on December 3.[127] The message read:

> Your despatch, which was answered by steamer on the 25th of November, seems to call for additional instructions.
>
> Should the Queen refuse assent to the written conditions, you will at once inform her that the President will cease interposition in her behalf, and that while he deems it his duty to endeavor to restore to the sovereign the constitutional government of the islands, his further efforts in that direction will depend upon the Queen's unqualified agreement that all obligations created by the Provisional Government in a proper course of administration shall be assumed, and upon such pledges by her as will prevent adoption of any measures of proscription or punishment for what has been done in the past by those setting up or supporting the Provisional Government. The President feels that by our original interference and what followed, we have incurred responsibilities to the whole Hawaiian community, and that it would not be just to put one party at the mercy of another.
>
> Should the Queen ask whether if she accedes to conditions active steps will be taken by the United States to effect her restoration, or to maintain her authority thereafter, you will say that the President cannot use force without the consent of Congress.
>
> Should the Queen accept conditions and the Provisional Government refuse to surrender, you will be governed by previous instructions. If the Provisional Government asks whether the United States will hold the Queen to fulfillment of stipulated conditions, you will say, the President acting under dictates of honor and duty, as he has done in endeavoring to effect restoration, will do all in his constitutional power to cause observance of the conditions he has imposed.[128]

On December 16 Willis once more interviewed the Queen, allowing her to have her most trusted adviser, J. O. Carter, present.

[126] Willis to Gresham, Dec. 9, 1893, enclosed in Willis to Carlisle, Dec. 9, 1893, Cleveland MSS.

[127] Sometimes dated Dec. 2, in printed documents.

[128] Gresham to Willis, Dec. 3, 1893, Instructions, III, 189-190; printed in *House Ex. Doc. 48, op. cit.*, p. 171.

She still clung to her former views, but at Carter's persuasion, rescinded the death penalty, reducing it to permanent banishment of all Revolutionists, including their families. She also promised to recognize the military obligations of the Provisional Government, because she believed they would be taken care of by the confiscated property of the exiles. Inasmuch as she objected to the Constitution of 1887, because the property qualifications for voting for Nobles discriminated against the natives, she desired to promulgate a new constitution. She also wished to limit the terms of judges to six years and to enlarge the Cabinet.[129]

In a third conference, on December 18, she still held to banishment and confiscation of property.[130] Faced with this determined attitude, Minister Willis exhibited his instructions, proving that her case was hopeless if she refused to yield. Even then she was adamant. However, on the same day, at the pressure of Carter, she suddenly changed her mind. At six in the evening, he brought word that Liliuokalani would give complete amnesty and would assume all obligations of the Provisional Government. In her letter of compliance, the Queen agreed that she "must not feel vengeful to any of my people" and "must forgive and forget the past"; she trusted that "all will hereafter work together in peace and friendship for the good and for the glory of our beautiful and once happy land." Furthermore, she asked Willis to bear a "message of gratitude from me and from my people" to President Cleveland; and promised that she would "prove worthy of the confidence and friendship" of the United States.[131]

* * * * *

[129] Interview enclosed in Willis to Gresham, No. 14, Dec. 18, 1893, Despatches; printed in *House Ex. Doc. 70* (53 Cong. 2 Sess.), pp. 23-26; and Thurston, *Memoirs,* pp. 462-463.

[130] Interview enclosed in same to same, No. 15, Dec. 19, 1893, Despatches; printed in *House Ex. Doc. 70, op. cit.*, pp. 26-28.

[131] Enclosures 1 and 2, in same to same, No. 16, Dec. 20, 1893, Despatches; printed in *ibid.,* pp. 29-30. Regarding his despatches touching the three interviews, Willis wrote Gresham a personal letter, marked "Important," in which he said: "As the contents of these three interviews might and doubtless would result in serious trouble if ever Known, I write in the interest of life, and peace, whether I cannot expunge No[.] 3 and write up only the formal parts of Nos. 15 & 16. If this is in Your discretion, I ask that it be done. The Queen has just Sent me a letter (not the first) announcing a conspiracy against her life. As to threats, social ostracism and other

Something of the tension between the American Minister and the Provisional Government, as well as an intimation of the philosophy upon which each was acting, is brought out by an unofficial exchange of views between Attorney General W. O. Smith and Minister Willis. Smith reported the conversation to the Executive Council and then proceeded to act as secretary to write the story up in that day's minutes.

Smith said he had asked Willis for permission to send despatches on the *Corwin* when it returned, because weeks might pass before another boat offered an opportunity for the Government to communicate with its Washington diplomats. Willis refused, and then went on to declare that he resented the local newspaper attacks upon Cleveland. He stressed that he was talking unofficially. Smith then answered that he would talk unofficially also. Both went to it, opening up their inner thoughts in (as the minutes said) an earnest and courteous manner.

Smith declared it was hard for his Government to understand Willis's secrecy; Willis denied any secrecy. He had come prepared to act, but certain contingencies arose to prevent his saying anything openly. He hoped to be able to talk the following Monday or Tuesday. Smith then stated he did not understand how the United States could justify its questioning of the right of the Provisional Government to exist after it had recognized that Government. He added that the whole affair looked like a bit of politics. Willis denied this charge warmly, maintaining that Cleveland was a man of the purest motives and highest honor. It was the United States[132] that was acting—acting "in accordance with the policy of a hundred years." Smith answered that it *must* have been a matter of personal opinion, because Harrison was for the treaty and he also had been the United States Government. When Willis asked what the Provisional Government would do if the Senate refused another treaty, Smith replied that it

similar petty annoyances to us, I have not thought proper to dignify them with an official statement" (Willis to Gresham, Dec. 23, 1893, in Gresham MSS.).

[132] Either Willis was not consistent, or else his visitor mixed up what he said, because Damon saw him later and reported that Willis had stated that "this Hawaiian Question was a quarrel between the present U. S. Administration and the previous Administration" (Minutes of the Executive Council, Jan. 2, 1894).

would wait until the next Administration came into office. Willis answered that this would be futile; Cleveland still had three years in his term, the Democratic party would be in power for the next twenty years, and Cleveland had a majority in both houses of Congress. Willis changed the subject by averring that it was hard to understand the local hatred for the United States. "Don't you know," he asked, "either of the two powers[133] in the harbor could crush you and you would have to seek help from the United States?" Smith replied that the Annexationists stood for a principle, and that that principle would not allow a monarchy to rule Hawaii.[134]

Honolulu was in a new fever of expectancy as soon as the *Corwin* arrived. It was the general opinion that Willis had received orders forcibly to restore the monarchy. President Dole said that he had lived in the city fifty years, but had never seen such a strain as that following December 14. He added: "The business of the entire community was practically suspended and its time and energy devoted to an exciting and absorbing consideration of the political situation and to military preparation to meet unknown contingencies."[135] The Government was anxious about what it should do with the Queen. On December 17 the Executive Council met first at W. C. Wilder's and later at Dole's home to discuss the advisability of taking her into custody. "But it was decided that it could probably not be done without costing much life, and perhaps her life, [and so] it was finally decided not to attempt it now."[136] Minister Wodehouse asked for permission to land troops from the British *Champion* in order to protect his Legation. The Council answered that the Provisional Government was fully able to guard him, but the request was "cheerfully" granted.[137]

Some strange stories have been told of the apprehension prevalent during what was generally known as "Black Week"; popular supposition had it that the American marines would attack the Provisional Government. These tales took several forms.

[133] He probably meant Japan and England.

[134] Minutes of the Executive Council, Dec. 16, 1893. Willis's version of the conversation with Smith is not extant.

[135] Dole to Willis, "Letter of Specifications," Jan. 11, 1894, which is enclosure 1, in Willis to Gresham, No. 31, Jan. 19, 1894, Despatches.

[136] Minutes of the Executive Council, Dec. 17, 1893.

[137] *Ibid.,* Dec. 18, 1893.

One version ran to the effect that Willis tried to bluff the Provisional Government into yielding. Thus Sereno E. Bishop declared that on the morning of December 18 "there had been increased stir on board of the *Philadelphia* and the *Adams*"; that crowds of natives lined the wharves expecting the marines to land; that many native police resigned rather than take an oath to fight for the Government; that the German Consul pleaded with Willis to do something to reduce the panic among the people; and that Willis refused, declaring he expected to accomplish his aims within forty-eight hours.[138] McElroy, writing much later, asserted that Willis, by a threat of force, pressured the Provisional Government to give in; that he ordered the marines on the two men-of-war to prepare to land; and that, in doing so, exceeded his instructions.[139] Perhaps these stories developed out of Minister W. R. Castle's statement at a Boston news conference in the fall of 1895. Said he:

> Just at the critical moment, however, when everyone in the city fully expected a conflict with the American troops, an intimation came to us, in a quiet way—I will not say how—that the troops had no idea of landing, and that no force would be used. The intimation was very slight, but it was sufficient to show us that the mustering of the troops on the deck of the ship was merely for effect. It was a big show of "bluff."[140]

Another version had it that Willis intended to use more than a mere threat or bluff; in other words, he planned to order a feint. According to this account, a junior officer landed in the midst of the crowd and went to a high official's residence, saying that the disembarking of the marines would be simply a display of force: that if the Provisional Government troops merely fired into the air, the marines would return to their ships.[141]

Still a third version was recorded by Musick, who quoted a secret message that was sent to Colonel Soper, Commander of the Provisional Government army, saying in substance: "If we land, for God's sake don't allow your men to fire on us, but move back

[138] In Alexander, *op. cit.*, p. 104.
[139] McElroy, *Cleveland, op. cit.*, II, 67.
[140] Printed in *Advertiser,* Oct. 2, 1895.
[141] Edmund Janes Carpenter, *America in Hawaii* (Boston, 1899), p. 223.

and take all your arms and ammunition with you. All we will be required to do will be to place the queen in the government building, then retire and leave her alone."[142] This story probably stemmed from Thurston's telegram to Dole of November 15 in which he said that Gresham differentiated between restoring the Queen and maintaining her in power.

Three versions, then, have been set down: (1) That Willis ordered the troops on the warships to stir about and indicate unusual activity, so as to make the Provisional Government give in to a bluff; (2) That the troops were actually to land, but were to retire the moment the Provisional Government army, by firing into the air, showed its intention to fight; (3) That the marines would disembark, the Provisional Government and its army would retire temporarily from the Government Building, the Queen would be replaced on the throne, and then the American forces would calmly withdraw. After that the Provisional Government could arrest the Queen and reestablish itself.

The first version is quite easily refuted and explained. Bishop said that the troops on the ships were astir on December 18, as if to bluff the Provisional Government. But what point was there in trying to bluff the Government before Willis had asked for its resignation and retirement, which he did not do until December 20? If there was any virtue in trying to overawe the Dole régime, the attempt should reasonably have occurred at the time when, and just after, Willis asked for its capitulation. Moreover, the activity of the marines on board the ships was explained in 1928 by Rear Admiral Albert S. Barker, who was Captain of the *Philadelphia* which was stationed at Honolulu during the autumn of 1893. According to Barker, Admiral Irwin declared at the time that he would feel disgraced if he had to restore the Queen, but that he had neither orders nor intentions of landing troops to aid her. American marines were, however, kept in readiness to put down rioting by either party, but were to help neither. This preparation, continued Barker, was thought by the Royalists and the Government to be for the purpose of somehow helping Liliuokalani. Barker added that the British and Japanese Commanders planned to land troops to help patrol the city if the United States at-

[142] John R. Musick, *Hawaii, Our New Possessions* (N. Y. and London, 1898), p. 384.

tempted to overthrow the Provisional Government. He denied that Willis intended to use either bluff or force when he asked the Provisional Government to step down, and submitted that Willis acquitted himself well in a difficult assignment.[143] Thus Bishop's story of troops astir on board the war vessels turns out to be merely a routine preparation to keep order in the city.

The second and third versions are even more absurd. That either Cleveland, Gresham, or Willis could wish to make the United States ridiculous by ordering American troops to retreat merely because a few ill-armed Provisional Government men had fired into the air over their heads, is hard to believe. Even more unbelievable is the story that the luckless Queen would be ceremoniously seated upon her throne by American bayonets, and that then the United States would figuratively wipe its hands of the affair by permitting her to be arrested and imprisoned by the Provisional Government. Such a procedure would have made of the United States a participant in the worst sort of *opéra bouffe* and the laughing stock of the world.

Aside from the argument of common sense, the records prove that no such folderol was even contemplated. Carpenter, while writing *America in Hawaii,* asked Assistant Secretary of State John Bassett Moore if there was any basis for the stories just mentioned. Moore, after a careful search through the files of the Department of State, said he was unable to discover any order for Willis to make a feint.[144] Nor are there any instructions of a similar kind in the records of the Navy Department.

A rumor got around Honolulu and into the *Star* that Admiral Irwin had moved his wife and children from their hotel to a warship for safety. Irwin simply called this a lie.[145] As a matter of fact Irwin had gone to the trouble of warning his men against taking sides and against wearing badges of either of the parties in Honolulu.[146] In brief, there is no evidence whatever that Willis

[143] Albert S. Barker, *Everyday Life in the Navy* (1928), quoted by Thurston, *Memoirs,* pp. 445-451. It is of considerable significance that Thurston, who had no reason to like Willis, quoted Barker.

[144] *Op. cit.,* p. 225.

[145] Irwin to Secretary of Navy, Feb. 8, 1894, No. 45057, enclosing clipping from the *Star.* Dole mentioned most of these indications of Willis's intention to land troops in his "Letter of Specifications," *op. cit.*

[146] Printed order in Cleveland MSS., folio marked "Printed Material 1893."

endeavored to gain his ends by the use of either force or bluff; if so, Admiral Irwin would have reported it. Instead (as even the Annexationist Sereno E. Bishop was constrained to quote), Irwin wrote on January 2, 1894: "Mr. Willis has never given me the slightest hint that there was ever any intention on the part of the United States Government to use force in order to restore the Queen. My own orders to preserve strict neutrality have been implicitly obeyed."[147]

The Republican press in the United States did not, however, know that fact. It expected war, and applauded the Provisional Government for its doughty refusal to give up in favor of a craven Queen. "These missionaries' children," said the New York *Sun* on December 14, 1893, "are men, self-respecting, honorable men, and smart enough, too; and they are ready, if necessary, to fight for all that freemen hold dear. The American spirit of '76 is in their hearts." Next day, upon hearing of the preparations to fight the United States, the *Sun* declared: "All Hail, Hawaii!"

* * * * *

The Provisional Government decided to make an official request of Willis to find out whether there was any basis to the rumors that the monarchy was to be revived. President Dole wished to know "if this report is true or if you are acting in any way hostile to this Government." He continued: "I appreciate fully the fact that any such action upon your part in view of your official relations with this Government would seem impossible; but as the information has come to me from such sources that I am compelled to notice it, you will pardon me for pressing you for an immediate answer."[148] As the *Advertiser* said, "this continued excitement MUST BE STOPPED."[149]

Minister Willis's reply to Dole's note was a request for an interview with the Provisional Government in order finally to have his say.[150] The meeting took place at 1:30 p.m. on December

[147] In Alexander, *op. cit.*, p. 120.

[148] Enclosure 1 in Willis to Gresham, No. 17, Dec. 20, 1893, Despatches; printed in *House Ex. Doc. 70* (53 Cong. 2 Sess.), p. 34; Minutes of the Executive Council, Dec. 18, 1893.

[149] Dec. 19, 1893.

[150] Minutes of the Executive Council, Dec. 19, 1893.

20,[151] two days after the Queen had complied with President Cleveland's conditions. Said the American Minister, in part:

> Upon the facts embodied in Mr. Blount's reports, the President has arrived at certain conclusions and determined upon a certain course of action with which it becomes my duty to acquaint you.
>
> The Provisional Government was not established by the Hawaiian people or with their consent or acquiescence, nor has it since existed with their consent. . . .
>
> In view of these conclusions I was instructed by the President to take advantage of an early opportunity to inform the Queen of this determination and of his views as to the responsibility of our Government. . . . I was . . . instructed, at the same time, to inform the Queen that when reinstated, that [*sic*] the President expected that she would pursue a magnanimous course by granting full amnesty to all who participated in the movement against her. . . .
>
> In obedience to the command of the President, I have secured the Queen's agreement to this course. . . . It becomes my further duty to advise you, Sir, the Executive of the Provisional Government and your Ministers of the President's determination of the question which your action and that of the Queen devolved upon him, and that you are expected to promptly relinquish to her her constitutional authority. And now Mr. President and gentlemen of the Provisional Government, with a deep and solemn sense of the gravity of the situation . . . in the name and by the authority of the United States of America, I submit to you the question, "Are you willing to abide by the decision of the President?"[152]

After recovering from their surprise and amazement,[153] the officials of the Government asked for several days in which to prepare an answer. In the laconic words of the Executive Council Minutes, "Mr[.] Dole told him we would return him an answer, and he withdrew." Instead of politely withdrawing and allowing the Pro-

[151] As will appear in the next chapter, Cleveland had on December 18 thrown the Hawaiian problem upon the shoulders of Congress.

[152] Enclosure 3 in Willis to Gresham, No. 17, *op. cit.* This is an astounding request, but it is clear from its words that no force was intended. The President had been appealed to by both parties as arbiter; hence the question: "Are you willing to abide by the decision of the President?"

[153] For press comment on Willis's demand, see *Advertiser,* Dec. 20, 21, 22.

visional Government to stall for time, now was the chance for Willis (if he had such intentions or instructions) to use his threats of force or to try the feint which Bishop and others said he had in mind. But he did neither; "he withdrew."

One reason for demanding time to make a reply was that the Government wished to await the arrival of the *Alameda* which was expected to bring news of the attitude of Congress; that body, having convened early in December would, it was trusted, denounce the President's program. The Government's request for time was wise, for the ship not only brought information of the Senate's attack upon Cleveland's Hawaiian policy, but also carried Thurston, who arrived just in time to be able to place his masterly ability at drafting papers in the service of the Government. The news about the Senate's attitude helped to lessen the tension, and on December 22 the *Advertiser* got out an extra issue to say that the crisis was ended. "Black Week" was over, although in the interim between Willis's demand for surrender and the arrival of the *Alameda,* plans for defense continued. The Government had even made arrangements to move to the Royal Hawaiian Hotel, out of cannon shot.[154]

Meanwhile Dole, presently aided by Thurston, was preparing his reply. So important was this work considered to be that at the meeting of the Executive Council for December 22, certain important outsiders were called in for advice. Besides Dole and Thurston, there were J. L. King, W. O. Smith, W. N. Armstrong, F. M. Hatch, A. F. Judd, W. R. Castle, A. S. Hartwell, J. W. Kalua, C. L. Carter, and H. N. Castle.

Finally at midnight of December 23, 1893, President Dole, in an extended memorandum, replied to Willis in the negative, basing his refusal to hand over the sovereignty to the Queen on nine definite and carefully considered points which can be briefed as follows: First, the Government was sorry to refuse the President's request that it surrender, but it was hopeful that its action would not alienate from it the friendship of the United States. Second, the démarche as issued by Willis was a new departure in diplomatic practice; the Provisional Government did not recognize President Cleveland's right to interfere in its affairs. Third, the Provisional

[154] Bishop, in Alexander, *op. cit.*, p. 108; Dole, *Memoirs,* pp. 111 and 127.

Government, having been recognized by the United States and by all the nations of the earth, could not now be tampered with. Fourth, the promise as made by S. M. Damon to the Queen that she would be heard at Washington was given on his own responsibility; he did not report to the Provisional Government that such an agreement had been entered into; and therefore the present régime did not accept or support what he may have said. Fifth, the Provisional Government never meant to allow an appeal by Liliuokalani to the United States. Sixth, if American forces illegally aided in the establishment of the new Government, that Government was not responsible for what American marines had done; this was a question for the United States alone; and the Provisional Government could not be destroyed to make amends to any former Queen. Seventh, if American forces had been absent, the Revolution would have taken place nevertheless. Eighth, the Provisional Government never knew until the publication of Gresham's letter of October 18 just what President Cleveland's intentions were. Ninth, the Provisional Government could not refute, comment upon, or judge Commissioner Blount's findings because they had never been officially submitted to it.[155]

These arguments are self-explanatory and require little expansion. They are as well founded as could reasonably be expected, considering that the Provisional Government had to make a case. The only point which cannot be defended at all is the declaration that the Provisional Government had never promised to allow the Queen an appeal to Washington.

Now that the worst of the danger was over, Dole and his colleagues could afford the time to express their exasperation at what Willis had attempted to do. The outcome was a lengthy protest, dated December 27, 1893, remonstrating against everything pertaining to the Hawaiian program of the Democratic Administration. Willis's "attitude" was objected to; in addition, his communications to the Provisional Government were "ambiguous" in that he never disclosed his or Cleveland's intentions for many weeks. Furthermore, the Government had never received a copy of Blount's report, and therefore could only guess at his conclusions. Willis's language, which hinted at the use of force to

[155] Enclosed in Willis to Gresham, No. 18, Dec. 23, 1893, Despatches; printed in *House Ex. Doc. 70* (53 Cong. 2 Sess.), pp. 36-42.

restore the Queen, was flayed because it produced "disquiet" among the people. He had held secret meetings with Liliuokalani and these conferences served to embolden the Royalists. As a consequence there was increased expense for military preparation because of Royalist threats to assassinate members of the Government. In view of all these grievances, Dole demanded assurances and explanations.[156] Cleveland thought this "a most extraordinary letter."[157]

Willis answered on the same day, calling for explanations also. He wished to know how his attitude had been unfriendly and just where and when he had ever hinted at the use of force to restore the *status quo ante*. He desired information on what communications from him had been "ambiguous."

In reference to Gresham's letter of October 18, he stated it was a domestic matter which could not receive diplomatic discussion.[158] President Dole answered on December 29 that the arrival of Cleveland's message to Congress, in which he had laid the Hawaiian problem before that body, removed all present danger and made further correspondence regarding Willis's attitude and ambiguity unnecessary.[159]

Willis was not satisfied with this cavalier shelving of the argument. He held that Dole's original protest had used expressions and had made charges which reflected upon the honor of both the President and himself. No doubt sick of the entire matter and deeply desirous of ending the controversy, Willis still felt he could not allow the Provisional Government's charges to stand on the record. In consequence he decided to attempt, by the use of personal persuasion upon certain conservatives, to have the charges withdrawn. He saw R. W. Irwin (not the American Admiral) who then informed the Executive Council that Willis was very much aggrieved and that therefore the letter should be withdrawn. Thurston and W. N. Armstrong advised that the request be refused, and it was.[160]

[156] Enclosure 1 in Willis to Gresham, No. 20½, Jan. 5, 1894, Despatches; printed in *House Ex. Doc. 79* (53 Cong. 2 Sess.), pp. 4-5.

[157] *House Ex. Doc. 76* (53 Cong. 2 Sess.), p. 1.

[158] Enclosure 2 in Willis to Gresham, No. 20½, *op. cit.;* printed in *House Ex. Doc. 79, op. cit.*, pp. 5-6.

[159] Enclosure 3 in *ibid.* Cleveland's message will be discussed later.

[160] Minutes of the Executive Council, Dec. 29, 1893.

Next Willis tried to work through the conservative Damon, who, he knew, was not in sympathy with the bellicose attitude of his Government.[161] At ten o'clock in the evening of December 30, Willis went to Damon's house on an unofficial visit to request that Damon try to convince his colleagues that they should withdraw their statement. He said he had warm feelings for the Americans in the islands and had their interests at heart, but that he could not overlook the arraignment of the President in the letter of December 27. If it was not recalled, he might have to remove the United States warships from the harbor. Again he used the political argument: "That the President was in power and had 100 majority in the House of Representatives and a majority in the Senate and he would act in such manner as he deemed it to be his duty; and in the interests and for the sake of Americans here he (Willis) hoped the matter would be dropped."[162] But the Government refused to drop it.

Dole replied on January 1, 1894, in an unsigned[163] communication which declared that the charges were not withdrawn, but that since the President no longer had the direction of the Hawaiian situation, the matter might end.[164] Willis, still dissatisfied, refused to subside, and, on the same day, called for "specifications" as to his unfriendly attitude, his ambiguity, and hints at the use of force.[165] It took the Provisional Government some ten days to prepare its "Letter of Specifications."

During the time these charges were being hurled back and forth, Admiral Irwin had penned a despatch to the Secretary of the Navy showing the disturbed state of public opinion. He reported on January 2, 1894, that the Provisional Government was still preparing for defense and that "the excitement is unabated." He continued: "The News papers assume that I, as Military Representative of the U. S., intend to use force to restore the Queen, at the same

[161] In fact Damon had nothing to do with and knew nothing about the letter when it was being drafted (Minutes of the Executive Council, Dec. 29).

[162] *Ibid.*, Dec. 30, 1893, and Jan. 1, 1894.

[163] Dole later said the letter was unsigned because of an oversight (EAC, Feb. 5, 1894).

[164] Enclosures 3, 4, 5, in Willis to Gresham, No. 20½, *op. cit.*

[165] Enclosure 6 in *ibid.* Willis probably never knew the fact, but the Government drafted a letter asking for his recall. The request was never sent because Dole and his advisers thought better of it (Dole, *Memoirs*, p. 128).

time they quote me as saying that I would not obey any order, which I considered unlawfull [*sic*], also that the officers and men under my command had assumed the same attitude." He felt that such rumormongering was devoted to the purpose of influencing American public opinion. Whatever the purpose, he declared that it was without foundation; he would follow a policy of neutrality, landing troops only to protect American lives and property. If the newspapers quieted down, he was certain that business would go on as usual. "Foreign influence, inimical to the interests of the United States is secretly at work here, as it is wherever we have any trade interests, and that influence will account for many of the mistatements [*sic*] in the papers." He went on: "Now, as the general public in Honolulu is fully aware of the above fact [that no force was intended] and have no longer any apprehension of any riot, and, as the perusal of the Presidents [*sic;* Cleveland's] Message has convinced every one that no force would be used to change the Government, it is criminal for anyone to make the mistatements [*sic*] referred to."[166] In another despatch the Admiral praised his men for their perfect discipline and good order while ashore on leave, in spite of "the most trying circumstances."[167]

The agitated state of public opinion was also indicated by the fact that Liliuokalani informed Willis, who relayed the fact to the Government through Damon, that she was fearful of being assassinated by Captain Good, who had been seen loitering near her residence. Damon said Good was all right, but that the Government would be glad to offer all the protection she needed. Willis was then told officially that the Provisional Government abhorred assassination and that members of the Government themselves had been warned of plots against them time and again. Willis replied that he had instructions to protect the Queen, but preferred that the Provisional Government do it.[168]

Before the "Letter of Specifications" was ready for presentation to Willis, he was handed a petition from the Hawaiian Patriotic League (Hui Aloha Aina); the natives wished it to be known that the agitation for a restored monarchy was not to be allowed to

[166] Irwin to the Secretary of the Navy, No. 43691, Bureau of Navigation; printed in *House Ex. Doc. 140* (53 Cong. 2 Sess.), pp. 9-10.

[167] Printed in *ibid.*, p. 10.

[168] Minutes of the Executive Council, Jan. 1 and 2, 1894.

die out. Supposedly representing 8,000 voters, it recited the grievances of the Kanakas since January 17, 1893, in ten typewritten pages. The League had been formed to preserve "the autonomy of the Country under the Native Monarchy"; it appealed to Cleveland against Stevens's "political crime" of being "in collusion with a cabal of a dozen aliens." The memorial was signed by an Honorary President, a President, four Vice Presidents, a Secretary, a Treasurer, and ten Executive Councillors.[169] About two weeks later, Samuel Parker, who described himself as "Premier and Minister of Foreign Affairs" in the Queen's last Cabinet, telegraphed Gresham from San Francisco, where he was on a business trip, to deny newspaper reports that the Queen had relinquished all hopes of restoration; "having submitted her Case to the Arbitration of the United States [she] will patiently await their verdict."[170]

Finally on January 11, 1894, Dole sent to Willis his lengthy and notorious "Letter of Specifications," which Willis called a " 'Stump Speech' of 50 pages."[171] The American Minister believed that Thurston, rather than Dole, had composed it, because of its general resemblance to other writings of the Hawaiian Minister to the United States.[172] It contained twenty-eight separate grievances against Blount, Willis, Gresham, and Cleveland for past acts. The onus of the charges came out of the complete Blount report which the Provisional Government had finally received on December 22. Much of the space was devoted to answering Blount's findings. Enclosed were affidavits of numerous Provisional Government officials who, under oath, declared there had been no secret agreement between the Revolutionists and Minister Stevens. Furthermore, Dole charged that the reason for the appointment of Blount was kept as long as possible from the Provisional Government, and that, when Minister Thurston inquired from Secretary

[169] Enclosed in Willis to Gresham, No. 24, Jan. 6, 1894, Despatches; printed in *House Ex. Doc. 76* (53 Cong. 2 Sess.), pp. 2-6.

[170] Parker to Gresham, telegram, Jan. 16, 1894, Notes from Hawaii.

[171] Willis to Gresham, private, Jan. 16, 1894, Gresham MSS.

[172] Same to same, private, Feb. 14, 1894, *ibid.* Willis was correct. Dole (*Memoirs,* p. 137) said Thurston drafted it at Dole's request; but Thurston (*Memoirs,* p. 472) asserted he only aided. See also W. N. Armstrong to Thurston, Feb. 8, 1894, M&E.

Gresham as to the object of the Commissioner's visit, he was refused any information.

Moreover, Blount's method was at fault; he interviewed sixty Royalists and only twenty Annexationists, only two of the Committee of Safety, only one of the Executive Council, only three of the Advisory Council, only two of the eight speakers at the mass meeting of January 16, 1893, and none of the five Commissioners who were sent to Washington to treat for annexation. The Provisional Government had never been requested to answer the charges made by Blount, a copy of whose complete report had arrived three days after Willis demanded the surrender of that Government.[173]

The paper bore in heavily upon the secrecy practiced by the Cleveland Administration in its Hawaiian program. As an example of the roundabout way in which the Honolulu officials came to know American policy, Dole quoted a passage from the *New York Herald* for November 8, 1893. He submitted that the Provisional Government should have been provided with this information through the regular diplomatic channels, instead of having to secure it through the newspapers. Said the *Herald*:

> A diplomatic bombshell will burst within the next few days and the report will be heard throughout the entire world.
>
> The bomb will be thrown by the accredited representative of the United States Government and he will hurl it against the badly conceived and worse managed Provisional Government of the Hawaiian Islands.
>
> If Mr. Willis and Rear-Admiral Irwin arrived in Honolulu on schedule there will be even livelier times in the capital city of the Hawaiian Islands, to-day, than there is in the metropolis of the United States. . . . Briefly stated, the present administration will do all in its power to restore the condition of affairs which existed in Hawaii at the time Minister Stephens[174] brought about the overthrow of Queen Liliuokalani. . . .
>
> This means that the Queen will be restored to her throne and the Provisional Government, representing

[173] Hastings was unable to get a copy until Dec. 8, when he sent it on to Honolulu (Hastings to Dole, Dec. 8, 1893, M&E).

[174] *Sic* in the copy sent by Willis to Gresham.

only a small part of the people of Hawaii, will soon be a thing of the past.[175]

Willis answered Dole's charges, explaining as best he could, the objections made against his conduct. He refused to discuss the Blount report because he felt it was outside his authority. Not believing Dole's protests against himself as justified, he demanded recantation or further proof.[176] Dreary, argumentative conversations, back and forth, lasted well into February before Willis was satisfied with Dole's explanations.[177]

These bitter recriminations, along with the fear of war between the Provisional Government and the United States, had rasped the feelings of all concerned; so much so that everyday social relationships between Willis and Hawaiian officialdom ceased. The same is true of the relations between Thurston and Gresham at Washington. Willis was certain that Dole intended to embarrass him by holding back his "Letter of Specifications" so long that Willis did not have time to copy it before the next ship left with mail.[178] Whether Dole was guilty of such a trick is not certain; but Thurston, upon returning to the United States, sent a copy of Dole's "Letter of Specifications" to Gresham on February 3, 1894, with the statement that he was doing it as a good gesture because Willis did not have time to copy the original.[179] Gresham sent it back unread, because "It is desirable that the contents of Mr. Dole's letter should reach the State Department in the regular way, through Mr. Willis."[180] Thurston had to take the rebuff silently because he could not tell Gresham that the suggestion had come from Congressman John F. Lacey[181] of Iowa and Senator John T. Morgan of Alabama.[182]

[175] Enclosure 1 in Willis to Gresham, No. 31, Jan. 19, 1894, Despatches. The letter was published as a pamphlet by the *Star* in Feb., 1894, with the subtitle, "An Indictment of American Diplomacy in Hawaii." A copy is in Official Dole Files, Archives.

[176] Enclosures 2, 3, 4, in Willis to Gresham, No. 31, *op. cit.*

[177] Enclosures 1, 2, 3, in same to same, No. 38, March 2, 1894, Despatches.

[178] Same to same, private, Jan. 12, 1894, Gresham MSS.

[179] Thurston to Gresham, Feb. 3, 1894, Notes from Hawaii.

[180] Gresham to Thurston, Feb. 4, 1894, Notes to Hawaii and M&E.

[181] Lacey to Thurston, Feb. 3, 1894, M&E.

[182] Thurston showed a copy of the letter to Senator Morgan, who, upon learning that Gresham had not as yet received it, told Thurston to take it to Gresham and Morgan would then "pull it out of him by resolution of the Senate" (Thurston, *Memoirs,* pp. 473-474). Gresham did not fall for the ruse.

Thurston's position at Washington vis-à-vis the Democratic Administration was just about as unpleasant as was Willis's vis-à-vis the Provisional Government. W. N. Armstrong told Thurston what was obvious: "I see that you and Gresham are not Kissing yet."[183] Soon the Hawaiian Minister was asking to be allowed to come home on leave or else he would resign. Being Hawaiian representative, he affirmed, was like "a bump on a log. . . . The Administration is still ugly in tone toward us—I would rather be Kicked than swallow Greshams [*sic*] bread, but for the good of the cause I swallow my spittle and smile like any other Villain."[184] Nevertheless Thurston stayed on the job, but did not darken the door of the State Department oftener than he had to. He said at another time: "I do not want to give him [Gresham] an opportunity to be ugly any oftener than possible."[185]

If anything, Willis's and Mills's situation was even worse in Honolulu. Both found that the hatred shown by the officials of the Government toward them and their entourage was almost unbearable. So harshly was Mills treated that Willis suggested he write a letter describing the insults he received, and Willis would then forward it to Gresham. Mills did so on January 2, 1894; he told how the Annexationists detested him because he had been Blount's secretary and because he tried to maintain a neutral attitude; he had been libelled in the press, especially by the *Star,* and even threatened with bodily harm. Willis enclosed Mills's note in a private letter to Gresham, in which he defended Mills, told of his own trials, described the press which was teeming with insults and epithets against "the damned Yankees," and praised the bluejackets and marines for their perfect discipline.[186]

By the middle of January, 1894, the tension began to be allayed. On January 12 Willis received Gresham's answer to the refusal of the Provisional Government to yield. "The President," Gresham said, "sincerely regrets that the Provisional Government refuses to acquiesce in the conclusion which his sense of right and duty and a due regard for our national honor constrained him to reach and

[183] Armstrong to Thurston, Feb. 8, 1894, M&E.

[184] Thurston to Dole, confidential, Feb. 21, 1894, *ibid.*

[185] Thurston to Hatch, confidential, March 9, 1894, *ibid.*

[186] Mills to Willis, Jan. 2, 1893 (*sic*), enclosed in Willis to Gresham, *"Personal,"* Jan. 3, 1893 (*sic*), Gresham MSS., Box 6.

submit as a measure of justice to the people of the Hawaiian Islands and their deposed sovereign. . . . The subversion of the Hawaiian Government by an abuse of the authority of the United States was in plain violation of international law and required the President to disavow and condemn the act of our offending officials, and, within the limits of his constitutional power, to endeavor to restore the lawful authority." The President, continued Gresham, could not construe the matter merely as a case wherein American officials must be reprimanded,[187] as the Provisional Government suggested. Because the President had done all he could do within his constitutional prerogatives, the problem had been laid before Congress.[188]

* * * * *

Thus ended, in ignominious failure, Cleveland's attempt to restore the Queen. The impartial student is forced to admit that, although ideally the episode did justice to the sense of honor of both Gresham and Cleveland, it was impractical; and furthermore that the policy ran into natural obstacles because it was conceived and executed in secrecy. As a matter of fact the scheme would have failed just as miserably had it been executed in the open.

At first blush the impression is given—because the President and his Secretary of State so long concealed their purpose from the Hawaiian officials—that they exercised the weapon of secrecy with deliberate intent. For example, Willis's confidential instructions to see Liliuokalani and effect a settlement if possible appear to indicate that the Administration, though not planning to use force, was acting as if to give to the Provisional Government the impression that force might be used. In addition, if one looks at the matter through the eyes of Hawaiian officials, he observes an apparent purpose to browbeat the Honolulu Government into giving up to the Queen; by refusing to deny in black and white that armed men were to be used,[189] the Administration seemed to be

[187] Yet this was exactly the attitude which the Morgan Committee of the Senate would soon be taking.

[188] *House Ex. Doc. 70* (53 Cong. 2 Sess.), p. 43.

[189] It will be recalled that Gresham always maintained he had told Thurston no force was intended; but Hawaiian officials said the statement was indefinite and ambiguous (Miscellaneous Archives, *op. cit.,* and Thurston, *Memoirs,* pp. 333-335). It is also worth reminding the reader that Henry

employing the threat of force to accomplish its policy of restoration. For, if Gresham had announced publicly that the President purposed to use merely his good offices to bring about an adjustment of the wrong perpetrated by Stevens, the Provisional Government would know, without peradventure, that no military suasion was to be exerted; and six or more weeks of tension and rasping of nerves in Honolulu might have been obviated. Under such conditions, the result would have been exactly what it turned out to be, namely, refusal of the existing Government to budge.

Such an interpretation—that Cleveland and his subordinates used secret and unfair methods including the threat of force—is fairly close to that which was taken by the Annexationists. It is, however, not the correct one. There is no reason for believing that Cleveland, at the time the Administration's Hawaiian policy was being laid down, proposed to use force, the threat of force, or the weapon of secrecy. The Provisional Government's charge of menacing secretiveness, in so far as there was justice in the accusation, arose out of the miscarriage of Cleveland's policy; that is, when the Queen in Willis's first visit wished to behead all her enemies, the execution of his instructions was delayed and then secrecy *was* essential. To have at that point stated publicly that Liliuokalani wanted blood would have ended any hope of ever carrying out the Administration's intentions, not to mention the possibility of exile or imprisonment for the Queen if the Provisional Government had at that time learned her extreme views.[190]

The absence of a cable lengthened this necessary period of concealment until Hawaiian officials became convinced that Cleveland meant to use military methods. Otherwise, why should Willis not talk, at least in order to allay public distress? In short, when the policy of restoration was being decided, it was confidently expected that no undue secrecy would result; Willis could, in a few days, get the Queen's consent to Cleveland's terms, inform the Provisional Government of the President's views, and then consider his instructions as fulfilled. Indeed, if Willis was disposed to hurry, it

James, in his *Olney, op. cit.*, p. 84, thought Gresham was willing to go beyond persuasion. Whether James was right or wrong, the important fact was that Cleveland did not so intend.

[190] Thurston had been pressing the Government to deport Liliuokalani for some time.

was theoretically possible for him to see the Queen on one day and the Government the next.

The program was foolish in the first place, and had Cleveland been able to foresee the complications that resulted from Liliuokalani's vengefulness and from the long-continued period of uncertainty, it is questionable whether he would have launched upon the experiment at all. In fact the scheme, no matter how carried out, was Utopian. Idealism had run away with common sense. To question the constitutionality of the Provisional Government, which had been recognized by both Harrison and Cleveland, was of doubtful validity in international law anyway.

* * * * *

It took a long time for affairs in Honolulu to settle back into a normal rhythm. To be sure, by January 11 Irwin could report that preparations for defense had ceased; that most of the sandbags had been removed;[191] and that he expected no rioting. But in a few days the Provisional Government would be commemorating its first anniversary, and Irwin was somewhat afraid of trouble then, although he hoped the officials would be wise enough not to celebrate.[192] Likewise, Willis wrote that "Since the 'war' with the 'U. S. forces' Ended, there has been perfect quiet"; however there was still considerable danger from "opera bouffe hostilities."[193]

The Provisional Government, however, was not wise enough, as Irwin had hoped it would be, to pass over January 17, 1894, without ceremonies. When he and Willis were invited to participate in the exercises celebrating the birth of the new order, they declined; upon their refusal, no foreign diplomats accepted the invitation.[194] Irwin expressed "sincere regret";[195] and Willis told Gresham he thought it best not to be present at the celebration of an event "which our President had decided to be a *wrong* done a weak & friendly Sovereignty [;] it Seemed preposterously absurd to go

[191] The final ones were taken away in the spring because the bags were rotting (Minutes of the Executive Council, March 29, 1894).

[192] Irwin to Secretary of Navy, Jan. 11, 1894, No. 43878, Bureau of Navigation; printed in *House Ex. Doc. 140* (53 Cong. 2 Sess.), p. 10.

[193] Willis to Gresham, private, Jan. 16, 1894, Gresham MSS.

[194] Enclosures in Willis to Gresham, No. 27½, Jan. 19, 1894, Despatches.

[195] Irwin to Dole, Jan. 16, 1894, enclosed in Irwin to Secretary of the Navy, Jan. 19, 1894, No. 44895, Bureau of Navigation.

in So Short a time & Congratulate them upon having done this wrong."[196]

Gresham approved Willis's decision to stay away.[197] The Annexationists, taking his action as a gross insult to their Government, seethed with anger. This ire came out in the fiery speeches and in the parade with its caricatures of Blount, Cleveland, and Gresham. Blount was represented by an individual carrying a rattrap on which were the words, "Blount's Instruments." The Portuguese marched down the street bearing banners with mottoes like "No Monarchy in Ours," "P.G. and Portugee, We're the 400," "Liberty or Death," and "America is Our Goal." Fireworks were displayed and a large American flag was raised while the band played "The Star Spangled Banner." In the addresses President Cleveland was roughly handled; and stress was placed on the argument that annexation was the manifest destiny of Hawaii. The chairman of the meeting said: "The Government is morally and financially sound, and upheld as it is by strong hands and willing hearts, it will live and prosper, until in the providence of God it shall be absorbed in the great American union." Much was said about the French, American, and English Revolutions, Bunker Hill, Magna Carta, and the Hawaiian monarchy whose "Runnymede had been passed in July of 1887." Regarding Cleveland's policy the following was asserted:

> There, on the one side, was the chief of sixty millions; here an armed body of a paltry thousand; there was the strongest of modern powers, with its army and its fleets; here were a few lonely rocks in the ocean without a fort upon its pinnacles and without a gun upon a deck; there was a great Government whose President had declared our dethroned Queen should reign again; here was a little band of men who said she must pass over their dead bodies first; there in our harbor were the broadsides of a possible foe; here on shore was a battalion behind its sandbags!

The Annexationist press flayed Willis for his absence. The *Star,* in a florid editorial, declared that they "Did very well without him. It is to be regretted that 'contingencies' should have arisen by

[196] Willis to Gresham, private, Jan. 16, 1894, Gresham MSS.
[197] Gresham to Willis, Feb. 9, 1894, Instructions III, 200.

which Minister Willis was unable to take note of yesterday's holiday and by which the *Philadelphia* and her consort were prevented from hanging up flags in place of their weekly washing." The editor doubted whether Willis believed in the justice of his acts, yet "He-Who-Must-Be-Obeyed [Cleveland], leaves his official employés small latitude of judgment when a question comes up between the rights of a free people and the prerogatives of a would-be dictator [Liliuokalani]." The *Advertiser* admitted that Willis had found himself in a dilemma, because the sovereignty of the Provisional Government had been recognized; and yet that sovereignty was being called in question by a demand upon the Government to surrender to the Queen. It blamed Cleveland entirely: "Hawaii is at peace with the American people, but at war with Mr. Cleveland, and Mr. Willis has chosen to cast his lot with that of the man who unquestionably is his master, and who claims to be the master of the American people too." In spite of its generally belligerent tone, the *Star* did try in one of its editorials to be charitable to the American Minister. "The mothers in Honolulu [it said], who, after the arrival of the *Corwin,* bent over their babes in prayer anxiously inquiring if the guns of the *Philadelphia* and *Adams* were shotted for them, gratefully thank him that he ordered the death angel to touch but not to rest on their pillows. It is now in order that we cultivate charity and forgiveness."[198] Willis was not invited to attend the celebration on January 17, 1895.

* * * * *

The military crisis had long been over and the sandbags were fast disintegrating, but the Provisional Government had learned one important lesson from the recent war scare. That lesson was that its citizen army was woefully weak and unprepared. The Commander, Colonel Soper, though a fine, honorable man,[199] lacked executive talent, military experience, and the ability to train his men. Among a number of instructions given to Thurston as he left for the United States, an important one was to report upon

[198] The speeches and newspaper clippings are all contained in Willis to Gresham, No. 30, Jan. 19, 1894, Despatches; printed in *Sen. Ex. Doc. 46* (53 Cong. 2 Sess.), pp. 2-17. The ceremonies were described by Julius A. Palmer, Jr., in *Memories of Hawaii and Hawaiian Correspondence* (Boston, 1894), pp. 42 *ff*.

[199] Thurston to Dole, March 24, 1894, M&E.

the qualifications of Major R. H. McLean, who had applied for the post of Commander of the Hawaiian army. Dole had heard that McLean was a drinker and wanted to know the facts. Furthermore, Thurston was told to get information about Krag-Jorgensen rifles and some other kinds of military equipment.[200]

Shortly after returning to Washington, Thurston had an interview with McLean at Philadelphia, and was highly impressed with him, although Thurston suggested another desirable candidate also. McLean, who was then head of the Cheltenham Academy, at Ogontz, Pennsylvania, seems to have thought that an interview meant an offer, for, within a few days he had accepted the place and asked Thurston to get Dole's confirmation.[201] Much to Thurston's and McLean's chagrin, they were informed that the post was not open any more because the commissioned officers of the Hawaiian army refused to serve under a stranger as their superior.[202] Thurston replied that he was now in an embarrassing position, and that McLean should be appointed whether the officers liked him or not; for, said he, the very existence of the Government depended upon a well-trained army.[203]

[200] Dole to Thurston, Jan. 5, 1894, *ibid.* On Feb. 28, 1894, a list of all munitions in the Ordnance Department showed 363 Springfield rifles; 179 Winchester 45/75 rifles; 69 sporting Winchesters made in 1886; 33 Winchester 45/75 carbines; 151 Remington-Lee 45/70 rifles; and a few other varieties (Dole Papers, Archives).

[201] Thurston to Dole, Feb. 11; McLean to Thurston, Feb. 15; Thurston to Dole, Feb. 15; and McLean to Thurston, Feb. 18, in M&E.

[202] Geo. C. Potter to Thurston, March 8, 1894, *ibid.*

[203] Thurston to Dole, March 24, and Thurston to Hatch, March 27, 1894, *ibid.*

VII. CLEVELAND'S POLICY AT THE BAR OF PUBLIC OPINION

The publication of Secretary Gresham's letter to Cleveland of October 18, 1893,[1] created as much commotion in the United States as it did in Hawaii. Closely as the secret was kept, rumors apparently had leaked out even before the letter appeared. Thus, on October 11 a lawyer of New York City told Gresham: "The action of the State Department in reference to Hawaiian matters has come as a thorough surprise here; but it is already plain that the sentiment of business and professional men here is overwhelmingly in favor of the course taken; and that the protesting 'Jingoists' are but an insignificant minority of any portion of the voters of this city."[2] Another personal friend, from Milwaukee, told Gresham that after the letter was printed it "made a decided stir through the country," and that he felt it "fully confirms the fact" of Stevens's conspiracy.[3] Still another said quite truly that the Hawaiian imbroglio was "one of the Several undesirable legacies bestowed upon the Change of Administration."[4] Schurz of course thought it was "admirably clear, strong and conclusive."[5] Henry Watterson declared: "Nothing could [?] be more conclusive in argument, or more incisive in Statement, than your Report [letter]. . . . The position therein taken is impregnable I think from both the standpoints of justice and policy." He added, however, with prescience: ". . . we shall have a fight on our hands, and I expect to do my share of it."[6]

Cleveland also received encomiums. A. B. Farquhar, president of the executive committee of the National Democratic organization, said: "You are entirely right. The people may not see it that way now, but they will later on."[7] One Mary Bedell wrote "a tribute

[1] Blount, pp. XVII-XXI.

[2] John DeWitt Warner to Gresham, Oct. 11, 1893, Gresham MSS.

[3] Charles E. Dyer to Gresham, Nov. 22, 1893, *ibid.*

[4] James C. Parsons to Gresham, Nov. 12, 1893, Gresham MSS. See also New York *World*, Nov. 14, 1893, which said the same thing.

[5] Schurz to Gresham, Nov. 11, 1893, CX, 24242, Schurz MSS.

[6] Watterson to Gresham, Nov. 12, 1893, Gresham MSS.

[7] Farquhar to Cleveland, Nov. 13, 1893, Cleveland MSS.

of proud thankfulness for the fine bravery" of the President in trying to right the Hawaiian wrong.[8] The Rev. Mr. Charles H. Malcolm, D.D., wrote to Mrs. Cleveland that "It is justice, and I trust your woman's heart will influence your good husband to bend his will" and restore the Queen.[9] Charles Francis Adams said: "Of the right and wrong of the question I know little; but I do know that it required courage in a public man to do what he is persuaded is right."[10] Cleveland and his colleagues received many letters of support,[11] and many of criticism.[12]

Alexander analyzed for Dole's benefit the reactions of those opposed to Cleveland's policy as follows: The Secretary's letter "had the effect of a bomb-shell, and created great excitement all over the country. The American eagle did scream. The public condemnation of the policy of restoration has been overwhelming." It was like "firing on Fort Sumter. . . . The secret and underhanded way in which the whole affair has been managed, the transfer of admirals, the pains that have been taken to keep the American people in the dark until after the elections [of November, 1893], and to deceive this legation, so as to explode the torpedo without warning at Honolulu, and to take the Provisional Government at as great a disadvantage as possible, is more worthy of a Machiavelli than of an American Secretary of State, and has been well exposed and justly commented upon by the press here."[13]

The Republican papers were vehement in their attacks. The New York *Sun* wanted to know "What accursed maggot in the brain of GROVER CLEVELAND has made him believe that it is part of the business of the United States to guarantee the existence of a monarchical government, and for that purpose to

[8] Bedell to Cleveland, Nov. 12, 1893, *ibid.*

[9] Malcolm to Mrs. Cleveland, Nov. 13, 1893, *ibid.*

[10] Adams to Cleveland, Nov. 18, 1893, *ibid.*

[11] For instance, Robert Duval to Gresham, Nov. 15, 1893, Gresham MSS.; the Democratic Club (colored) of Newport, R. I., to Cleveland, Nov. 16, 1893, Cleveland MSS.; and J. J. Abercombie, of the Military Order of the Loyal Legion, Illinois Commandery, to Gresham, Nov. 18, 1893, Gresham MSS.

[12] For instance, Sen. W. E. Chandler's long letter printed in the *New York Tribune,* Nov. 15, 1893; James H. Reall of Bloomfield, N. J., to Cleveland, Nov. 12, 1893, Cleveland MSS.; and E. M. Brewer to Schurz, Nov. 16, 1893, and Nov. 23, 1893, in Schurz MSS., CX, 24251 and 24264.

[13] Alexander to Dole, Nov. 19, 1893, M&E.

wipe out of existence the republican Government of Hawaii?" It thought that talk of impeachment was wild, however. Believing that Cleveland had been "Repudiated!" the *Sun* quoted a long list of papers which opposed his Hawaiian venture.[14] Murat Halstead denounced "The frostbitten lawyerism in the Gresham brief" and opined that Cleveland "must be not only mugwumped but also hypnotized."[15] The *New York Tribune* predicted that, if Cleveland's program led to bloodshed in Hawaii, he would be indicted before public opinion, more so than even Buchanan and Johnson.[16] The *Sun* said: "There is no principle of international law more undisputed than that the formal recognition of a government cannot be annulled but by an act of war";[17] the *Tribune* declared that "History is a thing that can't be unmade";[18] and most Republicans attributed Gresham's scheme to a desire to get even with Harrison.[19] Little wonder that Gresham informed Schurz: "My letter to the President seems to have created somewhat of a stir"; but he added: "Every statement contained therein was based on fact."[20] Even the Democratic New York *World* was unfriendly and wanted to "Ring down the curtain" on the Hawaiian "farce" which was becoming "tedious."[21]

The denunciation of Gresham's letter was widespread enough, but the howl which was raised upon publication of part of the Blount report on November 20 was tremendous.[22] The New York *Sun* thought it would be "A Thrilling Historical Scene" to see Willis "conducting the swarthy, purple-robed, and bespangled Polynesian to the bloody throne of her ancestors."[23] The *Tribune*

[14] Nov. 15, 1893.

[15] Halstead to the editor, *New York Herald,* Nov. 16, 1893.

[16] Nov. 17, 1893.

[17] Nov. 17, 1893.

[18] Nov. 18, 1893.

[19] *New York Tribune,* Nov. 19, 1893, and D. P. Baldwin, Logansport, Ind., to Gresham, Nov. 22, 1893, Gresham MSS. The *Tribune,* Nov. 27, 1893, asked: "Is there any one who doesn't believe that if the Hawaiian revolution had occurred in April instead of January Mr. Cleveland would be meeting Congress with an annexation treaty?"

[20] Gresham to Schurz, Nov. 16, 1893, Schurz MSS., CX, 24250.

[21] Nov. 12, 1893.

[22] See *Literary Digest,* VIII (Nov. 25, 1893), 76-77 for comments from both Democratic and Republican papers.

[23] Nov. 25, 1893.

insisted that Blount "was commissioned to make out a case against Minister Stevens and the previous Administration, and he obeyed orders";[24] he was "a faithful errand boy."[25] "That maggot," said the *Sun,* "in Mr. CLEVELAND'S head will have to be extracted by Congress."[26] The *Tribune* printed a long list of Democratic papers which were warning the President that his policy was wrong.[27] Rev. Oliver P. Emerson, secretary of the Hawaiian Board of Missions, who had voted for Cleveland in 1884, wrote a long letter to the President's secretary, justifying the Revolution, and saying of the Queen and her throne that "Only foreign troops could get her back to it, or keep her on it."[28] Charles L. Macarthur, editor of the Troy (New York) *Northern Budget,* who had been in Honolulu during the Revolution, sent a much-discussed letter to the New York *Mail and Express* of November 26, 1893, which was read and applauded by the Morgan Committee in his presence. Blount was much too reticent; and, what was worse, had visited only two islands and only one sugar plantation, that of the Royalist, Claus Spreckels. The report, he declared, was "a wicked perversion of the facts, as I had the opportunity of gathering them in Honolulu before his arrival and after. The story of a Stevens conspiracy is utterly absurd."[29] Said the *Mail and Express* editorially: "The voice is that of Gresham but the Claus are those of Spreckels."[30]

[24] Nov. 21, 1893.

[25] Nov. 23, 1893.

[26] Nov. 22, 1893.

[27] Nov. 23, 1893.

[28] Emerson to H. T. Thurber, Dec. 2, 1893, Cleveland MSS. Emerson was the first witness interviewed by the Morgan Committee, pp. 173-200.

[29] Morgan, pp. 695-702. If the reader wishes more examples of the Annexationist and Republican wrath against Cleveland's policy, he should peruse the multitude of editorials kept by Thurston and printed in his *Memoirs,* pp. 361-386. Thurston says that a Confederate colonel declared he would gather 1,000 ex-rebels and use them against the Queen, and that Senator John T. Morgan suggested the same idea (pp. 321-322 and 475-476). Lew Wallace's words as reported by Thurston are interesting: "I had not deemed it possible that anything could ever arise which would induce me to raise my hand against the old flag; but I swear to you that I would have done so in support of your government against the Presidents agression [*sic*] if I had been where I could make myself available" (Thurston to Dole, confidential, Feb. 11, 1894, M&E). Many others can be found in President's Files and in Official Dole Files, Archives.

[30] Quoted by *Advertiser,* Dec. 6, 1893.

The attitude of most Democratic editors was that of pointing out the dangers, while admitting the justice of restoration. The New York *World* called it "A National Humiliation" to read the depositions of Soper, Damon, Waterhouse, Wundenberg, Carter, Skerrett, and Swinburne, all of whom, it thought, had turned state's evidence. "The record thus made is one of the most scandalous and shameful in the whole history of the foreign relations of the United States."[31] Nevertheless this Democratic paper pointed out "The Absurdity of It," that is, of the attempt to right one wrong in Hawaii by doing another, when the United States was already overwhelmed by internal problems such as the panic, taxes, monopolies, and the Negro.[32]

Perhaps the most out-and-out defender of the Cleveland policy was the *New York Herald,* whose correspondent, Nordhoff, had recently been involved in a bitter hassle with the Provisional Government because of some of his revelatory despatches. This paper believed that "in every line of . . . [the report, there was] a most striking confirmation of the despatches sent to the HERALD by its special correspondent, Mr. Charles Nordhoff."[33] Stevens, it went on, was "simply a Confederate of the revolutionists";[34] and his act "goes into the archives of the State Department at Washington as the darkest chapter in the diplomatic annals of this country."[35] Nordhoff wrote to Gresham that "Blount's report is So strong & able a document that it must I think impress Congress, & the public will"; but he was sorry the President could not inform Congress about "an accomplished fact," namely, restoration.[36] Two days later he added: "Mr Blounts' report can't be successfully attacked; for the points are all so far as I see, Established on Provisional Government people's testimony. It is a very able piece of work."[37] Soon the New York *Sun* smelled collusion between Blount and Nordhoff, saying there was such similarity between some of Nordhoff's despatches and the testi-

[31] Nov. 21, 1893.
[32] Nov. 23, 1893.
[33] Nov. 20, 1893.
[34] Nov. 2, 1893.
[35] Nov. 22, 1893.
[36] Nordhoff to Gresham, Dec. 7, 1893, Gresham MSS.
[37] Same to same, Dec. 9, 1893, Cleveland MSS.; see also same to same, Dec. 12, 1893, Gresham MSS.

mony in Blount's report that Blount must have given Nordhoff information. It demanded a congressional investigation.[38] Nordhoff at once denied that Blount had passed on to him any material; he explained the similarity by asserting that those who testified to Blount kept copies of their statements and offered them to Nordhoff for his use. He never knew what Blount would say until he read the Commissioner's conclusions.[39]

Still another ardent defender of the Administration was Carl Schurz, editor of *Harper's Weekly,* who wrote an able leader in support of Cleveland.[40] Some readers did not like the *Weekly's* attitude. For instance, there was the pastor[41] of a Lutheran church in Washington, D. C., who wrote to Schurz: "Mr. Sec. Gresham has espoused the Cause [:] 1. Of Barbarism as against Civilization; 2. Of Heathenism as against Christianity; 3. Of Bourbonism as against Democracy; 4. Of Monarchism as against Independence." He would not read the magazine any more.[42] Likewise, W. N. Armstrong, who had been Attorney General under King Kalakaua, wrote to Schurz defending the Revolutionists and asking him to give the case a rehearing before making up his mind about the goodness of monarchical government.[43]

A considerable proportion of the letters coming to the Administration in support of its Hawaiian stand was composed of either missives from those who had something to sell or else from officeholders who, in many cases, felt it wise to show their colors. For example, T. E. Lawton, proprietor of the Mai Fai Lyceum Bureau of Boston, sent Cleveland a folder with a picture of Mme. Mai Fai, who was a lecturer on China, Japan, California and Colorado at the World's Fair and was well versed on Hawaii as well. "Would it not be a good idea [he asked] for the present administration to employ this lady, which the press reports will

[38] Dec. 5, 1893.

[39] Nordhoff to Gresham, Dec. 12, 1893, Gresham MSS.

[40] Nov. 25, 1893, p. 1118.

[41] W. E. Parson to Schurz, Nov. 23, 1893, Schurz MSS., CXI, 24268.

[42] Schurz later took a vicious cut at those clergymen, who, he said, were betraying Christian ideals when they opposed the granting of simple justice to the Queen (*Harper's Weekly,* Jan. 6 and 27, 1894, pp. 2 and 74).

[43] Armstrong to Schurz, Hampton, Va., Nov. 26, 1893, Schurz MSS., CXI, 24271. Armstrong was the brother of General S. C. Armstrong who, until his recent death, was head of Hampton Institute and who had defended the aims of the Revolutionists earlier in the year.

show to be a fine and able speaker, to deliver these lectures at Washington, D. C., and in and throughout the several states in behalf of our present and honestly managed administration?"[44] Noble C. Butler, a presidential officeholder in Indianapolis was so pleased with Gresham's policy that he claimed the Secretary got his inspiration from letters which Butler had sent him.[45] Ambassador Thomas F. Bayard informed Gresham from London: "I am greatly pleased with the dignity and justice of your treatment of the Sandwich Island matter—This Country is too great and aspires to too high a place in civilization to stoop [to] the small arts of trickery or bullying a scanty and feeble set of Islanders out of their rights—whatever these rights may be—"[46] This was the kind of idealism that Gresham admired. "I think [he told Schurz] the American people will respond to a frank appeal to their sense of right and justice but whether they do or not, I have done my duty."[47]

* * * * *

The Administration policy of restoring the Queen struck at the accomplishments of three men, above all others; and these three were in a position to reply.

The first was the recently retired President, Benjamin Harrison, whose reaction was briefly and succinctly put as follows: "If his [Cleveland's] policy suits him, mine suits me. . . . Unless my Administration is the object of unjust reflection in the action taken, I will have nothing to say to the public."[48]

The second was John L. Stevens, who saw the greatest achieve-

[44] Lawton to Cleveland, Dec. 4, 1893, Cleveland MSS.

[45] Butler to Gresham, Dec. 1, 1893, Gresham MSS.

[46] Bayard to Gresham, Nov. 25, 1893, *ibid.* For other letters of support, see local editors of California to Cleveland, Nov. 29, 1893, in Cleveland MSS.; N. W. McIvor to Edward H. Strobel of the Department of State, Nov. 28, 1893, *ibid.;* and citizens of Concord, Mass., to Cleveland, Dec., 1893, *ibid.* In the Cleveland MSS., Folio marked "Printed Material 1893," is a printed speech of P. W. Reeder, a tourist in Hawaii during the uprising of January, 1893, who said the Revolution was a conspiracy between Stevens and the Hawaiian-Americans. The *Cedar Rapids Standard* of Nov. 30, 1893, gave its entire front page to the speech. Reeder was a witness before the Morgan Committee (pp. 676-691) but could not give much information because he did not understand the native tongue.

[47] Gresham to Schurz, Nov. 21, 1893, Schurz MSS., CX, 24260.

[48] Quoted by *Literary Digest,* VIII (Nov. 18, 1893), 58-61.

ment of his career endangered. At first he was taken unawares, for, in his words, the Blount report was "so void of a real foundation of truth, so calumnious of the living and the dead, that I have no extended reply to make."[49] But he was not long without a defense, which, when prepared, was considerably more aggressive and vindictive than was Harrison's. In a lengthy justification of his part in the Hawaiian Revolution, which was read into the *Congressional Record,* he said:

> A deep sense of obligation to my country and an American's duty to defend an insulted, threatened, and struggling American colony, planted as righteously and firmly on the North Pacific isles as our Pilgrim Fathers established themselves on Plymouth Rock, demand that I shall make an answer to the astounding misrepresentations and untruths of Commissioner Blount's report. . . . Not only is the course of Gresham and Blount extremely un-American in its form and spirit, but it is also in direct opposition to the civilizing and Christianizing influence on the Hawaiian Islands, while it is playing into British hands. . . .

Stevens went on to say that he had followed Bayard's instructions of 1887 and therefore had precedent in his favor. "Not wishing to be severe on a neophyte in diplomacy, with little knowledge of the world's affairs outside of his own country," he could excuse some of Blount's statements, but not all. He defended his own actions by saying that because there had been a real menace in the Japanese, his assumption of a protectorate was necessary. Furthermore, there was not a semblance of truth in the allegation that Thurston and Smith had asked him for protection against the Queen. Moreover, it was "emphatically and categorically untrue" that he tried to aid the Provisional Government. The assertions of Parker, Cornwell, Colburn, and Peterson were false; all four of them were noted reprobates and liars. He concluded:

> Against all just expectations I have been forced to expose the anomalous, the un-American, and most unfair course of Blount and associates against my official conduct, my honor, and all that a public man holds most dear. . . . These strange and unpatriotic proceedings in the presence of our national rivals is making a shameful

[49] *Ibid.*

> page of American history, which our future, if not our present, statesmen and generation will repudiate and blot out by wise and effective measures.[50]

Stevens was going here and there making speeches in defense of his work. At Boston, December 16, he repeated the point that he had followed Bayard's instructions to Merrill in 1887 which in turn were based upon those written by Marcy in 1854.[51] The New York *World,* commenting upon Stevens's busy life devoted to self-defense, averred the country had had "quite enough of this untrustworthy jingo ex-Minister who could not tell the truth even in his official reports. . . . The most becoming thing that JOHN L. STEVENS can do is to keep quiet."[52] Nordhoff told Gresham that Stevens, in Blount's report, had been convicted out of the mouths of his own friends.[53] In a long article the *New York Herald* dissected the former Minister's defense under the title, "His Own Evidence Convicts Stevens."[54] A few days later, showing how Stevens had misinformed and deceived President Harrison, Nordhoff stated: "If He [Harrison] Values His Good Name and Fame Let Him Acknowledge His Hawaiian Error."[55] Blount offered to defend his report if Cleveland desired; but so far he had thought best to keep the peace. He added: "Poor old Mr Stevens! His mendacity in his review of my report is pitiable."[56] The New York *Sun* thought Stevens left nothing in the Blount document "save the prejudice, malice, and narrow-minded partisanship."[57]

The third man who felt it necessary to issue denials was Lorrin A. Thurston. As already mentioned, he submitted on December 5, 1893, just before leaving for Honolulu, a stiff note to Gresham denouncing the Blount report. He said the Commissioner's examination had been *"ex parte*[58] and conducted in secret." There was

[50] *Record* (53 Cong. 2 Sess.), Dec. 13, 1893, pp. 191 *ff*.
[51] *New York Tribune,* Dec. 18, 1893.
[52] Dec. 18, 1893.
[53] Nordhoff to Gresham, Dec. 12, 1893, Gresham MSS.
[54] *New York Herald,* Dec. 8, 1893. Nordhoff wrote the article.
[55] *Ibid.,* Dec. 12, 1893.
[56] Blount to Gresham, Dec. 16, 1893, Gresham MSS.
[57] Dec. 1, 1893.
[58] For a typical Annexationist analysis of the *"ex parte"* character of Blount's investigation, see Alexander, in Morgan, pp. 309 *ff*.

really nothing very new in this long defense[59] by Thurston, for it was practically a restatement of the traditional view held by the Provisional Government; much of it savored of the "Letter of Specifications" which has already been discussed.

* * * * *

This public argument, beginning in November, 1893, aroused a keen interest on the part of all interested parties to learn what Cleveland would say about Hawaii in his first annual message on December 4, 1893. Mention of Hawaiian affairs was brief, but it set Congress to debating. The President asserted he found himself in an embarrassing position upon entering office because of the treaty of annexation which had been sent to the Senate by the previous Administration. His decision was to withdraw it and send James H. Blount to inquire into the situation and secure the facts. The Commissioner's report showed that the constitutional government had been overthrown by the aid of American troops. The only honorable thing to do was to restore the former régime. To this end Minister Willis had instructions.[60]

The brevity of the President's statement disappointed everyone. The Philadelphia *Public Ledger,* saying that the Hawaiian part of the message was eagerly awaited by the public, declared that more explanation was needed; if the Royal Government had been subverted by the aid of American troops, the wrong should be righted, but the fact of American interference would have to be proved first.[61] The New York *World* admitted it was somewhat in the dark about Cleveland's Hawaiian policy as he expressed it in his message.[62] Thus, also, said the New York *Sun*.[63] The *New York Tribune* launched into a virulent crusade against Cleveland's usurpation of power, which the brief details of his message indicated. "If Congress permits President Cleveland [it said] to go on usurping its functions, we shall soon have a personal and not a constitutional Government."[64] Later it added: "He has committed a series of colossal blunders; he has transcended his con-

[59] Thurston to Gresham, Dec. 5, 1893, Notes from Hawaii; printed in *House Ex. Doc. 48* (53 Cong. 2 Sess.), p. 171.

[60] *Congressional Record* (53 Cong. 2 Sess.), Dec. 4, 1893, p. 4.

[61] Clipping of Dec. 5, 1893, in Cleveland MSS.

[62] Dec. 5, 1893.

[63] Dec. 5, 1893.

[64] Dec. 6, 1893.

stitutional authority; he has rejected an unparalleled opportunity; he has affronted Congress and the whole people by wrapping his proceedings in mystery; he has defied public sentiment; and finally he has brought about a state of affairs in Hawaii so critical that armed resistance . . . may be the only recourse."[65]

There were reasons why the Hawaiian portion of the annual message was so short. Many other matters of domestic importance had to be discussed; in addition, the President wished more information upon Willis's success or failure in his attempts to restore the Queen. The Republican press, however, kept hammering at the secrecy and mystery of the President's policy; daily the demands grew louder for the facts. Many editors feared Cleveland would have the country at war without its consent.

Already the President was preparing a special message devoted to the entire Hawaiian imbroglio. Mrs. Gresham, out of connubial loyalty, declared that her husband composed the entire paper, but James showed that it was really written by Olney; among the Olney manuscripts is a draft of the message, written by Olney, most of which Cleveland used.[66] Moreover, Olney himself said that Cleveland called Gresham in, asking him to prepare a special message on Hawaii; Gresham "did so, but, as the result did not cover the ground desired by the President, he asked me to see what I could do with it. I accordingly went over Mr. Blount's voluminous reports and other papers on the subject and prepared a draft which was accepted by him and forms by far the larger part of the message actually sent to Congress on the 18th of December [1893]."[67] Once again Olney entered the Hawaiian drama at a crucial moment.

The document was based entirely, as Olney asserted, upon Blount's findings. It reviewed the haste in which the Revolution had been accomplished, and told how, thirty-two days after that event—fifteen of which had been spent on the sea—the Commissioners had signed a treaty of annexation. The President believed that Minister Stevens had promoted the *coup* and that the Queen, in her protest to the United States, was justified. He pointed out that the weakness of the Provisional Government was proved by

[65] Dec. 14, 1893.
[66] James, *Olney, op. cit.*, p. 92.
[67] *Ibid.*, p. 200.

the fact that almost immediately it pleaded for the protection of American forces. All these considerations, said the President, made restoration the only honorable policy the United States could follow. It was true that Liliuokalani had so far refused to grant full amnesty, but as soon as she did, action would be taken. To this end the President felt that Congress should be given the full particulars, so as to provide him with the necessary authority with which to accomplish his purpose.[68] The prediction of the hostile *New York Tribune* of December 16, 1893, that the special message would probably be, "I have made a botch of it; the job is yours," was not far wide of the mark. The New York *Sun* called it a message of "Evasion and Suppression."[69] Former Minister Stevens said the allegations were grossly unjust and untrue.[70] Several days later the *Tribune* excoriated "That marvel of Georgia genius, Paramount Blount."[71]

Strangely or not, some of those papers which had supported Cleveland's Hawaiian policy most loyally were either very critical of the message or else were lukewarm. So ardent a proponent as Nordhoff now preached a hands-off attitude: "We have no further business to interfere in Hawaii"; and the *Herald* agreed.[72] So also the *World*, whose idea was that Hawaii should be let alone—"The country has heard quite enough of it";[73] and it quoted the *Boston Herald, St. Louis Republic, St. Louis Post-Dispatch, St. Louis Globe-Democrat, Atlanta Constitution,* and *Providence Journal* to the same effect.[74] "Carried to its logical extreme [continued the *World*], the President's contention would restore this continent to the Indians and surrender to the English, the Spaniards and the Mexicans a large part of our territory. It is not possible to conduct governments or to advance civilization on the refinements of ideal justice."[75]

The remarkable change in policy of papers like the *World* was probably as much the result of Alexander's missionary work as

[68] Blount, pp. III-XVI.

[69] Dec. 19, 1893.

[70] *New York Herald,* Dec. 21, 1893.

[71] Dec. 24, 1893.

[72] *New York Herald,* Dec. 21, 1893.

[73] Dec. 26, 1893.

[74] Dec. 23, 1893.

[75] Dec. 19, 1893.

of anyone else. He saw the editor and convinced him that the paper's past attitude had been wrong; however the editor, in spite of his conversion, still preferred independence to annexation. Alexander also interviewed Charles A. Dana of the *Sun,* Talcott Williams of the Philadelphia *Press,* Lyman Abbott of the *Outlook,* and President Timothy Dwight at New Haven. To those who already believed in annexation he gave more arguments, and to those who were opposed he used persuasion.[76]

Thurston severely criticized the Government at Honolulu for what he called its policy of starving the Legation; he felt that the Councils did not appreciate either the importance or the expense of the Legation's work of propaganda. He complained that he had received no funds for three months, nor any salary; and money was needed for pamphlets. He suggested that more documents be sent for his use; that pictures of Hawaii as well as 500 copies of the *Hawaiian Gazette* be given to American newspapers; and that a Bureau of Statistics be created in order to provide much needed information.[77] In spite of this apparent neglect of the Legation by the home officials, the Washington men sent all manner of information to Honolulu.[78]

* * * * *

Although most of the newspapers were not very friendly towards Cleveland's special message on Hawaii, he did receive some commendation. Sen. D. W. Voorhees of Indiana, whose vote would count, wrote in praise of that "great and powerful message." "There was but one opinion [he said] on our side of the Chamber and that was most Complimentary, in every respect to you. I am much mistaken if this splendid State paper does not Control the public Sentiment of this Country and of the world as but few official documents have ever done on a given subject."[79] President John J. Valentine of Wells, Fargo & Company thought: "To conclude . . . there is no such thing as international morals is pessimistic."[80] Felix A. Reeve of the Office of the Solicitor of the

[76] Alexander to Thurston, Feb. 4, Feb. 12, March 8, 1894; Alexander to Dole, Feb. 9 and Feb. 21, 1894; Hastings to Dole, Feb. 25, 1894, M&E.

[77] Thurston to Hatch, March 16 and 18, 1894, *ibid.*

[78] For instance, Thurston to Dole, Feb. 21, and Hastings to Hatch, June 7, 1894, *ibid.*

[79] Voorhees to Cleveland, Dec. 18, 1893, Cleveland MSS.

[80] Valentine to Vice President Dudley Evans, Dec. 26, 1893, Cleveland MSS.

Treasury was not so hopeful; he thought that the "moral sensibilities of our people have never before been so evidently vitiated as is manifested at this time with regard to the Hawaiian question."[81] The Rev. Mr. Vaughan S. Collins, secretary-treasurer of the Second General Conference of the Epworth League, said he was a prohibitionist, and yet could not refrain from expressing his "appreciation of your noble stand in this matter of Hawaii."[82] The *Omaha Bee* called the message "a plain, straight-forward, lucid history" which was related with "candor" and "sincerity." This editorial was sent to Cleveland, with the statement that it was "one of the wonders of the age—A fair minded editorial from the Omaha Bee."[83]

The London *Echo* praised Cleveland for teaching "the rulers and the Governments of the world a lesson."[84] Ambassador Bayard wrote to Gresham from London: "I fully agree with you—that our great Republic will perish 'if' we embark upon an Imperial system of acquisition of outlying dependencies—and that the methods employed under the late administration in the Hawaiian Kingdom were disgraceful to our Country, and will not be Sustained by the American people when they are fairly comprehended."[85] Oscar S. Straus sent Cleveland a Christmas note and his "sincere Congratulations upon your admirable Message on Hawaii. . . . Of your many great public Acts I regard this last the greatest."[86] The *New York Tribune* said, however: "President Cleveland, even with his sawdust doll, Queen Lil, did not have a pleasant or cheerful Christmas."[87]

Already the Administration forces in Congress were coming to grips with those opposed to Cleveland's program. One method of defending the President's cause was to get a good press by giving facts and documents to those who would support the policy of restoration. The close connection between Cleveland and Schurz

[81] Reeve to Cleveland, Dec. 20, 1893, *ibid.*

[82] Collins to Cleveland, Dec. 21, 1893, *ibid.*

[83] C. Franklin to Cleveland, Dec. 21, 1893, *ibid.*

[84] Clipping in Henry S. Hicks to Cleveland, Jan. 11, 1894, *ibid.*

[85] Bayard to Gresham, Dec. 25, 1893, Gresham MSS.

[86] Straus to Cleveland, Dec. 23, 1893, Cleveland MSS. There are numerous other congratulatory letters on the special message in this collection.

[87] Dec. 26, 1893. Cf., the Honolulu *Star*, Feb. 6, 1894: "'He's my Grover and I'm his Lil' is now the favorite song on the New York boulevard."

(editor of *Harper's Weekly,* who had intimate relations with the *Nation* and the New York *Evening Post*),[88] between Gresham and Schurz, and between Gresham and Nordhoff has already been learned. The historian, James Schouler, was allowed to read over the Blount testimony to write an article for the *Forum* of February, 1894.[89]

The endeavor to secure a good press was not the only means used to support Cleveland's Hawaiian program. The plan was well put by Nordhoff in a letter to Gresham: "I hope you will get some Senator to Study *Carefully* & thoroughly the testimony: & I suspect Col. Blount ought to be at his Elbow. And then use it *ruthlessly* in the Senate & House when the time Comes."[90] In short, the Administration forces in Congress must be supplied with ammunition. Blount had already offered to come and help, and was later called for.[91] It soon became clear that the Administration wheel horses in the Senate were to be George Gray of Delaware, Roger Q. Mills of Texas,[92] and William F. Vilas of Wisconsin.[93] George G. Vest of Missouri also was an able man who could be counted upon for real service, but his efficiency was weakened by his hatred of Cleveland.[94] Still another was John W. Daniel of Virginia who had indicated his stand as early as November 20, 1893, when he wrote to Gresham condemning the oligarchical character of the Provisional Government. "The Dole Govt. [he said] . . . is called a Republican Govt.—Wherein? Merely because it gives Republican names to usurpers."[95] Then there was Stephen M. White of California who informed Gresham

[88] The Honolulu *Star,* March 22, 1894, said the *Post* was the worst slanderer of Hawaii in the United States.

[89] On Jan. 22, 1894, Schouler thanked Gresham for the privilege of using the Blount documents (Gresham MSS). *Holomua* thought so highly of Schouler's article that a full page supplement containing it was issued on Feb. 13, 1894. The *Advertiser,* Feb. 23, 1894, said of Schouler: "Another good man gone wrong." Alexander considered the essay so important he thought he might write an answer (Alexander to Dole, Feb. 9, 1894, M&E).

[90] Nordhoff to Gresham, Dec. 9, 1893, Gresham MSS.

[91] Blount to Gresham, Jan. 31, 1894, *ibid.*

[92] According to Mrs. Gresham (*op. cit.,* p. 760), Mills was even more dependable than Olney on "the *sound morality* of the situation."

[93] *New York Tribune,* Dec. 9, 1893.

[94] Gresham, *Gresham, op. cit.,* p. 759.

[95] Daniel to Gresham, Nov. 20, 1893, Gresham MSS.

that he was coming more and more around to Gresham's side of the Hawaiian question;[96] but White did not play a leading rôle until 1898. The attitude of Voorhees of Indiana has already been noted. It was the policy of Gresham and the State Department to prime these Senators with facts and arguments, as well as to answer questions which they could not manage on the floor. Mills and Vest were given information time and again by Gresham, Cleveland, and John Bassett Moore.[97]

The critics of the Cleveland program got the start on its friends when, on December 5, 1893, Senator George F. Hoar of Massachusetts offered a resolution asking the President to lay before the Senate "copies of all instructions which may have been given to any representative . . . or any naval officer" in Hawaii since March 4, 1881. It lay over under the rules,[98] but met obstacles on December 6, when the Senate stopped the regular proceedings to hear resolutions on the placing of a statue of General James Shields of Illinois in Statuary Hall.[99] Later in the day Hoar was allowed to speak on his resolution; in a sharp address he defended the Provisional Government, accused Cleveland of committing an act of war, and objected strenuously to the manner in which Blount had been sent to the islands.[100] Touching this last item (the appointment of a diplomatic agent without consent of the Senate), Hoar remarked: "It seems to me . . . that the President . . . is adopting and getting into the habit of adopting rather extraordinary language in his dealings with the other branches of Government."[101]

Immediately the champions of the Administration came forward to answer Hoar's charges. The debate on Hawaii, which was to last intermittently until July 7, 1898, was on. Mills of Texas, aided by Gray of Delaware, took up the cudgel in opposition to Hoar. He denied that Cleveland's friendly interest in doing justice to the Queen was an act of war; asserted it was no business of

[96] White to Gresham, Dec. 24, 1893, *ibid.*

[97] Gresham, *Gresham, op. cit.*, pp. 759 and 770.

[98] *Congressional Record* (53 Cong. 2 Sess.), p. 19.

[99] P. 58.

[100] Pp. 61-62.

[101] P. 62. Hastings was not in favor of Hoar's hints of impeachment because that would unite the entire Democratic party behind Cleveland (Hastings to Dole, Dec. 13, 1893, M&E).

the United States what kind of government Hawaii had; and charged that the American forces had been responsible for the Revolution. Quoting liberally from the Declaration of Independence and from Blount's report, Mills counterattacked viciously. Just as Cato took figs from his toga and cried *Carthago delenda est,* said the Senator, so Stevens had "been writing letters telling us about how much sugar they produce, and what magnificent bananas hang from the trees." The speaker characterized the present régime as a military despotism upheld by American bayonets, and accused Stevens and Wiltse of conspiracy, filibustering, and buccaneering. Both had been working for the "sugar ring." "What a magnificent picture [he exclaimed] is presented by the representative of 67,000,000 of the most powerful people on the globe with the muzzles of their guns upon a poor defenseless woman whose property is about to be stolen from her! And they tell us she is not a Christian and that the Christian people are not on her side!" He reiterated that the sugar oligarchy was behind it all. "Is that day coming [he asked] when along Pennsylvania avenue we shall see a Hawaiian queen, not loaded with golden chains, but weighed down with sugar sacks on her back, coming to the Congress of the United States pleading in behalf of her poor, miserable, ignorant people for the right that we claim to have come direct from God to us, inalienable in its nature—the right to institute a government for themselves?"[102]

After Mills's rhetorical outburst, Vilas of Wisconsin advised the Republicans to wait until the President sent the documents, and then defended Cleveland against the jibes of Nelson W. Aldrich of Rhode Island.[103]

Hoar returned to the fray by asserting that when Cleveland recognized the Dole Government, and yet investigated it and conspired against it, he was acting like "Joab when he stabbed his neighbor under the fifth rib and said, 'Art thou in health, my brother?' "[104] There followed a hot, bitter clash of words among Hoar, Vilas, Mills, and Gray;[105] even John Sherman entered into the lists by declaring that Congress and the people had not been

[102] Pp. 62-64, 65-66, 67.
[103] P. 67.
[104] P. 69.
[105] *Ibid.*

treated in the open by the President.[106] That assertion required a new defense by Gray,[107] and then it was agreed that Hoar's resolution should be sent to committee.[108]

This, the opening clash between Cleveland's friends and the Annexationists in the Senate, indicated all too clearly that Vest, Gray, and Mills would need every bit of prompting they could secure from the Department of State, for Hoar was a difficult article to handle. Furthermore, this first skirmish presaged the lines of attack and of defense during the next six months of debate.

On December 11, Hoar renewed his obstructionist tactics by offering a resolution asking the President whether anyone had been appointed to represent the United States at Honolulu since the preceding March 4; whether such person had been accredited to the head of the Hawaiian Government; whether the appointment had been communicated to the Senate; and upon what authority such representative had been given entire control over the land and naval forces of the United States at Honolulu.[109] In defense of his resolution, Hoar lunged into the unconstitutionality of Blount's selection, and declared it was a usurpation of the dignity of the Senate.[110] Gray answered as best he could, but lamely.[111] Hoar came back with an onslaught upon "Lord Paramount Commissioner Blount."[112] Gray became so nettled that he lost his poise and declared petulantly: "I never professed to know as much as the Senator from Massachusetts, and I never expect to know as much as he knows about everything."[113] The debate on that day ended in the midst of bitter personal wrangling, accusations of misstatements, and rasped feelings.[114] Gray had been considerably worsted, for he found it difficult to justify Cleveland's choice of a diplomatic agent without Senatorial consent when the Senate was in session.

Vest of Missouri, perceiving that the Administration men

[106] P. 71.
[107] P. 72.
[108] P. 73.
[109] P. 127; *Sen. Mis. Doc. 13* (53 Cong. 2 Sess.).
[110] P. 128.
[111] P. 129.
[112] P. 130.
[113] *Ibid.*
[114] Pp. 132 *ff*.

needed ammunition, appealed to Gresham on December 11. He wanted precedents to prove "the power of the President to Send a diplomatic agent with *paramount* authority to a foreign government, without Consulting Congress." Next day he asked again, expressing doubt that Cleveland had the right to appoint Blount, and added: "I have every disposition to fight Hoar, but I'm afraid he can make trouble on the point I have Mentioned. Send me precedents."[115] Meanwhile the *New York Tribune* recorded that Hoar was going after Cleveland with vengeance for illegally appointing Blount.[116]

William P. Frye of Maine took up the attack on December 13, and Gray answered. Said Frye: "I affirm without hesitation that Mr. Blount in that report has not written one single unvarnished line of truth, nor given one unprejudiced opinion, nor rendered one important judgment." He proceeded to defend Stevens, his fellow citizen from Maine, by reading into his remarks Stevens's speech to his neighbors at Augusta upon his return from Honolulu. "I thank Heaven [Frye asserted] that no citizen of Maine ordered it [the flag] hauled down."[117]

Vest then had his turn; he spoke, declared he, not as a proponent of Cleveland, but as an American Senator. His lengthy address dissected, sentence by sentence, Frye's defense of "this man Stevens, this God-fearing, charitable, saintly old logician of Maine." In the course of his attack upon Stevens, he paid his respects to the American missionaries who went to Hawaii: "They have Christianized them [natives] out of their country; they have pursued the old New England fashion of taking possession in the name of God, and then dividing out under laws made by themselves." Vest also adverted to the undesirability of acquiring colonies. We "want no colonies," he announced; for, how were they to be governed? "It is proposed now that instead of having a compact, continental republic, as our fathers intended, we are to have a great, expansive territory-acquiring Government, extending even to the islands of the ocean and the uttermost parts of the earth."[118]

[115] Vest to Gresham, Dec. 11 and 12, 1893, Gresham MSS.

[116] Dec. 13, 1893.

[117] *Record,* pp. 190-191. Later in the day, John B. Gordon of Georgia objected bitterly to Frye's calling Blount, his fellow Georgian, a liar (p. 204).

[118] Pp. 194-196.

Vest then turned his attention to Hoar's criticism that Blount's appointment was illegal. He recited a list of several hundred diplomatic agents who had been sent on missions by various Presidents without Senatorial confirmation.[119] Gresham's clerks had done a good job. Even the New York *Sun* commended Vest for going into the heart of the matter.[120] Hoar tried to tear these precedents apart, aided by William E. Chandler of New Hampshire.[121]

White of California attempted to beat Hoar at Hoar's own tricks. His idea was that Stevens's authority at Honolulu had been terminated when the Queen fell, unless Harrison immediately honored him with a new letter of credence to the Provisional Government. Furthermore, whether Harrison had sent a new letter or not, his allowing Stevens to remain amounted to a new appointment; hence the Republicans had perpetrated the very misdeed for which they were criticizing Cleveland—appointing a Minister without consent of the Senate.[122]

On December 18, 1893, Cleveland sent the documents which Hoar had persuaded the Senate to request. The Republicans clutched at the opportunity of playing partisan politics. Hoar and Chandler wanted certain letters accompanying Cleveland's special message read in open Senate. The Democrats objected to wasting time in reading despatches which would be printed for the use of the Senate anyway. Voorhees thought it would be unfair to pick out one or two; all or none should be read. There followed a parliamentary snarl over the rules touching the reading of papers. Chandler said he wished three letters read; namely, those dated October 18, November 24, and December 3.[123] After charges by Administration men that the opposition desired to secure partisan advantage, the three despatches were read.[124]

[119] Pp. 196 *ff*. Gray added others, p. 199.

[120] Dec. 13, 1893.

[121] P. 205.

[122] White to Gresham, Dec. 24, 1893, Gresham MSS. White used this idea in a speech on Feb. 21, 1894 (*Record,* "Appendix," pp. 470-486).

[123] These letters have been discussed previously. That of Oct. 18 was Gresham's final instructions to Willis; that of Nov. 24 was Gresham's telegram telling Willis to demand that the Queen agree to amnesty; and that of Dec. 3 was Gresham's amplified instructions to the same purpose.

[124] *Record,* pp. 313-319.

Two days later Hoar attacked the President's message on Hawaii. He declared again that Blount's appointment had been unconstitutional, in spite of any precedents that might be unearthed; objected to Gray's "reviling me" and to Vest's "reviling the Puritans of New England"; and called Cleveland a dictator for commissioning Blount as his own "private agent."[125]

At the end of Hoar's address, Senator John T. Morgan of Alabama offered a resolution to the effect that the Committee of Foreign Relations, of which he was chairman, "shall inquire and report whether, and, if so, what irregularities have occurred in the diplomatic or other intercourse between the United States and Hawaii in relation to the recent political revolution in Hawaii, and to this end the said committee is authorized to send for persons and papers and to administer oaths to witnesses."[126] The resolution passed and the Committee worked steadily for two months. The fact that Morgan was a rabid Annexationist, and a leading Democrat at the same time, probably led the New York *Sun* to say on December 23, 1893: "Has the CLEVELAND policy of infamy not a single supporter in the Fifty-third Congress, even among the cuckoos?" Blount was asked to come to Washington and help the cause. Promising to do so, he added: "Senator Morgan cant [*sic*] go back upon himself for his party. . . . His investigating Committee is an outrage."[127] The New York *World* thought the idea of investigating the Hawaiian problem was foolish, for there were too many other matters of importance which needed attention.[128]

The Hawaiian Annexationists in Washington at once proceeded to organize and to secure the most favorable testimony possible. On December 26, 1893, Frank P. Hastings, Hawaiian *chargé* in the absence of Thurston, asked Gresham to get him permission to sit in on the hearings, and to give evidence to the Morgan Committee.[129] Annexationist members of the Committee were behind the move. Gresham rightly thought this was a peculiar request from the representative of a sovereign state, because the

[125] Pp. 430 *ff.*

[126] *Sen. Report 227* (53 Cong. 2 Sess.), p. 1. This document has heretofore been designated "Morgan."

[127] Blount to Gresham, Jan. 3, 1894, Gresham MSS.

[128] Dec. 28, 1893.

[129] Hastings to Gresham, Dec. 26, 1893, Notes from Hawaii; Hastings to Dole, Dec. 27, 1893, M&E.

investigation was a domestic issue; nevertheless he told Hastings to see Chairman Morgan.[130] When Hastings perceived that it was to be an examination of American officials alone, he withdrew the request.[131] Therein lay the significance of the Morgan investigation. The question had become a matter of domestic, or to put it more realistically, of partisan politics.[132]

Hastings continued to work hand in hand with the Annexationists in the Senate who were interested in, as he said, getting Blount's scalp. Senator Frye wanted to know what witnesses Hastings could produce. The latter named P. C. Jones, Alexander, Oleson, Spalding, and Emerson.[133] Alexander worked intimately with the Annexationist Senators. Spalding was on hand and did a good job of seeing important statesmen in the interest of the cause.[134] Both Hastings and Alexander pressed Dole to send affidavits from members of the Provisional Government for filing with the evidence.

The Hawaiian Legation thought it was extremely important to second the efforts of Senators Frye and Morgan. Knowing that Frye and Stevens were both from Maine, Alexander wrote with evident glee, that "Senator Frye is naturally particularly anxious to vindicate Mr. Stevens and discredit Blount"; he thought that Morgan, on the other hand, wanted an impartial report in order to further the cause of annexation.[135] Oleson feared that Morgan might be so influenced by the Administration as to side with it. "Gresham," he said, "is tricky and Cleveland obstinate and Willis conscious of failure, and the combination is a bad one."[136] Alexander, who thought better of Morgan, believed that Gresham was angry at Willis and wanted to make him the scapegoat. Hastings asked Morgan that Oleson and J. A. McCandless be allowed to testify.[137]

[130] Gresham to Hastings, Jan. 2, 1894, Notes to Hawaii.

[131] Hastings to Gresham, Jan. 3, 1894, Notes from Hawaii.

[132] Cf., New York *Sun,* Dec. 22 and 27, 1893.

[133] See Hastings's "Private Memorandum to the President," dated Dec. 22, 23, 24, 26, 1893, and Jan. 2, 3, 5, 6, 1894 (M&E) for more of what Hastings called "intrigue" between himself and the Morgan Committee.

[134] Hastings to Dole, Feb. 21, 1894, *ibid.*

[135] Alexander to Dole, Jan. 7, 1894, *ibid.*

[136] Oleson to Hastings, Jan. 8, 1894, *ibid.*

[137] Hastings to Dole, Jan. 11, 1894, *ibid.*

All the Hawaiian diplomatic representatives were aware of the danger in this type of intrigue; as Thurston said, they were not tying themselves up too closely with the Republicans, even though they were friends of annexation, because many Democrats and anti-Administration men were friends also.[138] Hastings admitted that, in view of the fact that both parties were using Hawaii as a political football, it was the duty of Hawaii's diplomats to win the best deal they could.[139]

Some of the Annexationists in Honolulu had interesting suggestions regarding possible witnesses. W. O. Smith wondered whether it would not be a good idea to bring Dole over. Cecil Brown, who was leaving on a trip to the United States, wanted to take C. B. Wilson, Joseph Nawahi, and J. W. Kalua along as witnesses, provided either the Provisional Government or the Morgan Committee would pay their expenses. To get such Royalists and/or natives to give their stories would prove that the Government was not afraid of what they would say; and besides, Wilson had promised to assert that he could have broken up the Revolution if the Cabinet had not been too cowardly to give the order. This statement, so Brown believed, would prove that the marines were not needed because the Revolution had been won without them.[140] Brown's hint that the Provisional Government might pay Wilson's expenses was a rather remarkable one, for no man was more hated by the Annexationists. The *Star* often referred to him as "the dull, brute power behind the throne . . . thief and paramour . . . the political lieutenant of the Queen."[141]

* * * * *

Meanwhile the House of Representatives had also become embroiled in the Hawaiian problem, in spite of the pressure of domestic issues, such as the tariff. Representative Robert R. Hitt of Illinois, speaking for the Republican minority, offered on December 6, 1893, a resolution which asked the President for copies of all correspondence to and from Honolulu since March 4, 1889.[142] Although the Democrat, James B. McCreary of Kentucky, reported

[138] Thurston to Dole, confidential, Feb. 15, 1894, *ibid.*
[139] Hastings to Dole, Feb. 11, 1894, *ibid.*
[140] W. N. Armstrong to Thurston, Feb. 13, 1894, M&E.
[141] Nov. 20, 1893, for instance.
[142] *Record,* p. 82.

Hitt's resolution back favorably from the Committee on Foreign Affairs, as a matter of routine, Hitt tried to make partisan capital out of it. Inasmuch as the public press, said he, was stating that one thousand Hawaiians were preparing to defend their homes against an invasion by American forces, information was sorely needed if the country was to be kept out of war. Hitt's resolution passed.[143]

The struggle in the House over Hawaii was really precipitated on December 18 with the President's special message (already discussed) and his message accompanying the documents asked for by Hitt.[144] After the reading of the messages, the Republican Charles A. Boutelle of Maine (who was soon to become as annoying as a hairshirt to the Democrats) arose on a question of privilege. At this point began the stormy debates on the Hawaiian question—debates which, in the lower chamber, would be characterized by the most partisan kind of bickering and which, time and again, threw that body into turmoil.

Boutelle began the rumpus by asking that certain of Willis's letters (out of which the Republicans expected to secure partisan advantage) be read in open house, instead of being sent to committee and perhaps buried.[145] The Speaker refused to accept Boutelle's claim that such a request was privileged (that is, should be acted upon at once), and forthwith the House became entangled over rules. The Republicans, although a minority, were adept at throwing sand into the gears of the Democratic machine. The reporter noted that there was "Confusion in the Hall."[146] After much time spent in parliamentary wrangling, the Democrats allowed three letters[147]—those of October 18, November 24, and December 2—to be read, with their own *consent,* and they wished it to be known that the concession was granted only out

[143] Pp. 220-221.

[144] Cleveland sent everything asked for except Stevens's No. 70 and Willis's No. 3. The reason for omitting these two despatches has already been explained: they contained personal references that might have caused international complications (*House Ex. Doc. 48,* 53 Cong. 2 Sess., pp. 1-2; and *Record,* p. 374).

[145] *Record,* p. 374.

[146] Pp. 474-475.

[147] It will be remembered that the Republicans in the Senate had demanded open reading of the same despatches.

of the goodness of their hearts. There was Democratic applause after Gresham's words, in his instructions to Willis of December 3: "You will say that the President can not use force without the authority of Congress." Boutelle arose again to offer a privileged resolution criticizing the President. Immediately there was such disorder that the sergeant-at-arms was called out to get the members back in their seats.[148] Though refused acceptance at the moment, the resolution reappeared later.

Next day William B. Cockran of New York tried the same device, namely, a privileged resolution. It ran to the effect that the President's message had indicated an attempt to bring about "a change in the territorial limits of the United States without any consultation with the House" of Representatives; that, because such matters ought to be referred to Congress, seven members be appointed to "examine into the rights, powers, privileges, and duties of the House . . . on all questions and proceedings affecting or involving the territorial integrity of the United States."[149] Just what Cockran had in mind when he charged Cleveland with trying to change the territorial limits of the United States is not clear; in any case he demanded that his resolution be sent to the Committee on Rules.

This maneuver was exactly to Boutelle's liking. In the midst of great confusion on the floor, he offered an amendment to Cockran's resolution. The President, said the amendment, had proved in his special message that "the rights and dignity of the House . . . as a coordinate branch of the Congress . . . have been invaded by the executive department in furnishing secret instructions to a minister" to conspire against the Government of Hawaii; and that such interference was contrary to American law.[150] When McCreary denied the privileged status of such resolutions and amendments, Boutelle went into a tirade; and Nelson Dingley of Maine cried: "Is nothing privileged if offered on this side of the House?" Boutelle proceeded: ". . . for all we know, under the instructions that have been read to this House, the armed forces of the United States may to-day have their bayonets at the throat

[148] P. 376.
[149] Pp. 397 *ff*.
[150] P. 398.

of a friendly government, with which, I believe, Mr. Speaker, the people of this country overwhelmingly sympathize to-day."

Boutelle's statement brought Republican cheers. McCreary objected again; Boutelle continued; disorder broke out once more on the floor; and Boutelle was directed to keep to the point, that is, to prove that Cockran's resolution and his amendment were privileged. He promised to do so, and went on: "I hold that it is our bounden duty at the earliest practicable moment to disavow and discredit and reprobate a public policy, unconstitutional in its inception, unpatriotic in its spirit, of gravest danger to the public interest, and calculated to bring the United States into discredit with the rest of the civilized world." Again there was applause on the Republican side.

Benjamin A. Enloe of Tennessee rose to make a point of order, but Boutelle continued to shout against "this shameful policy . . . originated by a renegade Republican [he meant Gresham] and a Democratic usurper." As he began to charge conspiracy, the Chair closed him down. Then he started his denunciation again, during which time the Speaker tried, in the midst of cries for the regular order and in great confusion, to decide whether Boutelle was really talking on a privileged resolution, and if so, whether his words were pertinent.

Finally, after a long period spent in argumentation, appeals to the rules, and precedents established during the Civil War, the Cockran-Boutelle motion was sent to the Committee on Foreign Affairs, against Republican objections that it should go to the Committee on Rules. The vote was 171 to 91; but 91 did not vote.[151] Before this tempest ended, however, Henry W. Blair of New Hampshire offered a resolution, which was later referred, "That this House is in favor of the annexation of the Hawaiian Islands to the United States."[152]

Two days later—December 21—the Republican attack against the embarrassed Democrats commenced again. Blair tried to secure unanimous consent for immediate action on a resolution calling for an investigation of the Hawaiian Revolution. It was later sent to the Committee on Foreign Affairs.[153] On the same day, Boutelle

[151] Pp. 399-401.
[152] Pp. 401, 446.
[153] Pp. 470, 478, 1833.

presented a resolution which quoted Blount's order of March 31, 1893, commanding Admiral Skerrett to haul down the flag; asked the Secretary of the Navy by what authority the naval forces had been placed under Blount; requested copies of all naval instructions sent to Honolulu since March 4, 1893; and wanted his resolution to be considered as a privileged one. It was sent to the Committee on Naval Affairs.[154]

The same day, however, saw some forward action on the part of the majority. McCreary, who had already authored a resolution upholding Blount and Cleveland, brought it back, slightly changed in wording, as the majority report of the Committee on Foreign Affairs. The resolution contained two clauses: (1) Stevens's action in using the naval forces "illegally" to overthrow the Royal Government and to help set up the Provisional Government (which was neither republican nor established in accordance with majority will) "was contrary to the traditions of our Republic and the spirit of our Constitution, and should be and is condemned." (2) Moreover, "we heartily approve" the President's statement that interference in the domestic affairs of another nation "is contrary to the spirit of American institutions"; furthermore, both annexation and protectorate were "uncalled for and inexpedient"; finally, the islands should have "absolute freedom and independence," and foreign intervention would "not be regarded with indifference by the Government of the United States."[155] Thus no words were minced touching Stevens's guilt and in doing honor to the Monroe Doctrine, but Cleveland received no support in his desire to do justice to the Queen. This was the resolution which the House finally passed.

At the same time the Republican minority of the Committee reported out a substitute resolution, originally introduced by Hitt. It also had two clauses: (1) Cleveland's order to the Dole Government asking it to abdicate "was an unwarranted intervention in the affairs of a friendly recognized government, contrary to the law of nations, the policy and traditions of the Republic, and the spirit of the Constitution." (2) Inasmuch as the Provisional Government had been recognized by the United States, the "highest

[154] Pp. 468-469.
[155] P. 1814; *House Mis. Doc. 44* (53 Cong. 2 Sess.).

international interests" required that it be left alone, and any foreign interference would be unfriendly to the United States.[156]

Both resolutions agreed in their support of the Monroe Doctrine, but with that they parted company. There was a head-on collision regarding what should be American policy towards Hawaii. Each condemned the other's intervention. In Democratic eyes Stevens's was heinous; Republicans denounced Willis's.

During the holiday recess, the Democrats who had been clearly taken off their guard by the vicious attacks of Boutelle, Blair and Hitt, prepared to seize the offensive when Congress reassembled. On January 1, 1894, Congressman Isidor Rayner of Maryland told Gresham that the Hawaiian matter ought to come up right away; the tariff could wait. He continued: ". . . instead of being upon the defensive we ought courageously to expose this great iniquity. There never was a case before a Jury in the land so overwhelmingly proven as this is." McCreary was to open the debate, and Speaker Charles F. Crisp had "promised to recognize me [Rayner] next. . . . I *wish you would remind him of this so that it is done.*" After talking about other details of the plan, Rayner added: "Do not forget to drop a line to Crisp." On the same day he sent a telegram to Gresham, wishing to see the Secretary on the Hawaiian problem.[157]

After the holiday recess the Hawaiian debate idled in the House until January 22, although on January 16 Hitt offered a resolution, which was referred, requesting the President to give all the information he had available on Hawaiian affairs.[158] Partly in answer to the requests of both houses, and partly on his own initiative, Cleveland began to submit Willis's despatches as soon as they arrived. On January 20 he sent to the House Willis's No. 20½ of January 5, with enclosures;[159] again on January 22 another message arrived containing Willis's No. 22 and No. 24, and Admiral Irwin's letter of January 2 to the Secretary of the Navy.

These letters gave to Boutelle his cue for another tussle. He arose on a question of privilege, stating that the documents just

[156] P. 1814; *House Report 243* and *House Mis. Doc. 42* (53 Cong. 2 Sess.).
[157] Rayner to Gresham, Jan. 1, 1894, Gresham MSS.
[158] *Record,* p. 513.
[159] Pp. 1122-1125; read in the Senate on Jan. 22, p. 1168.

read showed that the President was "still engaged in fomenting insurrection against a government with which we are at peace." Again, as was usual when Boutelle spoke on Hawaii, there were confusion, cries demanding the regular order, and argumentation over the rules. W. H. Hatch of Missouri asked that the House do something about Boutelle's repeated breaking of the rules. Finally Boutelle agreed to take his seat. Speaker Crisp said: "The trouble with the gentleman is that he violates the rule in doing even that." Boutelle rose again, but before he was able to speak at any length, Hatch interrupted to say that Boutelle had insulted the Speaker and demanded that Boutelle's "words be taken down." Another Democrat, John L. Bretz of Indiana, cried: "Is there not some way in which we can enforce the rules of this House?"

At this point the Democrats proceeded to discuss the tariff bill, but Boutelle, like a jumping jack, was on his feet again. Crisp called upon the sergeant-at-arms to put him in his seat. Faced by the mace, he sat down, but was up in a trice, demanding a roll call because he maintained there was no quorum. When Speaker Crisp appointed him as a teller to find out if there was a quorum, Boutelle asked, with impudent bravado, whether he was qualified to act as teller. The Speaker, losing his temper at such tactics, chose another to act as teller, whereupon Boutelle declared he wanted to serve inasmuch as he had not declined. There ensued a long altercation between Boutelle and Crisp whether the former's insolent question was tantamount to a refusal to serve as teller. Crisp insisted it did; Boutelle just as strongly contended it did not. As a result, he cleverly accomplished his purpose of tying up the House in order to delay the discussion of either Hawaii or the tariff. After interminable argument, the slow-moving, leaderless Democratic majority succeeded in getting its wishes accepted, and the House went into the Committee of the Whole on the State of the Union to discuss the tariff. Boutelle was still fighting and arguing as the decision was made.[160]

The Democratic majority was ready to take up the McCreary resolution which, on December 21, 1893, had been reported favorably from the Committee on Foreign Affairs. On February 2 Cleveland sent another of Willis's despatches, the reading of which

[160] Pp. 1189-1192.

gave to Boutelle a chance to obstruct by asking why the President had not sent the enclosures.[161] This move started the debate in earnest. McCreary opened in defense of his resolution by justifying Cleveland's policy, by decrying the recent partisanship, and by denying that the President ever ordered the Provisional Government to get out. The Republicans paid little attention until he charged that they did not wish Stevens's No. 70 published; Hitt arose to say they did. Leaning heavily upon the Blount report, McCreary made a long speech, although its effect was weakened by constant interruptions at almost every sentence by Blair and Hitt. In spite of obstacles, he did succeed in giving a list of precedents for Blount's unconfirmed appointment.[162]

Rayner of Maryland then held forth in support of McCreary's resolution. Declaring that he was no partisan, he said he was convinced, after a careful study of the facts, that Stevens was guilty and that the Republicans were endeavoring to cover up his "conspiracy." Rayner did not get very far before his opponents began to mob him with questions. John Van Voorhis of New York wanted to know how many were in the conspiracy; Rayner did not know. Between Republican questions, however, he was able to prove to his own satisfaction, "The Crime of an American Minister [Stevens]." He demanded that the Annexationists produce the private letters which Blaine undoubtedly had written in answer to Stevens's Annexationist despatches. He ended his discourse by asserting that he favored neither restoration nor annexation[163]—an attitude which would hardly be supported by Gresham and Cleveland.

Hitt answered for the Republicans by defending his own minority report in a speech which continued until next day, February 3. After deriding Blount's report, he proceeded to berate Cleveland for intervening "in behalf of the Messalina of the Pacific, a woman whose horrid blood-thirsty character, brought into the fierce light of publicity, has shocked the civilized world." In a passage filled with epithets, he declared that Willis—"the tiger protégé of Mr. Cleveland"—was chargeable with a "violation of the law of nations." "This is the first time," he insisted,

[161] Pp. 1813-1814.
[162] Pp. 1814 *ff*.
[163] Pp. 1825-1832.

"in all our history that an American anywhere has dreaded to see our armed ships and the flag of his country threatening him with hostility and monarchical rule." Hitt said he had little sympathy with the assertion that an American minority had raped Hawaii: ". . . if 2,000 Americans have such energy, pluck, business ability, character, honesty, and reputation that they own one-half or three-fourths of the property on the islands; if . . . they have $24,000,000 invested in one industry, is it to be made a reproach? I am proud of my countrymen!"

At this point in the address, Joshua F. C. Talbott of Maryland rose to ask Hitt a question; Henry U. Johnson of Indiana advised Talbott: "Sit down and do yourself honor." Once quiet had been restored, Hitt launched into a denunciation of "that pleasant romance brought back by the special commissioner." Hitt averred that, as a result of Blount's report, Cleveland thought Liliuokalani was a gentle-natured and kindly woman; on the other hand, Willis found her to be "more cruel and hideous than anything in the descriptions of Homer." This thrust brought cheers from the Republican side. Former Speaker Thomas B. ("Czar") Reed asked: "Why do not you gentlemen on that side cheer?" William W. Bowers of California, also a Republican, answered: "Oh! they can not cheer Americanism over there."

When he picked up the threat of his discourse next day, Hitt continued to berate the Queen for her desire to behead her enemies, condemned Willis's request for Dole to surrender, and praised Dole's reply. He accurately expressed Republican sentiment regarding the monarchy when he asked: ". . . is it for us, is it for the President of our Republic to pick up that tawdry, dishonored thing and attempt to force it back upon the shoulders of our kindred, of men of American blood, of American ideas, of American feelings?"[164]

The addresses of McCreary, Rayner, and Hitt set the standard of debating for the next week until a vote was taken. Generally speaking, little was added in spite of days and days of arguing, and page after page in the *Record* devoted to the Hawaiian problem. On February 3 Blair had his say in a long fulmination in which he defended annexation and drubbed Cleveland.[165] He

[164] "Appendix," pp. 440-449.
[165] Pp. 1832-1838.

objected strenuously to the fact that members of the Committee on Foreign Affairs were monopolizing all the time, and that others were not getting a chance. Then Hernando Money of Mississippi (later to be a Senator) had his inning for the Democrats.[166] William F. Draper[167] and Elijah A. Morse, both of Massachusetts, took up the gauntlet for the Republicans. By that time the debating period for February 3 had been completed, and yet there were dozens of members in both parties who desired to be heard, whether they knew anything about the question or not. Henry U. Johnson of Indiana said the Republicans wanted more time and asked that the debate be extended a day longer than planned. Richard P. Bland of Missouri objected because he had a silver bill pending "to supply some money with which to run this Government."[169] Nevertheless the Republican minority fought for more time.[170]

During these days the Hawaiian question overshadowed every other pressing issue, whether tariff, need of money, or plans to get the country out of the panic. Members fought for precious time to state their attitudes for the benefit of their constituents. On February 5 Morse of Massachusetts secured two and a half minutes in which to denounce the Democrats for favoring a white man's government in the South, and for supporting "a dissolute colored female" in Hawaii, whose "father was a colored barber." As he continued to rail against the President and the Democrats in unparliamentary terms, Joseph H. Outhwaite of Ohio rose to protest against such insults, and demanded that the words be taken down. Morse was ordered to send his manuscript to the clerk. The objectionable matter consisted in this: he had referred to "the cuckoos in the House and in the Senate" who were taking orders from "their master, the great Grover Cleveland." Morse objected to taking down the word "cuckoos" which, while in his manuscript, he had omitted when he spoke. He was forced to withdraw his language.[171]

[166] Pp. 1838-1844.
[167] Pp. 1844-1849.
[168] Pp. 1849-1851.
[169] P. 1851.
[170] *Ibid.*
[171] P. 1879.

After this interlude was over, the word battle went on. Johnson of Indiana defended Republican policies in a speech which required eight pages to print;[172] Josiah Patterson of Tennessee broke a lance for the Democrats in two pages.[173] The old rebel General, Joe Wheeler of Alabama, then made a talk but his remarks were never printed. Next came an address from the stormy petrel, Boutelle, who spoke so long and in such wearisome detail that even the Republicans probably did not listen. Most of the oration was in all likelihood never given, for it filled thirty-six pages in the "Appendix" of the *Record*. It was replete with long quotations, included practically all the documents since the beginning of the Hawaiian trouble, and traced the topic from the early years of Hawaiian history up to Willis's last published despatch.[174] After several more speeches,[175] it was decided to hold an evening session.[176]

As a vote on McCreary's resolution had been agreed upon for February 6, that day saw the lines grow tighter and the speeches shorter. Even at that, twenty-five pages[177] were filled before the previous question was ordered at 3:30 p.m. of that day. A resolution sponsored by Blair, which would approve the recognition of the Provisional Government, and which was offered as a substitute to Hitt's, was rejected, 165 nays, 90 yeas, 96 not voting.[178] With Blair's motion out of the way, the House speedily disposed of Hitt's substitute resolution, rejecting it by a vote of 161 nays, 98 yeas, 92 not voting.[179]

Defeated on their own resolutions, the Republicans proceeded to obstruct the Democratic majority. Reed of Maine offered a motion to recommit McCreary's resolution (that is, the majority report of the Committee of Foreign Affairs); it was lost by a strict party vote.[180] This Democratic success should have opened the way for the passage of the McCreary resolution; but the Re-

[172] Pp. 1880-1889.
[173] Pp. 1889-1891.
[174] "Appendix," pp. 543-570.
[175] Pp. 1893-1909.
[176] P. 1908. The evening session covered pages 1909-1921.
[177] Pp. 1942-1967.
[178] P. 1968.
[179] Pp. 1968-1969.
[180] P. 1969.

publicans still had tricks in their satchel. The vote on McCreary's resolution, when counted, stood: yeas 160, nays 2, not voting 189.[181] It was less than a quorum. The Republicans were using the old Democratic dodge of preventing a quorum when a measure came up for a vote.[182] When McCreary demanded a call of the House, no quorum was secured because of Republican absences.[183] In the midst of a great deal of confusion, in which the Democratic majority found itself helplessly impaled because of the lack of a quorum, a resolution was finally pushed through ordering the sergeant-at-arms to round up all members, illness to be the only excuse for absence. A vote was postponed until morning.[184]

On February 7 the struggle over the resolution was inaugurated by Reed of Maine, the former Speaker, who consumed considerable time in an altercation with Speaker Crisp about the rules. A vote was taken, but again a quorum was lacking.[185] Then followed an extended fight on the question of what really was a quorum. Reed injected himself into the argument by reminding Crisp of certain decisions Reed had made when he was Speaker. The Constitution was read from; the House rules were appealed to; precedents were invoked. The Constitution said a quorum was a majority. With four seats vacant, what was a quorum? One over half of those present, or one over half of the full membership? A member made the point that 177 would be a quorum because the House then had 352 on the rolls. In the last vote taken, there had been only 173 yeas as against 174 absentees. After seemingly endless parliamentary dickering and page after page of logomachy, Rayner asked for another vote. This time the McCreary resolution passed: 177 yeas, 78 nays, and 96 not voting.[186]

Before turning to other pressing problems, the Democrats hastened to put a quietus on Boutelle's resolution over which so much squabbling had occurred. His motion, which declared in

[181] Pp. 1969-1970.

[182] On Jan. 30, 1890, "Czar" Reed had ruled that those present but not answering the roll call were physically present for the purpose of a quorum. The Republicans in the present juncture were absenting themselves and could not be counted even under Reed's decision.

[183] P. 1972.

[184] *Ibid.*

[185] P. 2001.

[186] Pp. 2001-2017.

effect that Cleveland had invaded the dignity of the House was overturned: nays 158, yeas 94, and not voting 99.[187] Defeated, as he expected he would be, Boutelle had the last word: "Mr. Speaker, I do not know that it is exactly a parliamentary inquiry, but if the vote upon the resolution is to be understood as an abdication of the powers of the House, I hope gentlemen will interest themselves to find some friendly monarch somewhere who will restore them."[188] The Democrats, satisfied at what had been done, said nothing about this sally.

In short, the House by a strict party vote, had censured Stevens and upheld Gresham. It was a victory for the President,[189] but a Pyrrhic one; for it did not expressly support intervention against the Provisional Government. The independent press approved, and hoped for a similar expression from the Senate.[190] Republican editors contended that even those Democrats who voted for the resolution did so against their consciences; and that it could hardly be called vindication when only 177 out of 215 Democrats voted to uphold the Executive. Thurston likewise thought the President's policy had "severely soured on the stomachs" of members of the Democratic party.[191]

Both Hastings and Thurston, who had worked so hard giving

[187] P. 2008.

[188] *Ibid.*

[189] Gresham needed this expression of support from the House, for his Hawaiian policy had decreased his reputation in the country at large. Jacob D. Cox, dean of the Law School of Cincinnati College, thought: "The attacks on him [Gresham, were] very very *hollow,* as they sounded to my ears. It is a pity that party politics cant [*sic*] have a little dash of fairplay, but there is not a particle. It was thought good tactics by the Republicans to make a clap-trap issue on Hawaii & so Gresham must be attacked as if he were a mixture of fool & knave. . . . I think it is already Evident also that nobody of sense wants to annex Hawaii, any more than San Domingo. As for the descendants of the missionaries turned fillibusters [*sic*] & setting up an arbitrary white government over the natives which have been the *special exhibit* of Christian Churches in the line of *missionary civilization,* it is a satire on Christianity so coarse that one wonders whether it must not be an accusation by some resurrected Tom Paine" (Cox to Gen. G. B. Wright, Feb. 2, 1894, Cleveland MSS.). The New York legislature passed a resolution of gratification at Cleveland's Hawaiian policy. Senator David B. Hill presented it to the Senate (*Record,* Jan. 31, 1894, p. 1759).

[190] *Literary Digest,* VIII (Feb. 15, 1894), 367.

[191] Thurston to Dole, Feb. 11; and Thurston to ________, Feb. 11, 1894, M&E.

information to their friends in the House, were quite satisfied with the outcome. At first they believed that—inasmuch as restoration was now dead—the Provisional Government should come to some financial agreement with the Queen and end the matter for good. On second thought, however, Thurston said he felt it would be wiser to "Let her stew in her own gravy for a while and before long she will be in a position where she will appreciate the value of money more than she does now."[192]

Though the House had seemingly disposed of the Hawaiian question, there remained numerous loose ends to sew up. Cleveland continued to send Willis's despatches as they arrived.[193] On February 16 Boutelle had another chance to create trouble when his resolution of December 21, 1893, was called up.[194] This resolution, asking Secretary of the Navy Herbert by what authority the naval forces at Honolulu had been placed under Blount's orders, was reported back favorably on January 10, 1894. A long argument resulted when Boutelle demanded that the report have privileged status.[195] It was not until February 16 that the resolution was really discussed. Boutelle charged that politics had caused it to sleep in committee for two months. Although by that time the House had taken a stand upon the Hawaiian problem, the resolution passed.[196] The material asked for arrived on March 10,[197] and, when printed as a public document,[198] contained valuable information for the edification of the country.

Herbert replied that, inasmuch as the Hawaiian Islands were so far away, he permitted Blount to act as Admiral Skerrett's superior, so as more efficiently to carry out the President's instructions; and that the naval forces always acted under the civil branch anyway. The Secretary pointed out seven clear precedents for placing naval vessels and military forces under Presidential agents, the

[192] Hastings to Dole, Feb. 7; and Thurston to Dole, Feb. 15, 1894, confidential, M&E.

[193] Cf., *Record,* Feb. 13, 1894, pp. 2141-2142.

[194] Mentioned earlier.

[195] Pp. 630-632.

[196] Pp. 2247-2248.

[197] P. 2812.

[198] See *House Mis. Doc. 60, House Report 254,* and *House Ex. Doc. 140* (53 Cong. 2 Sess.).

most interesting being the cases of Polk's appointing Nicholas P. Trist to supersede General Winfield Scott during the Mexican War and Grant's selection of Orville Babcock to secure annexation of San Domingo in 1869.

On February 26 Boutelle offered another long list of resolutions, probably with the intention of reviving the Hawaiian fight, but he did not get very far. The resolutions adverted to the fact that in the past the United States had secured the recall of foreign diplomats who became *persona non grata* at Washington; therefore, the President, as a friendly gesture towards Hawaii, should recall Willis. As usual Boutelle demanded immediate consideration of his resolutions, but the Chair chose to see no privilege involved, and sent them to the Committee on Foreign Affairs, where they were buried.[199] The last important obstructive motion on the part of the Republicans was a resolution, March 3, 1894, by John F. Lacey of Iowa, who wished to rescind that part of the McCreary resolution, passed February 7, which had censured Stevens.[200] It got nowhere, partly because the House Democrats refused again to become involved, and partly because, by that time, public interest centered upon what was going on in the Senate.

* * * * *

Whereas the House had finally, in a clumsy and angry manner, arrived at a vote, the Senate was still wallowing in debate. On January 3, 1894, Frye offered a resolution which, had it passed, would have estopped any interference in Hawaiian affairs during the time of the Morgan Committee's work.[201] The next day Hoar sponsored a motion inquiring of the Secretary of the Treasury what sums had been paid to Blount and from what fund.[202] Still another was offered on January 8 by Chandler of New Hampshire asking the Judiciary Committee to look into the question whether the President might send diplomatic agents without the consent of the Senate.[203] At the objection of Vest, who said the Morgan Committee was considering that topic, it was withdrawn.[204]

In the midst of heated debating, Senator David Turpie of

[199] *Record*, pp. 2424-2425.
[200] P. 2574.
[201] P. 482; *Sen. Mis. Doc. 23* (53 Cong. 2 Sess.).
[202] P. 490; *Sen. Mis. Doc. 24* (53 Cong. 2 Sess.).
[203] P. 519; *Sen. Mis. Doc. 28* (53 Cong. 2 Sess.).
[204] Jan. 9, 1894, p. 567.

Indiana on January 8 laid before the Senate a resolution which read as follows:

> *Resolved,* That from the facts and papers laid before us by the Executive and other sources it is unwise, inexpedient, and not in accordance with the character and dignity of the United States to consider further at this time either the treaty or project of annexation of the Hawaiian territory to this country; that the Provisional Government therein having been duly recognized, the highest international interests require that it shall pursue its own line of polity. Foreign intervention in the political affairs of these islands will be regarded as an act unfriendly to the Government of the United States.[205]

This resolution became the storm center of an orgy of polemics which lasted off and on almost five months before the Senate found it possible to agree on an amended version. Turpie's original is significant for several reasons: (1) It favored Cleveland in that annexation was thrown overboard "at this time." (2) It offered an olive branch to the Annexationists because the Provisional Government was not to be disturbed by the United States. (3) As did the McCreary resolution, also, it expanded the Monroe Doctrine into the Pacific Ocean.

Speech-making in the upper chamber really began on January 10, when Cushman K. Davis of Minnesota (Republican) consumed several hours in detailing the history of Hawaii, the story of the Revolution, the weaknesses of the Blount report, and the virtues of Stevens. Aided and prompted by Frye, he continued his discourse on January 11, by objecting to any military interference in Hawaiian affairs and by condemning Blount's appointment as unconstitutional. He dissected the validity of the precedents offered by Vest and Gray, declaring that only seven of the 438 were really good. In the course of his oration he berated the idea of restoring a degraded monarchy, and expressed his sentiments about its demise as follows:

> Thus, Mr. President, the curtain fell upon the last scene of this harlequin monarchy. The stage lords and stage ladies vanished into the mass of the population. The

[205] P. 523; *Sen. Mis. Doc. 29* (53 Cong. 2 Sess.).

> queen of the play laid down her tinsel crown, put off her regalia, and reentered life through the stage entrance. The play had had its run. The engagement, which had not been successful, was ended and the theater was to be closed.[206]

On the same day Turpie defended his resolution by using testimony—especially Wundenberg's—from the Blount document. He demanded a plebiscite in Hawaii before annexation should be considered; he accused Stevens of being in a plot to overthrow the Royal Government, otherwise the Committee of Safety would never have appealed to him for protection; and, declaring that annexation would be "spoliation," he exhorted that if it ever came, let it be by "clean, pure, untainted" methods.[207]

In the middle of January, the copies of Hawaiian despatches, which had been requested by both houses, began to arrive;[208] as happened in the other chamber, these papers added to the general ill feeling. Hoar had an excellent opportunity for an attack and made good use of it by asserting that Willis's despatches describing the Queen's promise of amnesty broke the Constitution of 1887, which required all acts to be countersigned by a member of the Cabinet. At once the Massachusetts Senator was in a battle royal with his Democratic opponents.[209]

On January 23 Turpie reported his resolution back from the Committee on Foreign Relations, with the wording somewhat changed, but substantially as he wrote it. The Committee reported unanimously, save for Senator J. N. Dolph of Oregon.[210] The Committee report gave to Shelby M. Cullom of Illinois an excuse to have his say against both the Queen and Blount, the latter of whom he compared to André. Making use of recent despatches from Willis, he said: "The dusky madam stamped her foot and swore she would kill every mother's son of them and confiscate all their property besides. Imagine Messenger Willis, with tears in his eyes, begging the angry woman not to throw away this chance to become queen again."[211]

[206] Pp. 621-628 and 694-702.
[207] Pp. 702-707.
[208] Jan. 16, 1894, p. 849.
[209] Pp. 852-856.
[210] P. 1220; *Sen. Mis. Doc. 46* (53 Cong. 2 Sess.).
[211] P. 1233.

Next day, January 24, Vest offered a substitute motion which stated definitely that the United States would never annex; Turpie's resolution said nothing of the future.[212] Gray, however, saw no difference between the two resolutions. William M. Stewart of Nevada and Charles F. Manderson of Nebraska also offered amendments.[213] At this point Frye, quoting at length from a letter written by an American woman in Honolulu, made a frontal attack upon Willis's actions, and pointed out the disgrace and shame involved in American marines from the *Boston* fighting Americans in the islands. He pleaded that the whole question be terminated.[214] Sherman of Ohio then suggested that the archipelago be added as a county to California.[215] Dolph offered a resolution to recall Willis.[216]

A new protagonist for annexation entered the lists on January 29 in the person of Henry M. Teller of Colorado, who, after showing that annexation of territory was good old Democratic doctrine, said: "I am in favor of the annexation of the islands. I am in favor of the annexation of Cuba; I am in favor of the annexation of the great country lying north of us. I expect in a few years to see the American flag floating from the extreme north to the line of our sister Republics to the south. I expect to see it floating over the isles of the sea—not only these, but in the Great Gulf and in the West India seas." He declared that the United States now needed the Hawaiian Islands even more than in the past, in view of the proposed ship canal through the isthmus; he denied that it was difficult for a republic to govern colonies; and he refuted the charge that annexation would be a violation of the Monroe Doctrine.[217]

Teller's flag-waving imperialism was not answered until February 12 when Gray began a speech which was not finished until the next day. Aided by Senator James Z. George of Mississippi and bedevilled at every sentence by Teller, he went over the Blount testimony again to prove that the Revolution had been the result of a conspiracy with Stevens. Damon, Bolte, Cooper, and,

[212] P. 1308.
[213] *Sen. Mis. Doc. 49* and *50* (53 Cong. 2 Sess.).
[214] Pp. 1309-1310.
[215] P. 1311.
[216] P. 1447.
[217] Pp. 1574-1579.

above all, Wundenberg, were cited to establish the existence of a plot.[218] The Revolution, he concluded, arose from "a small junta" and the *Boston*. "That is the egg from which was hatched this revolution—the United States ship of war Boston; that is where the revolution started."[219]

On February 12, at the end of Gray's speech, Cleveland's message sending Gresham's version of the conversation between Thurston and Gresham on November 14, 1893, was read.[220] It did not allay the feelings on either side. Bearded again and again by Teller, Gray continued on February 13, spending most of his time defending the constitutionality of Blount's appointment, and holding that it was an employment rather than an office. He ended his address with an impassioned plea against such spread-eagleism as Teller had expressed. "Mr. President [he cried], there is one thing we may be very sure of—that when the flag of the United States is hauled up by the orders of a Democratic President, it will be hauled up under circumstances that will keep it where it is until the winds of heaven have blown it into rags. It will never be hauled up in dishonor; it will never be hauled up so as to put the great people, the symbol of whose power and authority it is, to the blush."[221] He hoped that, if expansion came, it might be without conspiracy: "If we are, Mr. President, ever to step from the shores of this continent out upon a career of empire and colonization let it be with head erect and above even the suspicion of dishonor, intrigue, and low dealing."[222]

The debate was certainly a stirring one, but by this time the arguments began to sound alike; speakers were prone to thresh and rethresh the same straw. On February 19 John W. Daniel of Virginia, in a discourse printed up in ten pages, defended Cleveland, went over the precedents for Blount's selection, and denied that the Commissioner was a spy.[223] He continued the next day, asserting that Harrison had been deceived by Stevens, that no republican government existed in Hawaii, and that the sugar

[218] Pp. 2080-2093.
[219] P. 2081.
[220] P. 2093.
[221] P. 2123.
[222] P. 2129.
[223] Pp. 2281-2291.

oligarchy was in control.[224] On February 21 White of California championed Blount and accused Stevens of plotting. When he asserted that Stevens had no final authority to recognize the new Government, Teller intruded into the speech to say that a Minister had the authority to recognize a revolutionary government subject to the final decision of the President.[225]

As February drew to a close, the Senatorial debates became more and more barren, and yet the arguing continued. Contests, wherein the philosophies of imperialism and anti-imperialism were evolved amidst the bitter give-and-take of personalities and partisan animosities, continued to fill the pages of the *Congressional Record* in spite of the fact that the country was getting tired of the Hawaiian muddle.[226] Nevertheless the Senate was not to see the problem buried. On February 26, as if to revive the dialectics, the report of the Morgan Committee was read into the *Record.*[227] This event of course gave more fuel to the controversy; hence the long oration, made by Frye on February 28, based on the testimony taken in the investigation. The speech continued into March 1.[228] The flagging interest of the public now turned to the Morgan report.

[224] Pp. 2309-2314.

[225] "Appendix," pp. 470-486.

[226] For instance, the *St. Joseph* (Mo.) *Gazette* said that the country was tired of hearing about Queen Liliuokalani and Hawaii; that international law required recognition of whatever government existed, without concern as to how it got into power; and that the Provisional Government should be left alone (clipping enclosed in W. A. P. McDonald to Cleveland, Feb. 20, 1894, Cleveland MSS.).

[227] Pp. 2408-2421.

[228] Pp. 2468-2475 and 2490-2502.

VIII. THE MORGAN REPORT AND THE SENATE RESOLUTION

The testimony and findings of the so-called Morgan Report, when published, printed up into a huge volume of 809 pages.[1] Almost all of the witnesses were Annexationists.[2] Several tourists who had been in Honolulu during the overthrow of the Royal Government were questioned about the facts as they saw them. Blount and Stevens were interrogated and, of course, were star witnesses. Others[3] included J. A. McCandless, one of the Committee of Safety; P. C. Jones, Minister of Finance in the Provisional Government until March 17, 1893; the sugar magnate Z. S. Spalding; William De Witt Alexander, the Hawaiian historian; and Lieutenant Commander W. T. Swinburne and Lieutenant Lucien Young, who testified on the naval side. Unfortunately, the facts as they might have been provided by Captain G. C. Wiltse, who, along with Stevens, was the key man in the decision to land troops, could not be secured, for he had died in the spring of 1893.[4]

One of the first topics to receive extended attention was the question whether John H. Soper accepted the command of the Revolutionary forces only after receiving assurances from Stevens. It was brought up during the quizzing of both Stevens and Blount.

On June 17, 1893, while Blount was in the midst of his investigation, he had written to Gresham as follows:

> It may be of interest to you to know that in an examination this afternoon of Col. Soper, commanding the military forces of the Provisional Government since the 17th of January last, he stated that at a meeting at the house of Henry Waterhouse, on the night of the 16th of January, composed of members of the committee of safety,

[1] It became *Sen. Report 227* (53 Cong. 2 Sess.), heretofore referred to as "Morgan."

[2] Liliuokalani (*op. cit.*, p. 256) said that everyone examined was her enemy; and that not one person, except Blount, spoke for the natives or for the Royal Government.

[3] Most of the witnesses offered testimony which was repetitive. These included McCandless, Jones, and Spalding.

[4] Morgan, p. 474.

> and some persons called in, he was offered the command of the military forces; that he declined to accept it until the next day; that in this meeting it was accepted by all as true that Mr. Stevens had agreed that if the persons seeking to dethrone the Queen got possession of the Government building and proclaimed a new government he would recognize it as a *de facto* government, that he (Soper) never accepted the command until after he had knowledge of this fact; that he is a citizen of the United States and claims allegiance thereto.[5]

Wundenberg, in his assertions to Blount, went even further by adding that Soper interviewed Stevens during the meeting and accepted the command when he returned.[6]

These statements, as given by Blount, seemed to be conclusive enough to prove conspiracy between Stevens and Soper; especially would that be true of Blount's letter of June 17, 1893, wherein he definitely quoted Soper himself. When the Blount report was printed, there arose in Honolulu a great clamor among the officials of the Provisional Government against what Blount had made Soper say. The latter at once declared that instead of going over to Stevens's home, he merely went out on the porch. Furthermore, on December 4, 1893, before an attorney, he swore that he had never told Blount anything:

> . . . that it is not true that affiant left the meeting of the citizen's committee held at Mr. Waterhouse's house in Honolulu, on the evening of January 16, 1893, either alone or in company with any other members of the committee until the meeting adjourned; that he did not visit Mr. Stevens, the American minister, alone or in company with others at any time on that day; that he did not report to said committee that he had full assurance from said Stevens that he, the latter, would back up the movement, nor did he report any remarks as coming from said Stevens. . . .[7]

This affidavit, which was printed in the Morgan report, no doubt with great satisfaction by the Annexationists, left the question hanging in mid-air. In brief, either Soper originally had lied to

[5] Blount, p. 98.
[6] *Ibid.*, pp. 26-27, 576.
[7] Morgan, p. 450.

Blount, or else Blount had lied to Gresham. It is difficult enough to see how Colonel Soper, a highly-esteemed American and commander of the Provisional Government army, could afford to tell an untruth. It is even more difficult to conceive of Blount, who had served for a generation in Congress and who had been Chairman of the Committee on Foreign Affairs in the House, deliberately perpetrating a falsehood. Perhaps the most charitable view is that Blount misunderstood Soper. Nevertheless it is to be said in Blount's favor that other independent witnesses, such as Wundenberg, supported the statement that Soper would not take command without assurances from the American Minister.

At all events, the members of the late Committee of Safety swore an affidavit that no agreement had ever been made with Stevens; that he had never recommended the overthrow of the Queen; and that, as a matter of fact, no American aid was needed to reduce the monarchy.[8] Furthermore, those present at the meeting of the Committee of Safety at the home of Henry Waterhouse sent a sworn statement that Soper had never entered Stevens's house at the time; in short, that Wundenberg was a liar.[9] W. R. Castle declared under oath that there had been no plot to land American troops or to assist the insurgents in any form whatever.[10] All these affidavits were used by the Annexationist members of the Morgan Committee to disprove Blount's charges.

The testimony of Stevens was considered to be most significant. Senator Frye did most of the questioning, although Gray took up considerable time in securing admissions which would justify Cleveland's policy. Much time was spent in asking Stevens about the truth of certain depositions made to Blount. Sample bits of colloquy follow:

> SENATOR FRYE. W. H. Cornwall [*sic*] testified—
> MR. STEVENS. He was one of the new cabinet.
> SENATOR FRYE. He states that Ministers Parker and Peterson called upon Minister Stevens and gave him to understand that the Government was able to take care of the situation, and asked him to keep the troops on board.

[8] *Ibid.*, pp. 590-591.
[9] *Ibid.*, pp. 591-592.
[10] *Ibid.*, pp. 586-587.

MR. STEVENS. Not true. . . .[11]

SENATOR FRYE. John F. Colburn testifies that Thurston in an interview with him and Peterson said that Stevens had given the committee of safety the assurance that if we two (that is, Colburn and Peterson) would sign a request to land the troops of the *Boston* he would immediately comply and have them landed to assist in carrying out this work.
MR. STEVENS. Nothing of the kind; as perfectly romantic as if born of another age. . . .[12]

SENATOR FRYE. The Queen's ministers delivered an address which is given by Mr. Blount in his report, in which they stated that Mr. Colburn and Mr. Peterson reported that a committee of safety had been formed at the house of Mr. L. A. Thurston and had made overtures to them to assist in dethroning the Queen, and they intended to go ahead, and that your assistance, together with that of the United States Government, had been guaranteed to them. Is there any truth in that?
MR. STEVENS. None; I never knew of it until I saw it in that report, as also that other inquiry about my promising Soper. You might ask me if that is in there.
SENATOR FRYE. Mr. Wundenburg [*sic*] further says that Mr. Soper was offered the position of commander-in-chief; that he hesitated to take it; that he and others went over to see you, and then came back, saying, "I understood them to say that Mr. Stevens had told them that if they would take possession of the Government building and read their proclamation, he would immediately recognize them and support them, or, failing to get the Government building, any building in Honolulu."
MR. STEVENS. I never heard anything about it until I saw it in Blount's report. It is pure fiction, absolute fiction, as well as that other statement that Soper wanted to take military command. . . . Soper never came to me to ask me anything about it. The first I knew of Soper being appointed to the command was one or two days afterward.[13]

Thus much of Stevens's testimony consisted in negations of charges made by those whose accusations appeared in Blount's

[11] *Ibid.,* p. 567.
[12] *Ibid.,* p. 568.
[13] *Ibid.,* p. 569; cf., Blount, p. 165.

findings. Samuel Parker deposed that the American Minister did not like the Queen's Marshal, C. B. Wilson, and had told Parker he would not favor the Royal cause as long as Wilson was in office: denied. Members of the Committee of Safety asserted that they had asked Stevens to delay landing the troops: denied.[15] Neumann, Wilson, and Dr. Trousseau declared that the Legation had been a meeting place of the conspirators, before and during the Revolution: denied, because Trousseau was a notorious liar.[16] The deposed Cabinet charged that the marines had been installed in Arion Hall in order to support the new Government: Stevens answered that the building was selected because it was the only one available having a reasonably central location.[17]

The witness was forced to admit several times that he had recognized the new Government without finding out whether it held the barracks and police station.[18] Moreover, he agreed that his knowledge of the forming of the Provisional Government came partly from rumors which he had heard through his daughter who learned them from gossips at the Legation gate.[19] His information as to when he sent the note of recognition was hazy; his recollection placed the time at five o'clock, but he said his wife and daughter thought it was a half hour later.[20] At any rate, he had written out his note of recognition before the Provisional Government notified him officially of its assumption of power; he held the note "in readiness, because it [the Revolutionary movement] was open as any railroad meeting would be in your city or mine."[21] But he did not know, until later, that the new régime had proclaimed annexation as its primary goal.[22] Senator Gray had Stevens on the defensive in the following passages:

SENATOR GRAY. When you sent the note of recogni-

[14] Morgan, pp. 572-573.
[15] *Ibid.*, pp. 566-567.
[16] *Ibid.*, pp. 570-571.
[17] *Ibid.*, p. 543.
[18] *Ibid.*, p. 553.
[19] *Ibid.*, p. 580.
[20] *Ibid.*, p. 547.
[21] *Ibid.* Stevens did not tell why he was able to have his note ready. The reason was that Dole had given him a copy of the proclamation some hours before it was issued (Dole, *Memoirs*, p. 78).
[22] Morgan, p. 577.

tion to the Provisional Government, to whom did you send it?
MR. STEVENS. I have no doubt I sent it to the minister of foreign affairs. Mr. Dole, under their organization, was President and minister of foreign affairs. Of course, the official usage is to send such notes to the minister of foreign affairs. I have no doubt I sent it to the minister of foreign affairs. I presume I conformed to the custom.
THE CHAIRMAN. Had you previously heard of the proclamation of the Provisional Government?
MR. STEVENS. Yes.
SENATOR GRAY. Had you a copy of that proclamation?
MR. STEVENS. I can not say.
SENATOR GRAY. Had you read that proclamation?
MR. STEVENS. I can not say that I had.
SENATOR GRAY. Could you say that you had not?
MR. STEVENS. I could not say that I had not.
SENATOR GRAY. Was any proclamation sent to you?
MR. STEVENS. Things had to be done very rapidly that afternoon. I had no clerk and I was a sick man, and it was impossible for me to make notes. I have no doubt I received the proclamation.
SENATOR GRAY. And you can not say one way or the other whether a copy of that proclamation was sent to you?
MR. STEVENS. I can not. I presume so. . . .[23]

SENATOR GRAY. Why did you not wait until the next day before you sent the note of recognition?
MR. STEVENS. For the reason that a half century of the study of government on both continents and 13 years of diplomatic experience would have told me it was right.
SENATOR GRAY. That was the result of your study?
MR. STEVENS. My study and experience would have told me so.
SENATOR GRAY. And your study and experience told you that it was right to recognize that government within an hour or an hour and a half?
MR. STEVENS. I do not accept it in that form.
SENATOR GRAY. I ask you as a matter of fact whether you did recognize it within an hour or an hour and a half?
MR. STEVENS. I do not think that material; probably within an hour and a half or two hours.[24]

[23] *Ibid.*, pp. 576-577.
[24] *Ibid.*, p. 580.

In defending what was nothing, if not loose, amateurish diplomatic technique, Stevens used the argument that the Royal Government had been dead since four o'clock of January 14—presumably the time of the second meeting of citizens at W. O. Smith's office. Because there was no recognizable authority, an interregnum existed,[25] and no basis of government rested anywhere until the mass meeting of January 16. The thousand citizens who gathered there were the government of Hawaii. However, with no agency of government existing, the troops had to be landed in order to preserve the peace. Said Stevens: "My only fear was that I delayed it [disembarking the marines] twenty-four hours too long."[26] Therefore, as soon as he heard of the establishment of a visible, organized government, he recognized it forthwith, in order to end the interregnum. The Queen's guards were too inconsequential to bother about—"Ten American soldiers were equivalent to the whole of them."[27] In fact the troops from the *Boston* had nothing to do with the dethronement:

> SENATOR FRYE. Mr. Wundenburg [*sic*] in his testimony says that the overthrow of the monarchy could not have been accomplished had it not been the general understanding that the American minister would make use of the troops. In your opinion, did the American troops have any effect on the overthrow of the monarchy?
> MR. STEVENS. Not the slightest.
> SENATOR FRYE. And whether the troops were on shore or not, your opinion is that the monarchy would have been overthrown?
> MR. STEVENS. Certainly.[28]

The above would seem to be rather tenuous argumentation; and yet Senator Morgan in his own "report" accepted it, justifying the premature recognition on the basis of the existence of an interregnum.[29]

When asked what his attitude had been toward annexation be-

[25] *Ibid.*, p. 540.
[26] *Ibid.*, p. 578.
[27] *Ibid.*, p. 569.
[28] *Ibid.*, p. 566.
[29] To be discussed later.

fore the Revolution, Stevens declared it was not his province to further annexation sentiment; but he admitted that a year after his arrival in Honolulu he foresaw that annexation "or something else" was "inevitable."[30] Although then favoring a protectorate, he soon felt that even closer union was necessary and he expected it to be accomplished by Hawaii's voluntary consent, as in the negotiations of 1854. "I followed Mr. Seward [he averred] for 25 years; I am a believer in his philosophy as to the future of America in the Pacific."[31]

The witness was forced to withstand hard probing in relation to the protectorate which he had proclaimed. His justification for the act consisted in the fact that the citizen troops had been away from their places of business for two weeks; furthermore, that the Japanese Government, which had sent an ironclad, was attempting to discover the sentiment of the Japanese in Hawaii. Stevens reminded the Committee that the Japanese Commissioner had informed him, before the Revolution, the Japanese wanted the franchise; moreover, a demand for political privileges had been made upon the Queen before her dethronement, and upon the Provisional Government as well. He estimated that between seven and eight hundred Japanese on the Island of Oahu had been in the Imperial army; these were a perpetual danger to the young Government, especially because rumor had it that they were in league with the deposed Queen who was supposed to have promised them certain rights and advantages if they supported her demand for restoration. In addition, Stevens said he feared the activities of the English Minister who was expecting a warship, and who desired a referendum on the question of annexation. The witness admitted that "we may have been unduly alarmed, but the Provisional Government was alarmed, and that was the state of the case."

The Chairman summed up the reasons for the declaration of the protectorate as follows: "To prevent other governments from coming in there to interfere." Stevens answered in the affirmative. This agreement of minds ended, on the other hand, when he objected to terming Foster's reaction a "disavowal."[32] When asked whether

[30] *Ibid.*, pp. 550-551.
[31] *Ibid.*, p. 551.
[32] *Ibid.*, pp. 553-556.

the new Government was in danger after Blount recalled the troops, he replied that there was no danger from the natives because they were unwarlike. "There is not [he concluded] the least danger of any attempt being made [by the Queen and natives to overthrow the Provisional Government] except by outside aid."[33]

Before he was through, Stevens had his say about Blount, who came "with a great deal of prejudice" and who was "very brusque with me in the start."[34] He repeated the (by then) well known charge that the Commissioner deliberately resided in a cottage owned by the Royalist, pro-English owner of the hotel, instead of accepting a house which Stevens and the Annexationists had arranged for him.[35]

* * * * *

Blount's testimony was just as interesting as was Stevens's. The first task of the Committee, when Blount appeared, was to try to find out whether, during his investigation, he had been prejudiced for or against the Queen. His attitude as expressed in his own words was:

> . . . I was impressed when I came to the investigation with the conviction that I had very much at stake. I had confidence in the integrity and high purposes of the President, and felt that I could give him no higher offense than to misinform him. I felt that any other than a truthful, an exhaustive, and impartial examination would bring about the contempt of the American people. I was, therefore, timid—over cautious, perhaps, in all my conduct in reference to it. I kept from their social life. I did not intimate any opinion to these people one way or the other. When I left those islands nobody had any idea, so far as I could gather, what my report was. Each side claimed in the newspaper that I was in favor of it. I studiously avoided communicating anything to anybody, and I turned the facts over and over again in my mind. I felt that I was alone, without anybody on earth to consult with, counsel with, and I often felt the need of somebody to advise with.[36]

The Annexationist members of the Committee asked numerous

[33] *Ibid.*, p. 561.
[34] *Ibid.*, p. 555.
[35] *Ibid.*, p. 559.
[36] *Ibid.*, p. 389.

questions in order to put Cleveland, Gresham, and Blount in a bad light. When they tried to make Blount admit that Cleveland had already prejudged the Hawaiian situation before he sent the Commissioner, Blount replied that Cleveland told him information alone was wanted; that the President said nothing of what he thought about the matter.[37] Charged with desiring restoration of the monarchy before he left the United States, Blount said: "I never dreamed of such a thing as the reinstatement of Liliuokalani; I never heard it suggested until my return to the United States." He admitted that Gresham had indicated he felt justice should be done the Queen, but that the President had no opinion whatever.[38]

Regarding his removal of the flag on April 1, 1893, Blount stated that the Secretary had given him permission to do so, provided it would not cause bloodshed; but he was to use his own discretion. Upon his arrival he was told by President Dole that the Provisional Government could preserve order without American assistance; and, feeling that he could not make a fair investigation until the protectorate was abolished, he ordered the troops to embark.[39]

The Committee wished to know what standing Blount had with the Provisional Government and with Minister Stevens. He answered that he did not inform the Hawaiian authorities of his powers, but merely presented his credentials. Nor did he read his instructions to Stevens because the Department of State sent Stevens what information it desired him to have touching the inquiry. He admitted he did read his orders to Admiral Skerrett because the Admiral commanded the American forces. The Provisional Government did not learn of his powers until he published his instructions on May 16.[40] Accused of making an *ex parte* report,[41] because he received more Royalist than Revolutionary depositions, he pointed out that he asked the members of the Provisional Government time and again for statements or for interviews, but they refused. Especially was this true of Henry E.

[37] *Ibid.*, pp. 387, 406-408.
[38] *Ibid.*, pp. 395-396.
[39] *Ibid.*, pp. 388, 397, 401.
[40] *Ibid.*, pp. 391-392, 398-399, 401.
[41] For instance McCandless made this charge, p. 637.

Cooper, who read the proclamation of January 17, 1893, and of President Dole and W. O. Smith.[42]

* * * * *

Lieutenant Commander W. T. Swinburne, who was in charge of the landing party, blamed Stevens for the early recognition of the new régime. Inasmuch as Wiltse could not speak for himself, Swinburne's testimony, coming from the highest ranking officer involved who was still alive, was important. He maintained stoutly that Wiltse had landed the forces to protect American property; and that if the Queen had asked for assistance, she would have received it.[43] To sustain his point, he introduced into his testimony a letter he had written to Commissioner Blount, on May 3, 1893, at the latter's request. In reference to the method whereby the insurgents had been recognized, it ran:

> . . . Wiltse asked if their Government had possession of the police station and barracks. To this the reply was made that they had not possession then, but expected to hear of it in a few minutes, or very soon. To this Capt. Wiltse replied, "Very well, gentlemen, I can not recognize you as a *de facto* Government until you have possession of the police station and are prepared to guarantee protection to life and property," or words to that effect. . . . As far as I can recollect, this must have been about 5 o'clock p.m. About half-past 6 Capt. Wiltse left the camp, and as he did so he informed me that the United States minister to the Hawaiian Islands had recognized the Provisional Government established by the party in charge of the Government building as the *de facto* Government of the Hawaiian Islands. About half-past 7 p.m. I was informed by telephone by Lieut. Draper, who was then in charge of a squad of marines at the United States consulate, that the citizen troops had taken possession of the police station, and that everything was quiet.[44]

Lieutenant Lucien Young, who, though under Swinburne, was Wiltse's confidant, stated what he would later print in his book; namely, that Wiltse sent the troops ashore on his own responsibility and, in fact, had them lined up and armed when Stevens

[42] *Ibid.*, p. 394.

[43] *Ibid.*, pp. 477-478. It is needless to say that Swinburne's statement did not coincide with Stevens's acts, for the Queen's Government did ask for aid.

[44] Blount, p. 57; Morgan, p. 488.

came aboard to talk the situation over and to report the request of the Committee of Safety for protection.[45]

Rear Admiral George Belknap, retired, who had been stationed at Honolulu during the troubles attending Kalakaua's election, was brought in by Annexationist members of the Committee in order to give evidence on the strategic value of the islands.[46] They secured what they wanted. "I think," said the Admiral, "it would be a suicidal policy on the part of the United States to allow Great Britain or any other European power to get any foothold on those islands."[47] He stressed the fact that Hawaii would make an invaluable naval base to command the Pacific Ocean, as well as a halfway station on the route to the Orient. He was certain that a few guns could protect Honolulu with ease.[48] The anti-Administration Senators also questioned him on what he thought of placing a naval force under a civil official, as had been done at Honolulu. He asserted that Blount's commission, whereby he ordered Skerrett to pull down the flag, was in direct violation of the Navy Regulations. He admitted that he would not obey the order of a private citizen, such as Blount, even if so instructed by the Secretary of the Navy; but he would obey such a person if commanded to do so by the President.[49] He also thought that the recognition of new governments was the province of the Minister and not of naval officers.[50]

Alexander was a valuable witness for the Annexationists and much store was placed by them upon his testimony. As a professor at Oahu College he had taught and knew the history of the islands, and a book he had written was referred to repeatedly; as Surveyor General under the monarchy, he knew the complicated details of the Hawaiian land system; as Privy Councillor and a member of the Board of Education, he had access to governmental

[45] Morgan, pp. 324-349. Young's book, *The Boston at Hawaii,* has received attention in an earlier chapter. Thurston (*Memoirs,* p. 412) charged that Secretary Hilary Herbert would not allow Young to publish his manuscript; and that it remained unprinted until 1898, when Secretary John D. Long gave his consent.

[46] Morgan, pp. 710-725.

[47] *Ibid.,* p. 710.

[48] *Ibid.,* p. 711.

[49] *Ibid.,* pp. 714-715.

[50] *Ibid.,* p. 720.

policy under both Kalakaua and Liliuokalani; and, as an ardent Annexationist, his depositions were very important to anti-Royalists. Morgan asked him many leading questions so as to take advantage of the Professor's scholarly reputation, and Frye requested his criticism of Blount's report in order to place the paper in the records.[51]

* * * * *

The report consisted of several statements, each representing the opinions of separate groups who could not agree upon a general conclusion. No majority being obtainable, the committee split up in the ratio of four-four-one. The *New York Times* referred to the document as "a rather picturesque bit of patchwork," and the *Philadelphia Record* called it "a mere incoherent yawp of jingoism."[52]

What was sometimes called the report proper—because it was so long—was written by Chairman Morgan; no other Senator signed it, although the Annexationist Republicans, while making their own statement, indicated general agreement with Morgan's conclusions. It seems that the Chairman had two purposes in mind: first, to gainsay everything the Blount report had asserted; second, to clear the name of every American official and to give to the United States a spotless slate. If Morgan hoped, by so doing, to bring the disparate elements in his Committee together so that a unanimous, or at least a majority, report could be made, he failed utterly.

Morgan's preamble oratorically dwelt upon the relations between this country and Hawaii as follows:

> Hawaii is an American state, and is embraced in the American commercial and military system. This fact has been frequently and firmly stated by our Government, and is the ground on which is rested that peculiar and far-reaching declaration so often and so earnestly made, that the United States will not admit the right of any foreign government to acquire any interest or control in the Hawaiian Islands that is in any way prejudicial or even threatening toward the interests of the United States or her people. This is at least a moral suzerainty over Hawaii. In this attitude of the two Governments,

[51] Alexander to Dole, Jan. 7, 1894 (M&E).

[52] Quoted by *Literary Digest,* VIII (March 8, 1894), 455.

> Hawaii must be entitled to demand of the United States an indulgent consideration, if not an active sympathy, when she is endeavoring to accomplish what every American state has achieved—the release of her people from the odious antirepublican régimé [*sic*] which denies to the people the right to govern themselves, and subordinates them to the supposed divine right of a monarch, whose title to such divinity originated in the most slavish conditions of pagan barbarity.[53]

This fulmination over, Morgan proceeded to berate the Queen. Her act of attempting to promulgate a new Constitution was revolutionary; thereafter no civil government existed. Subsequent to that act, none of her subjects respected her authority, and so an interregnum obtained. There was no civil power, and hence American troops had a perfect right to land and to protect American life and property. Sovereignty had returned to the people who reasserted it by forming a Committee of Safety.

> When the Queen found that her Government was opposed by a strong body of the people she did not attempt to reassemble the Legislature, but left the public safety in charge of a committee of thirteen men, organized by those who were endeavoring to preserve the peace and to restore the Government to its full constitutional powers by choosing an executive head. This condition of things continued from Saturday until the succeeding Tuesday, during all of which time the citizens of the United States residing in Honolulu had no protection of law. . . .[54]

The only hope of safety open to Americans (continued the reasoning of the Committee Chairman) was the *Boston,* whose men were landed to offer the protection due their countrymen. "In passing the palace on their way to the point at which they were halted, the Queen appeared upon the balcony and the troops respectfully saluted her by presenting arms and dipping the flag, and made no demonstration of any hostile intent."[55] The landing of the troops may have been invasion, but it was not war because there was no force to oppose them. When internal feuds break the central au-

[53] P. 2.

[54] P. 4.

[55] P. 5. The Senator did not perceive the inconsistency of arguing that there was no Government and of stressing that the troops saluted the Queen.

thority, declared the Senator, sovereignty disappears and any nation has the right to military interference.

> In this view of the facts there is no necessity for inquiring whether Minister Stevens or Capt. Wiltse, in arranging for the landing of the troops, had any purpose either to aid the popular movement against the Queen that was then taking a definite and decisive shape, or to promote the annexation of the Hawaiian Islands to the United States.[56]

At this point in the report, Captain Wiltse's instructions to Lieutenant Commander Swinburne (already discussed) were inserted in order to prove that the only reason for landing marines was to protect "our legation, consulate, and the lives and property of American citizens." The Chairman of the Committee found both Wiltse and Stevens innocent, for neither comprehended the fact that there existed a legal right to land the troops; while they were debating whether it was lawful to disembark, they really had the justification.[57] From January 12 until January 17, when the Provisional Government was established, there was no responsible Hawaiian authority. On that score the American troops had full right to remain until order was restored; because this was not achieved for several months, no charge of malfeasance could be launched against Stevens for protecting American life and property.

> The precise hour when or the precise conditions under which the American minister recognized the Provisional Government is not a matter of material importance. It was his duty, at the earliest safe period, to assist by his recognition in the termination of the interregnum, so that citizens of the United States might be safely remitted to the care of that Government for the security of their rights.[58]

Having given the American Minister and the Naval Commander clean papers, Senator Morgan—inasmuch as he had to lay the blame on someone—turned again to the Queen. Her protest to President Harrison was not well founded because she herself

[56] P. 6.
[57] P. 7.
[58] P. 19.

started the Revolution. This fact could be proved even in Blount's report, where the precipitation of the trouble had been laid to the lottery and opium bills. Her denunciation of the white people, when interviewed by Willis, and her determination to confiscate their property, proved the baseness of her character; and her desire to behead, and later to banish, the Provisional Government officials showed her to be unfit for a Christian crown.

Morgan placed the blame even farther back than upon Liliuokalani. In his opinion, it was the Cabinet which misled her by pressing for a new Constitution. The Ministers worked with the Queen in drafting it, but deserted at the last moment by appealing to the people.

> These men, whose conduct can not be characterized as anything less than perfidious, hastened to give to the President of the United States false and misleading statements of the facts leading up to, attending, and succeeding this revolution. To do this they made deceptive and misleading statements to Mr. Blount. Upon them must rest the odium of having encouraged the Queen in her revolutionary intentions.[59]

The Senator had a good word for the Provisional Government:

> Americans should not hesitate in their support of a government *de facto,* set up to oppose her [Liliuokalani], because she had not made a formal surrender of a place where a few soldiers and policemen had been stationed, who were powerless to hold it against the people then under arms. When a crown falls, in any kingdom of the Western Hemisphere, it is pulverized, and when a scepter departs, it departs forever.[60]

Americans who supported the movement against the Queen came in for their share of eulogy, also:

> If nothing but a decent respect for our national example was in question, if there was no question in Hawaii that concerned the people of the United States except that of a relapse of that Government into absolute monarchy, if there was no degradation of society involved in this falling away, no destruction of property and liberty in contemplation, there would still be enough in

[59] P. 24.
[60] Pp. 16-17.

> the conditions now presented there to excite the most anxious interest of our people. Citizens of the United States with wisdom, charity, Christian faith, and a love of constitutional government have patiently, laboriously, and honestly built up Hawaii into a civilized power under a written constitution, and they can justly claim the sympathy and assistance of all civilized people in resisting its destruction, either to gratify a wanton lust of absolute power on the part of the Queen, or the abuse of its authority in fostering vice and rewarding crime.[61]

Next the report turned to clearing the President's record by discussing Commissioner Blount's investigation. It disposed of the objection that Blount had been sent illegally by saying that there were precedents for appointments of Presidential agents without the consent of the Senate.[62] It was a necessary diplomatic power, for without it, foreign relations could not be cordial and friendly. The question—whether Blount had authority to remove the American emblem—raised the problem whether the United States could have two representatives at one capital, each exercising separate powers. Other governments granted authority to several representatives when conditions required; therefore the report concluded there had been no irregularity in giving Blount the necessary power to lower the flag. No limit could be placed upon a government in its diplomatic relations, said Morgan.

Turning to the President's policy, the Senator stated that if Cleveland had used force to restore the Queen, his act would have been illegal. He was, however, within his own rights in employing his good offices to reconcile the two parties. When the Provisional Government refused Willis's demand, the President's authority ended. The Queen having surrendered under the promise of redress from the United States, the President

> . . . could not have done justice to himself, to his country, to the people of Hawaii, to the Provisional Government, to Liliuokalani, without having made an effort to use his good offices for the purpose of ascertaining whether it was practicable that the Queen should be re-

[61] P. 12.

[62] The Chairman based his conclusions chiefly upon the precedent set by President Polk, who sent Nicholas P. Trist, with powers superior to those of General Winfield Scott, to make peace in Mexico. Trist's instructions were printed on pp. 44-45.

> stored to her authority, leaving the question to be determined by the people interested in Hawaii whether such restoration would be acceptable to them or not. If Liliuokalani had been restored to her throne by the consent of the membership of the Provisional Government, upon the terms and conditions of the proposition which she signed and delivered to Mr. Willis, the President of the United States would not have been in any sense responsible for her restoration, would not have espoused the monarchy, nor would he have done anything that was contradictory of American sentiment, opinion or policy. He would only have been the mutual friend, accepted, really, by both parties, whose intervention would have secured, with their consent, the final solution of that question . . . there is no reason for withholding approval of the conduct of the President of the United States in thus accepting and executing a function which he was entitled to perform, in submitting this question . . . to the contending parties. . . . Therefore your committee conclude to report that the President of the United States has not, in this particular, in any wise been a party to any irregularity or any impropriety of conduct in his high office.[64]

Even Blount was given a clean bill of health. He had, in a fair, impartial manner, presented an instructive report, but it was next to impossible to secure unprejudiced facts because of popular feeling.[65]

The only criticism lodged against American acts was in regard to the declaration of the protectorate. The Chairman decided that that had been done illegally and without authority. "It was disavowed by Secretary Foster and rebuked by Secretary Gresham, and the order to abandon the protectorate and haul down the flag was in accordance with the duty and honor of the United States."[66]

Among the letters which Morgan received about his "report," two are of some interest. One, from J. Alexander Fulton, an attorney of Dover, Delaware, indicated the hatred for Cleveland which was growing up even in his own party. After saying that he was doubtful of the President's right to appoint Blount, Fulton asserted: "As a life long Democrat, I deeply regret the position

[63] P. 25.
[64] Pp. 27-28.
[65] Pp. 24-25.
[66] Pp. 19-20.

Cleaveland [*sic*] has placed us in, not only in this matter but in many others. . . . How you people of the South ever supported his nomination I cannot understand. The party and the people never had a worse or more dangerous foe."[67] The other comment was from L. E. Robinson, of the Department of History in Mt. Vernon College, Mt. Vernon, Missouri: "That Report will be sanctioned by the intelligent students of American history as one of the fairest and ablest documents relating to our diplomacy, and setting forth in the soundest statesmanship the proper prerogatives of the executive in such emergencies."[68]

* * * * *

The conclusions of the Administration Senators were shorter, and more to the point. The statement was signed by those Democrats on the Committee who had been prominent in opposing annexation and in defending the President: M. C. Butler, David Turpie, John W. Daniel, and George Gray. They stated that they could neither censure Willis's actions as illegal nor Blount's appointment as irregular. But they did blame Stevens for his "active officious and unbecoming participation in the events which led to the revolution." There was nothing wrong in using good offices to brmg parties together, "but there is nothing in international law, in sound public policy, or in our past history and traditions which justifies a representative of this Government in interfering officiously or improperly in the domestic or political affairs of a foreign country, whatever may be the character of its rulers, its form of government, or its political condition." Stevens's "inopportune zeal" caused him "to exceed the proper limits of his official duty." His conduct was "directly conducive" to the overthrow of the Queen, the organization of the Provisional Government, and the scheme of annexation. They concluded that he deserved public censure.[69]

* * * * *

Another statement was prepared by those who, being Republican and Annexationist, were therefore opponents of Cleveland: John

[67] Fulton to Morgan, March 5, 1894, Morgan MSS., Box marked "1894-1896," Library of Congress.

[68] Robinson to Morgan, Feb. 24, 1894, in *ibid.* See also Z. S. Spalding, who wrote from Paris on May 5, 1894, to praise Morgan's "most admirable Report" (*ibid.*).

[69] Morgan, pp. 35-36.

Sherman, William P. Frye, J. N. Dolph, and Cushman K. Davis. They made the following assertions: (1) Blount's appointment as Commissioner was unconstitutional. (2) Orders of the Executive placing the naval forces of the United States under Blount and Willis were illegal. (3) Blount's order to haul down the flag was unlawful, for the protectorate had already been disavowed by Foster; furthermore, the interviews of Blount and Willis with the Queen were a violation of international law. (4) Recognition having been accorded to the Provisional Government, President Cleveland had no right to reopen the question. (5) Blount and Willis were not open to censure; the blame lay higher up.[70]

Hastings and Thurston, who, as has been seen, had worked closely with the Annexationists on the Committee, were so securely established on the inside that they could fairly accurately predict what the report or reports would say. Hastings prophesied that the main report would "ruffle the feathers on the *Cuckoos,* and, consequently, a minority report will be made by Gray, Turpie, and Daniels [*sic*]."[71] Thurston predicted that nothing further would be done; and several weeks later he asked Morgan what action would be taken on his report. Morgan replied: "None at all. It has accomplished its purpose already."[72] Indeed Thurston and Hastings were satisfied to leave well enough alone; for example, when Senator Anthony Higgins of Delaware wanted to offer a resolution asking Cleveland to return the treaty of 1893 to the Senate, they used pressure to stop him, feeling that such action would simply mean harm.[73]

On February 24, 1894, two days before the Morgan report was read into the *Congressional Record,* the Hawaiian Legation lost one of its most valuable helpers in the person of the historian, Alexander. It was felt that, after testifying before the Committee, his best work was done, and so he was permitted to leave for home. His missionary work was sorely missed by Hastings and Thurston. Because the secret commission to treat for annexation was never used, his most important contribution had turned out to be along the lines of propaganda. He continued his proselytizing

[70] *Ibid.,* pp. 33-34.
[71] Hastings to Dole, Feb. 21, 1894, M&E.
[72] Thurston to Hatch, March 2 and 27, 1894, *ibid.*
[73] *Ibid.*

the whole way across the continent. Writing from Oakland, California, Alexander declared he was delighted with the Committee's conclusions, although the words of his testimony were poorly stated. He added: "[Theophilus H.] Davies is here, a disappointed man. His lamentations are like unto those of Jeremiah. Morgan's report caused consternation to the Queenites. Occasionally I see a squawk from Julius A. Palmer, who picked up the mantle dropped by Nordhoff."[74] All Royalists were of course downhearted.

* * * * *

The discussion and study of the Morgan Report, as well as other matters, buried the Turpie resolution for several months. On March 20 Turpie tried to secure an agreement from the Republicans to vote on his resolution, but Dolph objected.[75] Senator George did, however, find time to make a long speech on that day defending Blount, going over precedents for his appointment, and in general rehashing the old story. Hoar, of course, fought back, and little was accomplished.[76]

The Hawaiian Legation favored the Turpie resolution and did all in its power to get action taken. Even Thurston, who by that time was back in Honolulu helping with the drafting of a new Constitution, used long-distance methods by writing to Senators Morgan, George C. Perkins of California, James H. Kyle of South Dakota, and Chandler. His argument to them was that as long as the United States allowed the determination of its Hawaiian policy to hang fire, the natives would be restless and the Provisional Government unable to solidify itself in power. All that was needed was a simple statement by the Senate that no intervention would be permitted.[77] Hastings used pressure upon those Senators close to him,[78] but the tariff pushed the resolution aside.[79]

[74] Alexander to Thurston, March 19, 1894, *ibid.*

[75] *Record,* p. 3128. Thurston predicted it would not pass because the Republicans did not like it (Thurston to Hatch, March 27, 1894, confidential, M&E).

[76] *Record,* pp. 3127-3138.

[77] Thurston to Hastings, April 26, 1894, M&E.

[78] The propaganda work of Hastings is clear from a letter which Kyle wrote (July 11, 1894), thanking him for information to be used in Kyle's speeches (M&E).

[79] Hastings to Hatch, May 26, 1894, *ibid.*

The matter idled[80] until May 22 when Kyle revived it by offering a substitute resolution to the effect that no force would be used to restore the Queen or to destroy the present Hawaiian régime; that the Provisional Government should be permitted to pursue its own policy; and that intervention by any foreign power would be considered an unfriendly act.[81] Two days later Kyle appealed for immediate passage of his resolution in order to end the rumors in the islands that the United States intended to reinstate the Queen. He averred that much hostility between parties existed in Hawaii; that the uncertainty was disturbing the business interests; and that there was need for the United States to express its attitude once and for all. The President would not and could not use force, said he; therefore let Congress declare its position forthwith. Frye and Morgan were in favor of this means of ending the subject.[82] Daniel agreed that the Administration intended no military methods without the consent of Congress; and Frye read excerpts from private letters to prove that the disturbed state of public opinion in Hawaii arose from a peculiar rumor which said the Senate would favor the employment of American troops to overturn the Provisional Government.[84] On May 25 Teller offered another resolution, similar to Kyle's and accepted by Kyle, in order to reach a vote; but Samuel Pasco of Florida asked why Turpie's was not passed.[85] After another day of discussion on May 28, Kyle waived his resolution on May 29, because it seemed possible to have a vote on Turpie's. "I think," said Gray, "it is in the interest of humanity and civilization that it [Turpie's] should be passed."[87] A vote was, however, impossible on that day.[88]

A widespread feeling existed that some sort of action ought to be taken, but division of sentiment remained as to the wording

[80] Cleveland continued to send all pertinent documents. See *Sen. Ex. Doc. 65, 77, 85, 92, 103* (53 Cong. 2 Sess.).

[81] *Record*, p. 5127.

[82] *Ibid.*, p. 5193.

[83] *Ibid.*, p. 5194.

[84] *Ibid.* These letters were probably from Thurston who was then in Honolulu.

[85] *Ibid.*, p. 5246.

[86] *Ibid.*, p. 5358.

[87] *Ibid.*, pp. 5434-5436.

[88] See Hastings to Hatch, May 26, 1894, M&E, for details about the devious maneuverings regarding the resolutions.

of the resolution. Both Turpie's original version and that of Kyle having failed, Turpie on May 31 reported a compromise draft from the Committee on Foreign Relations; it was, he said, an attempt to represent all shades of opinion. Because this was the statement the Senate finally enacted, its wording is important:

> That of right it belongs wholly to the people of the Hawaiian Islands to establish and maintain their own form of government and domestic polity; that the United States ought in no wise to interfere therewith, and that any intervention in the political affairs of these islands by any other government will be regarded as an act unfriendly to the United States.[89]

It was agreed that a vote should be had on this substitute; when counted, the result was 55 yeas, 0 nays, but 30 did not vote.[90] Many of the chief contestants on both sides were among those refusing to take a stand, because they were not satisfied with the phraseology. The non-voters included Mills, Daniel, George, Hoar, Kyle (away, but would have voted "yea" had he been present), Morgan, and Teller.

Because, at best, it expressed the majority opinion in one house of Congress only, the measure of course was not law and did not, in that respect, bind the Government. In the sense that annexation was impliedly condemned, the pronouncement was a kind of left-handed approval of Cleveland's policy. The original resolution, however, as offered by Turpie on January 8, actually stated its disapproval of annexation, but this had been extracted by May 31.

Thus both houses of the Congress rebuffed the Administration's policy of idealism. On December 18, 1893, the President asked power to do justice; in the resolutions passed by both chambers he received nothing. As neither was enacted in the same version by both houses, Cleveland never faced the unwelcome task of signing or vetoing; nevertheless it required no great amount of acumen to perceive that both Gresham and Cleveland were disappointed. Doubtlessly they had concluded long before this that Congress would not give them the warrant to interfere in Hawaii. The episode was one more evidence—along with others like the

[89] *Record,* p. 5499.
[90] *Ibid.,* p. 5500.

Wilson-Gorman Tariff—that the President had lost control of his party, more particularly in the Senate.

What he was thinking about, just before the Senate passed its resolution, is stated in a letter the President penned to Senator William F. Vilas of Wisconsin on May 29:

> I am sorry that the vast Hawaiian situation was talked today. The thing I care the most about is the declaration that the *people* of the islands instead of the *Provisional Government* should determine the policy, etc. I do not care much what is said or not said concerning annexation. . . . Can you not nail the endorsement of the Provisional Government, by putting in its place the more American and Democratic reference to *the People* as the source of power and control?[91]

The final, compromise resolution contained the words Cleveland desired.

Despite the legislative treatment which the President was receiving, Charles Robinson published in the *American Journal of Politics* for that very month a point-by-point defense of the President's Hawaiian program. "WHEN the history of the Hawaiian controversy comes to be written," he predicted, "after all the partisan clamor has died away, and every unpleasant incident of the passing record has been forgotten, the policy of the present administration will be fully justified at the bar of public opinion."[92]

* * * * *

Passage of the separate resolutions ended one era of Hawaiian-American relations *in re* annexation, and began another. These acts of the legislative department placed a "finis" to the story of the Hawaiian Revolution of 1893; for, although in the distant future a wave of Annexationist sentiment in the United States might bring about a union between the two countries, it was clear

[91] Allan Nevins, *Letters of Grover Cleveland 1850-1908* (Boston and N. Y., 1933), p. 353. Cleveland's attitude in respect to *"the People"* was not essentially different from Harrison's. According to Thurston, the latter had pressed Secretary Foster to include in the treaty of annexation a provision for a plebiscite and a statement that annexation was being accomplished by the will of the people (Minutes of the Meeting of the Commissioners at Wormley's Hotel, Washington, D. C., Feb. 10, 1893, M&C).

[92] "The Hawaiian Controversy in the Light of History," IV (May, 1894), 477-490.

that at that time no action of the United States would be taken to overturn the new Government and restore the monarchy.

To be sure, the fact that Cleveland would never receive the power to reinstate the Queen had been obvious from almost the very day Congress began to gnaw[93] at the Hawaiian problem, in December, 1893. Yet nobody could be sure, neither the Provisional Government which prayed for such a dispensation nor the Royalists who hoped against it. Repeatedly the Hawaiian Legation, as well as the Royalists, had pressed for a final decision. Was it to be intervention or not? For, if by some stroke of fate the Congress empowered Cleveland to undo Stevens's action, then the Revolution would either be nullified (by reconstitution of the Royal Government backed by American arms) or continued (by action of the displaced whites to unseat the Queen at the first opportunity when United States forces were absent).

The congressional notice to all concerned, that no action would be taken, established a policy by default. Both by failing to support the President and by failing to agree between themselves, the houses had ordained that the official United States attitude was to be one of doing nothing—a "hands-off" policy. At least one important forward step resulted. The passage of the Senate resolution cleared the air in Hawaii by informing both competing groups what the United States would and would not do.

For their part, the Royalists, who had depended so much upon President Cleveland for justice, perceived that if the Queen was to be restored they must do it themselves. At once there were secret maneuverings by the native leaders to revolt against the established Government. In planning such a move they forgot that both Congressional resolutions had made it evident that the new Government, now the recognized, legal régime in the islands, would receive aid from the United States in accordance with long-established custom. The shoe was on the other foot: instead of their receiving help from the United States to unseat the Provisional Government, the latter would get support to remain in power.

[93] In a despatch of March 2, 1894, describing the Morgan report, Thurston told Dole that the Senate was treating the Hawaiian question as a dog treated a bone: gnawed it a while, buried it, and gnawed it again. "The end has practically been reached already. . . ." (*Memoirs,* p. 483).

From the standpoint of the Provisional Government, the resolutions, although not all that was desired, were quite welcome. The Hawaiian Legation particularly favored Senatorial action, not only because it would end a long controversy and the continued uncertainty, but also because it would prove that no hostile action was to be taken against the Annexationist Administration in Honolulu. Hence, as soon as the Senate's resolution was received, it was read to leading natives to indicate that continued resistance on their part was useless because the United States intended to remain neutral.

Even before final passage of the Senate's resolution, the members of the Provisional Government perceived that a more stable system, which would carry on during the long pull, was needed in the islands. The hastily contrived government which was to rule provisionally, that is to say for a few weeks until annexation, had already been in power over a year. For some time a movement had been going on to reorganize the revolutionary administration into a permanent republic which could stand upright until the Republicans returned to power at Washington. It was patent that nothing need be either feared or hoped from the Democracy.

The key to what happened in the Hawaiian Islands was not in Honolulu but at Washington. Island politics reflected the attitude of American officials and the party in power at the capital of the United States. If a friend of annexation was President, then island politics reacted to that fact by expecting immediate annexation and hoping for the end of Hawaiian independence. If the American President was calculating in his attitude, then Hawaiian politics was oriented towards the problem of carrying on government more or less permanently until the wheel of fate changed the party predilections of the majority of Americans.

IX. THE SUMMING UP

Before he closes this book, perhaps the reader would appreciate a summing up of the essential facts, in so far as blame or credit is concerned. Without question, the counterclaims and charges, as for instance, between the Blount and Morgan reports, are confusing.

To the extent that an answer is possible, the matter may be summarized into the following considerations:

(1) There can be no doubt that Royal Government under Kalakaua and Liliuokalani was inefficient, corrupt, and undependable. That the powerful American minority disliked it is understandable, and that these same whites would wish to bring the islands under the control of the United States is equally understandable.

(2) Whether revolution against the existing Government by those whites was the proper course is not for the historian to decide. Such a decision becomes a matter of individual conscience; and if Thurston and his friends had concluded that good government was impossible under the monarchy and that strong methods were in order, what American is to gainsay such a conclusion? After all, violent revolution against tyranny was the American birthright established in 1776. Perhaps even more significant to the Hawaiian revolutionists than the menace from Royal misgovernment was the menace, real or imaginary, from Japan and Hawaiian Japanese.

Nevertheless the ordinary American believes—in fact must believe—in peaceful and orderly processes for redress of injustice, otherwise democracy is impossible. Therefore he could wish that the task at Honolulu had been done legally and without tumult, perhaps by using more patience until the native dynasty died out, or perhaps by purchase of its rights. On the other hand, if revolution was necessary, the observer has the right to prefer that it had been engineered in a way which would have been subject to less criticism—criticism in fact that helped to delay annexation, the very goal of the Revolutionists, for five years. For example, allowing Liliuokalani to surrender to the United States rather than to the insurgents was not only an egregious error; it also gave to the idealistic Gresham and Cleveland the feeling that such a grievous wrong must be righted in accordance with the basic standards of American justice.

(3) The rôle of Minister Stevens has already been analyzed. At this point it is required only to repeat that his actions during and after the Revolution can hardly be justified even politically, let alone morally. The premature recognition of the Revolutionists, for example, was a breach of international law; and the landing of troops—whether his or Wiltse's decision—with the injunction to prevent fighting of any kind made it impossible for the monarchy to protect itself.

(4) Whereas Harrison and Foster are to be condemned for a too hasty attempt to get their treaty accepted before the facts were known, Cleveland and Gresham are to be criticized for their impractical endeavor to undo what could not be undone without involvement in questionable international proceedings and complications. It is doubtful whether Gresham ever learned that there are certain international wrongs that cannot be righted, except by creating worse ills than those to be redressed. Both he and Stevens seemed to think it was acceptable practice for American diplomats to move in against any régime, especially small, weak ones, which they personally did not like.

Even granting that Liliuokalani's surrender obligated Grover Cleveland personally (she surrendered to the *United States* when *Harrison,* not Cleveland was President), one is constrained to insist that the most Cleveland should have done was to allow Willis to interview the Queen once; then, when she proved to be adamant, give up any hope of restoring a discredited Government which was sure to be overturned by the whites in a subsequent revolution. After-wisdom is of course easy; but assuming that the President desired some gesture which would attempt to right the wrong the United States had done to Liliuokalani, he should have considered that enough had been achieved to satisfy American honor when the Queen refused to follow a humane policy towards those who had deposed her. It is obvious that if restored she would never have dared to carry out any beheadings (any more than the Hawaiian Republic later dared to carry out its decrees of capital punishment for Royalist rebels in 1895). It is equally true that the Cleveland Administration, without perceiving the fact, had a golden opportunity to end all efforts at restoration with honor to itself and without unduly raising the ire of Annexationists. Cleveland could have said that he tried to do justice to the Queen in accordance with her appeal to the United States Government; she refused to cooperate; he wiped his hands of the entire affair. Such a course would have placed the blame (where much of it lay, anyway) upon the Queen; American honor would be vindicated; and the unpleasant impasses which have been described could have been avoided.

Had the Queen been amenable, accepting Cleveland's provisoes, the policy would still have been difficult. The Provisional Government would have been no more willing supinely to walk out at Willis's request earlier than it was when he asked it to do so later.

Nevertheless a more practical alternative and a wiser move for the President would have been to withdraw the treaty of annexation, let time take its course, and permit history to deal with Harrison and Stevens. Certainly when he threw the question into the turmoil of Congress he was asking for what he got: interparty and intraparty strife.

(5) From the standpoint of American sensibilities, it was fortunate that annexation did not occur in 1893. Had Harrison succeeded in forcing the treaty through the Senate, there would always have been certain unanswerable questions, each with an overtone of guilt, such as: Did the Provisional Government have the right to give away Hawaii's independence? Was it in power long enough to prove that it could stay, and by staying, claim the right to speak for the country? Was the United States receiving, as it were, stolen goods?

By 1898 such queries, if raised, could be raised with little real conviction. The régime had lasted five years, during which time its opponents had had ample time to overturn it and in so doing maintain that they spoke for the nation. The fact that the opposition did try to regain power in 1895 and that it failed proved, from the standpoint of the all-important nine points of the law, the right of the whites to speak for Hawaii. In 1898 no one could say that the United States was receiving stolen goods, for by that time the new Government had secured a good title.

BIBLIOGRAPHY

Newspapers

AUGUSTA, MAINE

Kennebec Journal (1892-93), State Library, Augusta, Maine.

HONOLULU, HAWAII

Daily Bulletin (1893-94), Library of Hawaii, Honolulu. Edited by Daniel Logan. Cited as *Bulletin.*

Hawaii Progress Holomua (1894), Bishop Museum, Honolulu. Cited as *Holomua.* Edited by Edmund Norrie.

Hawaiian Star (1893-94), Library of Hawaii, Honolulu. Cited as *Star.* Founded on March 28, 1893, the paper had Dr. J. S. McGrew as editor in chief and Walter G. Smith as managing editor. On June 3, 1893, McGrew resigned and Smith became editor in chief, in which position he served until May 6, 1894, when Arthur Johnstone took his place.

Pacific Commercial Advertiser (1893-94), Library of Hawaii, Honolulu. Cited as *Advertiser.* Edited by H. N. Castle.

NEW YORK CITY, NEW YORK

New York Herald (1893-94), Library of Congress, Washington, D. C.; James Gordon Bennett, proprietor.

Evening Post (1893-94), Library of Congress, Washington, D. C.; E. L. Godkin, editor. Cited as *Post.*

Sun (1893-94), Library of Congress, Washington, D. C.; Charles A. Dana, editor.

New York Times (1893-94), Library of Congress, Washington, D. C.; Charles R. Miller, editor.

New York Tribune (1893-94), Library of Congress, Washington, D. C.; Whitelaw Reid, proprietor.

World (1893-94), Library of Congress, Washington, D. C.; Joseph Pulitzer, proprietor.

SAN FRANCISCO, CALIFORNIA

Morning Call (1893-94), Library of Congress, Washington, D. C.; John D. Spreckels, proprietor.

San Francisco Chronicle (1893-94), Library of Congress, Washington, D. C.; M. H. DeYoung, proprietor.

Periodicals

The Friend (Honolulu) 1893-94; Library of Hawaii; Sereno E. Bishop, editor.

Harper's Weekly (New York) 1893-94; Library of Congress; Carl Schurz, editor.

Literary Digest (New York) 1893-94; Library of Congress; Isaac K. Funk, editor.

The Nation (New York) 1893-94; Library of Congress; E. L. Godkin, editor.

ARTICLES

Alexander, William De Witt, "The Uncompleted Treaty of Annexation of 1854," in *Papers of the Hawaiian Historical Society, No. 9* (read July 2, 1897).

Anderson, Russell H., "Some Aspects of Tariff Remissions on Sugar, 1876-1927," in *Annals of the American Academy of Political and Social Science,* CXLI (Jan., 1929), 149-159.

Beardslee, L. A., "Pilikias," in *North American Review,* CLXVII (Oct., 1898), 473-481.

Bryce, James, "The Policy of Annexation for America," in *Forum,* XXIV (Dec., 1897), 385-396.

Cooley, Thomas M., "Grave Obstacles to Hawaiian Annexation," in *Forum,* XV (June, 1893), 389-407.

Curtis, George Ticknor, "Is It Constitutional?" in *North American Review,* CLVI (March, 1893), 282-287.

Davies, Theophilus H., "The Hawaiian Revolution," in *Nineteenth Century,* XXXIII (May, 1893), 830-835.

———, "The Hawaiian Situation," in *North American Review,* CLVI (May, 1893), 605-610.

Dole, Sanford B., "Evolution of Hawaiian Land Tenure," in *Papers of the Hawaiian Historical Society, No. 3* (read Dec. 5, 1892).

Dozer, Donald Marquand, "The Opposition to Hawaiian Reciprocity, 1876-1888," in *The Pacific Historical Review,* XIV (June, 1945), 157-184.

Griffis, William Elliot, "Our New Fellow-Citizens," in *Outlook,* LIX (July 23, 1898), 722-728.

Herbert, Hilary A., "Reciprocity and the Farmer," in *North American Review,* CLIV (April, 1892), 414-423.

Hoffnung, A., "The Revolution in Hawaii," in *The Imperial and Asiatic Quarterly Review and Oriental and Colonial Record,* XV and XVI (Jan. and April, 1893), 406-417.

Hooley, Osborne E., "Hawaiian Negotiations for Reciprocity, 1855-57," in *The Pacific Historical Review,* VII (June, 1938), 128-147.

Jameson, J. Franklin, "Typical Steps of American Expansion," in *History Teacher's Magazine,* V (Feb., 1914), 39-44.

Kuykendall, Ralph S., "Lorrin Andrews Thurston," in *Dictionary of American Biography,* edited by Allen Johnson and Dumas Malone, 20 volumes (N. Y., 1928-37), XVIII, 517-518.

———, "Sanford Ballard Dole," in *ibid.,* V, 358-359.

Mahan, Alfred T., "Hawaii and Our Future Sea-Power," in *Forum,* XV (March, 1893), 1-12.

McPherson, John H. T., "James Henderson Blount," in *Dictionary of American Biography*, edited by Allen Johnson and Dumas Malone, 20 volumes (N. Y., 1928-37), II, 388-389.

Patterson, John, "The United States and Hawaiian Reciprocity, 1867-1870," in *The Pacific Historical Review,* VII (March, 1938), 14-27.

Robinson, Charles, "The Hawaiian Controversy in the Light of History," in *American Journal of Politics,* IV (May, 1894), 477-490.

Russ, William A., Jr., "The Role of Sugar in Hawaiian Annexation," in *The Pacific Historical Review,* XII (Dec., 1943), 339-351.

Schouler, James, "A Review of the Hawaiian Controversy," in *Forum,* XVI (Feb., 1894), 670-689.

Spaulding, Thomas M., "John Leavitt Stevens," in *Dictionary of American Biography,* edited by Allen Johnson and Dumas Malone, 20 volumes (N. Y., 1928-37), XVII, 618-619.

———, "Cabinet Government in Hawaii, 1887-1893," in *University of Hawaii Occasional Papers No. 2* (Honolulu, 1924), 1-22.

Spreckels, Claus, "The Future of the Sandwich Islands," in *North American Review,* CLII (March, 1891), 287-292.

Thurston, Lorrin A., "The Sandwich Islands," in *North American Review,* CLVI (March, 1893), 265-282.

Van Alstyne, Richard W., "Great Britain, the United States, and Hawaiian Independence, 1850-1854," in *The Pacific Historical Review,* IV (March, 1935), 15-25.

Woolsey, Theodore S., "Law and Policy for Hawaii," in *Yale Review,* II (Feb., 1893), 347.

Secondary Authorities

Alexander, William De Witt, *History of Later Years of the Hawaiian Monarchy and the Revolution of 1893* (Honolulu, 1896).

Blackman, William Fremont, *The Making of Hawaii: A Study in Social Evolution* (N. Y., 1899).

Bradley, Harold W., *The American Frontier in Hawaii: The Pioneers 1789-1843* (Stanford University, 1942).

Brookes, Jean Ingram, *International Rivalry in the Pacific Islands, 1800-1875* (Berkeley, 1941).

Callahan, James Morton, *American Relations in the Pacific and the Far East 1784-1900* in *Johns Hopkins University Studies in Historical and Political Science* (Herbert B. Adams, editor), Nos. 1-3, Series XIX (Baltimore, 1901).

Carpenter, Edmund Janes, *America in Hawaii* (Boston, 1899).

Chambers, Henry E., *Constitutional History of Hawaii* in *Johns Hopkins University Studies in Historical and Political Science* (Herbert B. Adams, editor), No. 1, Series XIV (Baltimore, 1896).

Conroy, Hilary, *The Japanese Frontier in Hawaii, 1868-1898* (Berkeley, 1953).

Dennett, Tyler, *Americans in Eastern Asia* (N. Y., 1922).

Field, Isobel, *This Life I've Loved* (N. Y., 1937).

Foster, John W., *American Diplomacy in the Orient* (Boston and N. Y., 1903).

Garvin, J. L., *The Life of Joseph Chamberlain* (London, 3 volumes, 1932-34).

Gresham, Matilda, *Life of Walter Quintin Gresham, 1832-1895* (Chicago, 2 volumes, 1919).

James, Henry, *Richard Olney and His Public Service* (Boston and N. Y., 1923).

Kingsbury, Henry D., and Deyo, Simeon L. (editors), *Illustrated History of Kennebec County, Maine* (N. Y., 1892).

Krout, Mary H., *Hawaii and a Revolution* (N. Y., 1898).

Kuykendall, Ralph S., *A History of Hawaii* (N. Y., 1926).

———, *The Hawaiian Kingdom, 1778-1854: Foundation and Transformation* (Honolulu, 1938).

———, *The Hawaiian Kingdom, 1854-1874: Twenty Critical Years* (Honolulu, 1953).

Latané, John H., *America as a World Power, 1897-1907* in *The American Nation: A History,* vol. XXV (N. Y. and London, 1907).

Laughlin, J. Laurence, and Willis, H. Parker, *Reciprocity* (N. Y., 1903).

Mahan, Alfred T., *The Interest of America in Sea Power, Present and Future* (Boston, 1898).

McElroy, Robert M., *Grover Cleveland: The Man and the Statesman: An Authorized Biography* (2 volumes, N. Y. and London, 1923).

Morgan, Theodore, *Hawaii: A Century of Economic Change, 1778-1876* (Cambridge, Mass., 1948).

Musick, John R., *Hawaii, Our New Possessions* (N. Y. and London, 1898).

Muzzey, David S., *James G. Blaine: A Political Idol of Other Days* (N. Y., 1934).

Nevins, Allan, *Grover Cleveland: A Study in Courage* (N. Y., 1932).

Olcott, Charles S., *The Life of William McKinley* (2 volumes, Boston and N. Y., 1916).

Palmer, Julius A., Jr., *Memories of Hawaii and Hawaiian Correspondence* (Boston, 1894).

Pratt, Julius W., *Expansionists of 1898: The Acquisition of Hawaii and the Spanish Islands* (Baltimore, 1936).

Robinson, Chalfant, *A History of Two Reciprocity Treaties: The Treaty with Canada: The Treaty with the Hawaiian Islands in 1876 with a chapter on the treaty-making power of the House of Representatives* (New Haven, 1904).

Stevens, John L., and Oleson, W. B., *Riches and Marvels of Hawaii* (Philadelphia, 1900) ; originally published as *Picturesque Hawaii* in 1894.

Stevens, Sylvester K., *American Expansion in Hawaii, 1842-1898* (Harrisburg, Pa., 1945).

Tansill, Charles Callan, *The Foreign Policy of Thomas F. Bayard, 1885-1897* (N. Y., 1940).

Taylor, Albert Pierce, *Under Hawaiian Skies: A Narrative of the Romance, Adventure and History of the Hawaiian Islands: A Complete Historical Account* (Honolulu, 1922, 1926).

Young, Lucien, *The Boston at Hawaii* (Washington, D. C., 1898).

Pamphlets

Creel, H. G., *Hawaii An International Crime* (Girard, Kan., 1915).

Hawaiian Gazette, Two Weeks of Hawaiian History January 14-28, 1893 (Honolulu, 1893).

Kennedy, Crammond, *Some Phases of the Hawaiian Question* (1893).

Tansill, Charles Callan, *Diplomatic Relations between the United States and Hawaii, 1885-1889,* in *Fordham University Studies, Historical Series No. 1* (N. Y., 1940).

Printed Sources

Barker, Albert S., *Everyday Life in the Navy* (Boston, 1928).

Congressional Record, 51 Cong. 2 Sess.; 52 Cong. 2 Sess.; 53 Cong. Special Sess. of the Senate; 53 Cong. 2 Sess.; 55 Cong. 2 Sess.

Dole, Sanford B., *Memoirs of the Hawaiian Revolution,* edited by Andrew Farrell (Honolulu, 1936).

Foreign Relations of the United States, 1887 (Washington, D. C.).

Foster, John W., *Diplomatic Memoirs* (2 vols., N. Y. and Boston, 1909).

Hoar, George F., *Autobiography of Seventy Years* (2 vols., N. Y., 1903).

House Executive Document 1 (50 Cong. 1 Sess.).

House Executive Document 47 (cited as "Blount"), *48, 70, 76, 79, 112, 140* (53 Cong. 2 Sess.).

House Miscellaneous Document 42, 44, 60 (53 Cong. 2 Sess.).

House Report, 243, 254 (53 Cong. 2 Sess.).

Hudson, Manley O., *Cases and Other Materials on International Law* (St. Paul, 1929).

Laws of the Provisional Government . . . Acts 1 to 42 (Honolulu, 1893).

Liliuokalani, *Hawaii's Story by Hawaii's Queen* (Boston, 1898).

Nevins, Allan, *Letters of Grover Cleveland 1850-1908* (Boston and N. Y., 1933).

Senate Document 214 (55 Cong. 2 Sess.).

Senate Executive Document 45, 76, 77 (52 Cong. 2 Sess.).

Senate Executive Document 46, 65, 77, 85, 92, 103 (53 Cong. 2 Sess.).

Senate Miscellaneous Document 13, 23, 24, 28, 29, 36, 46, 49, 50 (53 Cong. 2 Sess.).

Senate Report 227 (cited as "Morgan"), (53 Cong. 2 Sess.).

Senate Report 681 (55 Cong. 2 Sess.).

Thurston, Lorrin A., *Memoirs of the Hawaiian Revolution,* edited by Andrew Farrell (Honolulu, 1936).

Manuscript Sources

James H. Blount's Report, in the Records of the Department of State in the National Archives, Washington, D. C.

William E. Chandler MSS., Library of Congress, Washington, D. C.

Ciphers Received, No. 1 (November 5, 1888, to December 14, 1897), in the Records of the Department of the Navy in the National Archives, Washington, D. C.

Ciphers Sent, No. 1 (October 27, 1889, to May 31, 1898), in the Records of the Department of the Navy in the National Archives, Washington, D. C.
Grover Cleveland MSS., Library of Congress, Washington, D. C.
Confidential Official Correspondence, No. 1 and No. 2, in the Records of the Department of the Navy in the National Archives, Washington, D. C.
Consular Letters, in the Records of the Department of State in the National Archives, Washington, D. C.
Despatches from American Ministers in Hawaii to the Secretary of State, in the Records of the Department of State in the National Archives, Washington, D. C.
Sanford B. Dole Papers, Archives of Hawaii, Honolulu.
Foreign Office Files, Archives of Hawaii, Honolulu.
Foreign Office Papers, filed as Foreign Office. Miscellaneous Local, Archives of Hawaii, Honolulu.
John W. Foster MSS., Library of Congress, Washington, D. C.
General Correspondence of the Division of Officers and Fleet, 1887-1896, in the Records of the Department of the Navy in the National Archives, Washington, D. C. These records were formerly held by the Bureau of Navigation, hence in the footnotes are cited as "Bureau of Navigation."
Walter Q. Gresham MSS., Library of Congress, Washington, D. C.
Instructions of the Secretary of State to Ministers in Hawaii, in the Records of the Department of State in the National Archives, Washington, D. C.
Minutes of the Cabinet Council of the Monarchy, Archives of Hawaii, Honolulu.
Minutes of the Executive Council of the Provisional Government, Archives of Hawaii, Honolulu.
Minutes of the Privy Council of the Monarchy, Archives of Hawaii, Honolulu.
Miscellaneous Archives—Memoranda of Conversations with the Secretary of State, 1893-98, in the Records of the Department of State in the National Archives, Washington, D. C.
John T. Morgan MSS., Library of Congress, Washington, D. C.
Notes to and from Hawaii, in the Records of the Department of State in the National Archives, Washington, D. C.
Official Sanford B. Dole Files, Archives of Hawaii, Honolulu.
Richard Olney MSS., Library of Congress, Washington, D. C.
Proceedings of the Executive and Advisory Councils of the Provisional Government, Archives of Hawaii, Honolulu. Cited as EAC.
President's Files, Archives of Hawaii, Honolulu.
Protocol of the treaty of 1893, in the Records of the Department of State in the National Archives, Washington, D. C.
Carl Schurz MSS., Library of Congress, Washington, D. C.
Thomas M. Spaulding Collection, Library of the University of Michigan, Ann Arbor. These papers consist of typewritten copies of documents which are housed in the Archives of Hawaii, Honolulu. The copies

were made by Colonel Spaulding when he was stationed in Honolulu as an officer of the United States army.

Lorrin A. Thurston Papers, Archives of Hawaii, Honolulu.

United States, Minister to Washington; Archives of Hawaii, Honolulu. Contains the instructions of the Hawaiian Foreign Office under the monarchy to its Minister to the United States, and the despatches of the Hawaiian Minister at Washington to the Foreign Minister at Honolulu.

United States, Ministers and Commissioners to Washington; Archives of Hawaii, Honolulu. Cited as M&C. Contains the instructions of the Hawaiian Foreign Office under the Provisional Government to its representatives at Washington, and the despatches of the latter to the Hawaiian Foreign Minister. The contents are limited to the period of treaty negotiation during the first half of 1893.

United States, Ministers and Envoys to Washington; Archives of Hawaii, Honolulu. Cited as M&E. Contains the instructions of the Hawaiian Foreign Office under the Provisional Government to its representatives at Washington, and the despatches of the latter to the Hawaiian Foreign Minister. This file begins approximately at the point where the one cited as M&C ends.

INDEX

—C—

—I—

—J—

—Q—

—R—